MARTIN BUCER AND THE ENGLISH REFORMATION

To

My Wife and Nicholas-Martin

MARTIN BUCER

Photographic reproduction from the mezzotint by R. Houston

MARTIN BUCER
AND THE
ENGLISH REFORMATION

by

CONSTANTIN HOPF

D.Phil. (Oxon.)

BASIL BLACKWELL · OXFORD

MCMXLVI

Bucer . . . 'the pastor of nations . . .'

—John Milton *The Judgment of Martin Bucer, concerning Divorce . . . The Prose Works of John Milton* (London, 1916), vol. III, p. 285

'His remarkable piety indeed, and profound learning, has produced not a transient but an everlasting benefit to the church; whereby he has not only bound all godly persons, but myself more than all of them, under perpetual obligations to him.'

—Abp. Cranmer to Bucer's widow, April 20th, 1552. *Original Letters*, vol. I, p. 27

'Remember the readings and preachings of God's prophet and true preacher, Martin Bucer . . .'

—John Bradford in his *Farewell to Cambridge. Writings of Bradford:* sermons . . . (Parker Society), p. 445

'Itaque venit, adventui ab omnibus gratulatum est: ita deinde vixit, ut non sua, sed nostra causa eum huc advenisse constaret.'

—George Acworth in his oration, 1560. *Scripta Anglicana*, p. 938

'Ciuis erit coeli nemo, qui haud exulat ante. . . .'

—Roger Ascham in his poem on Bucer. *Epistol.* (ed. London, 1589-90), p. 491

PRINTED IN GREAT BRITAIN IN THE CITY OF OXFORD
AT THE ALDEN PRESS

CONTENTS

CONTENTS

LIST OF ILLUSTRATIONS

ACKNOWLEDGEMENTS

I WISH to express my sincere thanks to the Librarians and staff of the Bodleian Library, Oxford, for their courtesy and kind assistance, also to those of the British Museum, Cambridge University Library and National Library, Aberystwyth. I most warmly thank the Committee for Advanced Studies (University of Oxford) for their helpful grant towards publication. Last not least I want especially to express my profound gratitude to my supervisor, Dr. Claude Jenkins, for his kind help and most valuable advice.

ADDENDUM

Two à Lasco Letters (here, pp. 164-167) are already printed in Dalton, Hermann: Lasciana . . . (Beitrage zur Geschichte der evangelischen Kirche in Russland, iii. Band), Berlin, 1898, pp. 329-331 and pp. 333-334. Dalton however is ignorant as to the place where the MSS. are kept.

INTRODUCTION

INTEREST more recently shown in the study of the life and theology of the Strassburg Reformer, Martin Bucer, tends to throw new light on the special period of his life in England and on his relation to the English Reformation. The various references to Bucer's contribution to the work of the English Reformers are dispersed so widely over the large field of research on that period, scattered in volumes of English Church history and in studies relating to the Book of Common Prayer, that it is difficult for the general reader to obtain a comprehensive picture of Bucer's work in this respect.

Until Mr. A. E. Harvey in 1906 wrote his dissertation on *Martin Bucer in England* no effort had been made to give a special account of Bucer's relation to the English Reformation. Since then special studies of his teaching at Cambridge and his schemes for Reform of ecclesiastical, ritual and ceremonial, as well as of social and economic conditions prevailing in England, have tended to emphasize the importance of the last two years of his life in this country.

Wilhelm Pauck's monograph, on Bucer's *De Regno Christi*, '*Das Reich Gottes auf Erden*' (1928), traced theological and ecclesiastical as well as economic contrasts between the views of Bucer and those of sixteenth-century England. In doing so he provided not only new material but also a further confirmation of the contention that Bucer's work here in England formed a vital and inseparable part of the story of the English Reformation. Apart from Harvey and Pauck no detailed study of Bucer and England has hitherto been undertaken, and the lament of a modern writer (before he wrote that biography) that no good biography exists in English was justified.[1] The following pages contain the results of a more modest effort to concentrate attention on Bucer's relations with England and its ecclesiastical leaders directly and indirectly in a special field, and to elucidate so far as possible his aims and methods and the reactions of those whom he sought to influence.

His contribution hitherto mainly attributed to his *Censura* of the First Edwardian Prayer Book, has tended to underestimate and neglect a study of links with the English Reformation which are not restricted to that special liturgical chapter of the English Reforma-

[1] Eells, H.: *The Attitude of Martin Bucer toward the Bigamy of Philip of Hesse* (Yale University Press, 1924), p. 245: 'It is unfortunate that no good biography exists in English, for the failure of the historians to give credit to his influence on the Reformation is due more to ignorance than to a lack of such an influence.'

cf. also Note before our Bibliography, pp. 261 f.

tion, but which include as well other aspects and motives so vitally important for a fuller realization of the sources of the English Reformation.

Thus the task of this inquiry will be twofold: The material relating to Bucer already extant in works on the English Reformation and other material not yet referred to, has to be collected and arranged so as to provide a more or less comprehensive account of his contribution. This part of the book may help the student to form an opinion as to the extent of Bucer's influence.

The second and in some ways far more difficult branch of this inquiry will be the effort to discover how far it is possible, by research into manuscript sources and the works of Bucer, to add to existing knowledge. By this research it may be hoped that the theme of Bucer's contribution will be seen from a different angle. The Reformer of Strassburg has been described by Dr. Charles Beard in his celebrated Hibbert Lectures on the English Reformation as holding both geographically and theologically a middle position between Wittenberg and Zurich.[1] If what is attempted here be successful it may be claimed that at any rate he will be seen to have made a contribution to the Reformation as essential to its understanding as that attributed to Lutheranism and Zwinglianism, while it may prove not less interesting to readers from its kinship to the work of the English Reformers themselves.

By this twofold approach it is intended to give as complete an account as possible of Bucer in England, and to draw at the same time attention to other aspects, which had not been noticed.

It may be considered a serious omission neither to have given a full biography nor to have entered into a comprehensive discussion of Bucer's Theology — useful parts of a work of this kind, it will be readily conceded — but the omission will find justification in stating that a monograph or a discussion of the Reformer's doctrine lies outside the scope of the present book.

The chapters which follow are intentionally treated as separate studies, not running as a consecutive account. Their various and differing topics indicate the many-sided character of Bucer's influence and yet the resultant impression is found to present the lineaments not of a composite but of a single personality.

The first chapter is an introduction to the various aspects of Bucer's contribution. Some general survey of Bucer's life and work in England and of his correspondence and acquaintance with persons of

[1] Beard, Charles: *The Reformation of the Sixteenth Century*, Hibbert Lectures (New Impression, with an Introduction by Ernest Barker, London, new ed., 1927), p. 283.

social and ecclesiastical rank here is essential, in order to follow a detailed study of his influence. Links formed before he came to this country and his knowledge of English affairs, the appreciation of Bucer and the study of works of his by Englishmen at a time when he was still on the Continent, give the background against which the special chapters of this work are placed. The attempt to trace the more intimate acquaintance of Bucer with Englishmen is not less interesting than the effort to track down references to Bucer in many contemporary pamphlets and writings of that period. It reveals a most vivid picture to show not only Bucer's estimation in this country, but also a curiously assorted assemblage of men. From another aspect we are brought to realize in how great a number of English writings of that period Bucer's works are quoted as authority.

It is inevitable that in such a survey Bucer's relations with Cranmer should occupy a distinctive place. It is for that reason that this chapter includes a discussion of what seem to the writer to be some precarious assumptions in reference to the theology and eucharistic doctrine of Bucer and Cranmer put forward in a modern work (see pp. 35 ff.).

The second chapter attempts to give a detailed study of Bucer's relation with the history of the Prayer Book, with a comparison between his suggestions and the reforming principles expressed in the Articles for various dioceses and in the Royal Injunctions. The use made of Bucer's proposals by English theologians, in order to furnish their arguments with 'authoritative' material, tends to show that the ideas of the Strassburg Reformer formed common ground for many English theologians and had penetrated into many contemporary and later writings.

Bucer's work on the Prayer Book made him enter into the wide field of schemes for the Reformation in England, thus not limiting his work only to the Prayer Book but extending his influence to the sphere of contemporary theological discussions. His draft of the Ordinal and a discussion on the more modern literature on his connection with it will form another part of this chapter. The Reformer's observations on the Homilies seen in the light of the attack by Gardiner against them and in connection with the dispute on Justification, in which Bucer was involved at Cambridge, have also some relevance to Prayer Book questions. Finally, a discourse on the relation of Bucer to the Cologne *Consultatio* of Herman of Wied and its influence upon the Book of Common Prayer completes a synopsis which tends to a fuller realization of the importance of Bucer's work.

The study of the liturgical Reform leads consequently to the study in the third chapter of Bucer's ecclesiastical as well as social and economic proposals as set down in his *De Regno Christi*. The striking likeness between the Elizabethan Poor-legislation and Bucer's suggestions for Poor-relief, his doctrine on Marriage and Divorce contrasted with the general approach to that question in his time as compared with the relative chapters in the *Reformatio Legum*, and reference to Milton's translation and use of Bucer's chapters on Divorce, are all noteworthy. The stress laid by Bucer on Ecclesiastical Reform seems to coincide with similar suggestions of English Reformers like Latimer and others expressed in contemporary literature. Here also an intimate picture of Church conditions is given by Bucer in a letter to King Edward VI on the occasion of the dedication of *De Regno Christi* to the young king.

Another aspect to the question of Bucer's contribution is given in the fourth chapter on Bucer and the Vestment Controversy. The hitherto unpublished manuscript correspondence of Bucer and his contemporaries reveals some astonishing material in connection with the vestment controversy of Bishop Hooper. The original Latin copy of Bucer's letter to à Lasco, hitherto only known in its English translation (as extant in the Elizabethan pamphlets on the question and in Strype), letters of à Lasco to Bucer, a letter of Peter Martyr to Bucer, the original copy of Cranmer's letter to Bucer on the subject, William Bill's letter on similar topics to Bucer, as well as the copy of Hooper's notes[1] on the controversy, provide new material on the subject. A synopsis of that correspondence of Bucer and his contemporaries with an account of the writings in which English theologians made constant use of Bucer's judgement on the question, shows the importance attached to Bucer as an ecclesiastical authority in matters of ceremonial.

The official pamphlets under Elizabeth against the Puritan anti-vestiarian claim, contain Bucer's statements as authority against the Puritans. Cranmer, Parker and Whitgift are mostly indebted to Bucer as regards this question, while Hooper and the Puritans find in him a strong opponent. The contemporary literature and that of the period immediately after refer to Bucer's judgement as if with Bucer all opposition had to cease.[2] The study of this particular question results in the double conclusion that Bucer was a strong supporter of Anglicanism, used as such by Anglicans, and an opponent to Puritanism, and that the importance attached to his judgement here, might induce the conclusion that the use of vestments in the

[1] cf. my note in *J.T.S.* (July-Oct., 1943, no. 175-6), pp. 194-199.
[2] cf. Thomas Bell in his *The Regiment of the Church* (1606).

Church of England to-day can be attributed to its defence by Bucer.

The fifth chapter on Gardiner and Bucer, with a special study of the various controversies between them, shows the opposition Bucer and Protestantism had to face from the Roman Catholic side in this country. The doctrinal points opposed by Gardiner and so strongly and elaborately defended by Bucer, are points also vigorously defended by English Reformers, when attacked by the opposition party of Gardiner. The special reply to Gardiner on the topic of *Justification*, contained in Bucer's *Disputata*, which hitherto had been overlooked, when compared with Gardiner's letters on that question, shows that the controversy between the two men was not only on *Celibacy* or on the *Rights of Sovereigns*, and shows also, that the attack here launched against Bucer and the defence made by Bucer is very similar to the attack by Gardiner against the teaching of the Anglican Homilies, as defended by Cranmer and other men.

Thomas Hoby's letter to his brother Sir Philip Hoby on Gardiner's attack against Bucer shows that already, before Bucer's arrival, strong links existed between Strassburg and England.

Finally, by a special study of Bucer's Commentary on the Psalter and its early English translation another absolutely new aspect of research on Bucer's relation to England can be given. It will be shown that Bucer's Commentary was not only translated into English, thus providing the first printed English Psalter before Coverdale's Bible was issued, but also that his Psalms found their way into various editions of English Primers, and that the Psalter in 'Matthew's Bible' as regards notes as well as the superscriptions of the Psalms is strongly influenced by Bucer's Commentary, and in respect to the superscriptions entirely dependent on those from Bucer. Striking similarities in some versions of particular verses of Coverdale's Psalter with those of Bucer suggest the perhaps yet unguarded and premature conclusion, that Bucer's Psalter was consulted by those responsible for the edition of the English Bible, as his Psalter was known by the version in the Primers and by 'Matthew's Bible'.

A detailed research into the History of the English Bible, Coverdale, 'Matthew', the French Version of Lefèvre, Olivétan, Sebastian Munster and Rabbi Kimchi, was inevitable.

Apart from mention of Bucer's Psalter and its English translation in Catalogues (e.g. the 'Short Title Catalogue', Cotton's Edition of the Bible, etc.), and apart from a reprint of two psalms by Cotton and by Daniel Waterland, and another short reference to the Psalter in the article of the *D.N.B.* on George Joye, no attempt to work out the implications and to draw conclusions from its existence, has hitherto been made. The connection of the English translation with the version of the Primers was unknown and even denied.

The discovery here made during the time of the writing of our work seemed to be one of first rate importance, being neither noticed by Westcott, Driver, Dowden nor even more recently by *The Bible in its Ancient and English Versions*, edited by H. Wheeler Robinson (Oxford, 1940). But after research had been carried out at Cambridge University Library, at the British Museum, at Aberystwyth and at the Bodleian, consulting the various editions of Primers and of Bucer's Psalter, and the chapter had been completed, Mr. Charles C. Butterworth's new work, *The Literary Lineage of the King James Bible* (1941) was acquired by the Bodleian Library in June 1942, apparently one of the first copies in this country. Here I found that the author had drawn attention to the importance of Bucer's English version and to the fact that the version of the Psalms in the Primer was identical with his. Although I have come independently to the same conclusions, I can now claim only to have made a small new contribution and discovery as to the relation of Bucer's Psalter to that of 'Matthew's Bible', and another discovery of a Primer with Bucer's Psalms not mentioned by Butterworth.

Yet when we conceive Bucer's influence on the English Reformation under these different aspects, the importance of his contribution, hitherto obscured and sometimes ignored, stands out in clear light. Indirectly the attempt has been made to indicate that Strassburg was as strong a factor in moulding the English Reformation as Wittenberg and Zurich. Even more, that while Lutheranism had to fail under Henry VIII for political reasons, and while Zwinglianism and the Swiss Party did not succeed in playing any predominant part in the English Reformation, it was Bucer who was listened to and who in all sections of religious life in England can claim to have played a part he had already played on the Continent in Reform schemes like that of Cologne and in connection with the political scheme of the Landgrave of Hesse.

CHAPTER I

MARTIN BUCER AND ENGLAND

WHEN Archbishop Cranmer in October of 1548[1] wrote his letter of invitation to the Strassburg Reformer, Martin Bucer, it was not merely the gesture of a man who could offer hospitality to a person who had to leave his country for his religious conviction and who was in danger. That letter expressed also the expectation of the Primate, who, knowing Bucer and his work on the Continent, was glad to have the Reformer over here at his side in his not too easy task for the Reformation in England.

The man so cordially invited, so eagerly expected, had long before he came to England formed links with this country in meeting Englishmen and by his interest for the Reformation in England. His work as reformer at Strassburg, his co-operation with the Archbishop of Cologne, Herman von Wied, in his Reform scheme, his connection with the Landgrave of Hesse, the 'captain' of the Continental Reformers, his presence at all decisive Colloquies and Diets in matters of the Continental Reformation, his controversy with the Bishop of Winchester, and finally his own writings, had given him a good reputation long before his arrival. His correspondence with Cranmer and the share that he took in the judgement required of the Continental Reformers and Universities as regards the Divorce case of Henry VIII had already brought him into contact with English affairs.

In order to visualize his place and importance in the history of his time a rough outline of his life, work and contacts has to be attempted which might induce the student who is not only interested in Bucer's connection with England to turn to the biographies mentioned.[2]

Martin Bucer was born on November 11th, 1491, at Schlettstadt in Alsace. Not quite fifteen years old he became a Dominican. For ten years (1506-16) he lived with the Dominicans at Schlettstadt. Early in his life he came into contact with the Humanists (Erasmus, Beatus Rhenanus, etc.). From Schlettstadt he was transferred to the Dominicans at Heidelberg where he matriculated (January 31st, 1517) and took his degrees as Baccalaureus and Magister. He was present at Luther's Heidelberg Disputation in April 1518, a turning point in his life. Later he came into contact with Franz von Sickingen and

[1] cf. *Original Letters* (Parker Society), vol. I, pp. 19-20.

[2] cf. Baum, J. W.: *Capito und Butzer* (Elberfeld, 1860); Anrich, G.: *Martin Bucer* (Strassburg, 1914); Eells, H.: *Martin Bucer* (Yale University Press, 1931); or the article in *D.N.B.* by A. W. Ward; or the article in the *Realencyklopaedie für Protestantische Theologie*; etc.

Ulrich von Hutten at the Ebernburg where he also met John Glapion, Father Confessor to the Emperor. How much certain ideas, to which he would adhere throughout his life, took shape in those years, can be illustrated by one instance. In one of the conversations, Glapion spoke about the conquest of America by the Spanish. The narrative of the exploit of the conquest provides Bucer almost fifteen years later with an argument of suspicion against the discovery of new lands for the expansion of Christianity.[1]

Bucer's love and knowledge of the classical works, his wide range of reading of the Fathers and philosophers, of Aquinas and the Schoolmen can be traced back to the influences received in these early years.

Here in Hutten Bucer met the man who played the important part in that combat of wit which so much stirred the academic world with its immortal document, the *Epistolae Obscurorum Virorum*. After leaving Hutten Bucer was for one year chaplain at the Court of Pfalzgrave Frederick, first at Worms, then at Nüremberg.

In May 1522 he became Vicar of Landstuhl, a parish which belonged to Sickingen. For half a year (from November 1522 onward) he lived at Weissenburg engaged in preaching. In May 1523 he moved on to Strassburg. And here in the 'Silver-City', Argentoratum, he settles down to a ministry not only destined for the spiritual needs of its citizens, but also spreading all over the Continent, wherever wanted or needed by those who asked for it. Up to his escape from Strassburg to England, that city was the centre of Bucer's work. Here he contacted the theologians and schoolmen of that city. Here with men like Capito, Jacob, John Sturm and Paul Fagius, he plans and works out the religious and school-life of the town. Here he lays the foundation for the Evangelic Mass and here he carries out the fight against the Anabaptists. In collaboration with Sturm the famous Strassburg school is founded.

And from here Bucer sets out on his manifold and various missions which lead him to Switzerland or to the south of Germany or to the many Diets and Colloquies where his presence is needed—Augsburg, Worms, Speyer, Marburg, Ratisbon, to name only a few.

[1] cf. *De anima. cura* (1538), *Scripta Anglicana*, p. 301: '. . . Sic etiam grauis cernitur ira Dei in inuentione atque occupatione nouarum terrarum & insularum, de qua tamen tam magnifici aguntur triumphi, quasi hac ratione valde augeatur populus Christianus. Ibi enim nihil aliud agitur: quam vt primo, miseri illi homunculi & corpus & bona amittant, deinde vero etiam animam, per superstitiones quibus informantur a monachis mendicantibus. Ioannem Glappionem Caesareae maiestatis Confessionarium coram praestantibus hominibus querentem audiui: Hispanos in terris nuper inuentis, miseros homunciones tantopere ad laborem quaerendi eis aurum aliaque, vrsisse, atque torsisse, vt illi sibi ipsis mortem consciscerent, quippe quod eis tantus labor atque tortura intolerabilis esset.'

His advice in ecclesiastic and theological matters is asked by men from all camps. The *Tetrapolitana* is only one of the many instances in his continuous unceasing efforts to attempt an understanding in the Eucharistic controversy between Luther and his opponents.

Landgrave Philip of Hesse desires Bucer's help in the religious and political difficulties he has to face in Hesse. The Archbishop of Cologne, Herman von Wied, invites Bucer to Cologne for his Reform-scheme, which results in the *Consultation*, to which also the English Reformation is indebted.

There is hardly any place in the religious or political history on the Continent where Bucer's presence and advice cannot be traced: Roman Catholic theologians, Swiss theologians and Lutheran theologians converse with him. His insight as theologian and politician, as churchman and schoolman gave him authority to which most men willingly listened.

This short sketch, although incomplete and wanting so much in a description of the character and personality of the man, attempts only to lay greater stress on the fact that Englishmen met in Bucer a man of vast experience both theological and ecclesiastic as well as political, of fame matching that of any other great name of his age.

And here in connection with Strassburg we find Bucer's name mentioned in an English poem:

In Strasbrugh, that noble towne,
A Cyte of most famous renowne,
Wheare the gospell is frely preached.
And what dost thou their names call,
Which were counted in especiall,
The aduersaries of the masse?
Truly there where clarkes many one,
And gretly learned every chone,
  Whose names my memory do passe.
Howe be it, Hedius, Butzer. and Capito,
Celarius, Symphorian,[1] and wother mo,
In dede were reputed the chefe.
  Whose lyuynge is so inculpable,
  That their enemies with oute fable,
  In theym coulde fynde no reprefe.[2]

Strassburg, known as a centre of Reformation, had become a place

[1] Symphorian Pollio (Symphorian Altbiesser), cf. Ficker: *Handschriftenproben* . . . vol. II, p. 63.

On the poem cf. Herford, Charles H.: *Studies in the Literary Relations of England and Germany in the Sixteenth Century* (Cambridge, 1886).

[2] In *English Reprints*, 14 (Ed. by Edward Arber, London, September 20th, 1871), pp. 39-40.

of refuge for many religious refugees, not only on the Continent (Anabaptists, or men like Calvin, Peter Martyr, or Servetus), but also for Englishmen. The 'White-Horse-Theologians' of Cambridge, who had taken up the study of Protestant writings, had soon to leave or would have to face imprisonment under Wolsey. One of them, George Joye, fled to Strassburg at the end of the year 1527, and seems to have stayed there for some time. He writes from Strassburg:

> ... I would right gladly return and dare not, being exiled into a strange land among rude and boisterous people, with whose manners I cannot well agree, which is to me no little cross. ...[1]

But in spite of that nostalgic touch and unfavourable account of his reception at Strassburg, he not only stayed on but also continued his theological work and published several of his writings. And, as he refers later to Bucer's Commentary on the Psalms, in his controversy with Tyndale, and as he himself translated a Latin Psalter on the Continent, it is at least not unlikely that he came also into contact with Bucer.

By providing asylum to the Italian Divine, Peter Martyr, a lasting friendship was formed between him and Bucer which should carry them later through the exile both men shared in England. Martyr's letter from Strassburg to his Italian friends[2] is a living tale of praise of his host and of the hospitality extended to him, a tale which will have been the experience of so many exiles at Strassburg:[3]

> ... As soon as we were come hither, we were most lovingly received by Bucer into his house. Seventeen days I remained with him; in which time I spied wonderful examples of godliness as well in his doctrine as in his life. His house seemed to be a house of hospitality — such usual entertainment giveth he towards strangers, who are constrained to travel for the Gospel and for Christ's cause. He so well governeth his household, as in so many days' space I perceived not so much as a small occasion of offence, but found on every side matter of edifying. At his table there is no appearance either of excess or niggardness, but of godly moderation. In meats he maketh no difference of days, but eateth any sort of meat as it is laid before him without superstition, giving oftentimes thanks unto God through Jesus Christ for so many and so great benefits. Before and after meat, somewhat is recited out of the Holy Scriptures, which might minister for godly and holy communications. I may boldly affirm that I ever went from that

[1] Fol. Diij of 'The story of my state after the bishop had received the prior's letters', in *The letters which Johan Ashwel . . . with the answer of the sayed George* [Joye] . . . (Strassburg, 1528?).

[2] Peter Martyr to his colleagues at Lucca (December 25th, 1543), Gorham, G. C.: *Gleanings . . .* (London, 1857), pp. 20 ff.

[3] cf. Th. Hoby's diary; p. 9 in our work.

table better learned. For I always heard something which I never so thoroughly weighed before, or had not been so well satisfied therein. As touching other actions of his, I always found him occupied, and that in no private business, but in those things wherein he might help his neighbours; that is to wit, in daily sermons, in well governing of ecclesiastical matters, that curates might govern the souls committed unto them, that they should confirm them by holy examples; in visitation of schools of learning, that all the labour which is there bestowed may be referred to the furthering of the Gospel and commodity of the Church; in exhortations whereby he continually stirreth up and enflameth the magistrate unto Christian godliness. There is, in a manner, no day passeth over but he visiteth the Court. And because he is all the whole day occupied in these kinds of business, he hath appointed the night for his private studies and prayers. To say the truth as the thing is, I never awaked out of sleep in the night, but I found him awake. Then by studies he prepared himself to those things which in the day time he was to speak; then obtained he by prayers strength unto his actions in the day time . . .

Translations of works of Bucer into English and the reformer's interest in the state of religion under Henry VIII show another early link between Bucer and England.

In 1530 Bucer's Latin Commentary on the Psalms was translated into English and printed at Strassburg. A few years later — presumably about 1535 — another Strassburg pamphlet was translated into English and printed at London for William Marshall:

> A treatise declaryng & shewĩg dyuers causes takẽ out of the holy scriptur . . . that pyctures & other ymages . . . are ĩ no wise to be suffred in the temples or churches of Christen men . . . The authours of this little treatise ar the opẽ preachers of Argtẽyne . . .

The original German seems to have been drafted by Martin Bucer. It was translated into Latin by Jacobus Bedrot in 1530 and then about five years later translated into English.

In the divorce case of Henry VIII from Catherine of Aragon Bucer's judgement was also asked among those from Continental Reformers and Universities (1531).[1]

When John Fisher, Bishop of Rochester, had answered Luther's attack on Henry VIII and written against Luther's doctrine of the Sacraments as stated in his *De Captivitate Babylonica*, another Catholic, Thomas Murner, lectured at Strassburg against the Protestants and

[1] cf. Simon Grynaeus' Letter to Bucer (September 1531), *Original Letters* (Parker Society), vol. II, pp. 552-554, and other letters on Henry's divorce, op. cit., pp. 554-557. H. Eells in his *The Attitude of Martin Bucer* . . . (pp. 30-43) deals specially with Bucer's judgement in the affair.

their conception of the Eucharist, basing some of his arguments on those of Fisher. To this Bucer had replied (1524) in a small treatise, showing himself well conversant of Fisher's arguments and firmly taking the side of Luther.[1] His strong Protestant tendencies soon caused Bucer's writings to be banned in England until political events led Henry VIII to take a more favourable attitude towards Protestantism. Richard Bayfield, who had introduced into this country several Protestant books from the Continent, among them works of Bucer, was sentenced in November 1531 by Stokesley, Bishop of London. Among the prohibited books as named in the list drawn up at that occasion was Bucer's Psalter.[2]

The breaking away, however, of Henry VIII from Rome inspired Bucer and his fellow-reformers with new hope for the advancement of their cause. Gardiner's tract *De Vera Obedientia* with its deliberately Protestant phrases and its outspoken rejection of the Pope's supremacy induced Bucer and his Strassburg colleagues to rejoice and to believe that Henry VIII's policy was dictated by Protestant views.[3]

The English emissaries sent to Germany for negotiating with the Protestants, seemed to be proof for Bucer of England adopting schemes for Reformation. In April 1536 he dedicates his Commentary on Romans to Archbishop Cranmer, and refers to the scheme of a general Protestant alliance. And to Edward Fox, the Bishop of Hereford, one of the emissaries to Germany, he dedicated, in summer of 1536, his *Apologia de S. Coena Domini*, and he asks him at the end of this dedication to remember him to his colleague Nicholas Heath, who had also been to Germany as emissary.[4]

[1] *De Caena Dominica Ad* obiecta, quae contra ueritatem Euangelicam Murnerus, partim ipse finxit, partim ex Roffensi ac alijs pietatis hostibus, sublegit, Responsio Martini Buceri.

cf. also Kawerau, W.: *Thomas Murner und die deutsche Reformation* (Halle, 1891), p. 89.

[2] cf. MS. Lambeth 306, fol. 65. In 1540 we find the following list of prohibited books: (Historical MSS. Commission, Fourteenth Report, Append., Part VIII. The MSS. of Lincoln, Bury St. Edmund's and Great Grimsby Corporations, and of the Deans and Chapters of Worchester and Lichfield, etc. London, 1895, p. 183, xiii), Worchester Diocese: Then follow certain visitation detecta relating to heresy . . . , John Dydson's answers to articles, with a note of books found in his possession – *Lutherus in postill' Bucher in epãla Pauli ad Romanos et Zyngulus unica exposicio* – and many other sets of depositions during the visitation of 1540.

[3] cf. Bucer's letter to Vadian, January 17th, 1536, Arbenz, E.: *Die Vadianische Briefsammlung*, vol. V, II, pp. 298-299, and the preface written by himself and his colleagues (Capito and Hedio) to Gardiner's tract, cf. our work pp. 198-202.

[4] Metaphrases Et Enarrationes Perpetuae Epistolarum (Tomus Primus. Epistle to the Romans). Printed at Strassburg, March 1536. Preface dedicated to Thomas Cranmer '8 Cal. April 1536'.

Apologia D. Mart. Buceri de S. Coena Domini ex praefatione Enarrationum ipsius in quatuor Euangel. ad D. Edoardum Foxum, Episcopum Herephordensem desumpta. X. Cal. September 1536. (*Scr. Angl.*, pp. 670-681), prefixed to the 1536 edition of his: In Sacra Quatuor Evangelia, Enarrationes . . . (Bas. Joan. Herv. September 1536. Last sentence: 'Idē precor R.P.T. Collegae. V.D. Nicolao Haettaeo . . .' ibid. p. +7 verso.)

From now onward Bucer's interest is constantly directed towards England.[1] His correspondence during those years with Archbishop Cranmer and with Philip, Landgrave of Hesse, reveals the intentness with which he watched English affairs.[2] He deeply regrets the publication of the VI Articles by Henry VIII and the reaction against Protestantism, but he thinks Gardiner to be the person chiefly guilty. He also believes that the emissaries sent to England by Germany had not been conversant enough with the entire situation, and thus had also to be blamed for the failure of the negotiations. From the year 1539 onward, Bucer's attitude towards Gardiner, whom once he had praised in his preface to the bishop's *De Vera Obedientia*, had changed into an hostile attitude, as can be seen from his correspondence.

Gardiner, whom Bucer met for the first time at the Colloquy of Ratisbon in 1541, and in whom he had still hoped to find a person to resume negotiations, became to him the evil influence behind the scenes, and the bishop who was to blame for the break between Protestantism and England. From 1541 onward to the time of his death Bucer was involved in a constant controversy in numerous pamphlets with Gardiner.

Bucer's account of the proceedings at the Colloquy of Ratisbon in 1541 was soon translated into English by Myles Coverdale, and thus showed to the public that men such as the author had tried to come to a union with Charles V and the Roman Catholic Party on the Continent, but in vain.

Gardiner soon addressed two letters to Bucer, which were printed; these give an account of his conversation with Bucer and attack him most vigorously. The reply, eagerly expected by Bucer's English friends, did not come until 1548.

[1] cf. Otto Clemen: *Der Gothaer Briefcodex* A 406, p. 136 ff., letter XVI: Wolfgang Musculus to Myconius and Menius, Augsburg, February 7th, 1539: 'S.D. Literas vestras accepi, fratres in Domino charissimi, et tuas, Friderice, praesertim magna cum aviditate, propterea quod credebam me ex illis Anglicanae Ecclesiae statum tanquam ἀπὸ τοῦ αὐτόπτου ac omnium certissimo teste cogniturum. Tam enim horrenda de hoc rege apud nos feruntur, ut videatur Phalaridis [cf. *Phalaridis imperium.* Erasmi Adagia I, 10, 86, p. 344] aequare tyrannidem. Sperabam me cognita veritate habiturum, unde ψευδολόγοις ora obturarem. Sed bene habet, ad Bucerum me mittis, ex quo discam causae huius veritatem, qui id et poterit, quoniam absque dubio omnia abs te exacte didicit.'

[2] cf. his letters to Cranmer:

October 23rd, 1538?	*Original Letters,*	vol. II, pp. 520-526.
October 29th, 1539	,, ,,	vol. II, pp. 526-530.
September 3rd, 1548	,, ,,	vol. II, pp. 531-533.
December 23rd, 1548	,, ,,	vol. II, pp. 533-534.

Bucer's letters to the Landgrave (Lenz, Max: *Briefwechsel*):

September 16th, 1539,	Lenz, op. cit.,	vol. I, pp. 99 ff.
October 16th, 1539	,, ,,	vol. I, pp. 109 ff.
November 26th, 1540	,, ,,	vol. I, pp. 240 ff.
December 13th, 1544	,, ,,	vol. II, pp. 273 ff.

Myles Coverdale, who was then still on the Continent, was especially eager to obtain a copy of Bucer's answer to Gardiner, in order to translate it into English, which had been done by Thomas Hoby. He writes to Conrad Hubert (from Bergzabern, date uncertain):

> . . . And if you can by any means procure even one copy of Bucer's answer to the bishop of Winchester before the fair, I will take care that the Latin original shall be translated into English as soon as possible; which you need not doubt will be most acceptable to our brethren in the Lord throughout England. I wish, however, that it should be managed as secretly as possible, until it shall make its appearance both in Latin and English.[1]

It is unfortunately difficult to find out when Coverdale, who had already translated Bucer's Acts of Ratisbon into English, and who wrote in another letter to Conrad Hubert (May 22nd, 1544)[2] that he had been with Martin Bucer, and had made his acquaintance. If Coverdale, who speaks of Bucer in high terms of admiration, had been in contact with the Strassburg Reformer either personally or through his writings during the time when engaged on his English Bible, a valuable piece of external evidence for Coverdale employing Bucer's Psalter would be given.

It is in this connection that Bucer seems to have corresponded with Henry VIII on the matter of editing his work against Gardiner. For he writes in his *Gratulation*:

> . . . But when about the edition of this work sone after I had caused the moste royall and puyssant Prince of moste famous memorye, Kyng Henry the.viij. of y name to be made priuye, who made answere again that he had rather I should differ for a season the publisshinge abrode therof, for he trusted to come to passe that I should speake of this and other controuersyes in relygion at some tyme peacablie with winchester, & other learned of his realme, to thentent a godlye concorde and vnitie in religiō might be sought forth, and a farther instauration of the churches, which his purpose I might haue hindred, if winchester (whose bitternes in writinge he did in no maner wise aloue) shoulde haue byne prouoked to writ anie more openlie againste vs, And so this the kinges godlie

[1] cf. *Remains of Bp. Coverdale* (Parker Society), p. 520; cf. also, pp. 512-513.
[2] op. cit., pp. 510 f.
Hessius, who in his MS. (cf. Summary Catalogue of Western MSS. in Bodleian. Accessions 1922-23, n. 41549. MS. Clar. Press, c.5) refers to the same collection of letters at Strassburg, from which the letters in the Coverdale volume of the Parker Society are printed, ascribes Letter n. xx (pp. 512-513) in the Parker Society edition to Edmundus Britannus (Edmund Allen, who at that time was also on the Continent). The Letter to Hubert (pp. 519-20) is also ascribed to Edmundus Britannus by Hessius and is dated: February 16th, 1545, which date seems to be unlikely. (cf. Hessius, MS. cit. pp. 17 and 18.)

and prudent answere receued, when els (as I t[*h*]ought with my self) I should not seme by this my labour to profyt the churches anie thing: my worke which I had in minde to go forwarde withal I laid asyde againe: . . .[1]

In those years Sir Thomas Hoby, the brother of Sir Philip Hoby, had been sent to Strassburg by his brother to pursue his studies. Hoby, who was staying with Bucer and attending his lectures, then translated the *Gratulatio*, containing Bucer's answer to the epistles of the Bishop of Winchester, into English, prefacing the translation by a letter to his brother Sir Philip Hoby, a letter which is scarcely known. Hoby writes in his diary on his time in Strassburg:

Here I arryved the xvjth of October [1547] and remayned in Mr. Bucer's house, who was a man of no less integritie and purnes of lyving then of fame and learning. Him heard I in the Schooles in Divinitie, and sometime Peter Martir, Sturmius in humanitie, Paulus Fagius in Hebrue, and Dasipodius in Greeke, who in their faculties were the best learned of their time . . . Bucer and P. Fagius died afterward in England, whose deaths were not so much lamented of all menn as their lyves desired, and yet so lamented that they were celebrated throwghowt the wholl Universitie of Cambridge, both with orations and all kinde of verses in all three tungs after their deathe . . .

When Bucer had finisshed the little treatise he made unto the churche of England in answere to Stephan Bisshoppe of Wynchester's railing epistles unto him, I translated it ymediatlie into Englishe and sent it to my brother, where it was put in print . . .[2]

William Turner, who under the name of Wraghton, published a tract against Gardiner, had also been at Strassburg, and must have got some secret information about Bucer's conversation with the Bishop of Winchester. Gardiner in reply to Turner's writing accuses Turner of having given an unfair and untrue account of it.[3] An incident of that conversation, recalled by Bucer in his *Gratulatio*, must have excited some interest, for it occurs again in Nicholas Carr's letter at the occasion of Bucer's death, and Gardiner himself tried to disprove it.[4] Bucer had referred to Gardiner's temper, which

[1] Fol. Biiij verso f. in *The Gratulation*. In the Latin edition, pp. 11-12.

[2] cf. *The Travels and Life of Sir Thomas Hoby* . . . (The Camden Miscellany, vol. X (2), London, 1902, Camden Society, 3rd Series, vol. IV, pp. 4-6 and p. 65. cf. our work, pp. 203-204.)

[3] cf. *The huntyng and fyndyng out of the Romyshe foxe* . . . (Basle, 1543), fol. E vij. *The Rescvynge of the Romishe Fox* . . . The Seconde Covrse of the Hvnter . . . (1545), fol. K. viij ff.

cf. also here the chapter 'Gardiner and Bucer' p. 182.

[4] cf. *Gratulatio*, op. cit., p. 53.

cf. *Scr. Angl.*, p. 873.

cf. Gardiner's *Exetasis* (Lovanii, 1554), pp. 2-3.

displayed itself most curiously by the swelling of a vein between his fingers, when he got excited.

The translation of the *Consultatio* of Herman of Wied, Archbishop of Cologne, into English, needs mentioning here, as the work, of which Bucer was one of the chief compilers, influenced the Book of Common Prayer (cf. here pp. 94-96).

Another person from England, with whom Bucer corresponded before he came to England, was Richard Bonner, who in November of 1548 published his pamphlet 'A treatyse of ye right honourynge and wourshyppyng of our sauiour Jesus Christe in the sacramēt . . .', which he dedicated to Cranmer. Before he published the treatise, he seems to have asked some advice of Bucer to certain questions, as the answer of Bucer's letter to Bonner (September 4th, 1548) indicates.[1]

The contact Bucer made with England before his coming, is the prelude to the story of his activities here. Without it it would have been more difficult — not to say impossible — for Bucer to gain that influence and friendship he was going to receive.

English theologians knew him more intimately than they knew Luther or Zwingli or Calvin. His wise policy, his wide experience in matters of ecclesiastical reform schemes and in church conferences, had gained him not only fame but at the same time rebuke from his adversaries. But in spite of attacks from all sides, one thing was outstanding and perhaps the most convincing for English theologians: Bucer was the man of eirenic spirit, the man for Union, the man who tried to bridge the gulf. And the tragic story of the 'Interim', the story of the final break between Protestantism and Roman Catholicism, for the avoidance of which he had laboured for years on the Continent, shows also that Bucer, so eager for unity and peace, could not and did not accept a scheme for reform against his conscience, even if he would have to give up all hope for reunion. Bucer's heroic refusal to sign the Interim, which might easily cost him his life, and in consequence of which the old man had to leave his country, aroused much praise and admiration everywhere and stopped those critical minds, who liked to say that Bucer would sign any treaty for the sake of unity.[2]

Thus he came to England, known by his works, loved already by

[1] Corpus Christi College, Cambridge, MS. 113, 42: respondet quaestioni sibi propositae, utrum verborum Christi simplex recitatio in coenae Domini celebratione observatu sit necessaria.

[2] cf. on Bucer's attitude against the Interim:

(1) Dedicatory Letter of John Sturm to Francis Walsingham from Strassburg, February 23rd, 1577 (*Scr. Angl.*, fol. *a*4 verso and *a*5).

(2) Thirlby, Bishop of Westminster, Letter to Sir William Petre (April 3rd, 1548), Bucer said: he liked it in no wise (p. 19). The same to the Lord Protector (April 24th.

many Englishmen, admired for his resistance against the Emperor. He had been invited to go to Copenhagen.[1] But he had already left for the country where he thought not only to find a refuge for his body, but which seemed to him to promise also to give him that Church and religion in which he felt at home.

The time was opportune. The time of what the Abbé Constant has called 'schism' in England began to give place to the time of real scheming for Reformation.

Henry VIII had died and Gardiner, the Bishop of Winchester, was more or less silenced. The Government was definitely in favour of Protestantism, the young King as well as Protector Somerset and other influential persons. Cranmer saw his way clearly. All this helps to account for the fact that Bucer gained in England a hold which was not granted to Lutherans or Zwinglians. During their time of negotiation, the Lutheran emissaries had had to labour under unpropitious political omens in the policy of Henry VIII.

The strife between Lutheranism and Zwinglianism in matters of doctrine also did not help to give the impression in England that Protestantism would be a new and unified power for the Church and Christianity. The lack of unity among Reformers was often pointed at by their adversaries as proof that Protestantism would not be able to give the real Christianity which it claimed to offer. Thus it is not surprising that Bucer, who was known as the pacifying spirit, was much more warmly welcomed than one of the striving parties.

[1] cf. Letter of Joh. Sturm and the Strassburg 'Scholarchen' to the Rector and Professors of the University of Copenhagen, dated June 3rd, 1549 (vol. II, p. 85A, in Ficker, Joh. and Winckelmann, O.: *Handschriftenproben des sechzehnten Jahrhunderts* . . . (Strassburg, 1905).

1548); Bucer left (Augsburg) without signing the Interim (p. 22). Both letters in Calendar of State Papers, Foreign, 1547-53.

(3) Bucer in his Last Will. cf. Harvey, op. cit., p. 164, pp. 170-171.

(4) Thomas Hoby writes in his Diary:

'. . . This was the last time that ever I sawe Mr. Bucer, but afterward at times I receaved letteres from him. This Interim was not in my time receaved in Argentine, for that Mr. Bucer bothe writt and spake earnestlie against yt, yeven in Auspurck after he was sent for thither under th' Emperor's save conduct, and at his return preached openlye that in case they receaved it, they should liese him, as they did at lengthe: for he went from thense into England.' *The Travels and Life of Sir Thomas Hoby, Knight 1547-1564.* (Ed. for the Royal Historical Society by Edgar Powell, The Camden Miscellany, vol. X (2), London, 1902, Camden Society, 3rd Series, vol. IV, p. 6.)

§ I

MARTIN BUCER AND CAMBRIDGE

In a letter of October 2nd, 1548 (as already mentioned), Archbishop Cranmer had invited Martin Bucer, in a most striking gesture of friendship, expressing anxiety about his fate and safe conduct to this country.[1] Bucer thanked him in a letter from Strassburg (December 23rd, 1548).[2] But another few months were to pass before he could avail himself of the invitation. On March 24th, 1549,[3] Peter Alexander, a French refugee who at that time was staying with the archbishop, had written at Cranmer's special request repeating the invitation. In this letter he assured Bucer of a hearty welcome in England. He refers to Latimer, of whom he says:

ut Christum Simeon, ita te ille, tuique similes amplecti cupit.

Bucer's opponents seem to have thought differently of his presence in England. Burcher, one of the English partisans of the Swiss Party, wrote to Henry Bullinger on April 20th, 1550, when Bucer had been already one year in England[4]:

> In case of his [Bucer's] death, England will be happy, and more favoured than all other countries, in having been delivered in the same year from two men, of most pernicious talent, namely, Paul [Fagius] and Bucer.

On April 1st, 1549, Burcher had written to Bullinger:

> May the Lord preserve our England from both of them.[5]

Those words express clearly the feeling of the Swiss party against Bucer, and their anxiety, lest by his activities in England their chances for gaining ground with their own scheme for Reformation should be seriously impaired. But the Swiss party was not the only

[1] cf. *Scripta Anglicana*, pp. 190-191, and *Original Letters*, vol. I, pp. 19-20.

[2] cf. *Original Letters*, vol. II, pp. 533-534.

[3] cf. *Scr. Angl.*, pp. 191-192. cf. the similar letter of invitation to Paul Fagius (March 24th, 1549), *Original Letters*, vol. I, pp. 329-330.

On Alexander, Pierre, cf. article in *Biographie Nationale . . . De Belgique* (Bruxelles, 1866), and article in J. Ficker and O. Winckelmann,: *Handschriftenproben des Sechzehnten Jahrhunderts* . . . (Strassburg, 1905), vol. II, p. 73.

[4] *Original Letters*, vol. II, pp. 662-663. cf. also his letter to Bullinger (June 8th, 1550), *Original Letters*, vol. II, pp. 666 f. 'I am ignorant as to what the hireling Bucer, who fled from this church before the wolf came in sight, is plotting in England . . .' cf. also, op. cit., vol. II, p. 678. cf. also Bullinger's remark: 'I would really begin to hope for something better, if Bucer also were called by the Lord. . . .' (puoted by Eells, H., in his *Martin Bucer*, op. cit., p. 405).

[5] *Original Letters*, vol. II, p. 651.

one which felt disturbed by the prospect of strong advancement of Bucer's teaching in England. The Emperor Charles V, whose 'Interim' had caused Bucer to leave Strassburg, and who at first was delighted by not having any longer to face his opposition on the Continent, soon realized that England was in favour of Bucer and his teaching and thus opposed to his policy. In his instruction for Chantonnay to King Ferdinand he had stated at first (July 12th, 1549, Bucer had left in April):

> . . . et si est un grand point gaigné en ce qu'ils ont trouvé moyen de mectre Buccerus hors de la ville, qui est allé en Angleterre; . . .[1]

But his satisfaction changed to anger when he found that Bucer was responsible for English Church practice. Nicholas Wotton, Dean of Canterbury and York, wrote to the Council from Augsburg (September 1st, 1551), that he had had an audience with the Emperor on the matter of Holy Communion, and that he had argued for the use according to English practice as opposed to the Mass:

> . . . The Emperor said, he did not wonder they thought so in England now, for they had called to them, and received daily, all the greatest heretics of the time, as Bernardine, Bucer, and such others who were able to seduce any man. Wotton replied, that the Emperor might call Bernardine and Bucer, as it pleased him, but in England they were known for great, wise, learned men, notwithstanding which neither they nor a hundred such could have caused England to alter anything in those matters, unless the truth itself had very plainly appeared to them.[2]

But the welcome given to Bucer here could not be spoilt by the anger of his opponents.

The account of his journey and that of his fellow-travellers from Strassburg to England, a journey lasting about three weeks, is a thrilling story with a happy ending in their cordial reception by the archbishop at Lambeth:

> Sumpto itaque prandio Dovariae, postea equis dispositis Cantuanam ea nocte pervenimus; ubique ab illius loci episcopo hospitio suscepti, honorifice tractati fuimus. Vigesima quarta Aprilis Rotae [Rochester] pransi sumus. Noctu vero Gravesenii [Gravesend] pernoctavimus, quod est oppidum situm ad Tamisim fluvium qui cygnos alit in magna copia. Vigesima quinta Aprilis Londin-

[1] cf. in Druffel, August: *Beiträge zur Reichsgeschichte* (München, 1873), vol. I, p. 248.

[2] Calendar of State Papers (Foreign), 1547-53, pp. 166 f. cf. also Calendar of State Papers, Spanish, 1550-52, p. 349: The Emperor to J. Scheyfve, September 3rd, 1551. Also, p. 170: Simon Renard to the Emperor, September 1st, 1550: '. . . and in the third place they [scil. the English] fear that your Majesty may have still been more incensed by their reception of Bucer and brother Bernardin, whom your Majesty thrust out . . .'

um usque navigio horis quinque pervenimus. Eodem illo die statim post prandium, assumpti fuimus in Aulam Reverendissimi Episcopi Cantuariensis, Consiliarii Regii praecipui, qui tum sedem aulae suae habebat Lambeti in pago ad ripam fluminis ulteriorem, quasi e regione civitatis Londini. Is dominos nostros honorificentissime excepit, prolatis stolis, pro more gentis, quibus ipsos ornare dignatus fuit: et paucis diebus post ad Regem ipsum Edwardum sextum adduxit, qui non dico regium animum, sed magis paternum, etsi aetate juvenili adhuc erat, erga ipsos multis verbis et indiciis declaravit. Quam paternam benevolentiam multi procerum istius regni sequuti, illos quoque invitatos, plurimis beneficiis sunt prosequuti, inter quos primas partes sibi sumpsit Ducissa Suffolciae [Catherine Brandon, née Willoughby]; et protector regis, Dux Summersetensis.

Thus endeth the report of the perilous Odyssey of Bucer and his friends as given by Matthew Negelin.[1]

Before Bucer came to Cambridge he seems to have stayed from April to October of 1549 with the archbishop at Lambeth and at Croydon. During their stay with the archbishop in 1549 Bucer and Fagius were engaged on translating the Bible from its original sources into Latin and writing brief explanatory notes to the difficult passages of each chapter. Of these notes Bucer's annotation to the first eight chapters of S. Matthew are still extant in MS. form. The Latin translation has large notes added in the margin with remarks by Cranmer's hand also.[2] Sebastian Castalio in the Dedication of his Latin Bible to Edward VI (February 1551 from Basle) seems to allude to the work of Bucer and Fagius, when he writes:

. . . quod tu nuper hanc eandem transferendi libros sacros prouinciam, hominibus doctis mandauisses, sed unius obitu impeditus fuisses.[3]

Bucer's friendship with the archbishop was a great source of uneasiness for the Swiss Party. Hooper's remarks in various of his letters to Bullinger leave no doubt about it: he writes (April 26th, 1549):

[1] cf. the 'Itinerarium': Pierre Janelle (in *Revue d'Histoire et de Philosophie Religieuses*, 1928), *Le Voyage de Martin Bucer et Paul Fagius de Strasbourg en Angleterre en 1549* (pp. 162-177), pp. 173-174; cf. also pp. 176-177 in Negelin's Letter to Ulstetter. cf. also the letters of Paul Fagius to Ulstetter and to Hubert (*Original Letters* (Parker Society), vol. I, pp. 331-334), and Bucer's and Fagius' Letters to the Ministers at Strassburg (*Original Letters*, vol. II, pp. 534-537).

[2] cf. *Original Letters*, vol. I, p. 334 (Letter of Fagius to Hubert, Croydon, May 7th, 1549). cf. Corpus Christi College, Cambridge, MS. 104, 1: Martini Buceri in octo priora capita evangelii secundum Matthaeum. (Montague Rhodes James, Catalogue . . .). cf. also Strype: *Mem. of Abp. Cranmer* (ed. Oxford, 1840), vol. I, p. 279.

[3] cf. *Biblia*, Interprete Sebastiano Castalione . . . (Basle, 1551), fol. a.2. cf. also, Lewis, John: *A Complete History . . . of the Holy Bible* (London, 1739), pp. 179-180 and note q.

> . . . Peter Martyr and Bernardine so stoutly defend Lutheranism and there is now arrived a third (I mean Bucer), who will leave no stone unturned to obtain a footing . . .

and in another letter (May 31st, 1549):

> Bucer has very great influence with him . . .

and on June 25th, 1549:

> Bucer is with the Archbishop of Canterbury like another Scipio, and an inseparable companion.[1]

As early as September 1549 (September 26th) an annuity of one hundred pounds was granted to him by Edward VI,[2] and on December 4th, 1549, the king, in a letter to the Vice-Chancellor of the University of Cambridge (Walter Haddon), recommends Bucer as a new lecturer of Divinity and asks the University to accept him kindly.[3] Walter Haddon himself, in a letter to Dr. Matthew Parker, later Archbishop of Canterbury, requests Parker to present Bucer for his degree of Doctor of Divinity before the Vice-Chancellor, as the Master of Trinity College, John Redman, who could have been asked for that ceremony, was ill at that time. The letter has at the end the words *assensum est* in the handwriting of Parker.[4]

Bucer delivered an oration on the occasion of the conferment of the degree. He refers to the honour due to him, the 'senem, morbidum, inutilem, peregrinum',[5] who will do his utmost to justify the expectation of those who honoured him so unduly. He then enlarges on the subject of the reform of academic life and of the Christian standard of the University.[6]

In Cambridge Bucer lived in the same house in which later Nicholas Carr was to die.[7]

Life at Cambridge, in spite of illness and in spite of indisposition due to the English climate and winter, was made as pleasant as

[1] cf. *Original Letters*, vol. I, pp. 61, 64, 67.

[2] cf. Rymer, Thomas: *Foedera* . . . (London, 1713), Tom. XV, pp. 192-193: Pro Martino Bucero de Concessione ad Placitum.

[3] cf. Lamb, John: *A Collection of Letters* . . . (London, 1838), pp. 152 f. (MS. Corp. Chris. Col. Camb., CVI, 163.)

[4] cf. Lamb, op. cit., p. 153. (MS. Corp. Chris. Col., Camb., CVI, 166.)

[5] *Scr. Angl.*, p. 190.

[6] ibid., pp. 184-190.

[7] Letter of Bartholomew Dodington on the life and death of N. Carr, to Sir Walter Mildmay ('Cantabrigiae pridie Calend. Nouembris. 1570 e collegio trinitatis'), p. 62, verso: 'AEdes autem, ex quo matrimonium contraxit, easdem, quas olim sanctissimus vir, idemque theologiae apud nos regius professor, Martinus Bucerus, tenuit, de cuius obitu, omninoque de iustissimis laudibus epistolam nouendecim abhinc annis scripsit, ad D. Ioannem Chekum, patronum suum, quae impressa extat, digna, quae legatur ab omnibus . . .' 'Obijt in eisdem aedibus, quibus D. Martinus Bucerus, quasi fatale esset, illis duorum, doctissimorum virorum funera emittere.' (p. 63.)
Letter in Nicholas Carr: *Demosthenis, Graecorum Oratorum*. . . . (London, 1571).

possible by his many friends. The kindness shown to him by the Duchess of Suffolk, the kindness by King Edward, who presented him with an extra twenty pounds, in order that he might build a stove in German fashion, made Bucer feel immensely grateful. He writes in his preface to *De Regno Christi* with reference to the royal gift:

> . . . for he contributed in addition the magnificent gift of 20 pounds, with which I should arrange for a stove, not because being used to it, but being necessary for my old-aged body, weakened by illness.[1]

Great admiration filled Bucer for the young king, who had so kindly shown favour to him. Another gift to Bucer by King Edward was a 'poculum auratum' for his birthday (November 11th).[2] Bucer sees in him the young Josiah who will lead his nation to true religion.[3] He writes to Brentius from Cambridge (May 15th, 1550):

> The king . . . is godly and learned to a miracle: he is well acquainted with Latin, and has a fair knowledge of Greek; he speaks Italian, and is learning French. He is now studying moral philosophy from Cicero and Aristotle: but no study delights him more than that of the holy scriptures, of which he daily reads about ten chapters with the greatest attention. Some youths from among the principal nobility follow his example in these studies, and with good success. . . .[4]

Invitations by Cambridge professors to their houses soon followed. Matthew Parker became a good friend, a friendship which even went so far as to Bucer borrowing money from him.[5] Here at Cambridge he met with all the eminent Cambridge men, Walter Haddon,[6] William Bill, John Redman, Edmund Grindal, John Bradford, and with his Roman Catholic opponents, John Young, Thomas Sedgwick and Andrew Perne.

In discussions with men like Grindal, Parker, Sandys, Bradford, Bucer had an opportunity to form a clearer picture of English ecclesiastical and economic conditions so important for his work *De Regno Christi* and for his *Censura*.[7]

[1] 'adiecit enim praeclarum praeterea munus xx librarum, quibus pro corpusculi mei, sic fatigati senio, & morbo fracti, non tam consuetudine, quam necessitate, hypocaustum pararem.' (*Scr. Angl.*, p.a.)

[2] cf. Harvey, op. cit., p. 173.

[3] cf. Bucer's Letter to Edward VI here, pp. 127 ff.

[4] *Original Letters*, vol. II, p. 543.

[5] cf. n. xxxi-xxxiii, pp. 41 ff. in *Correspondence of M. Parker* (Parker Society, 1853).

[6] With Haddon's brother, James Haddon, Bucer seems to have been in correspondence. cf. Corpus Christ. Col. MS. CXIII, 5 (Bucer's letter to J. Haddon, May 22nd, 1550).

[7] cf. Sampson's letter to W. Cecil of March 8th, 1573 (Strype, John: *Annals* . . . (ed. Oxford, 1824), vol. II, i, pp. 392 ff.

John Bradford, who was at Cambridge, saw in Bucer his special friend.[1] He accompanied him on his journey to Oxford. He was present during the last illness of Bucer (*Scripta Anglicana*, pp. 874-875), and lamented his death grievously, so that even in the last days of his own life, when in prison, in his *Farewell to Cambridge* he reminded the city of Bucer and his teaching.[2] And it was Bucer's writings which comforted Bradford in prison and in expectation of death.[3] He read Bucer's Commentary to the Romans, and was specially moved by the explanation of Romans viii. 22: 'For we know that the whole creation groaneth and travaileth in pain together until now.'

The death of his fellow-exile and dear friend, Paul Fagius, on November 13th, 1549, affected Bucer deeply, as he writes in a letter from Cambridge to his colleagues at Strassburg (December 26th).[4]

In January of 1550 he began to lecture, and in spite of many interruptions caused by severe illness, carried on with his task even to a few weeks before his death. Besides his lectures on Ephesians, he apparently lectured also on the Gospel according to S. John, although Hooper's statement in a letter to Bullinger (March 27th, 1550) seems to suggest that the exposition on S. John was more on the line of sermons delivered on Sundays:

> Master Bucer is now lying dangerously ill at Cambridge. The subject of his lecture is the epistle to the Ephesians, and of his sermon, on holy-days, the sixth chapter of St. John.[5]

John Ab Ulmis in a letter to Bullinger (March 25th, 1550) writes:

> Bucer had entered upon the exposition of the sixth chapter of St. John, but is now, at the very threshold of his work, confined to his bed by a severe and dangerous illness. God, our merciful Father, knows what will be the result. We have almost entirely abandoned all hopes of his recovery.[6]

Hooper, in his letter to Bullinger, just mentioned, has a significant

[1] cf. Biographical note, pp. xx-xxiv in *The Writings of John Bradford, Letters, Treatises. . . .* (Parker Society, 1853).

[2] cf. op. cit., *Sermons, Meditations. . . .* p. 445.

[3] cf. *The Writings of John Bradford, Sermons, Meditations . . .* (Parker Society, 1848), pp. 350 ff.: 'The Restoration of all Things' (written after Bradford's condemnation, January 31st, 1555). p. 350: 'It is, through almost the whole, translated from the commentaries of the very learned Reformer, Martin Bucer . . .'

Myles Coverdale, who includes Bradford's 'Restoration of all Things' in his edition of the 'Letters of the Martyrs' (1564), makes the marginal remark: 'He meaneth that most godly & learned father, M. Martin Bucer' (op. cit., p. 355).

[4] 1549 is correct and not 1550 as given in the *Original Letters* (op. cit., vol. II, pp. 549 ff.).

cf. *D.N.B.* Article on Fagius, and Gorham, C., op. cit., p. 123.

[5] cf. *Original Letters*, vol. I, p. 81.

[6] cf. ibid., vol. II, p. 401.

passage as to the difficulties Bucer and any other lecturer had to be aware, when dealing with the Eucharistic question:

> Master Valerandus has recommended him [Bucer] by letter not to raise any controversy on the matter of the eucharist. He replied that he should teach nothing contrary to the opinion of Peter Martyr, which I sent you in manuscript about the middle of January.[1]

If this statement as regards Bucer's reply can be trusted, Bucer must have changed later his opinion, for he repeatedly criticizes, although in a friendly way, utterances of Peter Martyr concerning Eucharistic questions, which seemed to him to be too vague and to imply conceptions contrary to the doctrine of the Real Presence.

Whether Bucer observed the warning sent to him by Valerandus or not, he became involved in a far more serious controversy on account of his lectures. His letters to Grindal as well as to Cheke and his long and prolix review of his controversy with Young, show how much disturbed he was about it. The controversy took place in June 1550 on 'Justification by Faith only' and other topics between Bucer and Young, against whom Bucer had to defend later also his own views on Usury.[2]

In the course of his lecture on the Epistles to the Ephesians (January 1550)[3] he covered a wide field of theological and ecclesiastical questions. In a significant passage he pointed out the twofold danger theologians had to beware of. He stressed the fact that to pursue the study of theology meant neither to swerve to the right nor to the left of the path; ministers of the Word had to travel in their obedience and loyalty to their calling. The danger of acquiescing in a merely external conception of the ministry, as displayed by Roman Catholicism, is as grave as the other way of misinterpreting the ministry, as done by Anabaptism, which contemns the Church, Ministry and the Sacraments.[4]

[1] *Original Letters*, vol. I, p. 82.

[2] Letter to Grindal, *Scr. Angl.*, pp. 803-804.
Letter to Cheke, Harvey, op. cit., pp. 127 ff.
See also *Scr. Angl.*, pp. 711-712, letter of Bucer (3 Idus Augusti 1550) to the 'reader'.
Bucer's account of the Controversy: *Scr. Angl.*, pp. 805-862. Account, pp. 711-788, pp. 797-803. On Usury, pp. 789-796.
cf. also, Gorham, C.: op. cit., note on pp. 163-164.

[3] cf. Peter of Perugia's Letter to H. Bullinger (February 10th, 1550), *Original Letters*, vol. I, pp. 338-339, also Hooper's letter to H. Bullinger (March 27th, 1550), op. cit., p. 81.

[4] *Scr. Angl.*, pp. 519-520: 'Duo itaque hic sunt praecipitia diligentissime cauenda . . . cf. also *Scr. Angl.*, p. 556 (De vi et usu . . .). The 'via media' between the two extremes, the Roman Catholic conception of the Church and the Anabaptist conception of the Church, had been stressed by Bucer since he had to fight the two at Strassburg, and Bucer's stress for taking that 'via media' had become characteristic for his theology throughout.

The question of ceremonies, of the sacraments, of the necessity of the Church and its government, those are only a few topics of the same course of lectures.

When explaining the passage of Ephesians iv. 28, Bucer felt induced to enlarge on the question of 'Pleonexia' and usury. Some of his students, who could only pursue their academic life by lending their capital at interest, had asked for Bucer's advice as to how far taking of interest was permissible and justifiable. Bucer's reply in his lecture gave rise to a long dispute.

The Lectures on the Ephesians were posthumously printed. Immanuel Tremellius edited them in 1562 at Basle, eleven years after Bucer's death. Tremellius dedicated the Lectures by a prefatory letter (Heidelberg, September 17th, 1561) to Sir Nicholas Throckmorton. That was about sixteen years before Conrad Hubert, Bucer's colleague and amanuensis, edited by the kind assistance of Grindal Bucer's *Scripta Anglicana* (Basle, 1577). In that volume part of the lecture is included (pp. 504-538).[1] 'De vi et usu sacri ministerii Explicatio M. Buceri'[2] of the *Scripta Anglicana* (pp. 553-610) forms in Tremellius' edition part of the Lecture on the Ephesians (Praelectiones . . . pp. 108-154).

Tremellius edited the Lectures although he knew of Hubert's intention to publish Bucer's works, and although he knew that Hubert had a better and more correct MS. copy of the Lecture. Hubert was specially disturbed about Tremellius' manœuvre, pointing out in a letter (April 24th, 1562) that Tremellius' print of the section 'De vi et usu sacri ministerii' was full of mistakes.[3]

The lecture, with its firm ecclesiastical and doctrinal statements, furnished various English theologians with welcome material for their particular arguments. Whitgift in his controversy with Cartwright repeatedly makes use of Bucer's lecture.[4] Thomas Bell in his 'anti-Brownist' pamphlet makes reference to it,[5] so does *The Originall of Bishops* . . .[6] and George Hakewill in his *The Auncient Ecclesiasticall practise of Confirmation* (1613).[7] Bucer never finished the lecture, which was interrupted by that severe illness which finally led to his

[1] 'Explicatio Martini Buceri in illud Apostoli Ephes. iiii. Tolerantes vos inuicem . . .' *Scr. Angl.*, pp. 504-538.

[2] 'Coepta explicari Cantabrigiae in nomine Domini ix Nouembris, Anno sal. M.D.L.' (*Scr. Angl.*, p. 553).

[3] cf. Röhrich, Timotheus Wilhelm, 'Conrad Hubert', p. 273, in: *Mitteilungen aus der Geschichte*, vol. III, pp. 268 ff.

[4] cf. Whitgift, op. cit., vol. II, pp. 331 f.; vol. III, pp. 30-31, 64-65, 358, 360-361.

[5] Bell, Thomas: *The Regiment of the Church* . . . (London, 1606), p. 96, pp. 118-120.

[6] *The Originall of Bishops*. . . . (Anno 1641), p. 47, marginal note, reference to Bucer's De vi et usu . . . (*Scr. Angl.*, pp. 581-582).

[7] cf. p. 15.

death. Thus at the end of 'De vi et usu sacri ministerii' as printed in the *Scripta Anglicana*, the editor of that volume adds (p. 610):

> Huc vsque Explicatione sua progressus doctissimus Theologus, in morbum incidit grauissimum: cuius vehementia latius grassante, paulo post in Christo Seruatore felicissime obdormiuit, Cantabrigiae in Anglia pridie Cal. Martias, Anno salutis. M.D.L.I.

John Banck of Trinity College,[1] one of Bucer's students at Cambridge, took down notes of the lecture. These MS. notes, beautifully written, were dedicated by him with a prefatory letter to the Marquis of Dorset, Henry Grey.[2] They provide us with a further source of information to the lecture as printed in the *Scripta Anglicana* and in Tremellius' edition (*Praelectiones in Epist. ad Ephesios*, 1562). Here in Banck's lecture-notes we have the lecture as delivered to and reproduced by the student, whereas Bucer's own draft of the lecture provided the text for the two printed editions.

As Banck took down most faithfully even personal remarks of the lecturer ('. . . sed mihi videor quendam audire nescio quid ogannientem: Quid, Bucere, vis? An quomodo anabaptistae, ita nullos nobis ludos permittas? Quod si chartas tollas, quid putas suscipi a nobis oportere?')[3], and although he may on the other hand not have jotted down passages known to us from the printed editions, his notes are of interest in conjunction with the texts known to us.

The parts of Bucer's lecture are again clearly set out:

De vi, et Vsu sacri ministerij
De vi, et efficacia ministerij uerbi
De vi, et efficacia ministerij baptismatis
De vi, et efficacia coenae Dominicae.

A summary of the lecture is also given by Banck in his letter to the Marquis. The description of that part of the lecture which deals with the Eucharist found in the *Historia Sacramentaria* of Rodolph Hospinian[4] makes interesting reading when compared with that by Banck.

[1] On John Banck see article in Cooper, Ch. H., *Athenae Cantab.*, vol. I, p. 109; p. 542; and Garrett, Chr., *The Marian Exiles* (Cambridge, 1938), pp. 78-79 as to letters of Banck, cf. *Original Letters*, vol. I, pp. 303-309.

[2] MS. Coll. Gonv. et Caius 423; the letter to the Marquis is for the first time printed here: pp. 257-258.

[3] MS. Coll. Gonv. et Caius 423; cf. there also Bucer's own reference to the Continental Controversy on the Eucharist as put down by Banck: 'Ego quidem, fratres, magnos profecto labores in initio suscepi, totamque fere Germaniam peragraui, vt cum ijs, qui vtriusque partis principes erant, et cum illis item, qui in contentionem pertrahebantur, de tota causa, et controuersia sermones instituerem. Conueni Dominum Lutherum: et D. philippum: Conueni Zuinglium, et Bullingerum: et conueni quidem propterea, vt publicae concordiae, cui semper studui, consuleretur.'

[4] Rodolphi Hospiniani *Historiae Sacramentariae . . .*, Pars Posterior (Genevae, MDC.LXXXI), pp. 372-373: Paulo ante mortem in Cantabrigiensi Academia dictare

Though Banck thought so highly of Bucer's lecture, Thomas Horton, another student, was of different opinion when describing in a letter in terms of boredom the lecturer's incessant moral admonitions:

> . . . Dr. Bucer cries incessantly, now in [his] daily lectures, now in frequent sermons, that we should practice penitence, discard the depraved customs of hypocritical religion, correct the abuses of feasts, be more frequent in hearing and having sermons, [and] constrain ourselves by some sort of discipline. Many things of this kind he impresses on us even *ad nauseam*, for we are so insensitive that, notwithstanding, we sleep with both ears, we eat, we drink, we take wives, and expose them as it were to be gazed at, &c. but suddenly he concerning whom we are all heedless hammers on our inner doors.[1]

Being repeatedly seriously ill, he was thus hampered much in the execution of his lecturing duties. A most intimate letter to his physician at Strassburg, Johan Echt (May 13th, 1550, Cambridge), gives a clear account of the illness.[2] But in the early summer of 1550 he recovered suddenly and took a short vacation, staying at the home of the Duchess of Suffolk, and then visiting for about a week[3] his friend Peter Martyr at Oxford. Peter Martyr, who had already been informed by Bucer in a letter of his intention, was eagerly expecting him. In July Bucer, accompanied by John Bradford, came to Oxford. Laurence Humphrey recalls that event in his biography of Bishop Jewel, and the fact that Humphrey in 1572 can still give an analysis of Bucer's lecture at Christ Church on that occasion, shows the interest he attached to that visit and to Bucer's lecture. The account is scarcely known but for the fact that Strype

[1] English translation in C. H. Smyth, *Cranmer & the Reformation under Edward VI*, pp. 163-164. The letter by Horton was written to Francis Dryander (ex aula Pembruchiana Cantabrigiae, May 15th, 1550). This part (up to *ad nauseam et fastidium*) in its original Latin in Harvey, op. cit., pp. 48-49.

[2] Letter in Harvey, op. cit., pp. 122-127; translated extracts in Gorham, op. cit., pp. 145-146.

On Joh. Echt, cf. Adam, Melchior: *Vitae Germanorum Medicorum* (Heidelberg, 1620), pp. 72-73.

[3] 'Eleven days'. cf. Martyr's letter to Hubert, March 8th, 1551 (*Scr. Angl.*, p. 901) and *Original Letters*, vol. II, p. 491.

---

coeperat auditoribus suis explicationem de vi, & usu Sacri Ministerii: Cumque ad Coenam Domini pervenisset, promiserat explicare, quid ipse sentiat de hoc mysterio credendum esse: Tum, quam existimet veram, ac genuinam verborum Domini, & Spiritus Sancti de hoc mysterio intelligentiam, & interpretationem: Tertio, quibus nos verbis deceat maxime in commendando, praedicandoque hoc sacramento uti: postremo, ad fugiendam superstitionem Papistarum; tum etiam ad cavendas omnes hallucinationes, & iniquas de Fratribus suspiciones, quibus implicantur, qui de hoc mysterio, huc usque acriter contenderunt, etiam ad horum omnium respondere statuit argumenta, quibusquisque vel errorem suum tueri conatur, vel suam defendere in asserendo sua, & refutando placita & dicta Fratrum duritiem, sed morte praeventus absolvere non potuit.

mentions that Bucer lectured, so that it seems worth while to quote Humphrey:

> Bucer, accompanied beside others by John Bradford, that most excellent person and most faithful martyr, one of his most dear and intimate friends, went to Oxford, to see that University & Peter Martyr, a little before St. Mary Magdalen's day . . .[1]

From the beginning the Duchess of Suffolk had a liking for Bucer. Catherine Brandon, *née* Willoughby, was mentioned by Negelin in his account of Bucer's flight from Strassburg to England, among those who welcomed Bucer and his colleagues on their arrival in England. She soon became a real friend to Bucer, thus making Fagius already write jokingly in a letter to Hubert in May of 1549 (May 7th), that Bucer's wife ought to come soon to England, for otherwise Bucer would take another, as the Duchess of Suffolk liked him, 'who is now a widow'.[2] She sent her two sons, Charles and Henry, to Cambridge, where they attended Bucer's lectures and found in him a fatherly friend. A sincere and deep mutual friendship developed between Bucer and the Duchess and her sons. Bucer stayed with the family for a few days, as he mentions in his letter to Cheke.[3] The Duchess tried to make life for Bucer in his exile as agreeable as possible, and also tried to help him in business affairs. She writes twice to Cecil in connection with Bucer, the second letter being written only a few days before his death.[4] Her benevolence also took an even more practical turn. Her gift of a cow and a calf

[1] cf. *Writings of Bradford, Letters*, . . . op. cit., p. xxii. 'Anno. 1550. sub festum Magdalenae, quod tum erat apud nos receptum & celebratum, Oxoniam visendi Petrum Martyrem & Academiam causa, venit clariss. Sanctae Theologiae apud Cantabrigienses professor Mart. Bucerus, praeter caeteros Ioanne Bradfordo, optimo viro & constantissimo Martyre, qui ei ex intimis maximeque familiaribus erat, comitatus. Is in Collegio Christi concionatus est, seu ut ipse vocabat, praelegit, materia accepta ex Euangelio D. Ioannis capite decimo septimo: *Sanctifica nos* [sic] *o pater in veritate*, & quae sequuntur. Quod totum sic divisit, ut tres potissimum partes ea lectio amplecteretur: Pro quibus orabat Christus, Quibus de causis, & quid die sabbati sequente ex Math. septimo docebat nos cavere nobis, & attendere a Pseudoprophetis. Praecipuae partes erant de praecepto & propositione: ubi duo notavit, Quis & Quid moneret: tum de lupis rapacibus, & ovium simplicitate: Deinde regula & canone, unde Prophetae veri a falsis ex doctrinae & morum fructibus discernantur: postremo de proprietatibus quibusdam seu consequentibus, de uvarum ex spinis collectione, & de arborum inutilium excisione. De Scripturis autem & prophetia, illud utilissime observavit, ad eam quatuor valde conferre, Lectionem assiduam, precationem ardentissimam, conventus publicos, & privata colloquia. In Epilogo hortatus est ut veri prophetae, pastores, reges, ministri, miseris animabus prospiciant, nec eas fame vel siti perire sinant.' (Humfredus, Laur., *Iuelli . . . Vita* . . . (London, 1573), pp. 42-43).

[2] 'Sie soll sich bald auf die Fahrt machen, oder er [Bucer] wird eine andere kriegen, denn die Herzogin Suffoltzii will ihn haben; ist jetzt eine Wittfrau,' printed in Harvey, A. E.: *Martin Bucer*, pp. 41-42. It is a PS. to the letter printed in the *Original Letters*, vol. I, p. 333, which is omitted in the *Original Letters*.

[3] August 29th, 1550, cf. Harvey, A. E., op. cit., p. 127.

[4] Letter to Cecil, December 28th, 1549, Calendar of State Papers Domestic, 1547-80, p. 27, n. 58.

ibid., February 17th, 1551, p. 32, n. 6.

for Bucer's support and that of his house at Cambridge, gave rise to an anecdote, which for Bucer's friends seemed to have more serious implications, as deliberately invented by the 'papists'. Laurence Humphrey, in his biography of Bishop Jewel, recalls the story as an impudent attack against Bucer, at which Bucer only laughed.[1] When Bucer went once out to the field where the animals were kept, it was said that he was taught by them what to lecture. Bucer's reply, according to Humphrey, was only that those animals would be fine teachers, as they could neither speak Latin, Greek, Hebrew nor German, languages in which he himself was conversant. The fact that Humphrey attaches so much importance to this silly little anecdote, shows only how seriously everything was taken, when an intentional attack was suspected behind each small story.[2]

During Bucer's illness the Duchess nursed[3] him and was present with his friends, men like Bradford and others. His death was a hard blow to her; her two sons soon followed (July 16th, 1551) Bucer to his eternal rest. The many epitaphs on the occasion of Bucer's death contain also epitaphs on the death of the young Brandons

[1] Humphrey, Laurence, op. cit., pp. 260-261.

[2] In this connection another anecdote unfavourable for Bucer's fame ought to be mentioned. Humphrey, in the same work (p. 261), writes: 'Contra eundem Bucerũ coccisat Pontacus Burdegalensis [i.e. Bishop Arnaud de Pontac], eũm in Anglia moribundum dixisse, Iesum Christum non fuisse verũ illũ promissum Messiã, sed aliũ nobis expectandum. Quod prodigiosum figmẽtum. . . .'

With this story the account of a similar rumour as reported by Sir Richard Morysine to the Council (Augsburg, April 14th, 1551) ought to be given: 'Bucer's death has raised up again the bruit that was here, that we are become Jews. The tale is thus told: The King's Majesty asking Bucer how the Bishop of Rome's authority might be quite extinct? His answer was, "Sir, Messias is not yet come, and therefore the authority that Christ hath given him is to be accounted as none. Their Lordships see what lust they have to lie, that lie thus, not so much as colouring it with some likelihood of truth". Bucer is safely laid up, and our country not the worse of a mite that they, which know no more of Christ than his name and dwelling-place, do take us all for damned souls . . .' (Calendar of State Papers, Foreign, 1547-53, p. 88).

[3] cf. Roger Ascham, in his letter (June 18th, 1551) to Johann Sturm: 'Scriberem ad te copiose, qua pietate complexa est *Bucerum* nobilissima *Dux Suffolciensis*, qua cura curatione ipsa praesens noctes diesque illum fovit; nisi uxor *D. Buceri*, omnia illa opportunius commemoraret.' (*Rog. Asch. Ep.*, editio 1703, op. cit., p. 40.)

The passage in Peter Martyr's letter to Bucer (June 10th, 1550, cf. Gorham, op. cit., p. 151): '. . . your wife (as you write) has already gone into Germany' seems to explain why the Duchess and not his own wife nursed Bucer during his illness. (cf. Harvey, op. cit., p. 42, and note 5 ibid.)

But by 'Royal Patent' of Edward VI on 'the last day of March' 1551 a passport was granted to 'Mrs. Bucer' and several of her household. This seems to indicate that Bucer's wife was in England in March of 1551, having returned to England from Strassburg (cf. Acts of the Privy Council of England, New Series, vol. III, London, 1891, pp. 246-247). cf. also, *Original Letters*, op. cit., vol. I, p. 362, in Parker's and Haddon's letter to the guardians of Bucer's children. cf. also Smyth, C. H., op. cit., p. 164. As regards Mrs. Bucer's first coming to England, cf. Valérand Poullain's Letter to Bucer (June 8th, 1549), (pp. 240-243 in van Schelven, A. A., Zur Biographie und Theologie des Valérand Poullain. *Zeitschrift für Kirchengeschichte*, Neue Folge, X, Band XLVII, ii Heft, 1928, pp. 227-249). On Mrs. Bucer's visit to Germany, cf. also the PS. in Burcher's letter to Bullinger (Strassburg, June 8th, 1550), *Original Letters*, op. cit., vol. II, p. 667.

and vice versa. Walter Haddon's and Thomas Wilson's *Vita et Obitus Duorum Fratrum Suffolciensium, Henrici et Caroli Brandoni*, repeatedly dwells on the intimate friendship and admiration for Bucer by the Duchess and her sons, and gives many contemporary eulogies by scholars and famous men, in which Bucer and his two pupils are described in their friendship.

The friendship of Duchess Catherine with Bucer seems to have caused some talk with suggestions that she owed him money. Under Queen Mary when the Duchess fled to the Continent with her new husband, Richard Bertie, Coverdale, who also had become a refugee, was reassured by Bertie, that his wife

> as far as money was concerned, owed nothing at all either to our excellent father Bucer, or to any other persons.[1]

Thus writes Coverdale to Hubert (September 20th, 1555), even now connecting Bucer with the Duchess in her exile and distress, which is so movingly described in Foxe[2] and later in Thomas Deloney's garbled ballad: 'The Duchesse of Suffolkes Calamitie.'[3]

Bucer's acquaintance with the family of the Duchess of Suffolk seems to have brought him into contact with Lady Jane Grey, the daughter of the Marquis of Dorset, Henry Grey, who had married Frances, the half-sister of Charles and Henry Brandon.

Jane Grey, in a moving letter to Bullinger (July 12th, 1551), writes of Bucer:

> . . . I was bereaved of the pious Bucer, that most learned man and holy father, who unweariedly did not cease, day and night, and to the utmost of his ability, to supply me with all necessary instructions and directions for my conduct in life; and who by his excellent advice promoted and encouraged my progress and advancement in all virtue, godliness, and learning; . . .[4]

With the marquis, Henry Grey, Bucer had also corresponded.[5] And after Bucer's death John Banck of Trinity College presented the marquis with a MS. copy of Bucer's lecture at Cambridge.[6]

[1] Works of Coverdale: *Remains* (Parker Society), p. 528.

[2] Foxe, J.: *Acts and Monuments* (Ed. Townsend, 1849), vol. VIII, pp. 569 ff.

[3] *The Works of Thomas Deloney* (Ed. by Francis Oscar Mann, Oxford, 1912), pp. 389 ff.

[4] cf. *Original Letters*, vol. I, pp. 4-7.

[5] Bucer to the Marquis, December 26th, 1550, in Harvey, op. cit., pp. 134 ff. Extract in Latin and in Engl. translation: Strype, J.: *Mem. of Abp. Cranmer*, vol. I, p. 299.

[6] 'Tractatio Martini Buceri de privato ministerio quod *clericale* vulgo appellatur, deque vi ministerii publici et administrationis verbi et baptismatis, cum quibusdam quae de efficacia coenae Dominicae tractantur. *Locus communis* ad illustrissimum Principem D. Marchionem Dorcestriae: cum dicatione Latine ascripta ad eundem Dominum a Johanne Banck, data a Coll. S. Trin. Cantabr. Jul. 1551. Qui etiam ad eundem Buceri de *publico* ministerio disputationis rationem jam remiserat.'

cf. Montague Rhodes James, *A Descriptive Catalogue of the MSS. in the Library of Gonville and Caius College*, vol. II, n. 423 (Cambridge, 1908).

Jane Seymour, daughter of Protector Somerset, had also been in correspondence with Bucer.[1]

A special friendship existed between Roger Ascham and Bucer. Their mutual friend, the famous Strassburg scholar, John Sturm, brought them even closer together.[2] Ascham's friend and biographer, Edward Grant, writes of that friendship:

> Quis Bucero erat Rogero Aschamo carior? Quem majore amore complectebatur Rogerus Aschamus? Quem majore fide, observantia, studio venerabatur, colebat, observabat Aschamus? Hunc & aetate, prudentia, consilio patrem: & doctrina, moribus, vitae sanctitate, praeceptorem semper habuit diuque coluit.[3]

In autumn of 1549, when Bucer was still staying at Lambeth with the archbishop, Ascham met him there and made his acquaintance, telling him about the intrigues at the court of Princess Elizabeth, which induced him to take leave from the court, where he had been as tutor to the princess. In a letter from Augsburg on the day after Epiphany (presumably 1551)[4] Ascham reminds Bucer of their conversation and entreats him to write a letter to the princess on his behalf. As Bucer was very ill at that time, a few weeks before his death, he seems not to have been able to carry out the wish of his friend.[5]

Bucer's death filled Ascham with grief, seeing in his death and in that of the two young pupils, a special divine punishment. Thus he writes to Cecil (July 12th, 1552):

> God's wroth, I trust, is satisfied in punishing divers orders of the realme for their misordre, with taking away singular men from them, as learning by Mr. Bucer, counsell by Mr. Denny, nobilitie by the two young Dukes.[6]

In a letter to Sturm (January 29th, 1552) he refers to Peter Ramus and John Perion, the two great continental philosophers and theologians, and states that he prefers Ramus to J. Perion, and dislikes

[1] cf. *Original Letters*, vol. I, p. 2: Lady Jane Seymour to Bucer and Fagius, June 12th, 1549.

[2] cf. Roger Ascham, op. cit., Liber I, pp. 14-15 (Ascham to Sturm, April 4th, 1550) and passim.

[3] cf. Roger Ascham (editio 1703), op. cit., *Epistolae*, p. 15.

[4] cf. Roger Ascham, *Epistolae* (editio 1703), III, pp. 230-232. The letter is also of interest with its references to various political incidents (e.g. Andrea Doria, etc.). Bucer on A. Doria, cf. his letter (September 10th, 1544) to Rhenanus. Horawitz, A., *Briefwechsel* . . . (Leipzig, 1886), p. 518.

[5] cf. Katterfeld, Alfred: *Roger Ascham* (1879), pp. 74-77.

[6] Quoted from Mullinger, J. B.: *The University of Cambridge* . . . (Cambridge, 1884), p. 125, n. 1.

cf. also Thomas Becon's words: 'The death of those two most worthy and godly-learned men, I speak of M. Paulus Fagius, and of D. Martin Bucer, was it not a sure prognostication some great mishap concerning Christian religion to be at hand?' (*Works of Thomas Becon, Prayers and other Pieces* (Parker Society, 1844), p. 205.)

the latter's 'Ciceronianos'[1] in which Perion so ridiculously attacked Bucer and Melanchthon. To find a passage in Perion's work which would apply to this description by Ascham, has its difficulties.

The rôle of intercessor Bucer had to play also for other persons. He wrote to Princess Elizabeth (from Lambeth, August 27th, 1549), asking her to favour a young foreign scholar, whom he recommends in high terms of appreciation.[2] There was also the case of the famous historian of the Reformation, Sleidan, who, in order that he might carry out the task of writing the story, had to get special funds and support. He had been in England and had made contacts with Englishmen: he was known to Bucer and had asked the latter's intercession on his behalf. Thus Bucer wrote to Cecil, and to William Parr, the Marquis of Northampton. The matter seems to have been on his mind very strongly, making him dictate a letter even during a severe illness. His letter to Cecil (February 18th, 1550) he dictates to 'Joannes Quercetanus', a famous physician of the sixteenth century. He dictates:

> S.P. Vir clarissime, Accipies hic meas literas, quamlibet aegre dictatas ad summe doctum et pium Medicum D. Joannem Quercetanum. Sed te per Christum rogo, nosti supplicationem nostram pro Sleydano, si possis ulla ratione impetrare, dari responsum, in utram placeat partem. Nosti hoc decere administrationem Regni, et ceteris, et Religionis beneficio tantopere ornatam. Dominus prosequatur te, tuosque omnes beneficentia cumulatissima . . .[3]

In his letter to the brother of Catherine Parr he writes:

> . . . John Sleidan, a very learned and eloquent man, five years ago began to compile an history of this nature [i.e. the history of the Reformation], as the work he had published, did witness: but after he was much encouraged in this undertaking, and well furnished with matter, the calamities that befell Germany, for our own deserts, intercepted the pious attempts of this man, so very useful to the church. Nor doth it appear now from whence, besides the King's Majesty, we may hope that some small benignity may be obtained for Sleidan; since the salaries, which he received for this purpose from the German princes, failed; and he was poor . . .[4]

[1] Roger Ascham, *Epistolae*, I, p. 44.

[2] cf. Letter in Harvey, op. cit., pp. 119 ff.

cf. also Bucer's letter to Edmund Allen, chaplain to Princess Elizabeth (August 27th, 1549); *Original Letters*, vol. II, pp. 541 f. In the case of the great foreign Hebraist, Anthony R. Chevallier, Bucer also intervened by recommending him to Abp. Cranmer. (cf. Cranmer: *Miscel. Writings*, . . . (Parker Society, 1846), p. 436.)

[3] cf. Strype, John: *Memorials of Abp. Cranmer* (ed. Oxford, 1840), vol. II, pp. 1017-1018.

[4] Extract in English translation by Strype, J.: *Memorials of Abp. Cranmer* (ed. Oxford, 1840), vol. I, p. 278. The letter in its original Latin is printed in extenso in Hasenclever, Adolf, *Sleidan Studien* (Bonn, 1905), pp. 45-47.

Almost at the same time Cheke writes to Bucer (from Greenwich, May 11th, 1550) about Sleidan:

> . . . De Sleidani caussa & ceterorum sic habeto. Dominus Cantuariensis benivolus sed tardus est caussarum patronus: & in hac re opus est Consiliario Regio, idque ea animi magnitudine, qua par est ad honestas caussas cum moderatione, & judicio suscipiendas. Si quando *Εὐκαιρία* praetervolat, facilius quaeritur quam invenitur. Ego hortari Cantuariensem non cesso, & quod praeterea possum, efficio.[1]

To Secretary Cecil, Bucer and some of his friends had already written from Lambeth (August 13th, 1549) on behalf of some Frenchmen.[2]

Mutual admiration had brought Bucer and John Cheke together. The joy over the recovery of his friend Bucer from illness and his almost humorous advice given to him in his letter bear beautiful witness of a tender friendship:

> I hear you are grown stronger, and that all your weakness and sickness which had afflicted you is gone: for which I do earnestly, as I ought, give thanks to God, the Father of all comfort, who hath delivered you from so great a disease, and strengthened you to take in hand and undergo such an office in the Church. But pray take heed you be not too earnest in your beginning, and undertake more than the measure of your health will bear. We must so labour, as to think, not how soon, but how long we shall be able to perform our work. You know how far that of St. Paul reaches, *Use a little wine*; [cf. 1 Tim. v. 23: οἴνῳ ὀλίγῳ χρῶ] and how it may diffuse itself to all the actions of life. I do that to you which I could never induce myself to do to any else; that is, to advise that you be more remiss and moderate in this your almost intolerable labour of mind: for the greatness of it stretched beyond one's strength distresses the body, and disables it to take care for meaner things . . .[3]

Bucer sent an account of his disputation with Young to Cheke in a letter of August 29th, 1550.[4] He had also sent him (October 21st, 1550) his MS. of the *De Regno Christi*, with the intention that Cheke

[1] Roger Ascham, *Epistolae*, op. cit., pp. 433-434.

[2] Letter signed by Bucer, P. Alexander, P. Martyr and P. Fagius in: Strype, John: *Memorials of Abp. Cranmer* (ed. Oxford 1840), vol. II, App. cv, pp. 1034-1035.

[3] cf. J. Strype: *The Life of . . . Sir John Cheke* (ed. Oxford, 1821), pp. 54-55; cf. the original Latin in R. Ascham, *Epistolae*, pp.433-434.

Cheke, when at Cambridge, hearing Bucer expound Psalm 119, remembers still several years later in a conversation with Christopher Carlile the lecturer's praise of Castalio – cf. Chr. Carlile's letter to Castalio (3. Cal. Mai., 1562), in P. Colomesius, *Epistolae aliquot Singulares* (London, 1695), pp. 250-251.

[4] Letter in Harvey, op. cit., pp. 127-130. (On August 31st he wrote on the same matter to Edmund Grindal, *Scr. Angl.*, pp. 803-804.)

might present it to the King. He remarks especially that apart from Peter Martyr nobody had yet seen the work.[1] There is another letter of Bucer to John Cheke (December 3rd, 1550) on the matter of a certain fellow of Jesus College, Cambridge.[2]

A few days after Bucer's death Cheke wrote a letter of consolation (March 10th, 1551) to Peter Martyr, which shows how deeply he mourned the death of Bucer and how much he had admired him. Almost at the same time Nicholas Carr had written to Cheke at the occasion of Bucer's death. Those two letters were printed as a special little pamphlet in London already in 1551, showing the interest of the time in the admiration of those two eminent men for Bucer.

After a long and severe illness Bucer died on March 1st, 1551.[3] The story of his illness and death is most movingly told by Nicholas Carr in his letter to John Cheke: His last conversations, his patience during his illness, his prayers. One small incident told by Carr of Bucer's last hours is told with a special touch: Bucer's doctors, who attributed Bucer's failing strength to the change of the moon, were contradicted by the dying man, who said, 'It is He, it is He, who ruleth and ordereth all things'.[4]

His funeral was a great event for the university town, a crowd of about 3000 people were present, drawn to the funeral by the fame of Bucer's name. All eminent university representatives attended — and what seems to have been especially worthwhile mentioning by Carr — also the representatives of the town, the mayor and the corporation took part: 'Town and Gown together.' Orations and sermons were held. Walter Haddon gave a most moving discourse in which not only did he himself weep bitterly, but also the crowd wept and mourned so deeply, imagining they had lost a leader

[1] Roger Ascham, *Epistolae* (Oxford, 1703), pp. 434-435, n. XLVI. The presentation copy seems to be the beautifully bound MS. folio, now in possession of Pembroke College, Cambridge (MS. 217: *De Regno Christi*).

[2] 'De causa cujusdam Blithi collegii Jesu socii, qui papisticae superstitioni addictus praeter duo beneficia ecclesiastica sodalitio et optimo cubiculo adhuc fruebatur, et nepotem suum in sodalitio successorem instituere nitebatur.' MS. Corpus Christi College, Cambridge, cxiii, 6.

[3] There is some discrepancy on account of the exact date of Bucer's death. Martyr in his letter to Hubert (March 8th, 1551, *Scr. Angl.*, pp. 900-901) gives the date as February 28th (pridie Cal. Martias), thus the date is also given presumably by C. Hubert, at the end of Bucer's lecture printed in *Scr. Angl.* (p. 610). The entry of Bucer's death in King Edward's Journal is also under the date of February 28th. Nicholas Carr in his letter (*Scr. Angl.*, p. 867) gives it, however, as March 1st, 1551. With this agrees the Postscript note in the letter of the University to Edward VI (March 4th): 'Primo die Martii hujus anni 1551 obiit Cantabrigiae Martinus Bucerus et sepultus in choro Btae Mariae magnae.' (cf. Lamb, op. cit., pp. 154-155.) cf. also Harvey, op. cit., p. 91, n. 4.

[4] *Scr. Angl.*, pp. 874-875. English translation, in *Bradford's Works*, op. cit., *Letters*, pp. xxiii-xxiv.

As to malicious reports by Bucer's enemies in connection with his death, cf. Paulus, Nikolaus: *Luther's Lebensende* . . . (Freiburg, i. Br. 1898), pp. 46-47.

without whom they would be unguided. Parker preached a sermon on Wisdom, iv. 10-19 (selected).[1]

The next day a communion service was held attended by about 400 people, and John Redman preached. Bucer was buried in Great St. Mary's, Cambridge, and a tablet in the chancel indicates even to-day the place. Edmund Grindal is specially mentioned as one of the men who 'bore up Bucer's hearse, when he was carried to St. Mary's Church to be buried'.[2] King Edward VI has an entry in his Journal on the occasion of Bucer's death, referring to the multitude of people, to the men who spoke at the funeral, and to the greatness of Bucer.[3] Bucer's friends, Cheke, Martyr and Haddon were specially grieved and their correspondence is beautiful evidence for their friendship.[4]

The amount of contemporary pamphlets in connection with Bucer's death shows the general interest of the public.[5] But the

[1] cf. N. Carr's letter to J. Cheke (The 'Id. of March', 1551), *Scr. Angl.*, pp. 867-882, and J. Cheke's Letter to Peter Martyr (March 10th, 1551), *Scr. Angl.*, pp. 864-867. Parker's Sermon, *Scr. Angl.*, pp. 892-899.

[2] Strype, John: *The History of the Life . . . of E. Grindal* (Oxford, 1821), p. 9, and *Scr. Angl.*, p. 936.

[3] cf. King Edward's Journal of his own Reign, in Burnet, Gilbert: *The History of the Reformation of the Church of England* (2 vol., London, 1841), vol. II, ii Records, p. clxv.

[4] Letter of Cheke to Haddon, March 19th, 1551, *Scr. Angl.*, pp. 899-900.
Martyr to Hubert, March 8th, 1551, *Scr. Angl.*, pp. 900-901.

[5] Historia vera de vita, obitu, sepultura, accusatione haereseos, condemnatione, exhumatione, combustione, honorificaque tandem restitutione, beatorum atque doctiss. Theologorum D. Martini Buceri *e.* Pauli Fagii, quae intra annos xii in Angliae regno accidit. Conradus Hubertus, 1562.

A briefe treatise concerning the burnynge of Bucer and Phagius, at Cambrydge, in the tyme of Quene Mary, with theyr restitution in the time of our moste gracious souerayne Lady that nowe is. Wherein is expressed the fantasticall and tirannous dealynges of the Romishe Church, togither with the godly and modest regimēt of the tiue Christian Church, most slaunderouslye diffamed in those dayes of heresye. Translated into Englyshe by Arthur Goldyng. Anno 1562 . . . Imprinted at London in Fletestrete nere to saynct Dunstons Churche by Thomas Marshe.

In the Volume *Scr. Angl.*: *Historia de Accvsatione, condemnatione, exhvmatione atqve combvstione excellentissimorvm theologorvm D. Martini* Buceri, & Pauli Fagij. *Anno Dom.* M.D.LVI. (pp. 915-935). *Historia de restitvtione praeclarorvm organorvm Dei D. Martini Bvceri et Pauli Fagii temporibvs Restitvtae religionis in Anglia. Anno* M.D.LX. (pp. 935-945).

cf. also: Foxe, John: *Acts and Monuments* (1563) (Ed. Townsend, London, 1849), vol. VIII, pp. 258-296. 'The Order and Manner of the Cardinal's Visitation in Cambridge, with the condemning, Taking up, and burning of the Bones and Books of Martin Bucer and Paulus Phagius; Anno 1557, January 9.' – which is merely a reprint of Golding's translation.

Parker, Matthew: Howe we ought to take the death of the godly. A sermon made in Cambridge at the buriall of the noble clerck D. M. Bucer—printed by R. Jugge (1551?). A funerall sermon preached 1551 at the buriall of M. Bucer. printed by T. Purfoote (1570?). The Latin text of Parker's Sermon, see *Scr. Angl.*, pp. 892 ff. The Letters of J. Cheke and N. Carr: De obitu Mart. Buceri epistolae duae, item epigrammata varia cum Graecae tum Latinae conscripta in eundem. Lond. Re. Wolfii, 1551. Cheke's Letter to Peter Martyr (March 10th, 1551), also *Scr. Angl.*, pp. 864 ff. Carr's Letter to Cheke (Id. March. 1551); also *Scr. Angl.*, pp. 867 ff. Haddon, Walter: *G. Haddoni* . . . lucubrationes passim collectae & editae . . . Thomae Hatcheri . . . Londini—1567: De obitu D. Martini Buceri, pp. 83 ff; cf. also *Scr. Angl.*, pp. 876-878 and pp. 882 ff., and passim.

story does not end here with the burial of Bucer's body. Rest was even now not granted to the dead, who in his lifetime had never lived a restful life. Although Bucer had escaped by his death the fate of his fellow reformers in Mary's Reign, the 'inquisitors' would not rest until the dead should also receive ecclesiastical punishment and excommunication. John Mere, in his Journal, refers to the special stages of the proceedings.[1] The story of the 'inquisition' can be read in the end of the volume *Scripta Anglicana*. Witnesses, who knew Bucer and who would confirm his heretical views, had at first to be found. And it is a deplorable fact that among them were men, who at the death of Bucer had been his friends, men like Nicholas Carr. The trial started during the visit (January-February 1556-57) of the delegates of Cardinal Pole sent to Cambridge to make inquiries about the religious status of the university. A warrant 'de haeretico comburendo' was issued against Bucer and his friend Paul Fagius. The bones were dug out, chained and burnt at the market-place in Cambridge on a day (February 6th) when all the people from outside Cambridge came to the town, as it was market day. The peasants were amazed at details of the procedure, and could not understand why the bones, which certainly could not run away, had to be chained. With the bones, heaps of books of heretical content by the two reformers and others were burnt. During that performance assemblies and sermons were held in churches. And there is the story of Andrew Perne, who already to Bucer's lifetime had been one of the opponents at Cambridge — that he had to preach against Bucer, but after his sermon lamented his own doings.[2] That story is a further illustration to the accounts of Perne's character, whose changes from Protestantism to Roman Catholicism and vice versa gave welcome material to joking remarks about 'Mr. Turncoat'. The text of Perne's sermon was that of Psalm cxxxv: 'Behold, how good and joyful a thing it is, brethren, to dwell together in unity!' A most appropriate text in connection with the exhumation of the bodies of the two 'heretics' Bucer and Fagius.

Another sermon was preached by the Bishop of Lincoln, Thomas Watson. The whole episode seems to have had unexpected results for the 'visitors'. The public was not so deeply convinced of the necessity of such an ecclesiastical punishment on men, whose works

[1] cf. Lamb, John: op. cit., pp. 201-210, 213, 215-217.

[2] 'Increbuit fama, authores habuit ex illius familiaribus, illum aut statim dimissa concione, aut paulo ante quam eo accederet, percusso dextra manu pectore pene cum lachrymis, domui suae vehementer optasse, daret illi aliquis Deus, vt eius anima iam tum cum Bucero ageret. Satis enim sciebat, fuisse huius vitam eiusmodi, vt si alterius cuiusquam, illius imprimis animam coelo dignissimam ipse iudicarit.' (*Scr. Angl.*, p. 931).

and character was still alive in many an Englishman. The exhumation and burning was not cheered by the crowds. There is a contemporary woodcut of the burning.[1] The story of the burning spread throughout the country. Henry Machyn makes special mention of it in his Diary.[2] The de facto entry of the churchwardens of Great St. Mary (Easter 1556 to Easter 1557) provides an epitaph in involuntary satire to the proceedings:

> Item, payd for new halloweings or reconcylyng of our chyrche beying Interdycted for the buryall of Mr. Bucer and the charg thereunto belongeing, frankensens & swete purfumes for the sacrament, & herbes, &c. viij d. ob.[3]

And again the story does not end here. Under Queen Elizabeth (July 1560) the Church tried to make good for the injustice done to the dead reformers under Mary. They were solemnly reburied in Great St. Mary's. What actually was buried is difficult to say, as the bones had been burnt. Again sermons followed, one by Bishop Pilkington. The university orator, George Acworth, praised in public the men and abhorred the 'detestable' deed done to them under Mary. Again flowered epitaphs on the graves of the reformers. The story was soon written, the story of Bucer's death, the story of Bucer's exhumation, the story of Bucer's 'restitution'. It was translated into English as a small pamphlet by Arthur Goldyng in 1562:

> A briefe treatise concerning the burnynge of Bucer and Phagius, at Cambrydge, in the tyme of Quene Mary, with theyr restitution in the time of our moste gracious souerayne Lady that nowe is. Wherein is expressed the fantasticall and tirannous dealynges of the Romishe Church, togither with the godly and modest regiment of the true Christian Church, most slaunderouslye diffamed in those dayes of heresye.[4]

The story, together with the edition of Nicholas Carr's letters and that of Cheke, and the edition of Matthew Parker's sermon on the occasion of Bucer's death is a small contribution to the picture of religious instability in that period, till Protestantism got settled under Elizabeth.

[1] Reproduced in: Salzman, L. F.: *England in Tudor Times* (London, 1926). Plate LI: Burning of Bucer's Bones.

[2] Machyn, Henry: *The Diary of Henry Machyn 1550-63* (Ed. by John Gough Nichols, Camden Society, London, 1848, n. XLII), p. 124.

[3] Cooper, Charles Henry: *Annals of Cambridge* (Cambridge, 1853), vol. II, p. 185. There is another entry (April 5th, 1551) shortly after Bucer's death: 'Item for naylles to mend ye seates in ye chyrche where M.r Doctor Busur was buryed ij d.' cf. ibid. the account of the proceedings against Bucer and Fagius.

[4] Translated into Englyshe by Arthur Goldyng. Anno 1562 . . . Imprinted at London in Fletestrete nere to saynct Dunstons Churche by Thomas Marshe.

Words of Bishop Pilkington in his sermon on the occasion of Bucer's 'restitution' in their blunt attack on Roman Catholicism are as hard and unreconciling as words spoken by Marian churchmen at the occasion of the burning of Bucer's bones, and yet seem to be the prophetic vision of a man who foresaw the Reformation settled in England and Roman Catholicism overthrown:

> . . . it was a most apt example that was reported of their [i.e. the Bohemians] captain Zisca: who, when he should die, willed his body to be slain, and of his skin to make a parchment to cover the head of a drum: for it should come to pass, that when his enemies heard the sound of it, they should not be able to stand against them. The like counsel, he said, he himself now gave them as concerning Bucer; that like as the Bohemians did with the skin of Zisca, the same should they do with the arguments and doctrine of Bucer: for as soon as the papists should hear the noise of him, their gewgaws would forthwith decay . . .[1]

The short section of Bucer's life (not fully two years) in England almost fell into oblivion, because of the rich and important account of Bucer's religious and political activities on the Continent, which made the story of his time in England appear to be of small interest. The fact that soon after Bucer's death, in the reign of Queen Mary, many of his books were burnt and destroyed, and that the influence he had gained under Edward VI was made void, was unfavourable for any immediate and direct advance of Bucer's ideas under Elizabeth. So many of his works, which were rescued from burning and destruction under Mary, were only extant in MSS. and thus available to a limited circle of men. Gradually his works were printed. His lecture on the Ephesians was edited by Tremellius, his *De Regno Christi* (1557) was printed and an extract of it on the *Relief for the Poor* was translated into English, and finally, in 1577, in the *Scripta Anglicana* many of Bucer's writings were made known to the public. The interest of Hubert and of Grindal and of others of Bucer's friends had always been to get his writings published, in order to give them that place in theological literature in England they deserved.[2]

Several letters of Grindal[3] to Hubert concerning Bucer's works

[1] *The Works of James Pilkington* (Parker Society, Cambridge, 1842), p. 655.

[2] cf. also Ascham's letter to Sturm (June 18th, 1551) concerning the writing of Bucer's life and death. Ascham refers to the record on Bucer's death already written by Carr, and to the included talk by Redman at that occasion. (R. Ascham's *Epistolae* (editio 1589-90), pp. 56-59.)

[3] *Zurich Letters*, 2nd Series, 1558-1602 (Parker Society, 1845), pp. 17-20; (May 23rd, 1559), p. 24; (July 14th, 1559), pp. 51-52; (October 13th, 1560). cf. also Hubert's dedicatory letter to Grindal, Archbishop of Canterbury, dated from Strassburg, February 22nd, 1577. (*Scr. Angl.*, fol. *a2-a4*.)

from Boissardus, *Iconum Viros*, 1559

from Verpoorten, *Commentatio Historica*, 1709

and the edition of them, throw an interesting light on the endeavours made to get them printed. We learn also from that correspondence, that it was Grindal who instigated 'a certain learned man' to write the story of Bucer's exhumation and restitution.

In a letter of May 23rd, 1559, Grindal informs Hubert that he is sending him by messenger two MS. works of Bucer: Bucer's oration at the occasion of the conferment of the D.D. degree and his account of the controversy with Young. Those MSS. were kept by Matthew Parker, who was said to have some more MSS.

> but when he had brought them forth from the hiding-places, in which they had been concealed during the whole of these incendiary times, he found them gnawed by the rats and entirely spoiled . . .

Another difficulty for the editor of Bucer's MSS. will be the fact of his bad handwriting, which needs according to Grindal a *conjuror* in order to decipher it.[1]

In connection with the story of Bucer's exhumation, Grindal writes in the same letter:

> I am in doubt . . . whether I or Lakin undertook to send you the whole account of the exhumation of Bucer and Fagius. But lest you should altogether be disappointed of your wish, I have positively determined to write on the subject to Dr. Parker, who will, I hope, take care that a true description of the whole affair shall be prepared for me. Should he do this, I will take care that it shall be forwarded to you . . .

A few weeks later he writes again to Hubert on the same subject (July 14th, 1559):

> I trust, to send you in a few days the account of the burning of Bucer's [bones].

But more than a year was to pass till Grindal could keep his promise, to send the complete story, which then in 1562 was edited by Hubert at Strassburg: Grindal writes on October 13th, 1560, to Hubert:

> I send you at last . . . the promised account of the exhumation of Bucer and Fagius, which I have caused to be carefully drawn up by a certain learned man, who was a spectator of the whole tragedy.

One of the reasons given by Grindal for the delay is, that Archbishop Parker, Grindal himself, and Dr. Haddon, by virtue of power committed to them by Queen Elizabeth, had written letters to the Vice-

[1] Bucer calls his own writing: κακόγραφα; *Ioan. Calvini Opera*, vol. XI, p. 250.

Chancellor of Cambridge, Dr. Andrew Perne (!) to arrange some days for a ceremony to 'reinstitute' Bucer.[1] Perne and the university had answered this letter addressing it to Parker on 'tertio Nonas Augusti M.D.LV. [sic!]'[2] That gave Grindal final opportunity for sending Hubert the promised account.

In spite of all hindrances in connection with the Marian reaction, Bucer occurs as quoted authority in many controversial writings in the period after his death and later in Elizabethan times, and in writings of the seventeenth century. He is stated by his contemporaries to have had great influence on English theology and Church practice. In the controversy between Whitgift and Cartwright, Bucer is often quoted against Cartwright. Bishop Jewel in his controversy with Thomas Harding refers to Bucer. And in the controversy between Cranmer and Gardiner reference is made to Bucer's views on the Lord's Supper, and, strangely enough, Bucer's most strong adversary, the Bishop of Winchester, claims Bucer on his side against Cranmer.

The vestiarian controversy caused the Elizabethan theologians to publish and to translate into English Bucer's correspondence on the subject. John Boys, David Calderwood, Thomas Bell, Cornelius Schulting, Robert Parker, Bishop Cosin, Laud — to name only a few — refer constantly to Bucer and his writings.

Laud in connection with reference to Bucer's *Censura* writes disapprovingly of the English attitude of entertaining and valuing foreign scholars more than English scholars,[3] which only proves that Bucer's work and influence, in the short period of his staying in England, was recognized.[4]

[1] cf. *Zurich Letters*, 2nd Series, op. cit., p. 51, and ibid., n. 5, references.

[2] *Scr. Angl.*, pp. 944-945. The year must be, of course: M.D.LX.

[3] 'Howsoever, this hath been the common error (as I humbly conceive) of the English nation, to entertain and value strangers in all professions of learning beyond their desert, and to the contempt, or passing by at least, of men of equal worth of their own nation; . . .' (*Works of Laud*, op. cit., vol. III, pp. 351-352).

[4] cf. Richard Cox, Bishop of Ely, letter to R. Gualter (February 12th, 1571), *Zurich Letters*, 1558-1579, (Parker Society, 1842), pp. 234 ff.

cf. also account by Daniel Barbaro on his legation to England (May 1551): Bucer's persuasive influence in England against Papacy. Calendar of State Papers, Venetian, 1534-54, n. 703, pp. 346-347.

§ II

DISCOURSE ON 'SUVERMERIANISM'

This term is used by Canon Smyth in his *Cranmer and the Reformation under Edward VI* to describe the theological conception of the Strassburg reformer, Martin Bucer (specially in relation of Bucer's doctrinal teaching on the Eucharist). The term — so far not known in English literature — evoked a long controversy on the word itself.[1]

And as Canon Smyth states on p. 25:

> That Cranmer after his initial conversion from the Roman doctrine . . . never abandoned the Suvermerian theory of the Eucharist . . .

an explanation of the term or the tracing of its origin seems even to be of greater exigency. The study of the word itself reveals the following facts, which show that the word is based on a misinterpretation, misspelling and does not exist as such. In tracing the proper meaning of the original term, which has been misinterpreted later, it will also be necessary to answer the question, whether it is justifiable to apply the original meaning of the term to either Bucer or Cranmer, or whether the word should be replaced by another term, which would be more suitable to give expression to the particular theory of Bucer and Cranmer on the Eucharist.

We find the word mentioned in a letter of Bishop John Hooper to Henry Bullinger:

> . . . on the same day I was present at his evening sermon [scil. C. Hedio], where, among other things that he said, and which I heard with pain, he absurdly inveighed with great bitterness against the Suvermerians.[2]

[1] cf. *The Times Literary Supplement*, July 29th, 1926, p. 504.
cf. also Watson, E. W., in *J.T.S.* (January 1927), p. 202: 'The Saxon divines denounced the Swiss as *swermeros*; i.e. Schwärmer . . .'

[2] Dated from Strassburg, March 31st, 1549. *Original Letters*, vol. I, p. 50.
The original Latin has: Suvermeros (Latin: *Epistolae Tigurinae*, p. 32, n. xxvii), which has been rendered into the English 'Suvermerians' by the editors of the *Original Letters*.
It seems very unlikely that the word used by Hedio was meant as an attack against Bucer and the Strassburg group, as Hedio himself was one of the group, representing the same views as Bucer at Strassburg. For him the word must have had a different meaning, criticizing a group opposed to his teaching and to that of Bucer and his Strassburg friends. On the close relation and friendship between Hedio and Bucer see C. Varrentrapp: *Zur Charakteristik Hermanns von Wied, Bucers und Groppers*, p. 42, n. 2 in Zeitschrift für Kirchengeschichte, Bd. XX. 1 Heft (Gotha, 1899), and: Letter of Bucer to C. Hedio from Cambridge, October 14th, 1550, in Tim. W. Röhrich: *Mitteilungen aus der Geschichte der evgl. Kirche des Elsasses* . . . 3. Bd. (Strassburg-Paris, 1855), pp. 251-255.

In a footnote to this letter reference is made to an explanation given by Strype on the word:

'. . . The Saxon divines were exceeding hot against the Swiss divines, on account of their rejecting the doctrine of consubstantiation held by the Lutherans. In their ordinary discourses', Strype says, 'they styled them heretics, false prophets, Suvermeros, Sacramentiperdas.'[1]

This is the quotation from Strype in the footnote of the *Original Letters*. But the quotation is incorrect in one small and yet important point. The quotation has the term spelt: *Suvermeros*, whereas Strype writes *Suermeros*.[2]

This word *Suermeri* occurs also on the title-page of John Eck's *Replica*: '. . . Ego . . . offero me . . . Imp. nostro Carolo . . . ad aduersus Bucerum ac omnes Suermeros . . .'[3]

Andreas Althamer, a contemporary of the Reformers, gives an explanation of the word in his *Conciliationes Locorvm* . . . , giving also its origin: he spells it Suermeri . . . Schwermeri . . . Swermeri . . . *Svvermeri*. Althamer states that Luther gave that name to a certain group of theologians, who were the heretics of his time, who rejected baptism of infants, etc. The origin of the word is given by Althamer by stating that it comes from the German Schwarm.[4]

The Latin Suermeri would be in German *Schwärmer* or *Schwarm-*

[1] *Original Letters*, vol. I, p. 50, n. 3.

[2] Strype, *Mem. of Abp. Cranmer* (1840), p. 508.

[3] *Replica Joan. Eckii Adversus Scripta* secunda Buceri apostatae super actis Ratisponae . . . 1543.

cf. also the term (*Schuermerismum*) occurring in a letter to Calvin (October 24th, 1554), *Ioannis Calvini Opera* (Ed. W. Baum, E. Cunitz, E. Reuss), (Brunswig, 1876), vol. XV, col. 273 (in *Corpus Reformatorum*, vol. XLIII).

[4] cf. p. 211, verso, in Althamerus: *Conciliationes* (the Latin text of Althamer infra). The *Realencyclopaedie für Protestantische Theologie* refers to an earlier edition of the work in its article on Althamer: Diallage hoc est conciliatio locorum scripturae qui prima facie inter se pugnare videntur. Norimbergae, printed by Friedericus Peypus, 1527. Robert Watt in *Bibliotheca Britannica*: vol. I, Authores. Edinburgh-London, 1824, quotes another edition from 1528 under Althamer. The quotation from our edition seems to be from a later enlarged edition. cf. also the reference in the *General Index* to the Publ. of the Parker Society compiled by H. Gough (1855) on the word '*Swermerians*: heretics' (then the reference to Hooper's letter to Bullinger), 'they condemned the outward ministry of the word and sacrament, Rog. 237; said the baptism of infants was of the devil, ibid. 280.'

Conciliationes Locorvm scripturae, qui specie tenus inter se pugnare uidentur. Centuriae duae.

Andrea Althamero authore. Col. Norimbergae apud Iohan. Petreium. M.D.XLVIII.

p. 211, verso: Schwermeri enim magistro sathana excitati, magno furoris impetu illa impugnant. Sunt uero Suermeri, ne hoc in primis praeteream, haeretici nostri temporis, qui mox orta Euangelij luce inflati, magni haberi & esse cupientes, nouum dogma contra purum Christi Euangelium elegerunt ac susceperunt, contra paruulorum baptismum, quos sancta Ecclesia ab Apostolorum temporibus, referente Origene in sextum caput Epistolae ad Romanos, usa fuit: contendentes nullos infantes, sed adultos tantum, baptismate initiandos. Horrendum dictu, quantum suggillent paedobaptismum, Sathanae traditionem, magno pietatis zelo, tradunt esse.

Hi Swermeri etiam uicium originis omnino negant esse peccatum, clauium potestatem rident, Dominicam coenam euacuant, & diris modis corrumpunt. Ecclesiae

geister, employed by Luther against the Anabaptists and other sects closely related to them.

The rather precarious and ambiguous rendering of the term *Suvermeros* (Strype, Eck and Althamer: *Suermeros*) into the English *Suvermerians* by the translators of the *Epistolae Tigurinae* seems to have induced Canon Smyth to term Bucer's and Cranmer's conception on the Eucharist Suvermerianism.

Having discovered that the word Suvermerianism means nothing else than *Schwärmertum*, we have to enlarge on the implications arising. Was Bucer 'Schwärmer', what was actually termed by the Lutherans 'Schwärmertum', and lastly, can it be said that Cranmer never abandoned the Schwärmer theory of the Eucharist, that Cranmer in his Eucharistical outlook was a Schwärmer?

Undoubtedly, if the explanation given by Althamer (and Thomas Rogers)[1] were the only meaning of the word, neither Bucer nor Cranmer could be styled as such. Of Cranmer it is known that he was opposed to the teaching of the Anabaptists. As Strassburg was for a time the refuge for all kinds of sects, Bucer and his colleagues became acquainted with the teaching of the Anabaptists, and the teaching of other groups akin to that of the Anabaptists. It seems as if even at the beginning Bucer and the other Strassburg pastors were inclined to listen to their arguments. But already in 1533 a Synod was held at Strassburg against the Anabaptists. Their rather anarchic conception of the Church and her discipline could never be accepted by the Churchman Bucer. The overstressing of the 'inward voice' which did not allow the Anabaptists to proclaim the 'outward functions of the ministry', against the sacraments, and even against Scripture, had opened Bucer's eyes to the dangerous doctrine of the so-called 'Spiritualists' or 'Enthusiasts'. Three statements made by Bucer are an illustration of his attitude to those sects: (1) 'The sects

[1] Rogers, Thomas: on the XXXIX Articles (Parker Society, 1854) writes on p. 237: '. . . The anabaptistical Swermers, who both term all ecclesiastical men the devil's ministers; and also, as very wicked, do utterly condemn the outward ministry of the word and sacraments,' *and note* 6 *on the same page*: 'Hi Swermeri . . . ecclesiae ministros diaboli clamant, Nostrum ministerium in verbo Dei et sacramentorum dispensatione damnant. Althamer: *Conciliat. Locor.* Script. Noremberg, 1535. Loc. CXCI, p. 211.'

ministros diaboli clamant. Nostrum ministerium in uerbo Dei & sacramentorum dispensatione, damnant: ritus ecclesiae utiles in totum abrogant, et alia infinita ecclesiasticae politiae insano cachinno explodunt, coelum terrae miscent, omnia confundunt: Legitimos magistratus conuicijs proscindunt, ac tollere studuerunt: nihil omnino (p. 212) in ecclesia tollerant, nisi ab illis sit excogitatum: uetera auferunt, noua fingunt. Hi nouo uocabulo uernacula germanorum lingua ab apum examine, seu cestrorum strepitu & susurro ficta uoce *Svvermeri*, ab doctore Martino Luthero & alijs deinde uiris, sunt appellati: quasi dicas cestro aut furia agitati. Schwarm enim uulgari & teutonica uoce examen significat. Inde Suermeri, id est furientes, frenetici ac lymphatici accommodatissimo uocabulo: nihil enim illis est furiosius, obstinaciusque . . , (etc.). cf. also p. 214; p. 219, verso; p. 225 marginal note.

here have led to such utter contempt of the word of God, as if it were broken to pieces.' (2) 'They ought to enjoin upon themselves, that our faithful heavenly Father has promised to us His Spirit and Grace, as well as to those who lead you astray, and that they may err as well as we may err, and that because of these articles and Concordia they may not be afraid of anybody save Papists, Anabaptists, Schwenckfeldians and such like.' (3) '. . . and the word Schwermer or such like is not heard any longer by us.'[1] Those Anabaptists were mainly Balthasar Hubmaier, Hans Denk and Melchior Hofman. They ought to be distinguished from the other group of men, the prophets of the 'inward light', Karlstadt and the 'Zwickauer Prophets'—Thomas Münzer, Sebastian Franck, Schwenckfeld.

The word Schwärmer was not only used by Luther and his partisans against the Anabaptists: its usage was extended to all those who, by their 'Spiritualism', neglected the teaching of the Outward Word and the necessity of the Sacraments. Karlstadt was alleged by Luther to be a Schwärmer. He presented a new symbolical conception of the Eucharist, claiming that Christ at the Supper pointed to Himself and not to the bread and wine in saying: 'Hoc est corpus meum . . .' This explanation was the means by which Karlstadt thought to overcome any teaching of the corporal presence of our Lord in the elements of bread and wine. Luther attacks him strongly as being disobedient to the word of Scripture. So everyone who tried to interpret the presence of our Lord spiritually by means of a symbolical explanation, could easily be charged by Luther as Schwärmer, since this symbolical interpretation was at first represented by the Schwärmer Karlstadt.[2]

Yet it is interesting to find that Bucer almost from the beginning states that he has nothing to do with Karlstadt's doctrine, that the preachers of Strassburg neither taught 'that the true sacrament is

[1] (1) January 4th, 1533, to his friend Blaurer: Die Sekten haben hier das Wort Gottes in solche Verachtung gebracht, als ob es zerbrochen wäre, in Erbkam, H. W.: *Geschichte der Protestant. Sekten* . . . (Hamburg, 1848), p. 553.

(2) November 23rd, 1536: 'Sölten darbey auch zu hertzen furen, das unser getrewer hymlischer vatter uns uff unseren thail seinen gaist und gnad also wol zugesaget hat, als denen, die uch hierin irrmachen, und das sie sobald als wir irren mögen, Auch das ab disen artickulen und Concordi nieman mehr scheuent, dan Bäpstler, Teuffer, Schwenckfeldische und der gleichen.' D. Caspar Hedio, M. Bucer, M. Matheus Zell.: Brief der Strassburger Geistlichen an die Stadt Konstanz. Ernst Bizer: (Archiv für Reformationsgeschichte, Jahrgang 36, 1939), p. 223. The letter is signed by D. W. Capito.

(3) April 1st, 1537: . . . undd hört man das wort Schwermer oder derglichen by uns nit mer. In Bizer, p. 225 ff. Butzer's *Bericht an die Eidgenossen über seine Verhandlungen mit Luther in Schmalkalden und Gotha*, p. 228.

[2] cf. Anrich, p. 47, stating that by the representation of the symbolical conception of the Eucharist by Karlstadt, the personal enemy of Luther, Luther regarded any such conception as Schwärmerei. cf. K. Thieme, in his article 'Verzückung' in *Realencyclopaedie*: Quotation of Luther's opinion on Seb. Franck.

not in the bread and wine, nor do they teach Carlstadtianism'.[1] That was on February 13th, 1525. In October of the same year, Bucer, in a letter to Hans Landschad, gives a statement to the same effect.[2] Karlstadt had come to Strassburg in October 1524.[3] Bucer had become a citizen of Strassburg on September 22nd, 1524.[4] Thus very early he and his friends separated themselves from Karlstadt. Although Bucer attacked wherever he could the views of the Anabaptists — a fact which was also known to English theologians[5] — although Bucer moved away from Karlstadt and disliked the word Schwärmer,[6] is it still conceivable that Luther christened him with the nickname, which he used against all theologians who denied his Eucharistic Doctrine? As Luther included also in the term Anabaptists and other sects, one has carefully to state that here, if used against the Strassburg reformer, the term bears only relation to the Eucharistical conception and has no relevance to the general use of the word for Anabaptists and other sects.

In Bucer's treatise: Vergleichung D. Luthers und seins Gegentheyls ... of 1528, he alludes to the word as used by Luther against all those who did not share his Eucharistic doctrine. Yet it is used here by Bucer ironically with perhaps a touch of persiflage directed against himself, and we need not read it in the sense in which he

[1] A. Baum: *Magistrat und Reformation in Strassburg bis* 1529: p. 136, 10 declaration of predicants of Strassburg drafted by Bucer February 13th, 1525: Sie predigten weder, dass das wahre Sakrament nicht in Brod und Wein sei, noch lehrten sie carlstadtisch. cf. Eells Hastings, *Princeton Theolog. Review*, vol. XXIV, 1926: p. 230, n. 26.

[2] J. Schneider: *Ein Brief M. Butzers an den Ritter Landschad von Steinach über das h. Abendmahl* 1526, vol. V, pp. 105-116: in Archiv für Hessische Geschichte und Altertumskunde. Neue Folge, Ergänzungsband III, 2. Heft. Darmstadt, 1906, p. 108. ... Das yr nun schreyben, yr haben uch ym Herrn gefrewet mit uns, das wir der unsinnigen disputation D. Karolstadt nit anhangend, etc., strenger Herr, christlicher Bruder, Gott ist unser züg, das wir nichts denn seyn wort zu predigen begeren ... Mich verwundert (p. 109) auch, wie yr uns mögt zumessen Carollstadt meynung oder disputation ... (p. 114) ... Jr thut myr auch gewalt, das yr mich Karollstadt anhengig urteylet, mit dem (ich erkannte yn denn anders dan er sich dyss jar erzeygt hat) will ich nichts gemeyn haben. Das möchtet yr wol uss gemelter geschrifft an Hartmut vernummen haben. Bucer's letter to Hans Landschad, dated: Argent. October 22nd.

[3] A. Lang: *Der Evangelienkommentar M. Butzers* ... 1900, pp. 212 ff.

[4] cf. A. Baum, op. cit., p. 205.

[5] cf. John Boys (Dean of Canterbury, 1571-1625): *An Exposition of al the principall Scriptures used in our English Liturgie* (London, 1610-14) (Three Parts), refers in Exposit. to Psalms pt. I, p. 96, to Bucer's statement against the Anabaptists, Münzer, Hofman and the Swiss Anabaptists: (Bucer: Enarrationes in 4 Evangel. Editio 1536, pp. 597-598, commentary to John i.) *and* in the third part Boys quotes Bucer again on p. 75 against Anabaptists: (Bucer: Enarrat. Editio 1536, p. 413, Comment. to Matthew xx. 26). More explicit statements about his experiences with the Anabaptists and their views are given by Bucer in his Commentary on Zephaniah (Sophoniam), pp. 562, 572-573 in the edition printed: Oliua Roberti Stephani. M.D.L.IV. He had written his Commentary in 1528, as the dedicatory letter of his Commentary indicates IIII. Septemb. Anno Christi M.D.XXVIII.

[6] '... Mei per periphrasim, meque Schwermerlin, non proprio nomine meminit ...' Bucer in a letter to W. Farel (Strassburg, May 1st, 1528): in: Herminjard, A. L.: *Correspondance des Réformateurs* ... (Genève-Paris, 1868), vol. II, p. 132.

had been labelled by Luther. The dialogue between the Lutheran and the opponent to the Lutheran view on the doctrine of the Eucharist is presented by Bucer under two fictitious names: Seboldt (meant to represent the Lutheran) and Arbogast (the opponent). Seboldt visiting Arbogast at Strassburg is asked by the latter about the purpose of his visit: Arbogast: Was machst Du hier zu Strassburg? Seboldt: . . . Ich muss einmal lugen, was ihr Sakrament Schwermer hier zu Strassburg machen. Arbogast: Sakramentschwermer? . . .[1]

We know also that Bucer, soon after 1530, subscribed and consented to the Lutheran doctrine of the Sacrament, which gained him the enmity of the Swiss theologians.[2] We know that Bucer developed his own teaching on the Eucharist, founding a new centre of the Reformation, Strassburg. Strassburg was neither dependent on Wittenberg nor on Zürich nor on Geneva; it was the fourth place on the Continent from which the teaching of the Reformation went out. Canon Smyth, by intending to express by the term Suvermerianism the fact that Bucer and his teaching deserve a special rank among those towns of the Reformation which moulded independently from each other Protestant conceptions even in England would have been correct in his statement but for the fact that the word has precarious implications, of which he was not aware. One ought to choose a term for this special doctrinal conception as distinguished from Lutheranism and Zwinglianism. But it will not do any longer to term it 'Suvermerianism' (Schwärmertum), which does injustice to the Strassburg theology and would rank it among the Anabaptist and sectarian theologians. It is even more untenable to connect—as Smyth does—the term with Cranmer's doctrinal conception.

To call Cranmer a 'Suvermerian' (Schwärmer), because he shared Bucer's 'Suvermerian' views, leads us seriously to consider to which of these two men is done more injustice by bringing them into connection with this word, which was used as terminus technicus only for a special group of sects, who fell away from sound doctrine and Church discipline.

[1] Vergleichung D. Luthers und seins Gegentheyls vom Abentmal Christi. Dialogus Das ist eyn freundtlich gespräch gar nahe alles so D. Luther in seinem letsten buch Bekäntniiss genennt für gebracht hat . . . Anno 1528 Am letsten des Augsts . . . Strassburg xxj. Junii. M. Buczer, p. 1.

[2] Melanchthon de Bucero: Bucerus plane et clare affirmans praesentiam Christi (in sacra coena) satisfecit nostris omnibus, etiam iis, qui sunt duriores. (1537, Schmalkalden) in Seckendorf: Historia Lutheranismi, Lib. III, p. 153 additio (f).

That was at the 'Wittenberg-Konkordie' of 1536. cf. Letter of Andreas Friccius Modrevius to J. à Lasco, dated Crotovij die xx Junij MDXXXVI: *Epistola* IX, pp. 19 ff. in Gabbema, Simon: Illustrium & Clarorum virorum Epistolae . . . MDCLXIX.

Before that in 1530 Luther wrote November 7th: 'Sacramentarios, saltem Strassburgenses nobiscum in gratiam redire spes est.' Enders: *Briefwechsel Luthers*, vol. VIII, p. 312.

§ III

SOME NOTES ON BUCER'S EUCHARISTIC CONCEPTION

> He was the unwearied advocate of moderation and peace, but like too many who have attempted to steer between warmly contending parties, has been exposed to the imputation of insincerity and vacillation. — COOPER (*Athenae Cantabrigienses*) on Bucer.[1]

In a few lines of his *Diacosio-Martyrion* (1553), John White, Bishop of Winchester, characterizes Bucer's Eucharistic conception: Bucer's firm belief in a Real Presence — a Real Presence, however, which depends on the partaker's attitude of faith. Bucer's strong denial of the Christ-absence doctrine of the Swiss Reformers. His denial that Bread and Wine were mere signs or symbols.

The description does justice to Bucer's teaching. It becomes clear in those few lines, that Bucer was neither a Roman Catholic, believing in Transubstantiation, nor a Lutheran, believing in Consubstantiation and in the Presence of Christ apart from the attitude and belief of the receiver,[2] nor a Zwinglian, seeing in the Lord's Supper simply a memorial celebration. It is plain that Bucer attempted to steer clear of any prevalent Eucharistic conception, which tended in his eyes to misinterpret the true Catholic teaching of the Eucharist.

Thus White writes of Bucer:

> . . . *nam* scripsi da mihi veros
> Christi discipulos, erit illico Christus in illis,
> pascensque, aeternae, praebebit pabula, vitae,
> veri corporis esu, Et veri sanguinis haustu.
> Ergo, hunc, quid frontis, dicemus, Episcopum habere,
> qui, me, non timuit sic recta, et sana, docentem,
> sic quoque Catholicum, hac infamia inurere, tanquam
> non doceam verum corpus, verumque cruorem
> in caena tradi, sed signa et symbola tantum?[3]

[1] Cooper, Charles Henry: . . . *Athenae Cantabrigienses*, vol. I, pp. 103-104 (Cambridge, 1858).

[2] *Scr. Angl.*, p. 679.

[3] op. cit., fol. 94 verso. White, in his attempt to explain Bucer's doctrine employs Bucer's words in his *Defensio adversus Axioma Catholicum, id est criminationem R. P. Roberti Episcopi* . . . (i.e. Robert Cenalis, Bishop of Avranches), 1534: *Scr. Angl.*, p. 613: 'Da discipulos veros *Christi*, erit vtique *Christvs* in medio eorum, vereque pascet illos, ad aeternam vitam vero suo corpore, & sanguine. Quid iam dicemus frontis esse isti Episcopo, qui ausit de me scribere, scopum mihi in hac verborum Domini explanatione in eo consistere, vt probem in Eucharistia non esse verum Domini corpus & sanguinem: sed tantum signum aut symbolum eius?' The title of Bucer's writing against the Bishop of Avranches as given here, is that of the book published at Strassburg in 1534, from which the *Scripta Anglicana* (pp. 613-631) printed the part concerning the Eucharist.

In the defence of his doctrine, as early as 1534 Bucer pursues a line on the subject which he never abandoned in later years. By trying to avoid the dangers or misconceptions, apparent to him in either Roman, Lutheran or Zwinglian teaching on the Eucharist, he develops his own Eucharistic doctrine.

As Bucer's teaching on the Eucharist has been so ably described by Mr. Smyth in his book on Cranmer as a distinct and separate theory from that of Luther and Zwingli,[1] it can be hardly the task of this section of our investigation to enlarge further on Bucer's Eucharistic doctrine. Smyth's observation, that we are confronted with a third factor of Protestant teaching on the Eucharist, seems also easily to explain the contradictory judgements passed on Bucer as regards his doctrine: which has been defined as either Lutheran or Zwinglian, has been said to be a mixture of both, has been said to be inconsistent in teaching, changing from Zwinglianism to Lutheranism and back again to Zwinglianism.[2] After the Genesis of his Eucharistic doctrine, Bucer, although at times not so conscious of it, neither changed from Zwinglianism to Lutheranism nor vice versa, as being once in favour of the one doctrine and then of the other, but by conceiving the rights and wrongs of each of the two Reformed Schools of thought, imbibed ideas of the two which appealed to him. If we conceive his doctrine as a new and distinct contribution to the teaching of the Reformers, and yet being complementary to the two Protestant doctrines, it will be easily seen why those who detected similar lines of thought to those of Luther claimed him to be a Lutheran and those who thought to have detected lines of thought similar to those of Zwingli called him a Zwinglian.

Being in contact from the beginning with both movements and being acquainted with their theologies, Bucer could never extricate himself from their controversies, which also concerned him so much.

[1] cf. Smyth, C. H.: *Cranmer and the Ref. . . .*, p. 25, and passim. cf. also Abbé Constant, G.: *L'Introduction De La Réforme En Angleterre . . .* (Paris, 1939), pp. 182 ff.

[2] cf. Hallam, Henry: *Constitutional History of England* (Everyman's Library, no. 621, reprinted 1930), vol. I, pp. 88-89.

cf. *Calendar of State Papers* (Venetian, 1527-33), Ricio and Pazizoni, Milanese Secretaries to the Duke of Milan (July 12th, 1532), p. 343, n. 787.

cf. Schelhorn, I. G.: *Amoenitates Literariae* (Frankf. 1727), §§ 24-29, §§ 368-380.

cf. Verpoortenn, A. M.: *Commentatio Historica, De Martino Bucero, . . .* (Coburg, 1709).

cf. Brerely, John (pseud. for Anderton, James): *Luther's Life . . . and other Learned Protestants . . .* (At S. Omer's, 1624), pp. 88-104.

Since the 'Wittenberg Concordat' of 1536, Bucer was declared by his contemporaries on the side of the Lutherans.

cf. Prateolus, Gabriel: *De Vitis, Sectis, Et Dogmatibus Omnium Haereticorum . . .* (Cologne, 1569), pp. 104 ff. cf. De Animarum cura (*Scr. Angl.*, p. 260): '. . . nos, quos ipsi Lutheranos appellant . . .'

Being opposed to Roman Catholicism and the idea of the Mass, with its implications of the opus operatum doctrine, Bucer was afraid of the Lutheran insistence on the *Verbum externum* and its implication of Consubstantiation, conceiving that it might equal the Roman idea, working apart from faith or from the attitude of the recipient.

The other danger he had to face was that of Anabaptist teaching. Their stress on the *Verbum Internum*, the inward light, their opposition to Sacraments, Church order or discipline, as merely external functions, made him early realize the necessity for external parts of the Ministry, the government of the Church, and the need for the Sacraments.[1]

Against this background it is easier to conceive Bucer's attitude as regards the opposing parties in the 'Supper-strife' of the sixteenth century.

The greater part of his writings is concerned with the question of the Eucharist. Retrospective accounts of the history of the controversy are characteristic for Bucer's approach of the subject, for by this method he recalls the arguments of the various opponents and feels able to sum up and to crystallize what seems to him a valuable result.[2]

The extraordinary gift of combining and selecting, the striking balance between stressing the internal functions of the *Word* with the stressing of the external functions of the *Word*, find their explanation in his life and person, which was so deeply involved and concerned with that struggle of the Protestant Parties which he wanted to cease. It was to him the *saxum Sisyphi*,[3] which he had rolled for years, a burden under which he suffered, and yet which helped him to find his own way.

His whole desire, since the 'Sakramentsstreit' tended to split the Protestant Party, was to bring both groups together by proposing as basis a formula which could be accepted by both. He always thought that both were more or less desiring the same end, but the one party, by trying to avoid a mere docetically-spiritual conception of Christ in the Sacrament, stressed His presence to the extent of maintaining

[1] cf. his *De vera animarum cura . . .* (1538), *Scr. Angl.*, pp. 274 and 275. Also W. Pauck: *Das Reich Gottes auf Erden* (1928), pp. 6-7.
cf. also Stupperich, Robert: *Die Kirche in M. Bucers Theol. Entwicklung* (1938), pp. 90 ff.

[2] *Scr. Angl.*, pp. 615 ff. and pp. 673 ff. Characteristics of the different conceptions, *Scr. Angl.*, pp. 598-610. cf. also Melanchthon's and Bucer's *Sententiae* of 1534 (p. 1282 in M. Goldast: *Politica Imperialia*, 1614).

[3] cf. in his *Apologia . . . ad E. Foxum* (1536), *Scr. Angl.*, p. 679, and in his letter to P. Martyr (June 20th, 1549), *Scr. Angl.*, p. 547.

that the body of Christ was bitten with their teeth and locally present. The other party by trying to avoid the slightest tendency to the sacramental-sacrificial idea of Roman Catholicism or any idea of the inclusion of Christ in the elements, fell into the other extreme of making Christ absent from the Sacrament.[1]

His doctrine is complicated, and as his style is prolix and tiresome, it is difficult — it seems even to himself — to define exactly what his doctrine stands for.

The insistence on Faith seems to be the touchstone of his Doctrine. From here he can say that Christ is really present (by faith), that we feed on Him (by faith), from here he has to say, that he cannot subscribe the theory, as if Christ could not be present, as being lifted up to Heaven. From here he overcomes the doctrinal and scholastic subtleties of defining how it could be possible for the body of Christ to be present at different places at the same time. From here he avoids the discussion on the relation between the elements and the Body and Blood of our Lord. And here he can state that there is communion with Him, Koinonia with one another, as expressed by S. Paul in 1 Cor. x.

In order to substantiate the statements made here, it seems excusable to add the following observations upon:

(*a*) Bucer's and Luther's Eucharistic conception in relation to their respective conceptions of the *Verbum Dei* and *Faith*.

(*b*) The Christological implication for the Eucharistic Doctrine.

(*c*) Bucer's own testimonies as regards his doctrine in his correspondence during his time in England.

(*a*) Luther as well as Bucer favoured Augustine's saying: 'accedit verbum ad elementum et fit sacramentum.'[2] Both agree that the Verbum has decisive efficacy in the sacrament. And yet Bucer is not content with this statement unless he adds the second part of Augustine's saying: It is agreed, says Bucer, that by the 'word' all things are

[1] In a letter to the 'Italian Brethren' (December 23rd, 1541) Bucer writes: 'At inter agendum de Reconciliatione Ecclesiarum circa hunc locum deprehendi, nec Zuinglium nullam: nec Lutherum crassiorem illam, sed plane indefinitam praesentiam *Christi* in sacramento statuere.' (*Scr. Angl.*, p. 689). The letter as printed in the *Scr. Angl.* is but an extract of Bucer's original letter. Only the part of the letter referring to the Eucharistic question is printed. The entire letter is extant in a contemporary MS. copy (Rawlinson MS. D. 858, fol. 37 ff.). It must have been of some interest to English theologians, because it is prefaced in the MS. by the following remark: 'The trewe coppie of a lr̃e written by the greate learned diuine Mr. Martin Bucer, the chiefe preacher of Strazsburg vnto certaine men which fauored the trewe religion of our sauioure Jesus Christe, and did dwelle at Venise, Vicentia, and other citties of Italie:' cf. my note in *J.T.S.* (January-April 1943, no. 173-4), pp. 67-72: A Letter of Martin Bucer.

[2] S. Augustine: *in Joannis Evangelium Tractatus* LXXX. Ch. 3 (in Migne, Bibl. Patr. Lat. (1861) vol. XXXV).

accomplished (Verbo perficiuntur omnia), but as Augustine writes (at ut Augustinus scribit, non quia dicitur, sed quia creditur) not because it is said but because it is believed.[1]

Here a fundamental difference between Luther and Bucer appears in the difference of accent. Luther grants to the verbum Dei all power, that the *verbum ex se* can create everything and is efficient without and apart from the attitude and inclination of man towards it. Bucer grants this power to the word, but only in so far as it is believed. Its efficacy is dependent on faith of man as responsive to the word. Whereas the Lutheran would say: '... Our faith does not bestow (non largitur) the essence and truth on the words of Christ... we do not accept the body of Christ in the Eucharist because we believe, but because Christ says Hoc est corpus meum. The unbelief of some does not make it of no effect. For, what would be more absurd, than that faith should make the words of Christ true and real and our unbelief (as would necessarily be the case) make them untrue and false. A person perverse in faith might still have the sacramentum integrum ... the integrity of the sacrament is not dependent on the faith of the man, who consumes it.'[2] Bucer urges the necessity of the action of faith on the side of the receiver. The consequence is that he could never easily subscribe to the Lutheran doctrine of the *manducatio impiorum.*[3] If faith is not demanded as complementary to the action of the word, he fears that this definition of the outward word (*verbum externum*) borders dangerously upon the Roman Catholic idea of an opus operatum.

Bucer misunderstood Luther's doctrine of the Verbum Dei in this point: although Luther speaks of the verbum internum and the verbum externum, the verbum externum was never understood as outward action only, but was always in relation to the inward word: causing the response of man to it.[4] But he felt that there was not expressed enough the difference from the Roman teaching of the

[1] *Scr. Angl.*, p. 618 (in 1534), and the same idea in his sermon delivered at Augsburg (probably June 17th, 1531), p. 208 in Schubert, Hans von: *Zwei Predigten Martin Bucers* ... in *Beiträge zur Reformationsgeschichte.* (Gotha, 1896).

[2] Gerlach: *Antidanaeus* ... pp. 54-55: ... Quemadmodum vero fides nostra essentiam & veritatem verbis Christi non largitur, sed ipsius institutio & voluntas, vt videlicet corpus Christi non ideo accipiamus in coena, quia nos credimus, sed quia Christus de pane dixit: Hoc est corpus meum: Ita incredulitas quorundam, fidem verborum Christi de substantia coenae, non facit irritam. Quid enim absurdius, quam fidem nostram, verba Christi, *hoc est corpus meum,* vera & realia: incredulitatem autem (quod fieri necesse esset) eadem falsa efficere. Aug. lib. 3 cap. 14 contra Donatist. A person perverse in faith might still have the sacramentum integrum. Audis integritatem sacramenti non dependere a fide sumentis. (ibid).

[3] cf. *Scr. Angl.*, p. 623, where he contends against a similar assumption by the Bishop of Avranches.

[4] cf. Seeberg, op. cit., *Lehrbuch der Dogmengesch.* .. (Zweite Hälfte, 1898), pp. 266 and 267 f.

sacraments being instruments or means of grace. He feared that the doctrine of the verbum externum would be similar to that of an opus externum, where the words and symbols in the sacrament become mere 'canales et vehicula spiritus, instrumenta gratiae'.[1] So he felt, that by supporting Luther's doctrine of the verbum externum, there was the danger of falling back to Roman conceptions, although he had to admit that the verbum externum in the sense used by Luther was not the equivalent to the Roman opus externum, but was understood to be the word of God which at the same time acted internally by creating the faith of the partaker of the Sacrament, who listened to the word. He always felt inclined to believe that a doctrine of the verbum externum was apt to misinterpretation of the fact, that Christ only was working in the sacrament by His works, and not the Sacraments *ex se*. He felt the danger of ascribing to the ministers and to the Sacraments what belonged only to Christ.[2]

He had to learn, that Luther's teaching was to safeguard the Church from the denial of the necessity of the Church and Ministry, where Anabaptism and its partisans desired to abandon the functions of both:

> . . . Plurimum tamen, ut haec plane relegerem, etiam haeretici mihi contulerunt, qui omnem ecclesiae communionem evertere, et usum sacramentorum plane abolere conantur. Ex horum nanque [*sic*] furore didici causam, cur D. Lutherus, et qui illum sequuntur, de sacramentis atque sacro ministerio tam magnifice loqui soleant.[3]

He had feared that refusing to admit any 'tropus' explanation in regard to the relation of Christ's body and blood to the elements of bread and wine, and stating merely a local, substantial and corporal presence of Christ in the elements, would mean reintroducing the 'Papistical error' of an external work without faith.[4]

He believed, that by the external administration 'secluso spiritu

[1] *Scr. Angl.*, p. 675: in his Apolog. to E. Fox.

[2] ibid., p. 676, pp. 674 ff.: 'Semper enim verebar ne externis rursus actionibus ministrorum id tribueretur quod Christi est.'

[3] ibid., p. 675. Apolog. to E. Fox.

[4] Jacob Fabricius Dantiscanus in his account of the Wittenberg Concordia of 1536 *Scr. Angl.*, p. 651: The cause for the declaration of the Strassburgers, that the writings of Luther and his partisans attributed too much to the Sacraments, and stated a more crass union of Christ with the bread (. . . scripta D. Lutheri & suorum nimium sacramentis tribuere, crassioremque unionem *Christi* cum pane statuere, quam qualem S. Scriptura admittat) was 'quod tropus omnis ab illis hactenus in verbis Coenae negatus sit, & quod scripserint, Intellectum verborum *Christi* hunc esse: Hoc est corpus meum substantialiter & corporaliter, vel in pane adest corporaliter. Item quod sine ulla declaratione sacramenta tradantur esse canales gratiae divinae, nec concedant a nobis dici, quod spiritus *Christi* importet & augeat in nobis fidem, & quicquid in nobis boni est. Ex his certe visum nobis esse, talibus sermonibus de sacramentis Papisticum errorem in Ecclesiam rursum introduci & confirmari: quo fascinati homines salutem sine ulla fide in externo opere sacramenti collocant & quaerunt.'

Christi' the *sacramentum ex se* profiteth nothing, again not being fully assured, that the *verbum externum* of Luther meant Christ acting and creating the faith in the receiver, the verbum externum inseparably connected with the *verbum internum.*[1]

Bucer's attitude with regard to the contending parties in the 'Supper-strife', his anxieties and intentions are expressed by himself in his Last Will (1541) in a highly significant way, which sums up and supports what we have attempted to say:

> . . . Exorto enim certamine de sacramentis cum symmystae, Patres et fratres mei, Lutherus et qui illum in eo certamine sectabantur, sic de sacramentis loquerentur ut plerisque viderentur gratiam Christi externis symbolis et actionibus affigere, ego id incommodi vitare cupiens in contrarium malum, uti stulti solent, incidi, atque in sacramentis id magis urgere coepi, quod tesserae sint societatis christianae quodque sint signa exhibitiva gratiae et communionis Christi. Non negabam quidem usu vero sacramentorum fidem in Christum augeri et corroborari, nec aliud declinare cupiebam, quam viderer externis symbolis vel actionibus hominum virtutem aliquam salvificam tribuere, qua sacramenta et illis profuissent qui sine certa in Christum fide eis communicarent. Illud enim solum respiciebam et extare in Ecclesia volebam, Christum unum per spiritum suum dare et augere fidem et per fidem in se, salutem. Interim autem non satis intelligebam, eoque nec docebam, quam efficaciter Dominus, ad hoc ipsum, verbo et sacramentis suis utatur, in iis qui ipsum in his loquentem et agentem vera fide exaudiant et amplectantur. etc.[2]

(*b*) By expounding their Eucharistic doctrine the reformers revealed at the same time their Christology.[3]

Their insistence on definitions to express Christ's presence or absence in the Supper is only a logical inference from their conception of the Person of Christ. Thus Ridley had stated: The doctrine of the Presence of Christ 'giveth occasion to the heretics, who erred concerning the two natures in Christ, to defend their heresies thereby'.[4]

[1] p. 676: 'Ad hunc modum negare volui, verbum Euangelij & sacramenta ex se hoc habere, remota operatione Christi, vt spiritum salutis & gratiam adferant.'

[2] Bucer in his Last Will (1541) (cf. Röhrich, Timotheus Wilhelm, Martin Butzers Testamente, nach dem Original herausgegeben . . . in: *Beiträge zu den theologischen Wissenschaften* . . . Jena, 1851), p. 200.

[3] cf. O. Ritschl: *Dogmengesch. des Protestantism.* (1926) Bd. III, pp. 108 ff. cf. A. Barclay: *The Protestant Doctrine of the Lord's Supper* (Glasgow, 1927), pp. 76 ff. and pp. 92 ff. cf. R. Seeberg: *Lehrbuch der Dogmengesch.* (Zweite Hälfte, 1898), pp. 310 ff. cf. H. Tollin, *Servet und die Oberländischen Reformatoren* . . . (Bd. I, 1880) passim, & pp. 49 ff.

[4] *Works of Ridley* (Parker Society, 1843), p. 198, cf. also p. 200. cf. also Gerlach, Stephan: *Antidanaeus* . . . (Tubingen, 1580), p. 226, where L. Osiander is quoted: 'Qui corpus Christi ubique esse negant, dividunt operationes in Christo, & separatim alias Divinitati, alias humanitati tribuunt: qui est iamdudum damnatus Nestorianorum error.'

Although Bucer's Christology is very similar to that of the other reformers, he feels no logical coercion to apply its conclusions by philosophical or scholastic reasoning to his doctrine of the Real Presence.

The cogent reasoning of some of the theologians derived from their Christology, that as Christ is risen sitting at the right hand of God, He cannot be present in the Supper, seems to Bucer irreconcilable with his faith in Christ: Christ is present for the believer, and the denial of His presence, derived from scholastic reasoning on the physical limitations of a body, is to him a fallacious and dangerous conclusion.

By faith Christ, the *totus Christus*, God and man, is present in the Supper. This teaching safeguards him from falling into any logical and 'worldly' reasoning, which also cannot be proved by Scripture, and against the erroneous conclusion that Christ, sitting at the right hand of God, cannot be present in the Supper, and is therefore absent.[1]

Thus in his letter to Martyr (June 1549) he writes:

> For, though we should grant you, that He is circumscribed even in heaven by a physical place, how is that inconsistent with His being now truly present to us by faith; even as the sun, in whatever part of the world we behold him, is truly present to us by sight. Certainly all errors which can possibly arise from the name 'Presence', may be altogether excluded by such words . . . I have never felt disposed, nor am I up to this moment disposed, to come forward in that controversy. Whether Christ is circumscribed by any Physical place in the heavens, He sits at the right hand of God; He has left the world . . .[2]

Bucer's attempt to explain the presence of Christ in the Sacrament by employing the similitude of the sun, can already be found in his Commentary on the Gospel of S. Matthew. It then became a favourite illustration for theologians of the sixteenth century. Was Bucer the first to employ it? Ridley uses the illustration, Jewel uses it against Harding, and Gardiner uses it in his controversy with Cranmer, although Cranmer seems not to be satisfied with it. Harding and Gardiner actually refer to Bucer's passage in his Commentary.[3]

[1] *Scr. Angl.*, p. 606.
[2] cf. Gorham, op. cit., p. 90, pp. 91 f.
[3] cf. *Works of Ridley* (Parker Society), p. 13.
cf. *Writings and Disp. of Thomas Cranmer . . . The Lord's Supper* (Parker Society, 1844), pp. 89, 90-91. It is of interest to note that Gardiner refers to Bucer as opposed to Cranmer, cf. also pp. 19, 126, 223 & 225.
cf. Jewel, John: *The Works of John Jewel . . . The First Portion . . . The Reply to Harding's Answer . . .* (Parker Society, 1845), vol. I, pp. 498-499.

His Christology in connection with his doctrine of the Real Presence is often stated in his writings. In his *Censura*, the liturgical work, he includes also some doctrinal remarks and points out that Christ is in heaven and according to His human nature not everywhere 'diffused', He has left this world 'secundum praesentiam carnis', but is with us 'secundum divinam naturam, secundum virtutem, secundum spiritum'.[1] By the repeated and constant stress on Christ's presence *by faith*, Bucer attempted to avoid controversies and contentions, which endangered the Koinonia of the Christian Church. The solution of the problems theology had to face at his time, of the question of the relation between the Elements and Christ's Body (Transubstantiation, consubstantiation, communicatio idiomatum or elements = signa), of the question how a body could be present at different places at the same time, and of the question how the recipient could be in *communion* with the risen Lord, Bucer found by insisting on the approach to the Sacrament *by faith*. No 'worldly' reasoning would help to explain the 'mystery of Christ', nor would it help to bring together all the Christians in the various camps, who desired and needed Koinonia and remission of sins.

(*c*) It is highly significant that, by his contemporaries, Bucer's Eucharistic conception during the last years of his life, and especially during his life in England, was considered not to be Zwinglian but a belief in the Real Presence.[2] Contemporary correspondence[3] and writings[4] show that he himself was opposed to the memorial or Christ-

[1] *Scr. Angl.*, pp. 474-475. cf. also pp. 552 and 540, 20 and 690 on the union of the heavenly Christ with the believer.

[2] cf. à Lasco's Letter to H. Bullinger (April 10th, 1551), Gorham, C.: *Gleanings of* . . ., p. 248.

[3] cf. his letters to:
Peter Martyr (June 20th, 1549), Gorham, op. cit., pp. 82 ff.
Theobald Niger (April 15th, 1550), Gorham, op. cit., pp. 142-143.
Calvin (Whitsunday, 1550), *Original Letters*, op. cit., pp. 547 ff.
Brentius (May 15th, 1550), *Original Letters* (Parker Society), vol. II, pp. 544-545.
Hardenberg (October 22nd, 1549), *Scr. Angl.*, p. 863 f.
cf. also Bucer's Definitio Plenior S. Eucharistiae . . . ad petitionem D. Petri Alexandri Atrebatensis. *Scr. Angl.*, pp. 551-553.

[4] Bucer's *Censura* of the First Edwardian Prayer Book as well as his Lecture at Cambridge on *De Vi et Efficacia Coenae Dominicae* (*Scr. Angl.*, pp. 598-610) include statements of his on the Eucharist. In 54 'Aphorisms' Bucer attempted at Cambridge in 1550 to lay down his Eucharistic doctrine: Exomologesis, sive confessio D. Mart. Buceri de S. Eucharistia in Anglia Aphoristicos scripta, Anno 1550 (*Scr. Angl.*, pp. 538-545). An English translation (contemporary?) is to be found in Strype, John: *Memorials of Archbishop Cranmer* (Oxford, 1840), vol. II, pp. 855-869, n. XLVI. The 'Aphorismi' in Latin were already printed in 1557 in: Antidotus Valerandi Pollani Flandri, Aduersus Ioachimi Vuestphali . . . Consiliū . . . Aphorismi D. Martini Bvceri de S. S. Coena Domini. 1557 (pp. 42-57). In 1536 Bucer dedicated his *Apologia* . . . *De S. Coena Domini*, an extract from his *Prefatio Enarrationum in quatuor Evangel.* to the Bishop of Hereford, Edward Fox (*Scr. Angl.*, pp. 670 ff.). Fox, who had been one of the King's Emissaries to Germany for negotiations with the Protestants, had met with Bucer.

absent theory of the Eucharist, and that the Swiss Party saw in him their opponent,[1] and that men like Gardiner harped on the fact that Bucer was a Lutheran.[2] His final re-conversion to a more Zwinglian outlook, which seems to have occurred in the last few months of his life by his correspondence with à Lasco and in his incomplete lectures, has no weight in the discussion of Bucer's relation to the English Eucharistic outlook, as it could not have exercised any material influence.[3] A valuable source of information is the correspondence between Bucer and Martyr on the occasion of the latter's Dispute at Oxford in 1549.[4] Bucer confesses in his letter to Theobald Niger, that he could not influence Martyr in his 'propositions' for the Dispute, as it was before the time he came to England. But in his letter to Martyr he deals specially with Martyr's propositions, which he would have liked to have been presented differently. The letter is a prolix little treatise in itself. He warns Martyr that by his propositions, it might be inferred, that not only he, but also the English Church, did not believe in the presence of our Lord, but rather in His absence, in the Supper.[5] The presence of Christ – though only by faith – ought to be stressed against those who contend that He has left this world and that men remember and worship only the Christ in Heaven.

In his letter to Calvin (Whitsunday 1550) the following significant passage is to be found:

> We must observe in addition to these evils, that not a few persons, laying aside all desire after true repentance, faith . . . do nothing but dispute and contend, and often very profanely, how they may seclude Christ our Saviour from our sacraments and holy assemblies, and confine him to his place in heaven.[6]

How offensive this must have sounded for the Swiss Party can be seen from the fact that Beza, who edited the letter in the *Calvini Epistolae* (1576), in order to suppress the doctrine of the Real Presence, altered the pungent expressions into the vague words:

> They deliver upon the participation of Christ through the sacra-

[1] cf. R. Hilles to Bullinger (June 4th, 1549), *Original Letters*, vol. I, p. 266.

[2] cf. MS. Arundel 100: in Petrum Martyrem Florentinum malae tractationis Querela sanctissimae Eucharistiae nomine edita, authore Stephano Wintoniensi. cf. Janelle, Pierre: *Obedience in Church and State* (Cambridge, 1930), p. 207, note continued.

[3] cf. Smyth, C. H.: *Cranmer and the Reformation* . . . (Cambridge, 1926), p. 173; and Brerely, John (pseudon. for Anderton, James), *Luther's Life Collected . . . with a further shorte discourse . . . touchinge . . . Bucer* . . . (S. Omers, 1624), pp. 103-104.

[4] cf. Gasquet . . . *Edward VI and the Book of Common Prayer* (London, 1928, Revised ed.), pp. 215-216.

[5] cf. *Scr. Angl.*, pp. 548-549.

[6] *Original Letters*, op. cit., vol. II, p. 547. Latin in *Epistolae Tig.*, pp. 356 ff.

ments such things as are not sufficiently imbued with the sense of true piety.[1]

From a letter by Hooper to Bucer (June 19th, 1548) it appears also that Bucer had accused the Swiss of teaching the sacraments to be bare signs.[2] Although Bucer's language as regards the Eucharist is more than complicated, it remains that he teaches and stresses the fact that Christ is present, not absent, present by faith, not carnally, yet really.

Walter Haddon, in his oration at Bucer's funeral, expresses well the English sentiment towards the reformer's Eucharistic conception. He feels drawn to it because English theological thinking was much more akin to its conciliatory spirit than it was to that of the Continental contending parties, and because it emphasized rather the communion with Christ than made a matter of contest as on the Continent. Haddon deplores only the fact that by Bucer's death the English Church was deprived of a man who could have given a clear outline of his doctrine which so wisely could prevent the indulging of the Church here in a warfare similar to that raging at that time and which already had proved so fatal for the unity of the Church.[3]

§IV

NOTE ON BUCER AND COLET

Bucer's letter to the 'Senators' of Strassburg (1527)[4] contains a significant reference to John Colet's opinion on the interpretation of Scripture. By objecting in this letter to the allegoric interpretation, Bucer tries to strengthen his argument in claiming Colet as his authority. The Scriptures admit only one interpretation, the true interpretation, and any other method beyond that true interpretation misinterprets the singular and true sense of Scripture, leads to

[1] Joannis Calvini Epistolae et responsa. Editio secunda (with the life of Calvin by Beza), Geneva, 1576, p. 97: 'Accedit his malis quod non pauci omni verae poenitentiae, fidei, bonorum operum, communionis . . . vnum hoc agitent ac contendant, ac saepenumero admodum irreligiose vt de ea Christi per Sacramenta participatione, quae verae pietatis sensum non satis resipiant.' cf. 'The True History of the Edwardian Ordinal' (*Church Quarterly Review*, April, 1897), p. 131.

[2] *Original Letters*, op. cit., vol. I, pp. 47 f.

[3] *Scr. Angl.*, p. 890.

[4] Prvdentia aequitate, et pietate spectabilibus uiris, Senatoribus, inclytae urbis Argentoratensis Martinus Bucerus, Gratiam & pacem a Deo patre & Domino nostro Jesu Christo. (fol. A9-A10 verso), *dated* A.10 verso: Argen. 15 Kalend. Apriles M.D. XXVII. (Bodleian Library: Antiq. d. G. 1530-31.)

abuses, as can be seen by the distorted allegoric 'fancies' of his time.[1] Although Bucer praises, in the same letter, the Paraphrases of Erasmus[2] as an example of the right method of interpretation, he prefers Colet to Erasmus. He writes of Colet:

> . . . Nec est ut dicant ornatus, non doctrinae caussa ista adhiberi, par est siquidem & ornatum veritatis, verum & certum esse. Si oves Christi doces, non debes quicq̃ue eis proponere, nisi quod mentem ipsarum pascat, id autem tantum veritas est, & quidem Dei, nequamque tua commenta. Haec divinus ille, & doctissimus vir Johan. Coletus Anglus, per Erasmum Rot. identidem & merito sane celebratus, probe sensit, uti testatur eius ad Erasmum hac de re Epistola.

And Bucer comes to the conclusion:

> Allegoricas igitur istas nugas, ut optarim nullum prorsus locum in Ecclesiis habere, ita nullas uspiam adhibui.

Bucer, by mentioning here the letter of Colet to Erasmus, refers undoubtedly to the discourse between Erasmus and Colet on the subject of interpretation, as printed in the Enchiridion of Erasmus (1519).[3] By Colet's letter with his reply to the 'Erasmian arguments' a discussion was brought to an end, held between Erasmus and Colet at Oxford in 1499.[4] Bucer in referring to the letter may have been in possession of the Enchiridion. Deeply impressed by Colet's arguments, Bucer's Commentary on the Gospels (to which his letter to

[1] Bucer explains that Paul's and even Philo's allegorical interpretation of scripture (Paul, e.g.: 2 sons of Abraham in his Epistle to the Galatians) is quite different from the abusive alleg. interpretation of his time, where for example (as Bucer states) the six water-pots at the marriage of Cana become the six books of the Law, the water becomes the intellect of the Law, the wine becomes the Euangelion; or the five loaves are the five books of Moses and the two fishes represent the Gospels and the Epistles of Paul.

[2] In this connection Gardiner's remarks on the relation of Bucer with Erasmus seem of interest: a letter of Erasmus written to Bucer (November 11th, 1527) on Erasmus' opinion about the Protestant party was well known to Gardiner, the Bishop of Winchester. Gardiner, in his letter to Cranmer (July 1547), quotes a passage from Erasmus' letter as evidence for his own dislike of Protestantism. He must have read the letter of Erasmus which was printed in the 1529 Froben edition of Erasmus' Epistles. (cf. the letter of Erasmus in: Allen, P. S.: *Opus Epistolarum Des. Erasmi.*, vol. VII, n. 1901, pp. 229 ff. cf. Gardiner's letter to Cranmer in: Muller, James: *The Letters of Stephen Gardiner*, n. 125, pp. 316 ff. quotation, p. 333. cf. also Muller, op. cit., p. 360, note to p 333.)

[3] Enchiridion Erasmi. Jo. Froben (Basel, 1519), pp. 289-290: Colet's letter to Erasmus; pp. 291-294: Colet's *Responsio ad Argvmenta Erasmiana* the letter of Colet to Erasmus (probably October 1499), also in Allen, P. S.: *Opus Epistolarum Des. Erasmi.*, (Tom. I, 1484-1514), *Oxonii* . . . MCMVI, pp. 253 ff. no. 110. cf. also note to n. 108, pp. 245-246. But Allen does not bring in the *Responsio* of Colet which follows immediately Colet's letter in the Enchiridion.

[4] On the discussion see: Frederic Seebohm: *The Oxford Reformers* . . . (Everyman's Library, no. 665): pp. 70 ff.: Discussion between Erasmus and Colet on . . . the Inspiration of the Scriptures (1499).

the Senators of Strassburg was prefixed, in which he gives an account of his Commentary) bears the marks of Colet's statements. Outlining the method applied to the work on his Commentary, Bucer writes in his letter:

> Neque enim spiritus scripturis suis aliquid incertum, aut varium proponit, docet enim & ratione quidem absolutissima, igitur quicquid dicit, unum dicit . . .

Here the words of Colet in his discussion with Erasmus seem to form the background:

> Spiritus autem sanctus, qui sacrarum literarum parens est, quique est ipsa foecunditas, ut in se parit pro sua potentia unam & eandem simplicem veritatem, ita est necesse suo sermone veridico unum duntaxat sensum, eumque verissimum nobis educat. (*Ench.* 291/292.)

Bucer's restraint from allegoric interpretation in this commentary and his dislike of it in this letter can be ascribed to the lesson he learned from Colet. The Continental reformer, who later contributed so much to the English Reformation, was coming, for the first time, into contact with English theologians, indebted to one of England's greatest reformers of the pre-Reformation period, John Colet.

§V

BUCER'S REPLY TO THE 'ANTIDIDAGMA'[1]

(Additional Note on Thomas Sampson's manuscript translation)

At the Bodleian there is a printed copy of the *Antididagma* (1549),[2] which the Roman Catholic theologians of Cologne — the Chapter of Cologne — had written as reply to Herman von Wied's reform work. They had attacked Herman's reform scheme most violently and had objected as strongly to the Archbishop having called Martin Bucer to help him in his Reformation. The *Antididagma*, though splendid in its Theology, is invective in its tone. The Archbishop felt urged to reply to it and to contradict the charges and accusations brought against him and Bucer. The *Bestendige Verantwortung* was the answer

[1] In addition should be read: 'Capitulum Coloniense: An Episode in the Reformation.' *Church Quarterly Review* (January 1891), pp. 419 ff.
[2] (MS. Lat. Th. e. 4) *Antididagma* . . . 1549.

printed at Bonn in 1545. The theological part of the prolix reply has to be ascribed to Bucer. There, point for point the doctrinal arguments of the *Antididagma* were answered. But — as the work was written in German — it was only accessible to a limited number of readers. A Latin translation seemed advisable. The first manuscript Latin translation was done by Martin Brem, Bucer's amanuensis, who had followed him to England. The manuscript is still extant at Corpus Christi College, Cambridge. Bucer's reply was greatly valued by Archbishop Parker.[1] Brem's translation was also known to Conrad Hubert, for Grindal writes to Hubert (London, May 23rd, 1559) '. . . You told me that you had a copy of the answer to the *Antididagma*, turned into Latin by Martin Bremius . . .'[2] Not before 1613 was the Latin translation printed.[3] But it seems that the printed Latin translation was not that of Brem.

The copy of the *Antididagma* at the Bodleian contains also a manuscript Latin translation of the *Bestendige Verantwortung*. The copy is interleaved, and has on those inserted leaves the translation of the *Bestendige Verantwortung*. The translation was done by Thomas Sampson, Dean of Christ Church. On the front-leaf of the *Antididagma* in his own beautiful handwriting stands:

> Lectori. Habes hic adscriptum Responsum *Martini Buceri* quod ille Germanice scripsit et excudi curauit, dispositum ad quaelibet capita obiter Aduersariorum. Thomas Sampson.

As Sampson attempted to make his translation of Bucer's reply face the corresponding arguments of the *Antididagma*, the manuscript is not a consecutive straightforward translation, but is dependent on the text of the *Antididagma* so far as arrangement is concerned.

The manuscript is most beautifully written, frequently underlined or initialled by letters in red ink. To have the translation of Bucer's reply side by side with the arguments of the *Antididagma* was a great advantage for the reader. Sampson underwent hard work to complete the translation and to make the reply correspond to the relative pages of the *Antididagma*. Certain passages of Sampson's manuscript translation are verbatim the same as those in the printed edition of 1613.[4]

[1] MS. Corpus Christi College, Cambridge, 125 (cf. M. R. James, Catalogue of MSS. at C.C.C.C.). Another MS. translation is at the Bodleian, MS. Add. c. 97.

[2] cf. *Zurich Letters*, 1558-1602, 2nd Series (Parker Society, 1845), pp. 18-19.

[3] *Constans Defensio* . . . Auctore D. Martino Bvcero . . . Nunc primo e manuscripto Buceri in lucem editus . . . (Genevae . . . 1613).

[4] cf. e.g. *Constans Defensio* . . . pp. 157 ff. (De Imaginibus . . .) with the text of the corresponding interleaved pages to the *Antididagma*, pp. 47 ff. and in aliis locis.

CHAPTER II

MARTIN BUCER AND THE BOOK OF COMMON PRAYER

'Memor ergo quid Reuerendissimae P.T. & Ecclesijs Anglicanis cum primis debeam, quod datum mihi est hac in re videre, id studeam subscribere. Reuerendissima P.T. alijque tui ordinis, de his iudicabunt. Equidem cum primum in hoc Regnum venissem, quae publice dogmata quique ritus in Ecclesia essent recepti: videremque eo, num meum possem ministerium his solido consensu adiungere, librum istum Sacrorum per interpretem, quantum potui, cognoui diligenter. quo facto, egi gratias Deo, qui dedisset vos has ceremonias eo puritatis reformare, nec enim quicquam in illis deprehendi, quod non sit ex verbo Dei desumptum, aut saltem ei non aduersetur, commode acceptum. Nam non desunt paucula quaedam, quae si quis non candide interpretetur, videri queant, non satis cum verbo Dei congruere.'

BUCER: *Censura, Scripta Anglicana*, p. 456

WHEN Bucer came to England in April of 1549, the First Edwardian Prayer Book was just getting published and coming in use.[1] The introduction of a Book of Common Prayer of this type into the religious and public life of the people marks the most critical juncture in the History of the English Reformation. That Bucer should arrive at that very moment was thus the great chance for the advancement of the Continental Reformation in England. The welcome given to the Strassburg Reformer in this country — so different from that given to the Lutheran emissaries in previous years — can be explained by the decision taken by the English Reformers towards Protestantism.

It was natural that Bucer's interest should be concentrated on the Prayer Book and its reception by the people, since that might well reflect to him the attitude of England towards his own religious convictions. When reading the First Book of Homilies while still at Strassburg, he might have felt assured that the English Church had taken a firm stand on Protestant principles. Now by reading the Prayer Book 'per interpretem' he would be at once intimately attracted by some sections, as he recognized his own sentiments reproduced from the Cologne *Consultatio*, of which he had been one of the

[1] The dates of the first editions of the First Edwardian Prayer Book are: March 7th, 1549, May 4th, 1549, June 16th, 1549, July 30th, 1549.

chief compilers.[1] And yet to guarantee a permanent existence for the new Book as an expression of Reformed Liturgy and Doctrine, he could hardly be absolutely satisfied with all parts of it. Unless there were some further cleansing from expressions and passages, which might still be open to 'Roman' misinterpretation, the Reformation could not have seemed to him entirely successful. His first letter (April 26th, 1549),[2] which he wrote from Lambeth soon after his arrival in England to his Strassburg colleagues, thus deals mainly with the Prayer Book:

> The cause of religion, as far as appertains to the establishment of doctrines and the definition of rites, is pretty near what could be wished. Efforts must now be made to obtain suitable ministers, who will carry these wholesome doctrines into practice, and deliver them to the people . . . As soon as the description of the ceremonies now in use[3] shall have been translated into Latin, we will send it to you.
>
> We hear that some concessions have been made both to a respect for antiquity, and to the infirmity of the present age; such, for instance, as the vestments commonly used in the sacrament of the eucharist, and the use of candles: so also in regard to the commemoration of the dead, and the use of chrism; for we know not to what extent or in what sort it prevails. They affirm that there is no superstition in these things, and that they are only to be retained for a time, lest the people, not having yet learned Christ, should be deterred by too extensive innovations from embracing his religion, and that rather they may be won over. This circumstance however greatly refreshed us, that all the services in the churches are read and sung in the vernacular tongue, that the doctrine of justification is purely and soundly taught, and the eucharist administered according to Christ's ordinance, private masses having been abolished.[4]

The 'concessions' mentioned here by Bucer as 'made' show the

[1] cf. *The Order of the Communion*, 1548. Ed. by H. A. Wilson (London, 1908), pp. xxiv, xliii, 47 ff.

cf. W. Page: 'The First Book of Common Prayer'. . . (*Church Quarterly Review*, April, 1924), pp. 51 ff.

cf. also Brightman: *The English Rite*, vol. I, pp. cxlii.

cf. also Bucer's letter to his Strassburg colleagues (April 26th, 1549), *Original Letters*, pp. 535 f.

cf. also Dryander's letter to Bullinger (June 9th, 1549): 'A book has now been published, a month or two back, which the English churches received with the greatest satisfaction . . .' (*Original Letters*, p. 350.)

[2] He arrived at the Archbishop's Manor at Lambeth on April 25th, 1549.

[3] The English translation seems here to be incorrect, the Latin has: '. . . Ubi traducta fuerit in Latinum ceremoniarum descriptio, quod nunc fit, eam ad vos mittemus.' cf. *Ep. Tig.* n. CCXLVIII, pp. 349 f.

[4] *Original Letters*, vol. II, pp. 535-536.

policy of the English Divines, who, aware that their efforts might prove abortive, had to proceed cautiously. By ambiguous terminology in certain places, it was intended to avoid offending the still strong Roman Catholic Party, which had to be won over gradually. Thus Dryander writes to Bullinger (June 5th, 1549)[1]:

> You will see that the summary of doctrine cannot be found fault with, although certain ceremonies are retained in that book which may appear useless, and perhaps hurtful, unless a candid interpretation be put upon them. But in the cause of religion, which is the most important of all in the whole world, I think that every kind of deception either by ambiguity or trickery of language is altogether unwarrantable. You will also find something to blame in the matter of the Lord's supper; for the book speaks very obscurely, and however you may try to explain it with candour, you cannot avoid great absurdity. The reason is, that the bishops could not of a long time agree among themselves respecting this article, and it was a long and earnest dispute among them whether transubstantiation should be established or rejected. You perceive therefore by this certain proof, that there are no true and solid principles of doctrine in these men.

Thus for Gardiner it could appear that certain parts of the Prayer Book, specially the Communion Office, were 'well termed not distant from the catholic faith in my judgment'.[2]

And Bucer could write on the Communion Service of the First Prayer Book:

> Concerning this [office] I give the utmost thanks to God, who has given it to be drawn up so pure, and so scrupulously faithful to the word of God, especially at [considering?] the time at which this was done. For excepting a very few words and signs I perceive nothing in it at all which may not be drawn out of the Holy Scriptures . . .[3]

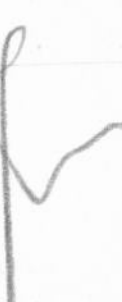

Although Gardiner and Bucer, the outstanding representatives of the opposing parties could interpret the Prayer Book as consistent with their respective doctrines, Bucer soon felt the need to turn over in his mind a project for a further critical revision. He did not object to ancient Church rites and ceremonies as handed down to the Church throughout the ages, so long as they had not been converted into 'superstitious papistical practices'. Here lies the difference from the Puritan Party, which disregarding ancient

[1] *Original Letters*, vol. I, p. 351, n. CLXXI.
[2] cf. C. H. Smyth, op. cit., pp. 234-235.
[3] *Censura*, p. 465, ch. vii; translation from C. H. Smyth, op. cit., p. 238. cf. also *Censura*, p. 456.

continuity, desired a Church disconnected from traditions and external practices. Bucer was too much of a Churchman not to see the faults of such a policy. His suggestions for improvements do not intend to overthrow tradition, and his constant reference to the Church Fathers and to ancient practices are evidence how much he valued that inheritance, to which the Church of the Reformation was so much indebted.

Bucer's work for revision of the First Prayer Book is his *Censura Martini Buceri super libro sacrorum, seu ordinationis Ecclesiae atque ministerii ecclesiastici in regno Angliae.*[1] When this work was for the first time printed in the volume of *Scripta Anglicana* at Basle in 1577, the editor, Bucer's colleague, Conrad Hubert, added to the title: 'ad petitionem R. Archiepiscopi Cantuariensis, Thomae Cranmeri, conscripta.'[2] The title itself (*Censura* ...) was put posthumously to the work by Hubert. It is not to be found in the two extant manuscripts from one of which it was printed.[3] The *Censura* was presumably written at the special request of Goodrich, the Bishop of Ely, who presented it to Cranmer.[4] It was finished on January 5th, 1551, less than two months before Bucer's death (on February 28th, 1551). The prefatory sentences already referred to show that Bucer was in general pleased with the tenor of the Prayer Book and that as Protestant Reformer he

[1] *Scripta Anglicana*, pp. 456-503.

[2] cf. Gasquet, op. cit., p. 259, n. 1; also C. H. Smyth, op. cit., p. 237, n. 2.

[3] cf. also n. 3 to p. 59 of this work.

The *Censura* is dated 'Nonis Januarij 1551' (and Bucer had died at the end of February 1551) added by Hubert: 'die XXV post defunctus'. Concerning the title, *Censura*, of Bucer's work, two statements are of interest: the first occurs in the controversy between Whitgift and Cartwright. Cartwright writes: 'But it is first of all to be observed of the reader, how and with what names those notes are called which are cited of M. Doctor [i.e. Whitgift] for the defence of these corruptions: they are called by Mr. Doctor's own confession, "Censures"; . . .' (op. cit., vol. III, p. 124.)

And Whitgift replies: '. . . To your second (cavil) of Master Bucer's Censures (though the book be not so intituled) the answer is short and plain: it was his judgment upon the first communion-book, in the time of king Edward . . .' (op. cit., vol. III, p. 125).

The second comes from Archbishop Laud: 'First, 'tis true, Bucer did make some observations upon that Common-Prayer-Book under Edw. VI. And he did it at the entreaty of Archbishop Cranmer. And after he had made such observations upon it as he thought fit, he writ thus to the Archbishop:– "Being mindful how much I owe to your most reverend Fatherhood and the English Churches, that which is given [me] to see and discern in this business, I will subscribe: this done, your most reverend Fatherhood, and the rest of your order" (that is, the rest of the bishops,) "may judge of what I write." Where we see, both the care of Bucer to do what was required of him, and his Christian humility, to leave what he had done to the judgment of the then governors of this Church. By which it appears, that he gave his judgment upon "that book", not as being the "censurer" of it, (as these men call him,) but as delivering up his animadversions upon it to that authority which required it of him. Much less was it such a "censure" as must bind all other men to his judgment, which he very modestly submits to the Church.' (Laud, op. cit., III, p. 351; cf. also there the original passage, erased later).

[4] cf. Gasquet, op. cit., p. 259, n. 1; cf. also Harvey, op. cit., p. 65; cf. also Brightman, op. cit., I, p. cxlii ff.

could subscribe to it. For his *Censura* he did not use the Latin Version of the Prayer Book done by Alesius, which we find prefixed to the *Censura* in the *Scripta Anglicana.*[1] He read the Prayer Book, as we have seen, 'per interpretem', and although when referring in his *Censura* to certain passages of the Prayer Book to which he wants attention to be drawn, he uses the English words of those passages, there is no evidence that he knew English well enough to understand the book in that language.[2]

Up to the edition of the *Scripta Anglicana* of 1577 the *Censura* was only extant in manuscript form.[3] It was thus only accessible to a few, not to the public as any printed book would have been. Therefore it was very little known up to the time of its printing twenty-six years after it had been written. Few knew of the important rôle it had played in the history of the revision of the 1549 Prayer Book, and of the suggestions for alterations and amendments, of which a number were carried out in the Second Prayer Book. This question is one of great importance for our present investigation. Many alterations were, no doubt, made by the English compilers of the Second Prayer Book which were often independent of Bucer's suggestions, or even

[1] cf. Dixon, R. W.: *History of the Church of England*, vol. III, pp. 293 ff.

[2] Against C. H. Smyth, op. cit., pp. 236-237.

[3] The MSS. are: (1) MS. Corpus Christi College, Cambridge 172, described by Dr. Montague Rhodes James (A Descriptive Catalogue of the Manuscripts in the Library of Corpus Christi College, Cambridge, Cambridge, 1912) as: Martini Buceri annotationes in librum precum communium. Exemplar autographum scriptum A.D. 1551. Inscribitur sed diversa manu ad episcopum Eliensem. Dated at the end (p. 118) Nonis Ian. MDLI Cambridge.

(2) New College MS. 317, now deposited in the Bodleian Library, described in the Catalogue (Henricus O. Coxe: Catalogus Codicum MSS. qui in Collegiis Aulisque Oxoniensibus . . . Pars I Oxford, 1853) as Martini Buceri de caeremoniis ecclesiae Anglicanae reformandis libellus, ad Edwardum VI; [*sic!*] dat. Cantabr. non Januar. 1551. Tit. 'Martinus Bucerus de caeremoniis ecclesiae Anglicanae'.

There are points of exceedingly high interest in regard to these descriptions. It will be noticed that both descriptions do not mention the word 'Censura', which appears to have been Hubert's own choice in 1577 by incorporating it into the *Scr. Angl.* Hubert might have been induced for his choice by Peter Martyr's letter (January 10th, 1551, cf. Gorham, op. cit., n. LXIII, p. 227) where Martyr speaks of his own work as 'Censura'. The Oxford MS. is a beautifully written copy of 55 folio pages in a contemporary hand, presumably that of Bucer's amanuensis. The handwriting is the same as that of Bucer's letter to Hooper (Rawlinson MS. D 346, fol. 16 ff.) and that of Bucer's letter to Cranmer (MS. New College 343, fol. 42 ff.). It has corrections, however, in Bucer's own hand, and is signed at the end by Bucer himself. The title-page differs in its writing from the other pages. It gives in a rude sixteenth-century hand the title: 'Bucerus De Ceremonijs Ecclĩae Anglicanae'. The different sections are headed by titles in red ink. The marginal references: 'Retinendum, Emendandum, corrigendum, tollendum', etc. (also in red ink) at once draw the reader's attention to the respective sections of the First Prayer Book, which Bucer wants either to be retained, altered or omitted. The wording of the sectional titles differs often from that of Hubert's printed copy. One small passage on the Confirmation Service is not to be found in the printed *Censura.* (cf. pp. 70-71 of this work.)

Gasquet and Bishop (op. cit., p. 259, n. 1) refer only to the Cambridge MS. It is thus of the most extraordinary interest to mention the Oxford MS. as it seems surprising that it should hitherto have almost entirely escaped notice.

ignored his advice. Changes were made which were neither wanted nor urged by Bucer, and yet there is clear evidence that his draft was consulted and used considerably.

Hubert's publication of the *Censura* in the *Scripta Anglicana* of 1577 is a significant turning point in a controversy which had already arisen. Any reference to the *Censura* before 1577 — claiming Bucer's responsibility and authority for the revision of the First Edwardian Prayer Book — was regarded with suspicion or considered as untenable by contemporaries who had neither seen the work nor knew of its effective influence. Those who did not know the work accused those who appealed to it of relying on a work of Bucer of which the authorship was not proved beyond doubt and which might be spurious. It was suggested that by quoting it they only wanted to find support for their own doctrinal and ritual views. A very notable example is to be seen in Thomas Cartwright's suspicions and objections as voiced in his controversy with Whitgift, concerning Whitgift's quotations from the *Censura* and his fondness for it. The controversy, stretching over years, began in 1572 and ended before 1577.[1] Hence Cartwright had not seen a printed copy, whereas Whitgift possessed the manuscript. Whitgift, on the other hand, was perfectly entitled to quote the *Censura*, of which he knew beyond doubt that it was Bucer's work. Cartwright knew only of the work by the quotations made from it by Whitgift who sometimes gave them in English. It is hardly surprising, therefore, that his opponent should be the more eager to see the original Latin text and to have it proved to be a genuine work of Bucer.

In this connection he writes to Whitgift:[2]

> But it had been for the credit of your cause, if you had shewed that out of those writings which are published and known to be his [i.e. Bucer's], and not out of those, whereof men may doubt whether ever he wrote any such or no; and, if he wrote, whether they be corrupted by those into whose hands they came. And, if you would take any advantage of M. Bucer's testimony, considering that a witness is a public person, you should have brought him out of your study into the stationer's shop, where he mought have been common to others as well as to you . . .

[1] Whitgift's Answer to the Admonition was sent to M. Parker, October 21st, 1572. Cartwright's Reply to it was published early the next year. Whitgift was far advanced in his Defence, June 4th, 1573. Cartwright's second Reply came out in two portions, 1575 and 1577.
cf. also Whitgift, op. cit., III, pp. x ff.
cf. also Pearson, A. F. Scott: *Thomas Cartwright . . .* (Cambridge, 1925), pp. 67 f., 86 ff., 103, et passim.
cf. also Frere, W. H.: *A History of the English Church*, pp. 181 ff.

[2] Whitgift, op. cit., II, pp. 533-534.

To which Whitgift answers:

> The book [i.e. the *Censura*] of M. Bucer's is forthcoming to be showed; and he affirmeth nothing therein contrary to his books published . . .[1]

In the nineteenth century Richard Laurence, Archbishop of Cashel, in the Bampton Lectures of 1804, maintained that Bucer's influence on English Prayer Book revision was unimportant. He supported his contention by reference to two letters of the Reformation period and says:

> The real fact indeed, with respect to the little influence either of Bucer's or Martyr's sentiments in the revision of our Liturgy, seems to have been put beyond all controversy by G. Ridley, in his Life of Bp. Ridley; and that by a reference to indisputable testimonies. He observes, pp. 333-334: 'A review of it was therefore determined; and many things were thought proper to be altered. Bucer and Martyr were desired to give their opinions also, as appears by a letter from Martyr to Bucer, January 10th, 1551; in which we see, that these foreigners in general agreed in censuring the same things. But they had no further hand in the alterations, than in delivering their censures separately to the Archbishop; for in the same letter Martyr says, *that what the points were, that it had been agreed should be altered, he knew not, nor durst presume to ask.* And as for Bucer, he died the latter end of the month, and could be no further concerned in it. And as the reviewers were not moved by them, but by some members of the Convocation, *so many alterations were agreed, before these Professors were consulted, as appears from the same letter.*'[2]

But in fact the letter, when read in its context, seems still to suggest that the Bishops did listen to the proposals of the two Continental Reformers, and it does not state that the proposals were returned or rejected, unread. And as by comparing the alterations made in the Second Prayer Book with Bucer's suggestions, a striking influence can be seen, this argument of the Bampton Lecturer hardly seems to hold good. The passage of the letter runs in its context (January 10th, 1551):

> And I thank God who has given us an opportunity of laying before the Bishops our suggestions on all these things. It has now been decided in their conference, as the Most Reverend informs me, that many things shall be changed; but what corrections they have decided upon, he did not explain to me, nor was I so bold as

[1] Whitgift, op. cit., II, p. 534.
cf. a similar remark made by Cartwright, op. cit., vol. III, p. 85.

[2] Laurence, Richard: *An Attempt to Illustrate* . . . op. cit. (3rd ed. rev., Oxford, 1838), pp. 246-247.

> to ask him. But I have been not a little gratified by what Mr. Cheke has told me; he says, that if they will not make the changes which have been considered necessary, the King himself will do this; and that, when Parliament meets, he will interpose his Royal authority.[1]

Too much importance has been ascribed to this letter in the effort to prove that Bucer's *Censura* was not considered as a possible basis for a revision of the First Prayer Book. But the letter was written only five days after Bucer finished his work. Martyr might just have had time to hand over the *Censura* to the bishops, but there had been very little time for them to read and consult it and to form their opinion of it. What use they could or could not have made of it would have to be judged by later results.

The second letter quoted by Archbishop Laurence is nothing at all to the purpose if our contention is correct. He quotes, on the authority of Beza, a letter of Bucer to a certain friend, written on January 12th, 1550, in which Bucer states that no foreigner is being consulted on the subject of rites. Archbishop Laurence uses that letter to prove that 'it had been incorrectly asserted that Bucer was the author of our Baptismal Service'.[2] As the letter was written in January 1550, a year before Bucer was asked to write the *Censura*, it cannot be claimed as evidence for the small influence of the foreigners, for during that year, 1550, Bucer's part played in English Church affairs can easily be illustrated by his correspondence on the Vestment controversy (where Cranmer specially asked his advice), and by other of his writings.

Secondly, this letter is inadequate to sustain the weight of the assertion as to Bucer's lack of connection with the Baptismal Service. Although the word 'author' seems to be an exaggeration, it is a fact that the Anglican Baptismal Offices derived a large contingent of their material from the Cologne *Consultatio*, of which, specially in regard to the Baptismal Service, Bucer can be claimed as the chief compiler. Thus, already before Bucer wrote the letter in question, his influence had been established on the First Prayer Book, and the remark in his letter can be interpreted only as referring to circum-

[1] cf. Gorham, op. cit., n. LXIII, pp. 228-229; and n. LXIV, pp. 231-233, another letter of P. Martyr to M. Bucer, as a reply to a letter of Bucer of January 22nd.

The Latin text of n. LXIII is to be found in: Strype: *Mem. of Abp. Cranmer*, vol. II, App. lxi.

[2] Richard Laurence, Bampton Lectures, 1804 (3rd ed., Oxford, 1838). On p. 246 Laurence quotes Bucer's letter (January 12th, 1550) from Beza's *Tractationes Theologicae*, vol. II, p. 323, ed. Geneva, 1570.

cf. Dixon, op. cit., vol. III, p. 281 note.

cf. Harvey, op. cit., pp. 74-75.

stances in January 1550, when he was not yet engaged on his *Censura* and when he had been in England for too short a time to be consulted on important ecclesiastical questions. Although lecturing and writing on Church conditions in England, his intimate relationship to English Church affairs began during the year 1550, when his judgement on the Vestment controversy and on the First Prayer Book was required by the bishops. It would, however, be going too far in the opposite direction to maintain with Durel that nothing was retained of which Bucer had not approved.[1]

We have noted that the interest and importance of the *Censura* was practically unknown at this time outside a strictly limited circle. But that circle included those who were the important agents in the work of revision that was going forward. If we look for evidence of the influences left by Bucer we shall find it later in the writings of Archbishop Whitgift who had at any rate first-hand sources of the formulas.

In his controversy with Cartwright, when stating the case of the Church of England against Puritan objections within or without, he employs repeatedly passages of the *Censura* as authoritative evidence, thus showing that the *Censura* was — at least by himself — regarded as a document which could properly be cited in a controversy as to Anglican rite, ceremonial and doctrine. Cartwright's objections to certain rites contained in the Prayer Book were those which were characteristic of all future discussions with Puritanism. It is, therefore, the more interesting that the official Church here represented by Whitgift tends to support arguments of defence by referring to Bucer's authority. The cross in Baptism, the ring in Marriage, Confirmation by Laying on of Hands, the Reading of Homilies, Private Baptism, vestments, etc., the chief and constant objections of the Puritans against the practices of the Church to which most of them still belonged, were already answered here by Whitgift, who felt himself in agreement with Bucer, to whom he refers on all those points mentioned as being opposed to the Puritan claims.

[1] On this letter of Bucer to a certain friend (January 1550) referred to by Abp. Laurence, J. Durel's statement (*Sanctae Ecclesiae . . . Vindiciae*, London, 1669, p. 147) is interesting:

'Idem dici debet de iis quae ex *Beza* ad *Balduinum* citantur. Sed & addo, egregie falli Clarissimum *Bezam*, quum ex eo quod *Cantabrigiae* anno 1550. scribebat *Bucerus*, scilicet, *Neminem extraneum de Ritibus rogari*, concludit, *Reformationem Anglicanam ex illius consilio & voluntate non fuisse institutam.* Nam utut res se habuerit, cum id scriberet, constat tamen ex illius ad *Cranmeri* Quaestiones jam memorata Responsione, ex *Censura ad librum Liturgicum* aliisque scriptis Anglicanis, ipsum de Ritibus aliisque ad ordinem & cultum Religionis pertinentibus, sententiam rogatum, & multa ex illius mente & consilio emendata in secunda Liturgiae Sacrae sub *Edvardo* recensione; nec Ritum ullum quem non probarit, postea in Ecclesia Anglicana retentum.'

cf. also: 'A briefe discourse . . .' (1566), pp. C verso – Cij and: 'An answere for the tyme . . .', pp. 127 f.

The Roman Catholic Divine, Cornelius Schulting, still living in the sixteenth century (about 1540-1604) mentions repeatedly Bucer's contribution as to the Prayer Book, a reference which bears even greater weight by the fact that he had a profound liturgical knowledge.[1]

The main evidence for Bucer's contribution to the Revision of the First Edwardian Prayer Book can, however, only be given by a minute study of his suggestions contained in the *Censura* in connection with the passages of the First Edwardian Prayer Book, on which he comments.

The following pages are an attempt at bringing together excerpts from the *Censura*, which seem to suggest close relationship to the Prayer Book and its revision. It is attempted also to include in this special study references to other contemporary Church documents (Injunctions, Articles, etc.), in order to show by this synopsis, how intimately Bucer was acquainted with English Church affairs.

Passages to be found in other writings of his which bear relevance to the Prayer Book and to the Book of Homilies, and the Ordinal (although these were not printed with the First Prayer Book) cannot be omitted in such an examination. We propose, therefore, to give a few notes from Bucer of general observations on Church rules and ceremonies, and then to add extracts from the *Censura* as to the various Offices of the Prayer Book, followed by Bucer's remarks on the Homilies and by his draft of the Ordinal, and a discourse on Bucer's relation to the Prayer Book through the *Consultatio* of Herman of Cologne.

Bishop Cosin's numerous and extensive references to Bucer's *Censura* (cf. 'Liturgica Sive Annotata Ad Divina Officia . . .', Notes on the Book of Common Prayer)[2] have also to be taken into account.

[1] His assertion, however, that the observation of the First Sunday in Lent is due to Bucer's reflection on it in his *De Regno Christi*, reflections which were made practicable in the Prayer Book, have to be taken cum grano salis, as we know that the Elizabethan Articles on the observation of Fasting Days, were caused by economic considerations. Schulting writes in his *Bibliothecae Ecclesiasticae* (Cologne, 1599), Liber IV, p. 134: 'Quadragesimam quoque, quod mirum est, obseruant Anglocaluiniani & per Quadragesimam retinent Dispositionem Officij Ecclesiastici nostri in Collectis, Epistolis, Euangeliis, ex quo conijcere licet Martinum Bucerum huius Formulae esse auctorem. is siquidem libro quinto [sic] de Regno Christi cap. 12. Quadragesimam, vt supra uerba eius induximus, commendat. Regina Elizabetha etiam ante paucos annot [!] publico mandato edixit . . .' On pp. 122-123 Schulting brought a long excerpt from the passage in question of Bucer's *De Regno Christi* (Lib. I, chap. xii).

[2] cf. Cosin, John: *Works of* . . . (Libr. of Angl.-Cath. Theology), V, 399 ff. (Oxford, 1855).

§1

GENERAL REMARKS

(1) Bucer criticizes the excessive ringing of bells by nights, on Saints days, etc. (*Scripta Anglicana*, p. 493).[1] Cosin (V, 417) ascribes rightly Grindal's *Inquiries* about abuse of ringing of bells in his 'Articles to be inquired of within the Province of Canterbury' (1576) to Bucer's objection (*Rem. of Abp. Grindal*, p. 160, n. 8 and 9).[2]

(2) He also severely objects to the disturbances of services by the noise made by boys, by people walking and talking (*Scripta Anglicana*, pp. 45, 495, 461).[3] People have to be taught to say the responses, which they do not. All ought to recite the prayer 'We do not presume' and the Thanksgiving after . . . together with the priest (*Scripta Anglicana*, p. 495) (cf. also Grindal, p. 170, n. 45).

(3) Another custom has to be abandoned:

> I am told that there are women of title who boldly demand memories to be celebrated when there are no communicants: and that there are mass priests, who celebrate memories in the very time and place that the ordinary ministers are celebrating the Communion.[4] (*Scripta Anglicana*, pp. 458-459.)[5] (cf. his objections to the prayer for the dead in the Communion Service.)

(4) The number of Saints days ought to be diminished. (*Scripta Anglicana*, p. 493.)

(5) He desires a clear statement on the Degrees of Affinity and

[1] 'Ad quam enim vel decentiam, vel ordinem religionis, ad quam disciplinam fideiue aedificationem conferat ille tam multus & intempestiuus campanarum abusus, quem superstitiosi & copiosi homines aliquanta solent cereuisia a stultis iuuenibus, quos interim oblectat inanis tintinabulorum sonitus, & ineptae fabulae, quas interim potu excitati non suo loco conferunt? Quam etiam tintinabulorum concussionem illi nunquam adhibent insolētius dies & noctes, quam ad festa sua superstitiosa, vt ad diem animarum, atque in festis conceptionis ac praesentationis Mariae, Georgij & aliorum Diuorum, de quibus plus extat fabularum, quam verae historiae. Et quam rationem habet & noctu & diu ita campanis perstrepere: quibus tamen temporibus nemo ad templum cogitat? Vsus sane huius sonitus alius esse non debet, quam vt populus ad sacrum se vel Reipubl. coetum aut praeparet, aut veniat.'

and *Scr. Angl.*, p. 494: 'Necesse itaque erit statuere, vt campanae non pulsentur, nisi cum populus monendus & conuocandus est ad sacrum coetum, aut ad res necessarias Reipublicae. Deinde, vt pulsentur certis differentijs ac notis, vt populus queat agnoscere ad quid vocetur. Nunc enim confundunt sonitum tintinabulorum, vt populus non scire possit, ad quam rem, ad conciones, vel ad alias sacras caeremonias, vel ad praecandum pro aegrotis, vel ad publicum aliquod negocium euocetur.'

[2] cf. also Frere, W. H., and Kennedy: *Visitation Articles and Injunctions* . . . vol. II, p. 286, n. 19: Hooper's *Injunctions* (1551-52).

[3] cf. Frere, W. H., op. cit., vol. II, p. 245, 12 and 13, Ridley's *Injunctions*, 1550.

cf. also, Bucer: *De Regno Christi* (*Scr. Angl.*, p. 46): '. . . atque hinc agnoscere, quam horrendam ij faciant diuinae Maiestati contumeliam, qui templa Domini habent pro deambulacris, locisque tam prophanis, vt in illis quaeuis impura & prophana cum similibus suis garriant & pertractent . . .'

[4] Engl. trans. cf. Dixon, op. cit., vol. III, p. 283.

[5] cf. also Calderwood, D.: *Altare Damascenum*, p. 726.

Consanguinity (p. 487).[1] A suggestion which was carried out by Archbishop Parker. (Strype: *Life of Abp. Parker*, I, 174-176. 'Parker table.' Cf. Wilkins' *Concilia*, A.D. 1563, tom. IV. 245. Cf. also, Grindal, op. cit., pp. 174-175, n. 60.)

(6) He proposes a Confession of Doctrine (*Scripta Anglicana*, p. 501). Cosin (V, 469) thinks that the Articles of Religion in 1552 met his suggestion.

(7) Need for Synods and Visitations (*Scripta Anglicana*, p. 503. cf. Cosin, V, 469).

CEREMONIES

The last paragraph in the First Edwardian Prayer Book: CERTAYNE NOTES FOR THE MORE PLAYNE EXPLICACION AND DECENT MINISTRACION OF THINGES, CONTEINED IN THYS BOOKE contains the following passage:

> As touching kneeling, crossing, holding up of handes, knocking upon the brest, and other gestures: they may be used or left as euery mans deuocion serueth without blame.[2]

Bucer referring to those ceremonies,[3] comments very strongly on them, which undoubtedly led to the omission of this passage in the Second Edwardian Prayer Book. He writes (*Scripta Anglicana*, p. 493-494; English: cf. Dixon, op. cit., vol. III, p. 291):

> There is 'still found' a studied representation of the execrated Mass (execratam Missam), in vestures, lights, bowings, crossings, washing of the cup, breathing on the bread and cup, carrying the book from right to left of the table, having the table where the altar was, lifting the paten and cup, and adoration paid by men who nevertheless will not communicate.[4]

In another passage of his *Censura* (p. 465) he again refers to the same paragraph of the First Prayer Book. The Scottish opponents to Laud, who complain of the liberty of gestures as indicated in that paragraph of the First Prayer Book, claim Bucer on their side against Laud. But they quote him incorrectly, as Laud rightly observes. They quote his passage:

> nunquam satis *execrandos* Missae gestus; and would have them to be abhorred, because they confirm to the simple and superstitious, ter impiam et exitialem Missae fiduciam.[5]

[1] cf. Bucer's *De Regno Christi*, II, chap. XVII in *Scr. Angl.*, pp. 87-88.

[2] cf. the *First* and *Second Prayer Books of King Edward the Sixth* (Everyman's Library, no. 448), pp. 288-289.

[3] Cosin, op. cit., V, pp. 418, 476.

[4] cf. also: W. H. Frere: *Visitation Articles*, vol. II, pp. 241-242; Ridley's *Injunctions* (no. 2), 1550; vol. II, pp. 191-192, n. 2, A Draft for Visit. Articles, 1549. cf. also Grindal, op. cit., pp. 159-160, n. 7.

[5] Laud, op. cit., III, pp. 350 ff.

Laud states against them, that Bucer did not refer to the gestures he wanted abandoned, but to the Mass. For his words are: 'nunquam satis *execrandae* Missae gestus'. Although Laud's observation in regard to Bucer's correct text are right, it is also true that Bucer was not too fond of retaining those ceremonies, as quoted in the passage accordingly altered in the Second Prayer Book.[1]

MATTINS

The first rubric: 'The Priest beeyng in the quier, shall begynne . . .' was extended in the Second Prayer Book, differing from the First Prayer Book. Bucer had some effect there, as he had not been satisfied with the rubric:

> That it was an anti-Christian practice for the choir to be severed from the rest of the church, and for the prayers there only to be said, which pertained to the people as well as to the clergy; that the separation of the choir from the body of the church served for nothing else, but to get the clergy some respect above the laity, as if they were nearer to God than laymen are: that a pernicious superstition was thereby maintained, as if priests alone were able to procure God's favour, by reading and reciting a few prayers: that in the ancient times of the Church, their temples were built in a round form, and not in a long figure, as ours are; and that the place for the clergy was always in the midst of those temples; and that therefore this custom of the division of churches from chancels, and of the priest's saying service in them, was an unsufferable abuse, to be forthwith amended, if the whole kingdom would not be guilty of high-treason against God. (Cosin's translation, Cosin, V, 436-437, Latin: *Scripta Anglicana*, p. 457.)[2]

In his lecture 'De vi et usu' . . . at Cambridge (commencing November 1550) Bucer speaks about the lessons chosen in the Prayer Book (*Scripta Anglicana*, p. 564):

> De legendis Scripturis, gratia Domino, probe constitutum est in Ecclesijs Anglicanis: si idonei modo instituerentur Lectores, qui dignam diuinis mysterijs, quae lectionibus sacris recitantur, adhiberent grauitatem atque religionem.[3]

[1] cf. *Scr. Angl.*, p. 494, at the end: 'Iam quod ad manifesta signa attinet & repraesentationem veterum superstitionum, siue εἰδωλολατρίας ἢ λιψανολατρίας, siue nephariae Missae his profecto interdici debet singulari seueritate: . . .'

[2] David Calderwood in his *Altare Damascenum*, referring to this passage of the *Censura*, brings it in connection with Cartwright's remark: 'Audivimus ex Cartwrighto non in decima quaque Ecclesia populum audire integrum officium, qui post Buceri tempora floruit.' Calderwood: *Altare Damascenum*, p. 634.

[3] In his lecture on the Ephesians at Cambridge (*Scr. Angl.*, p. 522) Bucer expresses gratefulness to God for the rendering of the services in the Church of England into the vernacular, and the opposition to 'Popery'.

THE BAPTISMAL SERVICES

Public Baptism

Bucer approves of the form of service, and of its administration in the presence of the congregation. But it should be done when the greatest number of the congregation would be present, and that time would be, according to Bucer's suggestion, immediately 'priusquam S. coenae administratio incipiatur . . .' Baptism ought to go hand in hand with the Communion Service, as the 'gemina Ecclesiae sacramenta'. This his suggestion was, however, not accepted in the Second Prayer Book (cf. *Censura*, p. 477. cf. Cosin, op. cit., V, 482, who quotes Bucer).

In the first prayer (Almighty and everlasting God . . .) Bucer wants the omission of the words: 'and by the Baptisme of thy . . .' to 'away of synne'. However, this passage to which he objected was not omitted in the Second Prayer Book. The reason for his objection was that the statement had no scriptural warrant, and serves to encourage the superstitious idea, that some mysterious sanctifying virtue is communicated to the Baptismal water, etc.

His objection is the more astonishing, as he did not object to the same clause of the prayer in the Office of the Cologne *Consultatio*, of which, specially in regard to this service, he was responsible as compiler (*Censura*, p. 479. cf. the section in this work on the *Consultatio*).

On the use of the 'white vesture' and the Sign of the Cross he admits the ancient use of the 'Crysome', but he prefers its use to be omitted as liable to superstitious abuse: 'Sublata itaque haec signa malim, quam retenta. Si autem retineri omnino contingat, opto vt salutaris eorum vsus quam diligentissime doceatur & vrgeatur' (*Censura*, p. 478). It was accordingly omitted in the Second Prayer Book. The Signing of the Cross he wants retained, not only because its use is very ancient, but also as it has an express signification of the 'Passion of Christ' (*Censura*, p. 479). It was accordingly retained in the Second Prayer Book.

Whitgift, against Cartwright's and his partisans' objection to the Sign of the Cross, claims Bucer as his authority for retaining it (Whitgift, op. cit., III, pp. 123 ff.).

The words in the prayer connected with the Sign of the Cross, he wants to be altered in their form, not because they were not holy, but because they are addressed to the child, which does not understand them. He suggests as words for that prayer: 'Da huic, o Deus, infanti, figmento tuo . . .' This proposal was not accepted in the Second Prayer Book (*Censura*, pp. 479 f.; cf. also Calderwood: *Altare Damascenum*, pp. 825-826, 828-829).

In the prayer 'Almighty and immortal God' he wants the words 'that they coming to thy holy Baptism' to be altered into 'that they brought to thy holy Baptism'. This was, however, not altered in the Second Prayer Book. The words Bucer wanted to be altered are only to be found in the Prayer Book: they do not stand in the prayer of Sarum Use (which is the source of this prayer) nor do they occur in the Formula of Luther who revised this prayer for his *Taufbuechlein*.

Concerning Rubrics

The rubric after the prayer 'Almightie and everlastyng God, heavenly father', which indicates that a part of the service was done outside the Church, he wants to have altered, which was accordingly done in the Second Prayer Book.

Bucer is also opposed

(1) to Exorcism

(2) to 'Anointing upon the head'

(3) to the prayer on blessing the water of the font (cf. *First Edwardian Prayer Book* in Everyman's Library, op. cit., p. 245). Numbers 2 and 3 were accordingly omitted in the Second Prayer Book.

PRIVATE BAPTISM

This office seemed to imply for Cartwright and his followers, that it was done by women. He objected to it. Whitgift again, by translating a passage of Bucer's *Censura* (p. 481), tries to convince Cartwright of the right and necessary use of the service (Whitgift, op. cit., II, pp. 533-535).

CHURCHING OF WOMEN

Bucer objects to the statement of the last rubric of that office: 'The woman that is purified, must offer her Crysome and other accustomed offeringes.' This was accordingly altered in the Second Prayer Book (*Censura*, p. 490. cf. Cosin, op. cit., V, 500).

In connection with his *Censura* on the Baptismal Services his doctrinal views as regards Baptism ought to be mentioned. In the Dispute with Young, Perne and Sedgwick in June 1550 at Cambridge, on Justification and other theological topics, an interesting passage of the discussion between Sedgwick and Bucer on Baptism in connection with Justification occurs:

> The question is, whether Catechumens, not yet baptized, can be claimed as justified, and whether their good works before Baptism are good works in the eyes of God.

SEDGWICK Are Catechumens justified?

BUCER If they believe in God sincerely, they are justified.

SEDGWICK As they are not baptized and as they are not members of the Church yet, therefore they are not justified, and yet they do good works.

BUCER If they believe, they have eternal life according to God's testimony and are truly already members of Christ and of the Church, and being truly justified they of necessity do good works. Justification is not first conferred on them by Baptism, but it is sealed, confirmed and increased to them.

SEDGWICK They are not washed, therefore not regenerated. John iii. 5.

BUCER refers to the story of Ambrose and the sisters of the Emperor Valentinian. God has not tied his saving efficacy to Sacraments. We shall therefore say rightly (if we affirm) that those who condemn the Baptism of Water, the laver (lavacrum) of regeneration, cannot enter into the kingdom of God. But with regard to those to whom it could not be applied — without their fault — (e.g. the thief on the cross) — it forbids that we should consign them to Gehenna.

SEDGWICK For entrance into the Church two things necessary: Faith and Baptism.

BUCER If the second cannot be obtained, otherwise the first may suffice.

SEDGWICK Augustine and other Fathers think that those who have not been baptized perish. Catechumens were kept for twenty days in the ancient Church from Baptism. They were desirous for Baptism. But if they died during that period, what about their salvation?

BUCER If they believed and had sincere desire, they had eternal life.[1]

CONFIRMATION

(1) In the manuscript copy of the *Censura* (New College, D 317, fol. 37) we find a passage as regards to the Confirmation Service, which is omitted in the printed *Censura*. The passage is headed *De ipsa Confirmationis Descriptione* and deals with the questionnaire at the beginning of the service:

In hac primum praecipitur, vt Confirmandi rogentur ab Episcopo vel Confirmatore, quisquis sit, quid Compatres, et Commatres eorum pro eis promiserint ad Baptisma. Id totum optarim mutari, ad eam rationem, quam supra in descriptione Baptismatis

[1] cf. Gorham, op. cit., n. XLV, pp. 158-160, who translates the passage from the *Scr. Angl.*, pp. 730-732. The quotation here is only the gist of the dispute, based on Gorham's translation.

exposui,[1] vt interrogentur Compatres et Commatres, num velint operam dare, vt pueri Catechismum discant: atque deinde ipsi sua ipsorum & conscientia, & ore, diabolo renuncient, et fidem suam confiteantur.

This suggestion was not accepted by the compilers of the Second Prayer Book.

(2) That Bucer approved the imposition of hands is alleged by Whitgift in his controversy with Cartwright in connection with the disapproval by the Puritans of this rite as 'the first step of Popery in this confirmation'. Whitgift quotes a passage from Bucer's lectures on the Ephesians held at Cambridge in 1550, and translates the passage into English:

The sign of imposition of hands bishops only did give, and that not without reason; for, whether the covenant of the Lord is to be confirmed to those that are baptized, or whether they are to be reconciled that have grievously offended, or whether the ministers of the church are to be ordained, all these ministries do best become those to whom the chief care of the church is committed. (Whitgift, op. cit., III, pp. 360-361.)[2]

The words said before the imposition were approved by Bucer:

Oratio quidem recte fit super pueros qualibet aetate, et quicquid habeant fidei, dum se patiuntur doceri Euangelion *Christi*. (*Censura*, p. 483, cf. Cosin, V, 489.)

(3) With regard to the concluding rubrics in the formula, Bucer suggests that the children shall be instructed not 'once in six weeks' but every Sunday and holiday (*Censura*, p. 485; cf. Cosin, V, 491-492). The rubric in the Second Prayer Book was accordingly altered.

[1] cf. *Censura*, p. 481.

[2] From the Latin: *Praelectiones in Epist. ad Ephes.* (Basil., 1562), cp. 4, p. 122.

Calderwood: *Altare Damascenum*, p. 354: 'Quid ergo sibi vult', inquit Parkerus, 'quod in privatis aedibus administretur? quod saepe tenelli confirmentur, priusquam ad perfectam aetatem per Canonem Aurelianensem debitam pervenerint? quod confirmentur quicunque Catechesin Anglicanam verbotenus recitare possunt, quam vel triennalis quisque discere poterit, & Martini Buceri judicio imperfecttior est? quod & si lege Anglicana, ni fallor, capax coenae Dominicae sit, qui confirmatur, confirmentur tamen, qui modo Catechesin recitare possunt, qui sese examinare non possunt, vel rite sese ad mensam Domini praeparare, ad quam etiam non nisi multos post annos accedere solent?' . . . *As marg. note to this passage*: De polit. lib. 3, c. 16, sect. II. Robert Parker: *De Politeia Ecclesiastica* . . . (1616), Lib. III, p. 181. cf. also pp. 181-186.

cf. also George Hakewill: *The Auncient Ecclesiasticall Practice of Confirmation* . . . (London, 1613), who refers to another passage of Bucer's lecture on the Ephesians: (Hakewill, p. 15) . . . 'and of *Bucer*, affirming that if any Church held this Rite or Signe, as he calleth it, to be peculiar to the Apostles times; I would not too hardly censure such a Church (saith he) yet would I endeauour to draw it from that conceit'. In the margin: 'In 4. ad Ephe. Si quae Ecclesiae contenderent hoc signum fuisse Apostolorum tantum, has Ecclesias damnare equidem non possem, a sua tamen opinione eas quoad liceret, reuocarem.'

In the same rubric the words in brackets: 'which are not yet confirmed' were changed into 'which have not learned their catechism'. Bucer wanted those words of the rubric in the First Prayer Book omitted (*Censura*, p. 485. cf. also Cosin, V, 487-488 and Grindal's Injunctions, op. cit., pp. 161-162, n. 13 and 14). In the same rubric the remark: '. . . which can say the articles of their faith . . .' was disliked by Bucer, who wanted Confirmation not to become a mere or bare recital (Cosin, V, 488). Not accepted for the Second Prayer Book.

(4) The Catechism inserted in the Confirmation Service was regarded as far too short by Bucer (*Censura*, pp. 485-486). But Cosin's assertion (Cosin, V, 491) that Cranmer, owing to Bucer's criticism, 'set forth a larger catechism' is wrong, as Cranmer's Catechism had been published in 1548 before the *Censura*.

MATRIMONY

Cosin quotes here in his notes (V, 492-493) the *Censura* more frequently, finding Bucer especially pleased with the office as compiled in the First Prayer Book. The only objection of Bucer seems to have been as regards this office, that he thought the third cause for which marriage was ordained ought to get the first place as it was the principle on which marriage ought to be founded: 'Mutual society.'[1] But the sequence was not altered in the Second Prayer Book.

Whitgift, in his controversy with Cartwright, defends his position and the use of the Prayer Book regarding this rite, by referring to Bucer as authority. The Communion Service for married people immediately following the service is to be retained as lawful (Whitgift, op. cit., III, pp. 356-357). The ring in marriage, the symbolism, being put on the fourth finger, was specially liked by Bucer, who enlarged on that point (*Scripta Anglicana*, p. 489). Whitgift (III, pp. 353 ff.), who points out to Cartwright how this ceremony was approved by Bucer and that it would be well to retain it, gets as reply from Cartwright a criticism of Bucer's attitude:

> I see that sometimes Homer sleepeth . . . to make such fond allegories of the laying down of the money, of the roundness of the ring, and of the mystery of the fourth finger, is . . . very ridiculous and far unlike himself. And . . . that he will have the minister to preach upon these toys, surely it savoureth not of the learning and sharpness of the judgment of M. Bucer. (Whitgift, op. cit., III, p. 354.)[2]

[1] *Scr. Angl.*, p. 488.

[2] cf. Calderwood, op. cit., p. 869: 'In hoc Buceri testimonio gloriantur Formalistae, cum tamen multa alia non emendent quae Bucerus in sua censura reformari volebat.' Calderwood quotes then the passage of Cartwright's criticism on Bucer.

VISITATION OF THE SICK

Bucer calls this office (*Scripta Anglicana*, p. 489) an order, which is made 'ad divinarum Scripturarum regulam quam convenientissime'. Whitgift gives an English rendering of Bucer's opinion:

> And those things which are commanded in this behalf do well enough agree with the holy scriptures; for to receive the communion of the Lord, and to be partaker of his table, doth not a little avail unto the comfort of the afflicted consciences, if it be received according to the Lord's institution.[1]

Bucer's only objection is against the rubric referring to the 'anointing' of the sick person. This was, accordingly, omitted in the Second Prayer Book.

Peter Martyr, Bucer's colleague at Oxford, who had read the draft of the *Censura*, and who himself had submitted his criticisms on the First Prayer Book to the bishops, expresses in a letter (January 10th, 1551) his surprise that a rather significant matter should have escaped Bucer's attention in regard to this office:

> ... I have only wondered how you could have omitted to disapprove the order which is given in the Communion of the Sick, if it shall happen to be on the Sunday on which the Lord's Supper is celebrated, that the Minister should, in that case, take with him a portion of the elements, and so should administer the Communion in the house of the sick person. In which matter, it offends me that they do not there repeat those things which particularly belong to the Lord's Supper; since I agree with you in thinking that the words of the Supper belong more to men than to bread or to wine. I stated, that it clearly seems to me, that all things that are necessarily required for the Lord's Supper, should be both said and done in the presence of the sick person, and of those who communicate with him. And it is, indeed, wonderful that they should scruple to say those words in the presence of a sick person, which might be very profitable to him, though they choose to repeat them, uselessly, whenever it happens during communion in the Church that wine is wanting in the cup, although the per[sons] who take the Sacraments, have already heard them. These are the points which I have considered as of some m[oment]; and I do not fully understand why you have omitted them. But in all those matters which you have judged to need amendment, I [am of] your opinion.[2]

[1] Whitgift, op. cit., II, p. 545.
Cosin, op. cit., V, 495, who states '... that it is made ad divinarum Scripturarum regulam convenientissime', omitting, in his quotation, the 'quam' after 'regulam'.
cf. also Calderwood, *Altare Damascenum*, p. 874.

[2] Gorham, C.: *Gleanings of some scattered ears* ... No. LXIII, p. 228. The Latin text in: J. Strype: *Mem. of Abp. Cranmer*, II, App. lxi.

Unfortunately there is no answer to this letter by Bucer, owing presumably to the fact of his illness and his death at the end of the next month.

COMMINATION

Well approved by Bucer (*Scripta Anglicana*, p. 491).[1] He suggested to have it three or four times a year. It was altered in this sense in the Second Prayer Book. To the nine maledictions, he adds a tenth. But his suggestion (all his maledictions are different from those of the Prayer Book) was not accepted.[2]

THE HOLY COMMUNION

Although Bucer suggests many alterations and amendments specially in this service of the 1549 Book, it is significant that he does not object against the Sequence of the ancient Canon retained. He is too conservative and indebted to Church traditions, which in themselves by not being open to misinterpretations recommend a ceremonial worthy to be observed, to advocate such a violating infringement as carried out in the service of the Second Prayer Book. His section of the *Censura*, dealing with this service (the longest section of the *Censura*) contains also his doctrinal statements on the Eucharist, which explain his suggestions for alterations and amendments. They are of vital interest for the study of his views and those of the English Reformers at that time.

The intimate study of the service by Bucer becomes evident in his lengthy suggestions, which reveal his approval of certain parts, to which the Swiss Party would never have consented, and they show also how carefully they were considered by the English Reformers by the alterations made in the Second Prayer Book.

His suggestions as to the Rubrics

(1) The First Prayer Book provided a Second Communion for Christmas Day. To this Bucer objected, pointing out that no special importance should be laid on a particular Feast Day, as of perhaps higher value than another.[3]

This was altered accordingly in the Second Prayer Book.[4]

[1] cf. Cosin, op. cit., V, 500; cf. Grindal, op. cit., p. 158, n. 3.
[2] cf. Dixon, op. cit., III, p. 290 and note.
[3] cf. *The First Prayer Book* in: Everyman's Library, p. 40: 'At the Seconde Communion.' cf. *Scr. Angl.*, p. 465, chap. vi, and p. 495, chap. xxvii. cf. also *Scr. Angl.*, p. 60, *De Regno Christi*, II, v. cf. W. H. Frere: *Visitat. Articles* . . . vol. II, p. 195, n. 10: A Draft for Visit. Articles, 1549.
[4] cf. Cosin, op. cit., V, 456.

(2) Then shal folowe this exhortacion at certaine tymes when the Curate shal see the people negligent to come to the holy Communion . . .

This rubric in the Second Prayer Book was added according to Cosin on Bucer's suggestion.[1] Rubric 6 at the end of the Communion Service in the Second Prayer Book, with its statement that every parishioner shall communicate at the least three times in the year, is also claimed as due to Bucer, by this passage in his *Censura* (cf. no. 9 of this section).

(3) The vestment rubric at the beginning of the service of the 1549 Book was silently omitted in the Second Prayer Book, as Bucer objected against this rubric, which might be misinterpreted ('occasion of superstition').[2]

(4) No part of the service must be read upon holidays, etc., when there was no communion; the order appointed by the book being 'a dumb show, borrowed from the Roman antichrist'.[3]

(5) Morning and Evening Prayer must not be read in one place, and the half-communion service at another; that is, at the altar; nor, that the one should be said in a surplice only, and the other in a cope . . .[4]

(6) The Sacrament must not be administered in private houses, nor in chapels annexed to other churches, nor in chapels of noblemen, for fear of superstition.[5]

(7) Liberty should be given for use of leavened and common bread as well as wafers and unleavened. But the words 'no less received in part than in the whole', might be omitted for fear of transubstantiation. He is pleased that the bread should be 'fragilis' and wafers instead of the holy loaf at the offertory, which he calls 'officium gratae pietatis in pastorem et Ecclesiam'.[6]

This rubric was used by Stephen Gardiner for affirming that the Prayer Book was 'well termed not distant from the catholic faith in my judgment'. Referring especially to the words of the last sentence, against which Bucer in right anticipation had objected (the words are: 'And menne muste not thynke lesse to be receyued in parte then in the whole, but in eache of them the whole body of our sauiour Jesu

[1] Everyman's ed., op. cit., p. 382. Cosin (op. cit., V, 468), quotes Bucer's Latin passage (*Scr. Angl.*, pp. 495-496).
[2] *Scr. Angl.*, p. 458. Cosin, op. cit., V, 474.
[3] *Scr. Angl.*, p. 458, chap. iii. Cosin, op. cit., V, 475. cf. Calderwood, *Altare Damascenum*, p. 726.
[4] *Scr. Angl.*, p. 459. Cosin, op. cit., V, 475.
[5] ibid., p. 459. Cosin, op. cit., V, 475.
[6] *Scr. Angl.*, p. 459. Cosin, op. cit., V, 475.

Christ'). Gardiner states that this sentence is truly 'agreeable to the Catholic doctrine'.[1]

(8) He disapproves of those who think they receive Christ more fully in the Sacrament of His Supper than in Baptism or in preaching of the word, or who think that more preparation is needed for the one than the other (*Scripta Anglicana*, chap. xxvii, pp. 460, 496; Cosin, op. cit., V, 475).

(9) Instead of exhorting the people to receive Communion once a year at the least he suggests an exhortation 'to set before them the greatness of their fault, if they refused to communicate or went away from the sacrament, so often as it was celebrated' (*Scripta Anglicana*, p. 461; Cosin, op. cit., V, 475).

The first exhortation in the Second Prayer Book in the Communion Service, commencing: 'We be come together at this time . . .' seems to have been inserted on this comment by Bucer (cf. n. 2 of our section).

(10) He thinks it a practice open to superstitious misinterpretation, to give the Sacrament in people's mouths and not into their hands, as prescribed in the seventh rubric at the end of the Communion Service in the First Prayer Book (*Scripta Anglicana*, p. 462). Accordingly in the Second Prayer Book service we find in the rubric at the distribution of the Sacrament the words: '. . . to the people in their handes kneling' (Everyman's Library, op. cit., p. 389).

(11) He makes the suggestion for a Collection for the Poor at the Offertory (*Scripta Anglicana*, chap. iv, p. 463; Cosin, op. cit., V, 476).[2]

(12) He approves of the custom that the men shall sit on the one side, the women on the other. But he wants the altar so placed that both parties may hear what is said at it (*Scripta Anglicana*, p. 464; Cosin, op. cit., V, 476).

(13) He disapproves of the rubric which states that the minister should only provide for so much bread and wine as sufficient for the people, which is apt to misinterpretation, as if the elements in themselves were *sacred*. The direction might imply the view of the 'Papists' that the nature of the elements were changed, and Christ were 'interned' in the elements. He states explicitly, that 'extra usum', when the Communion is over, bread and wine might be put to any common use (*Scripta Anglicana*, p. 464; Cosin, op. cit., V, 476).

[1] Quoted from Smyth, C. H.: *Cranmer and the Reformation*, p. 235, n. 11. cf. *First Edw. Prayer Book*, op. cit., p. 230.

[2] In the First Prayer Book the collection for the poor is now replacing the ancient offertory. But it was still too little observed and in too few parishes for Bucer.

(14) He disapproves the use of gestures of kneeling, crossing, etc., as tending to retain 'popish' rites and upholding the Mass (*Scripta Anglicana*, chap. v, p. 465; Cosin, op. cit., V, 476. cf. also our section on Ceremonies).

(15) He approves the Homilies as good, yet he stresses the point of the need for good preachers as well. Homilies ought not to be cut. And he makes suggestions for a larger number of Homilies, suggesting new subjects (*Scripta Anglicana*, chap. vii, p. 465; Cosin, op. cit., V, 476-477. cf. also our section on Homilies).

(16) He likes the singing of the Sanctus, but not as it is done in some churches, when the priest says the prayer 'for the State of Christ's Church' (*Scripta Anglicana*, ch. viii, p. 467).

His suggestions as concerning the prayers

(1) In the Prayer for Christ's Church militant here in earth, he objects to the clause, commending the souls of the departed to God. He suggests another clause instead: to beseech Almighty God, that we, following the example of His saints in the constant profession of our faith and obedience, may, together with them and all other departed in the faith of Christ, at His second coming have a glorious resurrection (*Scripta Anglicana*, ch. ix, p. 467). According to Cosin (op. cit., V, 477) this his suggested clause is 'now used in the form of bidding the prayers before sermon, and in the Burial of the Dead'. The objected clause was omitted in the Second Prayer Book.

The Bidding of the Bedes, referred to by Cosin, has the following clause:

> Finally, let us praise God for all those which are departed out of this life in the faith of Christ, and pray unto God, that we may have grace to direct our lives after their good example: that, this life ended, we may be made partakers with them of the glorious resurrection in the life everlasting.[1]

(2) In the Prayer of Consecration he objects to the clause:

> Heare us (o merciful father) we besech thee; and with thy holy spirite and worde, vouchsafe to bl+esse and sanc+tifie these thy

[1] Brightman, op. cit., vol. II, p. 1055, 'The Bidding of the Bedes', 1604. cf. Canon 55, 1603. The respective passage in Bucer's *Censura* runs: '... His itaque de causis optarim ego commendationem defunctorum & precem pro aeterna eorum pace, praetermitti: & in locum huius commendationis & precationis preci praecedenti, qua oratur concedi nobis exempla Diuorum eorumque in fide constantiam, atque praeceptorum Dei observantiam sequi, ista subijci, Quomodo una cum his, & omnibus qui ad te nos hinc in fide nominis tui praecesserunt, possimus in adventu filij tui gloriose prodire ad resurrectionem vitae, atque collocari ad dexteram filij tui, & audire laetam illam vocem, venite benedicti, &c. Nolim in voce illa (somni pacis) dare occasionem placendi sibi ijs, qui affirmant, defunctos in Domino dormire etiam animis, vsque ad extremum diem' (*Scr. Angl.*, chap. ix, p. 468).

> gyftes, and creatures of bread and wyne, that they maie be unto us the bodye and bloude of thy moste derely beloued sonne Jesus Christe.

He suggests instead:

> . . . blessing and sanctifying us, that with true faith we might receive the Body and Blood of Christ in these holy mysteries, as heavenly food (*Scripta Anglicana*, p. 468;[1] Cosin, op. cit., V, 477-478).

The Latin of the passage in the 1549 Prayer Book of the words 'that they maie be unto us' has 'ut fiant nobis' (which rather seems to imply a change), undoubtedly led Stephen Gardiner, the Bishop of Winchester, to include this passage into the list, by which he wanted to support his claim that the Book of Common Prayer was 'not distant from the catholic faith', as this passage might imply transubstantiation (cf. Smyth, op. cit., p. 235, III).

Laud was reminded by his opponents of the passage as objected to by Bucer, but he replied: 'Well if these be the words, how will they squeeze corporal presence out of them?' (Laud, op. cit., III, pp. 353-354).

(2a) He objects also to the making of the crosses over bread and wine, as directed by that passage, and against the marginal direction: 'Here the priest must take the bread into his hādes.' Accordingly, in the Second Prayer Book, the crosses and the marginal note were omitted (*Scripta Anglicana*, p. 472; Cosin, op. cit., V, 478).

Regarding Gardiner's statement and that of Laud, Bucer's objections seem justified. His objection against the passage of the prayer for Christ's Church, concerning the departed souls, was also based on sound suspicion against misinterpretation, as Gardiner wanted to prove by that passage, that it supports the Catholic conception of the Mass as a propitiatory sacrifice (cf. Smyth, op. cit., p. 235, IV).

(3) In the prayer of oblation he objects (*Scripta Anglicana*, pp. 472-473) to the clause:

> and commaunde these our prayers and supplicacions, by the Ministery of thy holy Angels, (cf. Everyman's Library, op. cit., p. 223).

'which he wishes to be changed into that form we have after the participation' (Cosin, op. cit., V, 478). The passage objected to was entirely omitted in the prayer of the Second Prayer Book (cf. Everyman's Library, op. cit., p. 390).

[1] Audi nos o misericors Deus pater, atque benedic nobis, & sanctifica nos verbo ac Spiritu S. tuo, vt corpus & sanguinem filij tui ex ipsius manu his mysterijs vera fide percipiamus in cibum potumque vitae aeternae. Qui filius tuus in ea nocte qua tradebatur, accepit, &c.

(4) On the Prayer of Humble Access, Bucer enlarges especially (*Scripta Anglicana*, p. 473) as he thinks it extremely important, as expression of an Eucharistic view, which maintains the *Real Presence*. He makes a special point in saying that the words of that prayer: '. . . so to eat the flesh of thy dear Son Jesus Christ, etc.,' ought to be kept, as affirmation of a doctrine, which is opposed to any Christ-absent conception of the Eucharist. That prayer was kept in the Second Prayer Book.

Cosin's assertion concerning Bucer's remarks on this prayer is of special interest, as it shows on the one side that Bucer took not the line of the Swiss Party and their English partisans as regards to the Eucharistic doctrine (which Bucer proves also in his letter to Peter Martyr, June 20th, 1549),[1] and shows on the other side that the compilers, by altering certain passages for the Second Prayer Book, did not follow the rigorous suggestions of the Swiss Party on this point. Cosin writes concerning those words, of which Bucer clearly states that they ought to be kept, that Bucer was so strongly recommending them as he was

> fearing that upon the common exceptions taken against them, (which exceptions he answers at large), they also would be changed or left out of the book; for he knew very well that this was the intention of the Protector, and that for this reason Cranmer had sent for his censure upon the book; and, indeed, all things were presently ordered and altered according to his mind and censure (Cosin, op. cit., V, 478-479).

Although it has been said that Cosin's statements have to be taken cum grano salis,[2] his words deserve to be considered more seriously in the context on Bucer's contribution to the Prayer Book by his *Censura*.

Letter to Theobald Niger, concerning Bucer's opinion of Martyr's Disputation on the Eucharist:

> *Dr. Peter Martyr's* Disputation was planned, and his propositions communicated, before I came into England. I could have wished a modified Proposition, composed in words altogether different, and those [the words] of Scripture. I am well assured, however, that he by no means wished that the Supper of the Lord should be [viewed as] a mere administration of Bread and Wine; he acknowledges the presence and exhibition of Christ; but, since the Zurich

[1] . . . nec ecclesiam Anglicanam uspiam in eam venire suspicionem quasi nihil in coena Domini agnosceretis, quam vacua *Christi* signa, per quae absentis modo *Christi* debeat excitari recordatio . . . *Scr. Angl.*, p. 549. cf. also his letter to Theobald Niger (April 15th, 1550) in Gorham, op. cit., n. XXXVIII, pp. 142-143. Latin in *Scr. Angl.*, p. 862. cf. also Gasquet, op. cit., p. 216.

[2] J. T. Tomlinson: *The Prayer Book, Articles . . .*, pp. 180 ff.

people have here many and great followers, this excellent man was drawn, I hardly know how, to consent to use the word 'Signification', although he added 'efficacious', by which he understands the exhibition of Christ, as he himself explains it in the Preface to his Disputations; in which [Preface], by my advice, he added many observations to his own, and withdrew some [the Disputations were already published]; for he is most desirous of a pious concord. Those who had hitherto listened to my explanation of this Mystery, especially those who care for the kingdom of Christ, approved it. Up to this time nothing further is established in this kingdom concerning that controversy, than that Transubstantiation is not to be affirmed. In the Public Prayers, however, at the Lord's Supper, a true exhibition of the Body and Blood of Christ is expressed in words exceedingly clear and weighty [*solidis*]. In truth, I know in whom I have believed; and I have made my Confession both in writing and in words wherever it was my duty to do so; in that [course] the Lord will preserve me. You know the piety and erudition of that excellent man; therefore as far as you have any influence over those who have taken offence at his Disputations, reconcile them by the Preface to those Disputations. When we cannot obtain all that we wish, it is our duty, as far as lies in our power, to bend to the glory of God those things which are given us, especially when they come from men so pious and learned. Take in good part these suggestions, which I have dictated because I am unable to write. May you and all yours fare well: salute my friends.

Cambridge, April 15, 1550. Martin Bucer.[1]

(5) For the same reason he wants (*Scripta Anglicana*, p. 473) the following words in the prayer after the Prayer of Consecration retained:

> . . . humbly besechyng thee, that whosoeuer shalbee partakers of thys holy Communion, maye worthely receiue the most precious body and bloude of thy sonne Jesus Christe (Everyman's Library, op. cit., p. 223).

Those words were omitted, for obvious reasons, by the compilers of the Second Prayer Book. Bucer's strong appeal, with its explicit reference to the words in this prayer and to the words in the Prayer of Humble Access, for retaining them, his silence on changing the sequence of the Canon, are strong evidence that he took a conservative line different from that of the Swiss Party, and that alterations were made, not suggested by Bucer, who otherwise was followed so much by the compilers of the Second Edwardian Prayer Book. Bucer's attitude concerning these special points (the words in those

[1] From Gorham, op. cit., pp. 142-143, n. XXXVIII. Latin text: *Scr. Angl.*, p. 862.

two prayers, the silent recognition of the Canon) is the best illustration for the contention that he was not in favour of the Swiss with their neglect and contempt of Church tradition. It shows at the same time that he, although not accepting Luther's Eucharistic doctrine with its cogent consequences, believed in a real presence of Christ in the Supper, and did not accept the Zwinglian view.

§ 11

THE HOMILIES

The First Book of Homilies, which caused grief to Stephen Gardiner, the Bishop of Winchester, was the source of much rejoicing for the Strassburg Reformer. Bucer realized that English divines had expressed their doctrinal convictions in the same way as he himself had argued against Gardiner. In his *Disputata Ratisbonae*, he had included his reply to Gardiner on the same topic, against which Gardiner objects now in the Homily:

> *Defenditvr oratio articvli Conciliati Ratisbonae* . . . Iustificare nos fide, quatenus illa apprehenderit misericordiam Dei in Christo, & non quatenus habet cha[ri]tatem sibi adiunctam.[1]

Gardiner's objections to certain passages of the Homily on Salvation are practically the same as those which he had made in his controversy with Bucer some years before. Gardiner writes from the Fleet prison to Somerset (October 14th, 1547):

> The booke of homilies in the sermon of salvation teacheth the clere contrar[ye] to the doctrine established by thacte of Parliament; even as contrarye as *includethe* is contrarie to *excludethe* . . . The homile speaketh the vertues to be present in the manne justified, and howe faithe excludeth theim in thoffice of justifieng . . .[2]

In finding the teaching of the Homilies in agreement with his own teaching and that of his fellow-Reformers, Bucer realized that the time in England for Protestantism was opportune. Still at Strassburg, reading the Homilies, he was more than ever convinced that his hope for a Theology and Church, in which he would feel at home, would not be in vain. The firm stand of the Homilies on

[1] cf. p. 538 of the *Disputata*. The Homilies in certain passages argued as Bucer had argued against Gardiner in their controversy.

[2] James A. Muller: *The Letters of Stephen Gardiner*, p. 382. The reference to the Act of Parliament is to the 'King's Book'.

doctrines, as that on justification, made it more easy for him to decide to take refuge in England, the land which promised to be a shelter from his enemies and also to give him that spiritual home he was looking for. His *Gratulation* to the Church of England written in Latin (Martinus Bucerus in ministris Ecclesiae Argentoratensis, November 1547), and soon translated into English by Thomas Hoby, who was at that time his pupil and guest at Strassburg, gives him ample opportunity to begin with an eulogy on the promising course adopted by the English Church, as seen in the Book of Homilies. Thus he writes:

> For it chaũced now of late dayes that youre sermons or Homelies came vnto oure hãdes, wher with ye godlye & effectiouslye exhorte youre people to the reading of holye scripture, and therin expounde to the same the faithe (wherby we holde our christianitie, & iustificatiõ wherevpon al oure healthe consisteth) and other most holye principles of our religion, with a most godly zeale. For these foundations truely layde, what may then longe after wante in youre churches to the ful perfection of Christ hys doctryne and discipline . . . ye prepare awaye for them, and specially in expoundynge so plainelye and substancially the nature and efficacye of the trew and Christiane fayth . . . & separate it so religiously frõ the dead faythe . . . By thys so happye & perfect a restitutiõ of Christes doctryne ye so enlarge al christes kyngdom with your mẽ, y[t] there can remaine for no long season any remnant of the olde leuen in anye parte of the ceremonyes or discypline . . .[1]

In 1550, a year after his coming to England, Bucer was involved in a dispute with Young[2] at Cambridge. The main point of the controversy was just that article on justification as expressed in the Homily. He was the more eager to defend his position since he realized that much more was at stake than losing the dispute. He wrote to Cheke on August 29th, 1550:

> . . . Cumque domi legissem ista fidei nostrae dogmata esse regiis homiliis definita, ea profecta spe in Angliam veni, ut nemini licere in pub[licis] vel praelectionibus, vel disputationibus, haec dogmata serio contendendo, convellere, putarim . . .[3]

That this doctrine should again become matter of discussion caused him great anxiety, since, as we have just seen, he had entertained the hope that the teaching of the Reformers was accepted once for all.

[1] Translation by Thomas Hoby: The gratulation . . . fol. *a*iv, verso – *a*v, verso. Latin text: *Scr. Angl.*, p. 171, *Gratulatio*, pp. 3-4. This treatise contains part of his reply to the Letter of Bp. Gardiner.

[2] John Young (1514-80), Master of Pembroke Hall, Cambridge, cf. Article in *D.N.B.*

[3] cf. Harvey, op. cit., n. VI, p. 130.

His lengthy account of the dispute with Young in the *Scripta Anglicana*,[1] and also the fact that he wrote to Grindal[2] (on the same issues as to Cheke) asking him to submit his statement to Ridley, then Bishop of London, show how deeply he was stirred by the controversy. On the other side, Gardiner, who had tried to warn English churchmen of the danger of the Protestant doctrine, had to realize that now those very points, to which he never wanted to consent in his argument with Bucer, were accepted in the Homilies, thus opening the doors of the Church of England to Bucer and his Protestant friends.

In the discussion with Young, Bucer stressed the point that no good works could be done before justification, which he taught in accordance with Holy Scripture, the ancient Church and the Homily on Good Works of the Church of England, as he maintained. Young did speak of Good Works even preceding justification 'per gratiam praevenientem'.

The following excerpts of that discussion, which is minutely and at length described by Bucer in the *Scripta Anglicana*, show the dispute as relevant to the Homily on Good Works.

p. 800: (BUCER)

Indicaui & consensum Ecclesiarum Anglicanarum, ex sermone de bonis operibus, cuius partem aliquam ab initio feci recitari, in qua praedicatur, hominem ante & extra fidem iustificantem, non posse facere vllum bonum opus, quod acceptum sit & placitum Deo: sicut nec palmes fructum, nisi manserit in vite: impossibileque esse, vt placeat talis homo Deo, atque omnem vitam huiusmodi hominum fide, & fide *Christi* iustificante carentium, esse peccatum, cunctaque eorum opera mortua, vana, mala, tenebras, peccata. Quae omnia in ea Homelia docentur ex verbis Domini, Ioh. 15. & Matth. 6. & ex Roman. 14. & ex Ebrae 11. Adducuntur ibi & Ambrosij & Augustini atque Chrysostomi authoritates . . .

That Bucer claimed this Homily for himself against Young, caused Young and his friends to complain that Bucer had suggested that Young was not loyal to the authorized doctrine of the English Church.

p. 800:

. . . subieci in praelectione mea, dicti loci ex Homilia De bonis operibus recitationi & ponderationi grauem obtestationem ad

[1] cf. the account of the Controversy: C. Gorham: *Gleanings* . . . p. 163 ff. The controversial passages on Justification were treated in connection with the Homily on Good Works.

[2] Letter to Grindal, August 31st, 1550: *Scr. Angl.*, pp. 803-804. English translation in Gorham, op. cit., n. XLVII, pp. 163 ff.

> omne auditorium, ne quis vellet ex eo quod adducerem & confessionem Anglicanam ex Homilia regia, ostenderemque hanc cum verbis Domini & Spiritus sancti, atque cum fide & confessione veteris Ecclesiae consentaneam, Iungique assertionem ei contradicere, occasionem arripere, Iungum arguere aut insimulare contemptus Ecclesiae Anglicanae, aut inobedientiae aduersus Maiestatem Regiam, quorum criminum, nec ego illum accusarem. (cf. also, pp. 801, 805 ff., 834-835, 857-859).

Finally, Bucer sums up with an appeal to the reader to decide himself, whether it has been conclusively proved or not, that his doctrine is in agreement with the English Homily:

> p. 862:
> . . . inde fiat & de hac quaestione iudicium. Vtra vero doctrina, mea vel Iungi, per Homiliam Regiam, De bonis operibus, probetur aut reprobetur. iudicetur ex prima eius Homiliae parte.

It is scarcely to be wondered that Bucer should be gratified to find in the existence of the First Book of Homilies the indication and adoption of a definite course for the Church of England, which, if followed, could be consolidated and improved, thus guaranteeing entire success for the Protestant interest. In spite of the fact of the attack of Young and his followers, this would be more easily achieved, since Gardiner had ceased to fill the important part he had played under Henry VIII.

Bucer suggests in the *Censura* a greater number of Homilies and provides new titles (18) for a new series. Some of his suggestions may have influenced the choice of subjects for the Second Book of Homilies.[1] Strype states that Bucer and Martyr, on Cranmer's request, wrote some notes amounting to a sermon on the subject of Rebellion. Certainly Cranmer's Sermon on Rebellion was influenced by Martyr's notes. For public as well as ecclesiastical reasons the subject was of great importance at that time, as the Homily on Rebellion proves.[2] For Bucer, however, the Homilies would only achieve their purpose of helping to reform the Church, if the English Church authorities would not merely concentrate on supplying certain apparent

[1] *Scr. Angl.*, p. 466.

[2] J. Strype: *Mem. of Cranmer*, vol. I, p. 268, referring to the Devon Revolt of 1549, says: 'Martin Bucer also wrote a discourse against this sedition, as well as Martyr' (cf. MS. Corpus Christi College, Cambridge, 103. 32). Cranmer 'thought it convenient that these learned foreigners should give some public testimony of their dislike of these doings. Bucer's discourse, subjoined to Martyr's, began in this tenor: Quae dici possunt ad sedandos animos plebis, et ab omni conatu seditioso absterrendos (quod ad rem ipsam attinet) inscripta sunt omnia, in reverendissimi D.N.M. Ven. Collegae nostri Pet. Martyris Schedis, ut nostra adiectione nulla sit opus, tamen ut consensum spiritus testemur, haec subiecta libuit annotare, &c.' cf. Cranmer's sermon, pp. 190-202 in *Misc. Writings and Letters of Th. Cranmer* (Parker Society, 1846).

deficiencies, but would set themselves to deal with the principal failures, which had caused those particular defects.

Thus concerning Homilies he stresses repeatedly in his other writings and correspondence the importance of educating able ministers, who by their theology will teach the congregations doctrines in accordance with those of the Homilies. Until that education of reliable ministers is performed, the Homilies are the best safeguard against any inefficient preaching by uneducated clergy. The Homilies as well as all the other suggestions for Church reform, as indicated in the *Censura* and other writings of the same trend, have to be envisaged in a general scheme of Reformation, which will not be achieved *ex parte* but only *in toto*.

In connection with his approval of the Homilies Bucer's scattered statements on the education of the clergy and the pitiful conditions of the ministry, as they presented themselves to his mind, ought to be read. Thus he writes to Calvin from Cambridge (Whitsunday, 1550):

> . . . you may find parishes in which there has not been a sermon for some years. And you are well aware how little can be effected for the restoration of the kingdom of Christ by mere ordinances, and the removal of instruments of superstition . . . And even our friends are so sparing of their sermons, that during the whole of Lent, which nevertheless they still seem to wish to observe, with the exception of one or two Sundays, they have not once preached to the people, not even on the day of the commemoration of Christ's death or of his resurrection, or on this day. Sometimes, too, many of the parochial clergy so recite and administer the service, that the people have no more understanding of the mysteries of Christ, than if the Latin instead of the vulgar tongue were still in use . . .[1]

On similar lines he writes to Bishop Hooper at the middle of November of the same year.[2]

The connection of the question of the Homilies with that of the theological education of the clergy becomes a strong argument for Whitgift against Cartwright's and his partisans' objections to the Homilies.

[1] *Original Letters* (Parker Society), vol. II, pp. 546-547.

[2] *Scr. Angl.*, p. 706. Eng. Trans. Gorham, C.: *Gleanings* . . . n. LV, p. 201.

cf. also: *Scr. Angl.*, p. 466: 'Ingens enim per regnum pastorum numerus est, qui sacra sic perturbate, leviter, praecipitanter, non recitant, sed impie demurmurant, ut populus non plus ea quae leguntur intelligat, quam si lingua recitarentur Turcica aut Indica.'

cf. Frere, W. H.: *Visitation Articles* . . . vol. II, p. 296, n. 34; Hooper's Interr. 1551-52; also vol. III, pp. 166-167, n. 8; Bentham's *Injunctions for Coventry* . . . 1565. *De Regno Christi*, *Scr. Angl.*, p. 60: 'The sacrificers recite it so indistinctly that it cannot be understood, although it is in the vulgar tongue.'

Whitgift writes:[1]

But of reading homilies in the church I have something spoken before; now it shall be sufficient only to set down Master Bucer's judgment of this matter in his notes upon the communion-book, which is this:

> 'It is better that, where there lacks to expound the scriptures unto the people, there should be godly and learned homilies read unto them, rather than they should have no exhortation at all in the administration of the supper.'

And a little after:

> 'There be too few homilies, and too few points of religion taught in them. When, therefore, the Lord shall bless this kingdom with some excellent preachers, let them be commanded to make more homilies of the principal points of religion, which may be read to the people by those pastors that cannot make better themselves.'[2]

Cartwright replies:[3]

And as for Master Bucer's authority, I have shewed before how it ought to be weighed, and here also it is suspicious; for that it is said that his advice was that, when the Lord should bless the realm with more learned preachers, that then order should be taken to make more homilies, which should be read in the church unto the people. As if M. Bucer did not know that there were then learned preachers enough in the realm, which were able to make homilies so many as the volume of them might easily have exceeded the volume of the bible, if the multitude of homilies would have done so much good. And, if the authority of Master Bucer bear so great a sway with Master Doctor, that, upon his credit only, without either scripture, or reason, or examples of the churches primitive, or those which are now, he dare thrust into the church homilies, then the authorities of the most ancient and best councils ought to have been considered, which have given charge that nothing should be read in the church but only the canonical scriptures.

Additional Note

A yet unpublished letter of Alexander Alesius to Edward VI bears some relevance to the Homilies. It has to be remembered that Alesius provided a Latin version of the First Edwardian Prayer Book, which is printed in the *Scripta Anglicana* prefixed to Bucer's *Censura*. From this version Cosin derives his knowledge of the First

[1] Whitgift, op. cit., III, p. 346.
[2] cf. *Scr. Angl.*, p. 466.
[3] Whitgift, op. cit., III, pp. 346-347.

Edwardian Prayer Book. This version was full of deliberate inaccuracies, as Dixon remarks in detail in his History.[1] The version was not used by Bucer for his *Censura*, although he states that he read the First Edwardian Prayer Book *per interpretem.* Strype, in his *Memorials of Archbishop Cranmer*,[2] deceived by the title of Alesius' translation of the First Edwardian Prayer Book, commits himself to the wrong statement, as if Alesius had translated a German work of Bucer into Latin. Strype's incorrect statement occurs in the article on 'Alesius' in the *D.N.B.* But A. W. Ward in his article on 'Bucer' in the *D.N.B.* draws attention to Strype's blunder and to the wrong statement in the article on 'Alesius', by referring to Laurence's Bampton Lectures.[3]

The letter of Alesius, which confesses to be 'ex autographo', is to be found in the Bodleian (MS. Smith 67, fol. 59-61, n. 21). The following extract is of interest: its importance does not seem hitherto to have been noted.

Alexander Alesius to Edward VI.

Lipsiae, duodecimo Calendas
Quintilij anno 1551

. . . Significandum autem duxi vestrae majestati me pio studio erga incrementum Religionis et amore majestatis vestrae et consolatione piorum hoc luctuoso tempore Ordinationem Ecclesiasticam in inclyto Regno majestatis vestrae vertisse in linguam Latinam, ut haec praeclarissima cura Regiae majestatis vestrae quamplurimis innotesceret, et jussi hanc versionem submisse offerri vestrae majestati, si forte vacaret inspicere. Cum infima autem subdictione peto a vestra majestate, ut hoc factum meum in bonam partem clementissime accipere velit. Brevi etiam edentur duodecim illae orationes, in quibus doctrina religionis est praeclare exposita, propositae cum mandato majestatis vestrae legendae Dominicis diebus a pastoribus Ecclesiarum in inclyto Regno majestatis vestrae, et alia quaedam majora volumina, de quibus intelliget majestas vestra ex reverendissimo in Christo Patre et Domino Archiepiscopo Cantuariensi. Is enim expositurus est Regiae majestati vestrae me non tantum vacuum ex Insula esse dimissum sed propemodum necessitate etiam coactum discedere . . .

[1] Dixon, op. cit., vol. III, pp. 294 ff., 294 note.
[2] Strype: *Mem. of Cranmer* (ed. Oxford, 1840), vol. I, p. 579.
[3] Laurence, Richard: *An Attempt to Illustrate those Articles* . . . 3rd ed., 1838, pp. 221-222. Bampton Lecture for the year MDCCCIV.

§ III

THE ORDINAL

> . . . we should advise nobody to study the real history of this matter [i.e. the composition of the Anglican Ordinal] who has not nerve enough to recognize how close the Church of England lay in those days to mere Protestantism.
>
> (*Church Quarterly Review*, January 1878, p. 269.)[1]

In the eyes of such eminent authorities as Dr. W. H. Frere and Dr. F. E. Brightman,[2] there are unmistakable signs of dependence of the Anglican Ordinal, in sections not connected with the Roman Rite, upon Bucer's *De Ordinatione Legitima Ministrorum Ecclesiae Revocanda.*[3] This may be said in spite of the fact that there seems still to linger some doubt about the actual date at which Bucer wrote his treatise, so that the question seems still to be open, whether his work can be claimed as a source preceding the Anglican draft or whether Bucer wrote his work already knowing the Anglican draft and giving his own revised version of the Anglican Ordinal.

Another authority, Dr. W. K. Firminger, even regarded Bucer's *De Ordinatione Legitima* as 'Latin translations of the First Edwardian Ordinal, and not a draft which lay before the compilers of the First Ordinal'.[4] It is necessary, therefore, to examine the question in order to form an opinion whether this view should be adopted or if there is real ground for supposing that Bucer's work already completed lay before the compilers of the First Edwardian Ordinal.

When Bucer's *Scripta Anglicana* were published in 1577 by his former colleague, Conrad Hubert (Bucer had died in 1551), reference in the index to the works written in Germany is made by an asterisk[5]; no such asterisk, however, is attached to the *De Ordinatione*, which means that it was written in England. This fact, however, does not necessarily imply that he wrote it at a stage when the Anglican draft was already known to him. For, as Bucer arrived in England in April 1549 and then stayed for some months with Archbishop Cranmer, he may have written his *De Ordinatione* during that time at the

[1] I am informed by my supervisor, Dr. C. Jenkins, that this article was written by Canon R. T. Smith, 'The Anglican Form of Ordination', pp. 261-290, *Church Quarterly Review*, No. X, January 1878.

[2] W. H. Frere: *A New History of the Book of Common Prayer* (ed. London, 1941), p. 662 and passim.

F. E. Brightman: *The English Rite*, vol. I, pp. cxxxi ff., vol. II, pp. 930 ff. cf. also: C. H. Smyth: *Cranmer and the Reformation* . . . pp. 228 ff.

[3] Bucer, *Scr. Angl.* (Basle, 1577), pp. 238-259.

[4] W. K. Firminger: 'The Ordinal', in *Liturgy and Worship*, pp. 671 f.

[5] fol. β 2.

request of Cranmer, who planned a new *Ordinal*, the wording and structure of which, however, was not yet completed.[1]

Firminger argues that as Bucer's draft is not dated, and as Bucer refers in his *Censura* of the First Edwardian Prayer Book, to the 'nuper edita ordinationis formula', his draft was a revision of the First Edwardian Ordinal, and that the passages of Bucer's draft which seemed to suggest an influence on the Anglican Ordinal, were mere translations from the English draft.

Although it is true that Bucer mentions the 'nuper edita ordinationis formula', his own draft can still be claimed an independent one. In the pages of his *De Ordinatione* preceding the actual *Ratio Ordinandi*, Bucer, in speaking of the preparation and examination for the persons to be ordained, refers repeatedly to 'our churches' or 'our church',[2] meaning his church at Strassburg, as an explanatory marginal note put by the editors of the *Scripta Anglicana* to this section proves:

> Hanc in examinando oblatos, ad ecclesiae ministeria, religionem, nostra ecclesia, sic reuocare studuit. (p. 243). Marginal note: 'Ecclesiae Argentin. in oblato ad examinandum religio.'

The last sentence immediately before the actual formula for Ordination runs:

> Vt itaque ista nostrae Ecclesiae, quoad possent omnia, in vsum salutarem reuocarent, ad hunc fere modum, sacram ordinationem faciendam instituerunt: *Ratio Ordinandi* (p. 255).

Bucer, by way of describing the Ordination use of the Continental Church, seems to suggest a formula suitable for the English Reformers, who at the stage of compiling their Ordinal fell back on his descriptive draft, which, however, they modelled to their own liking.

It may be assumed that if Bucer intended to give in his *De Ordinatione* his criticism on an Anglican draft already laying before him, or if a revision of the Anglican draft was intended by him, he, according to the method adopted in his *Censura*, would have attempted to outline doctrinally why he thought it necessary to alter and to revise

[1] Brightman: pp. 170-171 in *Liturgy and Worship*.
Harvey: *Martin Bucer in England*, pp. 57-58.
C. H. Smyth: *Cranmer* . . . p. 230.
A. H. Drysdale: *History of the Presbyterians* . . . p. 31, n. 3: 'the very first word of which [i.e. Bucer's *De Ordinatione*] *Quaeritur* de ordinatione legitima . . . is sufficient to show that the tractate was drawn up in answer to a request for a statement of his views.'

[2] cf. also, op. cit., pp. 243-244, 254.

the already existing Anglican formula. He would have made explicit reference to it.[1]

There is another passage at the end of his *Censura*, referred to by Firminger:

> Atque hinc sciat Reuerendiss. P.T. factum, vt istam de quaerendis, formandis, examinandis Ecclesiarum ministris, & restituto crucifixi patrimonio, appendicem excussioni libri Sacrorum, quam Reuerendissima P.T. solum a me petijt, adiecerim (*Scripta Anglicana*, p. 503).

To this is added as a marginal note by the editors of the *Scripta Anglicana*:

> Hunc, certa de causa, praemisimus sub inscriptione, De ordinatione legitima ministrorum Ecclesiae.[2]

On these facts Firminger builds his argument, that the 'passages of Bucer's appendix . . . are therefore Latin translations of the First Edwardian Ordinal . . .' an argument which, with its conclusion, is still open to question.[3]

Differences of Bucer's form from the Anglican Ordinal, not less remarkable than the resemblances, seem also to suggest that the English Reformers, by using certain parts from the Strassburg Reformer's production, had, on the other hand, their own definitely fixed views which they did not change in spite of Bucer's work. Bucer, supposing that he wrote his treatise as an explicit criticism of the already complete Anglican Ordinal, would have attempted to state doctrinally that his differences from it were necessary in order to avoid a 'Papistical' interpretation of the Anglican Ordinal, which might imply a 'Roman' conception of specially conferred gifts of grace.

His own treatise, although referring to three Orders, provides only one form of ordination:

> Cum autem tres ordines sint presbyterorum & curatorum Ecclesiae, ordo Episcoporum: deinde presbyterorum . . . & Diaconi vel adiutores (p. 259).

He also has only one form of words for use in the act of ordination, regardless whether a bishop, a priest, or a deacon is to be ordained,

[1] cf. also, R. T. Smith: We ought not to alter the Ordinal, p. 145 '. . . it would not have been possible that he should have proposed a substitute for the English Ordinal without mentioning or alluding to his reasons for dissatisfaction with it.'

[2] On this marginal note Firminger remarks: 'His editors in the margin say that they have included Bucer's appendix to the *Censura* under the heading *De Ordinatione Legitima*, etc.' (Firminger, p. 672). But *De Ordinatione* is not 'included' to the *Censura*, but is to be found in quite a different part of the *Scr. Angl.*

[3] cf. also n. 1 on p. 672.

MARTINVS BVCERVS.

Natales, Bucere, tuos Germania Jactat,
Natalibus felix tuis.
Quis verò et quantus fueris, tua scripta loquuntur,
Ad littus orbis ultimum.

cum priuillegio.

from Verheiden, *Praestantium Aliquot Theologorum . . . Effigies . . .*, 1602

whereas the Anglican Ordinal has its three distinct sets of words. His words are:

> The hand of Almighty God, the Father, the Son, and the Holy Spirit, be upon you, protect and govern you, that ye may go and bring forth much fruit by your ministry, and may it remain [with you] unto life eternal. Amen[1] (cf. Smyth, op. cit., p. 230).

He states, however, his opinion as to the way in which distinction may be made between ordaining a bishop and ordaining a priest or deacon by saying (*Scripta Anglicana*, p. 259):

> So let ordination be attempered to each: so that when any Superintendent, that is Bishop, is ordained, everything may be somewhat more [fully?] and more gravely done and finished . . . than when a priest of the second or third order is ordained. So also let some distinction be made between the ordination of a priest of the second and of the third order.[2]

Bucer's suggestion for *a somewhat more fully and solemnly* administered rite for the ordination of a bishop and priest as distinct from that of a deacon, would, in case he had the Anglican Ordinal before him, have made it imperative that he should give reason why he could not agree to the distinctions as made in the Anglican Ordinal. His one set of words for use at the time of the imposition of hands, even omitting any reference to the gift of the Holy Ghost in ordination, suggest a doctrinal conception of ordination different from that of the Anglican Ordinal. All the more strongly would he have objected to the Anglican words. Abbé G. Constant is thus entitled to write:

> Cette formule diffère totalement de celle de la Ratio ordinandi de Bucer, qui semble avoir inspiré en grande partie les autres prières du presbytérat. Bucer dit en effet: Que la main de Dieu . . . etc. Ceci prouve que dans les rites et prières jugés essentiels, la Commission de 1550 se sépara nettement de Bucer. Il en est de même pour la suite de cette prière, avec la porrection du calice et du pain (Constant: *l'Introduction de La Réforme* . . . p. 314, n. 226).[3]

To this can be added the statement of Dr. W. H. Frere, that the compilers of the Anglican Ordinal, while accepting much of Bucer's plan and drawing largely upon his exhortations and examinations,

[1] 'Manus Dei omnipotentis, Patris, Filij, & Spiritus sancti sit super vos, protegat & gubernet vos, vt eatis, & fructum vestro ministerio quamplurimum afferatis, isque maneat in vitam aeternam. Amen.' *Scr. Angl.*, p. 259.

[2] Engl. transl. cf. Smyth, C. H., op. cit., p. 230.

[3] cf. *The Times Literary Supplement*, January 17th, 1942, p. 31: 'The Reformation in England.'

rejected his doctrinal standpoint.[1] It is a further question whether by those different forms of words used for the three Orders in the Anglican Ordinal there was intended a difference as to the special gift of grace conferred on the ordinand (as they seem to imply), or whether the Reformers not regarding ordination as a sacrament of the Gospel saw no *doctrinal* meaning in the variations, but wanted only to express the distinction between different *ecclesiastical* grades.[2] For Bucer the imposition of hands at ordination does not seem to have been conceived mainly as connected with the special gift of the Holy Ghost conferred on the candidate.

The influence of Bucer's form of ordination can be seen distributed over the three distinct services in the Anglican Ordinal. Passages of his *De Ordinatione* are thus to be found in those parts of the three Anglican services where the structure of his rite follows parallel lines.

The parts in the Anglican Ordinal where direct dependence on Bucer can clearly be inferred are:

(1) Choice of Lessons;

(2) Questionnaire: all eight questions in the Form for Ordaining of Priests from Bucer. Four of the seven questions for deacons, which are also the same in the questionnaire for priests, are so, of course, also taken from Bucer.[3]
Three questions for bishops (two common with the two other rites, and one common with the question in the formula for priests) are also from Bucer;

(3) The challenge for 'any impediment' in the rite for priests;

(4) The allocution (rite for priests): It 'reproduces all but a few lines of that of Bucer, with the effect that the teaching-office and the personal life of the priest are didactically emphasized as they had not been in the Latin rite'. (Brightman, op. cit., I, p. cxxxv.)

[1] cf. Frere, op. cit., p. 662.

For Bucer (*Scr. Angl.*, p. 255) the imposition of hands in ordination *represents* the direction, corroboration and protection of the hand of God, by which the person ordained is able to perform (praestare et perficere) his ministry to the glory of God and to the 'salus' of the church; and: Significat etiam tradi ei potestatem, vt vice *Christi* Ecclesiam doceat & gubernet: Seque etiam, quod est boni pastoris, hostiam, si opus sit, per fidem & salutem Ecclesiae libenter impendat.

[2] Constant in 1911 in another paper on the subject admits the 'vagueness' of those formulas which seem to justify to him a catholic interpretation: L'époque où ces formules furent introduites est celle en effet du compromis, celle où le vague des expressions permet encore l'interprétation catholique. Il en aurait été autrement si l'on avait admis la formule unique pour les trois ordres que proposait Bucer dans son *De Ordinatione* . . . (livre qui inspira cependant plus d'une prière des ordinations anglicanes) . . . (p. 489, n. 4); and (pp. 489-490): Dès 1543, en effet, l'archevêque rejetait l'ordre (Ordination) en tant que sacrement: ce n'était plus un rite conférant une grâce spéciale, mais une sorte de transmission officielle de la juridiction ecclésiastique que détenait le roi.

G. Constant: in *R. d'H.E.*, vol. XII, 1911, pp. 479-495.

[3] cf. also here, p. 119, note 1.

(5) In rubrics;

(6) Prayers.

The hymn *Come Holy Ghost* was already in the ancient rite (Sarum Use) and thus accepted by Bucer as well as by the Anglican Ordinal.

The parallelisms between Bucer and the Anglican Ordinal have been illustrated by comparison of the framework of the services, of questions, lessons, prayers and exhortations, in Brightman's *The English Rite* (vol. II, pp. 932 ff.).

Dr. Brightman gives, of course, a conspectus of other sources as well for the Anglican Ordinal from Ancient Rites. But the passages where the connection of that Ordinal with Bucer's draft can be shown, may fairly be claimed in support of the argument, that Bucer's *De Ordinatione* played its part in the history of the draft of the Anglican Ordinal, although the English Reformers kept their independence as regards their doctrinal conception of ordination.

Additional Note

On the conception of the distinct Orders as being of ecclesiastical necessity for the sake of order and discipline, the 'Originall of Bishops' writes:

> The beginning of which kind of subordination of many Bishops unto one chiefe, if it were not to bee derived from Apostolicall right: yet it is by Beza fetched from the same light of Nature and enforcement of Necessity, whereby men were at first induced to enter into consociations, subjected one unto another; and by Bucer acknowledged to have been consentaneous to the law of Christ, and to have been done by the right of the body of *Christ*.[1]

The importance of a strict examination and of an observation of discipline in life is urged by Bucer at the end of *Censura* (*Scripta Anglicana*, pp. 501-502). And in this connection Cosin's statement is of importance with his concluding words, which seem to intimate that at least to that part of the Ordinal Bucer could not extend his influence, as the Ordinal followed there 'Ancient Constitutions': 'In the form of Ordination of Ministers (which was then extant) he moved to have a stricter examination of them for their life and man-

[1] Marginal note: Atque hoc consentiebat legi Christi, fiebatque ex jure corporis Christi. M. Bucer. de vi & usu S. Ministerii. (inter scripta ejus Anglicana pag. 565). *The Originall of Bishops* . . . p. 74. In the same pamphlet, pp. 45-48, English translations of passages from Bucer relating to the subject (1) from *De Regno Christi* . . . lib. 2, chap. xii, p. 67 (*Scr. Angl.*); (2) from De animarum cura . . . p. 280 (*Scr. Angl.*); (3) from De vi & usu & Ministerij, Camb., 1550, pp. 581-582 (*Scr. Angl.*).

ners, even from their infancy, than was then required. Nor did he like the trial of them by a sermon, which was deceitful. But the ancient Constitutions and Canons had taken order for this matter before' (Cosin, V, 469).

§ IV

DISCOURSE

on the *Consultatio*[1] of Herman of Cologne, Martin Bucer and the First Edwardian Prayer Book

The dependence of the First Edwardian Prayer Book in certain parts on the *Consultatio* of the Archbishop of Cologne, Herman von Wied, is a well-known fact to any student on the subject, and can be studied in all commentaries on the Book of Common Prayer.[2]

In connection with a study of Bucer's contribution to the Anglican Prayer Book, it is of special importance to note the fact that certain parts of the *Consultatio*, parts which influenced the Prayer Book, were drafted by Martin Bucer, who was one of the compilers of the Cologne Reform book and theological adviser to Herman von Wied. The Baptismal Service and the Communion Service of the *Consultatio*, those two offices which chiefly contributed material to the 1549 Prayer Book, are known as Bucer's compilation. Melanchthon writes; '. . . legi de caeremoniis Baptismi et Coenae Domini quae ipse [i.e. Bucer] composuit.'[3]

Conrad Pellican writes in his *Chronikon*:

> Reformationem archiepiscopi Coloniensis germanice impressam legi diligenter et sic placuit, ut voluerim ab omnibus episcopis reliquis sic inchoare; infirmiora quaedam erant, quae essent tempori et incipientibus permittenda; et de causa eucharistiae nihil inveni, quod displicuit: notavi adfuisse tam Philippi Melanchtonis

[1] The work was written originally in German. It was translated into Latin by A. Hardenberg. In 1547 an English translation was made from this Latin version by John Daye (at London) with the title: 'A simple and religious consultation, of us, Herman by the Grace of God Archebishop of Colone . . .' In 1548 a second and amended edition to this English translation was made.

[2] cf. Brightman, F. E.: *The English Rite* (London, 1915), vol. I, pp. xlv ff. and passim in text.

cf. (Procter and Frere): Frere, W. H.: *A New History of the Book of Common Prayer*. . . (Rev. and re-written . . . London, 1941), passim.

cf. C. H. Smyth, op. cit., pp. 37, 41, etc.

G. Constant: *La Transformation* . . . (1911), pp. 44-45.

[3] *Corpus Reformatorum*, vol. V, 2707.

> candidius ingenium et Buceri studium illi solitum et nimis perplexitati aptum.[1]

Bucer employed for his draft of both services Lutheran Church Orders, for instance that of Nuremberg. The contribution by those two special services to those of the Prayer Book may thus be described as a composition partly from Lutheran Church Orders with suggestions from Herman, compiled by the Strassburg Reformer, Bucer.

On the relation of those services to the Prayer Book (and by specially mentioning the Nuremberg Service, reference is indirectly made to Bucer) Richard Hilles writes to H. Bullinger, June 4th, 1549:

> ... we have an uniform celebration of the Eucharist throughout the whole kingdom, but after the manner of the Nuremberg churches and some of those in Saxony; for they do not yet feel inclined to adopt your rites respecting the administration of the sacraments. Nor do I doubt but that master M.B. [Martin Bucer] and the other learned men from Germany and Italy, (who are here with the most reverend the archbishop of Canterbury, and are lecturing in the universities of this country,) teach, nay, exhort and persuade that there is no occasion for it, and perhaps even, that it is not becoming. Thus our bishops and governors seem, for the present at least, to be acting rightly; while, for the preservation of the public peace, they afford no cause of offence to the Lutherans, pay attention to your very learned German divines, submit their judgment to them, and also retain some popish ceremonies.[2]

Cornelius Schulting, a Roman Catholic divine, still living in the sixteenth century, states:

> Nam in Regno Angliae seruant Coenam ex ritu & ordinatione Buceri longe dissimili modo atque ordine quam qui receptus est a Lutheranis in Saxonia.[3]

When Bucer, in writing his *Censura* on the First Edwardian Prayer Book, comments on just those Offices of the Prayer Book which originally derived material from the equivalent parts of the *Consultatio*,

[1] Bernhard Riggenbach: *Das Chronikon des Konrad Pellikan* (Basel, 1877), p. 168. Luther writes: 'But affected by the articles [i.e. the *Consultatio*], I was soon involved in the Book and in the articles on the sacrament, for there the shoe pinches me hard and I find that I am not pleased everywhere there with all parts ... That I can well scent that chatterbox ('Klappermaul'), that man Bucer.' – English translation, from De Wette, W. M., *Dr. Martin Luther's Briefe* ... (Berlin, 1828), vol. V, pp. 708-709.

[2] *Original Letters* (Parker Society), vol. I, p. 266.

cf. also, ibid., p. 344: John Brychman's letter to H. Bullinger (December 10th, 1549): '... For the emperor had strongly urged upon the English ambassadors the settling a form of religion agreeable to the Interimistic doctrine. But upon due consideration they confirmed by public decrees throughout the kingdom the form established by master Bucer.'

[3] Cornelius Schulting: *Bibliothecae Ecclesiasticae* ... (Cologne, 1599), vol. IV, p. 152.

of which he was the compiler, it would be expected that he would not suggest changes.

But in his *Censura* relating to the Baptismal Service of the 1549 Prayer Book we find just the contrary. Here he objects to the passage of one of the prayers, which he had incorporated in the Baptismal Service of the *Consultatio*, whence it found its way into the Prayer Book service. The passage is in the first prayer of the service, which begins: 'Almighty and everlasting God . . .':

> . . . and by the Baptism of thy wellbeloved son Jesus Christ, thou didst sanctify the fludde Jordan and all other waters to this mystical washing away of sin.

> 'This statement', he observes, 'has no scriptural warrant, and serves to encourage the superstitious idea that some mysterious sanctifying virtue is communicated to the baptismal water, some magical mutation, such as there is so strong a propensity in men to fancy, and of which there are so many examples in the church of Rome. Add to which, that baptism should be a sacrament of the remission of sins is a privilege the Lord has earned for us, by his Baptism on the cross. And although water is used on the occasion, yet this remission is not the work of water, but of the Lord Christ.'[1]

The same passage occurs in the prayer of the *Consultatio* (the source for the *Consultatio* and for the Prayer Book is the prayer in the *Taufbuechlein* of Luther):

> . . . which didst consecrate Jordan with the baptism of thy son Christ Jesus and other waters to holy deeping and washing of sins.

Bucer's objection is the more surprising as he did not object to this clause in the prayer of the *Consultatio* some five years before, when he was involved in the draft of that work.

By this special examination of the *Censura* and its passages bearing relevance to those of the Prayer Book, it has been attempted to show how intimately Bucer was acquainted with the Prayer Book.

Alterations have been made in the Second Prayer Book which are not due to Bucer. To quite a number of suggestions made by Bucer no attention was paid by the compilers of the Second Prayer Book.

[1] cf. Roberts, A.: *A Review of the Book of Common Prayer* . . . (London, 1853), pp. 20-21, who translates the passage from the *Censura*, p. 479. The passage begins (not translated by Roberts): 'In prima precatione super infantem, optarim ista omitti Vnd by the baptisme of thy vuelbeloued sonne, vsque vue beseche the, &c. Quibus verbis memoratur Deum per Baptisma sui benedicti filij *Iesv Christi* sanctificasse fluenta Iordanis, & omnes alias aquas ad hanc mysticam peccatorũ ablutionem. Scriptura enim haec non praedicat . . .'

And yet, to deny the fact that the *Censura* played its distinct part in the story of the Revision of the First Prayer Book, seems to be difficult, unless one refuses to recognize the often striking similarity of his suggestions with those carried out in the Second Prayer Book and in other English Church documents of that period.

However, it should be noted at the same time, that some of the alterations made in the Second Prayer Book, which were not urged by Bucer, seem to be of a most severe character, infringing vital parts of liturgical and ritual life: the sequence of the Canon, so painfully severed in the Second Prayer Book, was never for Bucer an object to alteration.

The omission of the words:

> humbly beseeching thee, that whosoever shall be partakers of this holy Communion, may worthily receive the most precious body and blood of thy Son Jesus Christ. Grant us therefore gracious Lord, so to eat the flesh of thy dear Son Jesus Christ and so to drink his blood in these holy mysteries . . .

was made although Bucer had specially those words recommended as well expressing the Eucharistic doctrine.

Those two examples show that by these alterations it was intended to go far beyond the scope desired by the Church. The tendency of introducing a specially pointed doctrine as regards the Eucharist, by omitting any 'doubtful' reference as to the presence of Christ in the Supper, is clearly indicated by these examples. It was not shared by Bucer, and thus proves again how much nearer he was to the views of the English Church than the Swiss Party, to whose influence those alterations have to be ascribed.

It has also been attempted to show how far Bucer's suggestions reflect on Church conditions and disputes on ceremonies, which were the main subject for projects made by the English Church as stated in such Church documents as Injunctions and Articles. His *Censura* only focuses Bucer's general impressions on English Church conditions, such as are to be found in others of his writings and his letters.

He himself states at the end of the *Censura* that he trespasses beyond the task set him by the bishops, when he deals also with the question of ordination, as the Ordinal was not attached to the First Prayer Book, on which only his criticism was asked. His attitude as regards the Homilies had to be considered as well, as the Book of Homilies with its express doctrinal statements cannot be disconnected from any reflection on the Prayer Book.

His orthodox views as regards Church traditions and rites show him in definite line with the Church of England as opposed to Puritanism, and are proof that he, as claiming to be on the side of the Church of England, was better listened to than would have been the case, if he could have been considered as favouring Puritanism.

To see his *Censura* and the suggestions and criticisms otherwise made by him in their right proportion, it has to be remembered that for Bucer the Reformation would not be achieved by concentrating on special minor points which needed obvious reforming, but that he stressed repeatedly and most strongly the fact that the Reformers had chiefly and first to see the main point in question, the Reformation of the whole body, without which any other zealous effort of reforming minor abuses would be useless.

All special suggestions for alterations or amendments made by him were only useful and promising of success if they were viewed together with the bigger issues of a reform scheme for Church administration, education of the clergy, training suitable ministers, establishing Church discipline and *moral*.

Cosin's observation in his Notes gives the best characteristic of such intentions for Church reform, when he writes of Bucer and his *Censura*:

> Bucer also, in the last chapter of his Censure [pp. 498 ff.] upon the book, urged very earnestly for the restitution of the lands and goods which laymen had taken away from the Church, and which they bestowed upon their pleasures of hunting and feasting, &c., threatening and forespeaking a general calamity and destruction that would come upon this kingdom unless such restitution were made, worse than Germany, or Israel and Judah suffered. But in this particular they never gave ear to him, which they did in altering and lessening the service of the Church.[1]

[1] Cosin, op. cit., p. 469.

cf. also the Puritan Manifesto referring to Bucer's stress on Christian life and prophesying of hard times for the Church if Christians would not obey God's commandments: '. . . the unquenchable flame of Gods vengeance, which followed shortlie after the like foretelling of that reverend father to this realme and church of England: – "If we refuse to submit our necks and whollie to undergoe the yoke of Christe, and to see such apparant sinnes and enormities punished, and to take awaie so horrible and fearfull contumelies, wherwith the sonne of God in these iniquities is dishonored and reproached; surelie the axe is put to the roote of the tree, our miseries stand ready on a suddaine to overwhelme us, the grievous examples of Gods judgements shall be executed against us, for the threatenings of allmightie God can not possible faile, which thinges when I consider and muse of with my self (allthough I can never waie and looke into them deepelie enough) thei make me to tremble and quake, and do enforce me to admonish upon everie occasion offered, whosoever I can of the same." ' *The Puritan Manifesto* (1586) translated the passage from Bucer's *Censura* (*Scr. Angl.*, p. 503).

cf. Peel, Albert: *the Seconde Parte of a Register Being a Calendar of Manuscripts* . . . (Cambridge, 1915), vol. II, p. 26; cf. also vol. II, pp. 7 and 9. The manifesto says of Bucer (p. 7): '. . . that deepe, learned, politique, and experienced souldiour in God[s] Church . . .'

CHAPTER III

BUCER'S 'DE REGNO CHRISTI'

> ... your Lordship shall see him [sc. Bucer] so well and so fully set forth the wants of the things of Christ's kingdom in this kingdom, that your lordship shall see what is wanting, and what is to be had and planted. He that concludes, that to have the church governed by meet pastors and ministers taketh away the authority of Christian magistrates, is by Bucer sufficiently confuted....
>
> Th. Sampson to W. Cecil, March 8th, 1573
> (Strype: *Annals* (ed. Oxford, 1824), II, i, p. 394)

It is to Bucer alike in his correspondence and in his *Censura*, that certain credit is due for insisting that a Reformation in England will be achieved not by concentrating on suggestions for remedies of special abuses in Church ceremonies and practices, but by reflecting on an entire social, ecclesiastical and economic Reform of the English system of Church and State. The way for this will be prepared by outlining a general scheme of Church discipline and order, sound doctrine and a conscientious Christian life for every member of the community. 'An intensive educational campaign by preachers was more important and would be more effective than a policy of legal discipline.'[1]

The crying need of the time was the reform of practical abuse rather than the framing of new prayer books and articles of belief. The renaissance of discipline in the personal life of the Christian in general as well as of the politician as such, the renaissance of the Christian responsibility to Christ and His Kingdom will bring the reformation of all other social and ecclesiastical evils.

Thus Bucer wrote his *De Regno Christi*, the work by which he tried to amplify and to round off the suggestions for the Reformation as expressed in all his other writings. That work tries to focus his various proposals on the special outstanding problems, which were regarded at the time as of pre-eminent urgency in any scheme of Reformation. Thus he had written the *Censura* contemplating a ritual and ceremonial reform as already laid down in the First Prayer Book. Thus he had given his advice in the Vestment Controversy. Thus he had written to men like William Bill, who had asked for his advice on similar matters. Thus he had given his opinion on the burning question of the abolition of altars.[2] The *De Regno Christi* is his final word,

[1] cf. Powicke, F. M.: *The Reformation in England* (Oxford, 1941), pp. 88 ff.
[2] cf. Gorham, op. cit., pp. 209 ff.

summing up all his life work for the advancement of the Reformation. From it alone all his other writings will be understood as a whole. The work 'contains the most absolute and perfect effigy of all Christian doctrine, not only expressed in colours, but also expressed in distinct lineaments', writes Nicholas Carr to John Cheke (March 1551). The *De Regno Christi* was Bucer's 'swan song'. He dedicated it to King Edward VI, as can be seen from the preface of the work and from his letter to the king, which we have added as an appendix to this chapter.[1] Like others Bucer expected the young king to be the new Josiah, who would be able to execute that scheme of Reform, which he had laid before him in the book. King Edward's small treatise on similar topics suggests that Bucer's draft had left an impression which he tried to set into practice.[2] But in the reign of Mary the work fell into oblivion and never gained that influence which it might have achieved had Edward not died so early.[3]

It was printed for the first time at Basle (1557), six years after Bucer's death, and in 1577 was incorporated into the volume of the *Scripta Anglicana*. In 1558 it had been translated into French and published at Geneva. The chapters on the 'relief for the poor' were translated into English and published as a separate little volume (presumably in 1558), contributing most valuable material to the characteristic laws relating to the poor in the Elizabethan time.

John Milton (1644) — almost a hundred years after Bucer's death—being engaged on his work upon Marriage and Divorce, discovered Bucer's chapters on the subject in his *De Regno Christi*, and translated them into English, full of praise and joy at having found in Bucer an ally and authority. The *De Regno Christi* is an extensive folio volume divided into two parts. The first part is of more or less doctrinal character concentrating on suggestions how to create a Christian State. Some might even call it a 'Christian Utopia'. Suggestions and detailed proposals mainly contained in the second part are practical and reveal an intimate knowledge of English economic, social and ecclesiastical conditions under Edward VI. Bucer, the foreigner, during the short period of his two years in England, surprises the

[1] cf. also Bucer's letter to Cheke, to whom he sent the MS. that he might present it to the King (October 21st, 1550), *Rogeri Aschami Epistl.* (ed. 1703), op. cit., pp. 434-435. His letter to Edward VI, see here pp. 127-130.

[2] A Discourse about the Reformation of many abuses (Burnet, Gilbert: *The Hist. of the Ref. of the Church of England* (London, 1841), vol. II, pp. clxxv ff.; cf. also vol. I, pp. 405-406).

[3] The Roman Catholic divine, Cornelius Schulting (at the close of the sixteenth century) in his *Hierarchica Anacrasis* provides a special chapter for a very critical examination of *De Regno Christi*. cf. 'Examen sive Discussio Duorum Librorum De Regno Christi Martini Buceri, quibus Disciplinam et Politiam Ecclesiasticam fuit complexus' (*Hierarchica Anacrasis* . . . (Cologne, 1604), Liber. III, pp. 87 ff.).

reader by his immensely practical comment on current affairs in England, which suggests that he must have devoted a great deal of his time to consulting leading personalities as well as contemporary writings concerning those aspects. This is affirmed by the following statement which we find in Sampson's letter (March 8th, 1573) to Cecil.[1]

> Bucer wrote his book in England, being but a stranger; yet of England most aptly, touching the state of it, to the king of England: but by report of his familiars in Cambridge. And they were the same which are now archbishops of York [i.e. Grindal] and Canterbury [i.e. M. Parker], bishop of London [i.e. Sandys], Bradford, and such like. I know not what conference they had with him when he made the book; but I am sure, that since his death, in private talk, they have much approved his book . . .

Whether Bucer knew More's *Utopia* and derived information from it remains an open question, although certain striking similarities seem to point that way: the crying need for a remedy of the land question, the system of enclosures (the cause of so many economic grievances), which had made so many people homeless and unemployed, thus adding a new crowd to the large number of beggars, was felt by More in the reign of Henry VIII as well as by Bucer under Edward VI: thus More[2] writes:

> For one Shephearde or Heardman is ynoughe to eate up that grounde with cattel, to the occupiyng wherof aboute husbandrye manye handes were requisite . . .[3]

And his suggestion to employ criminals in mines (cf. *Scripta Anglicana*, p. 138) in order to convert their idle prison-life into some useful work for the good of the common weal, seems to sound again More's reflection:

> Suche as amonge them were convicte of great and heynous trespaces, them they condempned into stone quarries, and into mienes to digge mettalle . . .[4]

But Bucer's work differs from More's *Utopia* in its wide scope of suggestions and by its Christian implications, demanding an ethical and political as well as ecclesiastical Reformation of England. Castigating obvious abuses in Church as well as in State and at the same time

[1] cf. Strype: *Annals* . . . (ed. Oxford, 1824), vol. II, pt. i, pp. 392 ff., p. 394.
[2] More, Thomas: *Utopia* (Everyman's Library, no. 461, 1937), p. 24.
[3] And Bucer writes almost in the same tone: '. . . Quem lanae quaestum aiunt nunc eo excrevisse, ut plerisque in locis unus occupet pro ovium suarum pascuis, tantum agri, quanto paulo ante alebantur et vivebant supra mille homines.' *Scripta Anglicana*, p. 136.
[4] More, Thomas: *Utopia* (Everyman's Library), p. 28.

giving a practical suggestion or admonitory hint as to the Christian duty of man, he is much more akin to Latimer in his sermons. His indignation about the abuses in the Church, pluralism, lack of education, irresponsibility as regards the ministry, is as great as his keen reproach, that the Government imposes too hard a pressure on the Church in order to get more revenues from it. He speaks against extortion by moneylenders and merchants, he proposes provisions to be made for the poor, he pleads for a reformation of the system of laws.[1] He gives hints as to how to improve the agricultural, mercantile and export situation of the country. He discusses the system of enclosures, and speaks of the necessity for cornfields and cultivated ground and vegetables, and thinks that by making the women learn to weave, the country would be relieved from the expense of importing linen. Being a Churchman his main interest is, of course, concentrated on a restoration of Christian discipline, Christian education in schools and universities, on asking for laws to improve the moral standard of the nation as regards marriage, and for an improvement of laws for the criminals, etc. From here only, from the Christian domain, as he repeats so often, will come the advancement of the Kingdom of Christ in England. A sound relationship between Church and State can be achieved only if Christianity is not left to the Churches only, but if it penetrates and infiltrates all secular affairs, being the dominant thinking from which all action will spring. Secularism in science and in politics acting by its own reasoning cannot be tolerated in a Christian State, because it ignores the characteristic features of Christianity, features which distinguish such a State from a pagan organization. In Christian England the first impulse has to come from Christian considerations even in matters which at first sight seem to demand other reflections. Already in his inaugural lecture on the occasion of receiving his degree of Doctor of Divinity at Cambridge in 1549, he laid stress on that point.[2]

Here already Bucer laid down the main principle of his *De Regno Christi*, and by illustrating it with an example from the academical

[1] *Scr. Angl., De Regno Christi*, chap. LVI, pp. 148: Bucer states that the laws are written in an obsolete language unintelligible for the layman, unscrupulous lawyers exploiting the situation by trapping people and robbing them of their money. The King ought to appoint men to revise the laws and correct them.

[2] 'Atque in horum omnium examinatione, prima duci ratio debet religionis. Christianam enim religionem nostrae scholae profitentur, ac praecipuae quoque ipsae Ecclesiarum partes sunt . . . Nec audiendi sunt, qui dicunt: Ille non profitetur Theologiam, sed philosophiam, vel artem medicam, vel scientiam legum, non est igitur in eum aliquid inquirendum de religione: Philosophiam profiteri, mederi corporibus, respondere de iure, potest etiam Turca, & Iudaeus: sed non in schola, & Ecclesia Christianorum, qui tantarum artium professiones, & omnia honesta munera, tantum ad *Christi* membra deferunt.' *Scr. Angl.*, pp. 186-187.

sphere, stresses even more considerations on which every Christian ought to base his life and activities.

His allusion to the practice of dealing severely with certain crimes whereas other crimes are regarded as less vicious because they affect not the immediate personal concerns of men but ought to be punished more severely because here the breaking of the law affects God's commandments, not only man's, arises from the same trend of thought.[1] The work has recently been made the subject of a special study by an American scholar, W. Pauck.[2] In the scope of the present work our task has to be confined to some particular observations on various aspects of *De Regno Christi*, which seem to show another kind of contribution made by Bucer to the English Reformation. As will be seen the stress on practical and moral reform, which is one of the main characteristics of the English Reformation compared with the doctrinal and more theoretical stress made by the Continental Reformers, brings Bucer's immensely practical suggestions into close connection with those of the English Reformers. Hence it is that men like Latimer have much more in common with Bucer than with Luther, because of the fact that they saw the new life as only coming if an entire Reformation in all walks of life could be attempted. The challenge to clergy as well as to the citizen, the censure of the social, moral and political evils had to be taken in account in a scheme for such a Reformation.

Thus to round up the account of the manifold aspects of Bucer's contribution to the English Reformation, doctrinal, liturgical, exegetical or ceremonial, some of his practical suggestions as contained in his *De Regno Christi* must be added:

(*a*) His demand for an ecclesiastical Reform;
(*b*) His teaching on marriage and divorce;
(*c*) His outline of a legislation for the poor.

It will be clear that all three points stand in some direct relation to the English Reformation.

The description given by Bucer in his letter to Calvin of the ecclesiastical conditions in England contains an account of special facts, which seem to him to be so characteristic that he repeatedly refers to

[1] 'Quid autem causae dicemus, cur in furta sic animadvertantur acriter: ad stupra vero & adulteria, vitia cultus divini, depravationem doctrinae coelestis, qua continetur hominum praesens & aeterna salus, ad blasphemiam divinae Maiestatis, tantum non a nimis multis corrideatur: nisi quia pecunia & externae opes tanto sunt hominibus chariores, quam Deus ipse, sempiterna ipsorum salus, pudicitia, & honestas?' *Scr. Angl.*, *De Regno Christi*, p. 163.

[2] Pauck, W.: *Das Reich Gottes Auf Erden* . . . (1928). cf. also the short survey by Pauck given in *The Princeton Theological Review*, vol. XXXVI, 1928, pp. 80-88.

them in others of his letters and writings when dealing with the question of the Reform of the Church.[1] As those letters were written in the course of the year 1550 when he was engaged in drafting the *Censura* and the *De Regno Christi*, it is not surprising that often the same trend of thought occurs in either of these works or in his letters. His correspondence thus provides an additional source of information to the proposals made in his *De Regno Christi*. At the end of the *Censura* also he refers to the same subject, mentioning the universities especially as places whence the Reformation ought to come. The offices and duties of the bishops, so deplorably neglected, have to be restored in order to become again centres of Church life and discipline. Visitations and the administration of parishes by well-educated and responsible ministers, who observe their duties regularly and who preach intelligible and sound sermons, are other features in the programme of the Reformation. Abuses in rites and ceremonies and private masses have to be severely rejected as well as the increasingly unconscientious conception of the ministry in the minds of the clergy. Despoliation of churches and their revenues by unscrupulous ministers who look only after their own advantages, has to be stopped by abandoning the system of pluralism and by admitting to the ministry only men who are theologians and not provided merely with the equipment of laymen. Homilies ought to be read so long as there is no guarantee that a sound sermon can be preached. His suggestions on this particular point are also mentioned in the *Censura*.[2] By removing such obvious obstacles in the academical and ecclesiastical sphere it will be easy to improve minor defects which come from the side of the congregations such as lack of church attendance and disturbances during service time, caused by 'babbling' and 'walking' people.

'It is from these colleges that the swarms of faithful ministers ought to have been sent forth from time to time,' writes Bucer to Calvin (op. cit., p. 546), thus stressing the point that the universities are the starting place for a scheme of reform. Nobody ought to be allowed to study there and to enjoy benefits, who is not prepared, by being destined to render services either to Church or State, to study and to

[1] Martin Bucer
to Calvin (Whitsunday 1550), *Original Letters*, vol. II, pp. 545 ff.
to Brentius (May 15th, 1550), ibid., pp. 542 ff.
to Hooper (middle November 1550), Gorham, op. cit., pp. 200 ff.
to à Lasco (October 20th, 1550), see pp. 151 ff. of this work.
to Cranmer (December 8th, 1550), Gorham, op. cit., pp. 214 ff.
to Henry Grey, Marquis of Dorset (December 26th, 1550), Harvey, op. cit., pp. 134 ff.
to William Bill (November 17th, 1550), ibid., pp. 143 ff.

[2] The section on the Homilies may be referred to under this head, see pp. 81 ff.

teach diligently. So Bucer wrote in his *Censura* (p. 497), and almost the same words occur again in the *De Regno Christi* (p. 61). Many 'pseudocanons' languish in those universities making it impossible for younger and more able men to take their places[1]: more serious even is the system of pluralism:

> . . . very few parishes have pastors qualified for their office. Most of them are sold to the nobility; and there are persons, even among the ecclesiastical order, and those too who wish to be regarded as gospellers, who hold three or four parishes and even more, without ministering in any one of them; but they appoint such substitutes as will be satisfied with the least stipend, and who for the most part cannot even read English, and who are in heart mere papists. The nobility too have, in many parishes, preferred those who have been in monasteries, who are most unlearned, and altogether unfit for the sacred office; and this, merely for the sake of getting rid of the payment of their yearly pension . . . (Bucer to Calvin, *Original Letters*, p. 546).

In this connection a passage in Bucer's letter to à Lasco (October 20th, 1550) is most relevant. This passage has been omitted in the English translation of the letter under Queen Elizabeth and is here for the first time published:[2]

> nam & Episcopi & nobiles mercedem hinc reddunt oeconomis suis, & alijs ministris: & uni tria, aut quatuor tradunt sacerdotia, qui ne uni seruiat: ut illi collatores eo maiorem de prouentibus Ecclesiasticis partem sibi retineant. Cuius enim quaeso inuentum, poscere primi anni fructus & decimas? Vel tum [?] quarum exactione sic vigilant, ut contingat toties per mortem, vel alias vacantibus sacerdotijs illos, ex uno sacerdotio, in uno anno ter primos fructus, adeoque trium annorum fructus percipere. Cuius iam, quod hodie uendunt in aula facultatem sacerdotia plura occupandi? Et quibus hanc uendunt facultatem, nisi sceleratissimis, nemo enim alius emeret. Cuius quod Episcopi dant dilationem suscipiendi muneris Ecclesiastici ad annos decem, aut duodecim, hominibus qui nunquam Ecclesiae uolunt ministrare, ut interim tamen fruantur (hi) bonis sacerdotiorum? Cuius, quod pueris nobilium, Archidiaconatus conferuntur, prouentum ducentarum librarum . . . his enim id efficitur, ut frequentes inuenias in Anglia Ecclesias, quae in sex & septem annis nullam audierunt concionem . . .

[1] 'Sed Antichristi lues & haec Collegia grauissime inuasit, vt plerique in illis, instar improborum monachorum & pseudocanonicorum, bonis horum Collegiorum ociosi abutantur, plane impio inibi ocio marcescentes, et consenescentes: atque iunioribus qui se verae Theologiae & Ecclesiarum ministerijs cupiunt mancipare, locum & facultatem praeripientes.' (*Scr. Angl.*, p. 61.)

[2] cf. p. 157 of this work.

Thus he draws the conclusion expressed in his reference to the 'prorsus exitialem parochiarum desolationem'[1] in the *Censura*.

Jeremy Collier,[2] in his *Ecclesiastical History of Great Britain*, gives an excellent summary of Bucer's *De Regno Christi* and especially of the chapters concerning ecclesiastical reform. Bucer proposes as remedy for all those evils, a strict and profound theological education of the young clergy. As regards the bishops he desires that their time should not be so much occupied by having to attend to secular matters. They should visit their dioceses every year. Suffragans over every twenty parishes ought to be appointed. Provincial synods ought to be held twice a year.[3] In the *fifth law* (pp. 74 ff.) he suggests the preservation of the revenues of the Church. Its funds ought only to be disposed to persons duly qualified, thus preventing simony. On no account should bishoprics or benefices be charged with pensions to secular men, who neither officiate in the Church nor are really indigent. The obvious deficiencies in the government of the Church are no excuse for the State to take everything from the Church. For, if the Church is thus robbed of its property and revenues how would it be possible to train young clergy and to give them a sufficient education? Bucer does not shrink from criticizing the State's attitude towards the Church by imposing high taxes on the Church and by demanding money from it. The king ought not to imitate 'Rome' by exacting from the churches first fruits and the tenth. The Church, of course, ought to pay taxes, but not on the scale demanded. Out of the exchequer large pensions could be paid as has been done for support of the clergy and of the poor. Bucer writes that he has been informed of the exhaustion of the king's treasure by war, but that does not entitle him to rob the churches. And if he wants to avoid that imputation of sacrilege, the king ought to drop the demand for first fruits. Bucer knows that the king's advisers will remind him of the policy of his father:

> Ditavit tam multos ex ministris suis de bonis monasteriorum et Ecclesiarum S.M. tuae pater: cur non filius paternam sequeretur liberalitatem, et in suos ministros?[4]

The courtiers will certainly try to persuade the king of the justice of their case by exploiting the deplorable state of the churches, but their arguments spring from covetousness and greed. Bucer tries to meet these arguments: they would object that the churches gained

[1] *Scr. Angl.*, p. 498.

[2] Collier, Jeremy: *An Ecclesiastical History* . . . (ed., London, 1845), vol. V, pp. 397 ff.

[3] 4th law, *De Regno Christi*, p. 73.

[4] *De Regno Christi*, p. 77.

their property and estates by impostures (indulgences).[1] The abbeys and colleges thus are illegally acquired accessories of the Church, and can be re-taken by the State. But — and Bucer admits the wrongs of a past ecclesiastical system and episcopal government — the State by taking those estates from the Church, which by now have become places of learning and education for the advancement of religion, does not only commit the same mistake once committed by the churches, but deprives the Church and country of the possibility of creating a sounder religious system.

§ I

BUCER'S TEACHING ON MARRIAGE AND DIVORCE

Bucer's teaching on marriage and divorce was too far advanced in its warm defence of divorce and re-marriage in cases, e.g. of desertion, and in its condemnation of divorce merely *a mensa et a thoro*, to make any effective impression on English matrimonial law in his time. The traditional and orthodox view of the Church, not recognizing divorce *a vinculo* was deeply rooted in the law system of the sixteenth century and linked with the sacramental conception of marriage. Bucer's view was regarded as being lax and licentious.[2] The French translator of Bucer's *De Regno Christi* even considered it necessary to indicate in the preface to the work Bucer's somehow different view from those of other scholars at his time, when he writes:

> Au surplus, il traitté du mariage, & du diuorse, autant amplement qu'auteur qui ait escrit de nostre temps, en quoy lon pourra facilement voir sa grande diligence, sutilité, & profond sauoir. Mais d'autant qu'il est different de l'opinion & intelligence de plusieurs sauans & excellens personnages, qui ont de plus pres regardé la verité, & plus approché du vray sens de l'Escriture, & de l'intention du Seigneur, en ce poinct du mariage, & du diuorse: i 'ay bien voulu admonnester le lecteur, de ne se troubler & offenser en telle diuersité, ains de se tenir tousiours à la conclusion & arrest qui est auiourd'huy practiqué en ceste matiere aux Eglises mieux reformées, suiuant la resolution qu'en ont donnée plusieurs bons seruiteurs de Dieu encore viuans, qui ont du tout

[1] *De Regno Christi*, p. 79.

[2] cf. Burcher's letter to Bullinger (*Original Letters* (Parker Society), vol. II, pp. 665-666).
cf. also: Cope (Copus), Alanus: *Dialogi Sex* . . . (Antwerp, 1573), pp. 160-161.

> regard à ce qui est exprimé en la parole de Dieu, & au sens plus conuenable à l'analogie de la foy. Et ne doute point de ma part, que Bucer n'eust adheré à leur opinion, comme la plus saincte & plus veritable, si le Seigneur ne l'eust retiré de ce monde tantost apres auoir fait cest' oeuure . . . (pp. +iiii, iiii verso).

In 1644 Milton published *The Judgment of M. Bucer concerning Divorce* and his own *The Doctrine and Discipline of Divorce*. He had translated Bucer's chapters relating to the subject in the *De Regno Christi*[1] to a certain extent into English and rejoiced to have found in Bucer an ally and an eminent ecclesiastical authority for his own views.[2]

The attempt made by the compilers of the *Reformatio Legum*[3] in its article *De Adulteriis et Divortiis* to introduce a proposal for a law allowing divorce on other grounds than only on that of adultery and making provision for a section on re-marriage, seems to express Bucer's views. That article states that adultery ought to be harshly punished as well as desertion. That the innocent party in a case of adultery may be allowed to re-marry after a period of one year or six months. That would apply also to the innocent party in case of desertion or protracted absence, with this reservation that if the person returned and could give any reasonable excuse for his absence, the wife ought to return to her former husband. The article also allows re-marriage, if one of the party is victim of deadly hostility or incorrigible harshness. Divorce is not allowed in cases of trifling disagreement or incurable disease. The fundamental difference from all former matrimonial legislation is to be found in the passage that separation *a mensa et a thoro* is to be abolished. Permission for re-marriage and abolition of separation brings this article of the *Reformatio Legum* in absolute contrast to medieval Church law which would not recognize divorce *a vinculo*.

In its essential points the law of the *Reformatio Legum* agrees with Bucer's views as expressed in his chapters of the *De Regno Christi*. Bucer, however, would have the permission for re-marriage and for divorce also extended to the case of leprosy, which was not granted by the *Reformatio Legum*.

Bucer, as well as his opponents, tried to establish their case by constant reference to the Fathers and to the ordinances of the Christian emperors as laid down in the Codex Justinianus and other sources.

[1] *De Regno Christi*, Liber II, chaps. xv-xlvii (*Scr. Angl.*, pp. 86-134). Milton's translation quoted here from the edition of *The Prose Works of John Milton*, vol. III, pp. 274 ff. (Bohn's Libraries, London, 1916.)

[2] cf. Masson, David: *The Life of John Milton* (London, 1873), vol. III, pp. 255-261.

[3] *Reformatio Legum Ecclesiasticarum*, Londini MDCXL: De Adulterijs et Divortijs (pp. 47-56, 21 chapters).

A special treatment of the loci classici of the Bible, mainly Matthew v, Matthew xix, the equivalent passages in Mark and Luke, Romans vii and 1 Corinthians vii and references to the Old Testament passages (Deuteronomy, Malachi) formed an essential part of treatises on the subject.

A definition of marriage leads Bucer to consequent conclusions on divorce, re-marriage and celibacy. The New Testament passages had been already explained in his Commentary on the Gospels and on the Epistle to the Romans. Although those commentaries were written nearly twenty years before he wrote his *De Regno Christi*, his opinion has not changed. Thus Milton, for instance, includes in his translation of Bucer's chapters from *De Regno Christi* a passage of Bucer's commentary on S. Matthew, as being of the same opinion.[1]

Resting his arguments on 'They shall be one flesh' (Genesis ii. 24), Bucer lays stress on the point, that all conditions and actions which prevent the realization of this demand are impediments for marriage. If those impediments exist the marriage cannot rightly be called a marriage according to God's law. Thus if a woman commits adultery, if a partner deserts the other partner, if incurable disease or impotence, if threats of endangering the life of one partner do occur in married life, the marriage according to God's law is already broken, since all these actions and others make it impossible for the couple to be one flesh. And therefore, since the marriage bond has already been broken, divorce ought to be granted legally. Marriage is not indissoluble, as the contract has been broken by one of the partners:

> there is no true marriage between them, who agree not in true consent of mind; so it will be the part of godly magistrates to procure that no matrimony be among their subjects, but what is knit with love and consent.[2]

But divorce means not separation *a mensa et a thoro* only:

> For although they also disjoin married persons from board and bed, that is, from all conjugal society and communion, and this not only for adultery, but for ill usage, and matrimonial duties denied; yet they forbid those thus parted to join in wedlock with others . . . And they pronounce the bond of marriage to remain between those whom they have thus separated . . .[3]

Separation *a mensa et a thoro* has to be abolished therefore and

[1] In his translation of the end passage of chap. xvii of *De Regno Christi*, Milton writes: 'And because this same worthy author hath another passage to this purpose, in his comment upon Matthew, chap. v. 19, I here insert it from p. 46.' Milton's trans., op. cit., p. 289.

[2] cf. chap. xix in Milton's translation, p. 290. cf. also chap. xxviii, p. 298.

[3] Chap. xxii, Milton's trans., op. cit., p. 292.

divorce granted, which means that the person divorced is allowed to re-marry, for 'the sentence of divorce and second marriage is one and the same'.

In his definition of marriage the following passage is of interest:

> Now the proper and ultimate end of marriage is not copulation, or children . . . but the full and proper and main end of marriage is the communicating of all duties both divine and human, each to other with utmost benevolence and affection.[1]

This passage seems to reflect Bucer's suggestion in his *Censura* on the Marriage Service (*Scripta Anglicana*, p. 488), that the third cause of marriage as stated in the service in the beginning exhortation (mutual society) ought to get the first place, as main characteristic of a 'godly' marriage.

Another significant feature in those chapters of Bucer's *De Regno Christi* is the suggestion to provide a definite statement in matrimonial law, by which anybody may know in which degrees of affinity it is permissible to marry and in which degrees of consanguinity it is prohibited (chap. xvii, *Scripta Anglicana*, p. 87 f.). This proposal seems to stand in close relation to the 'table of degrees of affinity' issued by Archbishop Parker in the reign of Queen Elizabeth. For the ordinary person the situation as regards to those degrees was so confused and unintelligible, that a legal statement by authority was considered necessary and desirable. By subtle and casuistical interpretations of those degrees and by special investigation by experts, it had been possible to establish the proof that a certain marriage was void because contracted on grounds of a prohibited degree. Here was the loophole in the strict and rigid observation of the canonical matrimonial law, which otherwise would never recognize a divorce. But if it had been proved that the marriage had been null and void from its beginning, the partners were not regarded as married at all. In cases of divorce, desirable, but of course unobtainable in case of a valid marriage, people eagerly took to the pretence that the marriage had been void from its beginning and suggest proof of this by having unearthed some degree of relation, which came under those prohibited.[2]

The passages of the Fathers and of Scripture enlisted by Bucer, and by all who were engaged on the problem of marriage and divorce, are of wide range. It is curious to observe that a certain passage cited by Bucer in favour of his argument is used by another writer as

[1] Chap. xxxviii, Milton's trans., op. cit., p. 305.

[2] Dibdin, Sir Lewis, T.: *English Church Law and Divorce* (London, 1912), p. 24.

proving the contrary.[1] Quotations from the Fathers were usually taken so far as they had any relation to the loci classici of Scripture above mentioned. Ambrose, Augustine, Chrysostom, Cyprian, Epiphanius, Jerome, Origen, are the most frequently cited authorities.

In an appendix contributed to *English Church Law and Divorce* by Sir Lewis Dibdin and Sir C. E. H. Chadwyck Healey (London, 1912), Dr. Claude Jenkins draws attention to certain *Collectiones De Divortio* by Archbishop Cranmer.[2] The significance of those *Collectiones* is to be seen in the fact that this selection of statements of Scripture and of the Fathers on the matter seems to suggest that it was the intention of the compiler to prove that divorce was unlawful. He refers to passages which are also used by Bucer, but in support of the contrary conclusion.

For instance, both Bucer and the *Collectiones* refer to S. Jerome's 'Epitaphium Fabiolae'. The *Collectiones* state (p. 112):

> *Idem* in Epitaphio ffabiole. 'Si arguitur . . . vulnus accepit'. *Si arguitur quare repudiato marito non innupta permanserit*, facile culpam fatebor, dum tamen referam necessitatem. She was young and could not endure perpetual widowhood. *Persuaserat sibi et putabat a se virum iure dimissum*, nec euangelij vigorem noverat, in quo nubendi vniuersa causatio viuentibus viris foeminis amputatur.

This extract is brought in the *Collectiones* in context with other statements against the permissibility of divorce or re-marriage.[3] Bucer, who also alludes to that passage, states that Jerome

> defended Fabiola, a noble matron of Rome, who, having refused her husband for just causes, was married to another . . . But some one will object, that Jerome there adds, 'Neither did she know the vigour of the gospel, wherein all cause of marrying is debarred

[1] e.g. Ambrose (on 1 Cor. vii), quoted by the *Collectiones* (p. 111) under section B, seems to have been regarded as authority, not admitting the possibility of dissolution of marriage for anything save adultery: 'And he (the Apostle) did not subjoin, as he did of the woman, *but if she have departed* that he should remain as he was, *quia viro licet ducere vxorem si dimiserit vxorem peccantem*, because he is not bound down by the law in the same way as the woman. For the man is the head of the woman.'

Bucer makes reference to the same passage of Ambrose in chap. xxxiv: 'D. Ambrosius . . . aperte agnoscit: esse viro quidem concessum, vt vxore adultera repudiata, aliam ducat: negat autem idem permitti vxori in virum. rationem vero huius suae opinionis nullam adfert aliam, quam quod vir sit caput mulieris, & quod inferior non omnino hac lege vti debeat qua potior.' (*Scr. Angl.*, p. 110.) Reference to the same passage of Origen on Matthew vii is made by the *Collectiones* as by Bucer. The *Collectiones* quote it under section B, as apparently speaking against the dissolution of marriage (p. 107). Bucer alludes to it in chap. xxxiv (*Scr. Angl.*, p. 97).

[2] Op. cit., Appendix E, pp. 104 ff.

[3] Under the head: 'Quod non liceat post divortium viuente priori coniuge secundas nuptias contrahere', reference is made to S. Jerome's statement as regards Fabiola (*Collectiones*, p. 106). S. Jerome's passage here quoted is cited by the *Collectiones* also under section B (p. 112) in context with other quotations, but it remains doubtful whether Jerome's passage was considered to be pro or contra.

from women, while their husbands live; and again, while she avoided many wounds of Satan, she received one ere she was aware'. But let the equal reader mind also what went before: 'Because' — saith he — soon after the beginning 'there is a rock and storm of slanderers opposed before her, I will not praise her converted, unless I first absolve her guilty . . .' Jerome by 'the vigour of the gospel', meant that height and perfection of our Saviour's precept, which might be remitted to those that burn; for he adds, 'But if she be accused in that she remained not unmarried, I shall confess the fault, so I may relate the necessity' . . . (chap. xxii, Milton's trans., op. cit., vol. III, p. 293).

The *Collectiones* (op. cit., pp. 106, 113 ff.) make Augustine their strongest authority against divorce and re-marriage. Bucer, on the other side, writes:

But the words of our Lord, and of the Holy Ghost, out of which Austin and some others of the fathers think it concluded, that our Saviour forbids marriage after any divorce, are these . . . [Matt. v. 31, 32; xix. 7, etc]. Hence therefore they conclude, that all marriage after divorce is called adultery, which to commit, being no ways to be tolerated in any Christian, they think it follows, that second marriage is in no case to be permitted either to the divorcer, or to the divorced. But that it may be more fully and plainly perceived what force is in this kind of reasoning, it will be the best course, to lay down certain grounds wherof no Christian can doubt the truth . . . (Chap. xxv, Milton's trans., op. cit., p. 296; cf. also chap. xxxi, *Scripta Anglicana*, p. 105).

In connection with Bucer's treatment of the places of Scripture, which are relevant to the problem, his exegetical remarks concerning the passages in S. Matthew and its equivalent contexts in Mark and Luke, and his observation on the seventh chapter of the Epistle to the Romans are worth-while mentioning.

On the passages in S. Matthew he observes in agreement with the observation made in the *Collectiones*, that Matthew records the saying of our Lord 'That whosoever shall put away his wife, saving for the cause of fornication, causeth her to commit adultery' (Matt. v. 32) differs from that recorded by Mark and Luke, who state only 'Whosoever shall put away his wife, and marry another, committeth adultery against her' (Mark x. 11; Luke xvi. 18), omitting the special reference to *stuprum*. He says:

Apud Matthaeum quidem, inquiunt, pronunciat haec Dominus nominatim de illis, qui cum alijs iunguntur matrimonio, facto diuortio non fornicationis caussa. Apud Lucam autem & Marcum, vbi exceptionem istam non expressit de contrahentibus alteras nuptias post quacunque de causa factum diuortium. Hinc itaque concludunt, obstringi adulterij crimine omnem virum, qui vxorem suam repudiat & alteram ducit: & repudiatam ipsam, si viuente priore viro copuletur alteri, etiamsi adulterij causa factum diuortium sit. Cum iam adulterij admittere flagitium nemini possit Christianorum concedi, nec ferri in quoquam, putant consequi, coniugia altera siue repudiatorum, siue repudiantium vlla de causa, superstitibus ijs qui repudium miserunt vel acceperunt, nemini posse Christianorum vllo pacto permitti, aut in quoquam tolerari. (*Scripta Anglicana*, p. 99; cf. also ibid., p. 105).[1]

This observation as regards the difference in the reports of the Gospels is also observed in the *Collectiones* although they come to another conclusion (cf. *Collectiones*, p. 124, n. 2; p. 126, n. 7).[2]

As regards Romans vii. 2 (For the woman which hath an husband is bound by the law to her husband so long as he liveth . . .) Bucer maintains, that this text cannot be employed as an argument against divorce or re-marriage. Already in his Commentary to the Epistle to the Romans (1537) he had stated that this text had nothing to do with the question of marriage and divorce, and since it was an example taken from the Mosaic law, which permitted divorce and remarriage 'nihil ex praesenti loco colligendum esse contra diuortium'.[3] Now in stating his opinion of the passage almost thirteen years after he had written his commentary on the Romans, he writes on the same lines:

> Here it is certain that the Holy Ghost had no purpose to determine aught of marriage or divorce, but only to bring an example from the common and ordinary law of wedlock . . . Besides it is manifest, that the apostle did allege the law of wedlock, as it was delivered to the Jews; for, sayth he, *I speak to them that know the law*. They knew no law of God, but that by Moses, which plainly grants divorce for several reasons. It cannot therefore be said, that the apostle cited this general example out of the law, which God

[1] cf. also one of the questions (number 5) in the *Collectiones* (p. 122): An exceptio illa (excepta fornicationis causa) etiam in luce marci et pauli locis, qui de his rebus tractant, est subaudienda.

Answer (*p.* 123): Ad quintam respondemus quod exceptio ista uidelicet nisi causa stupri est subaudienda in Luca, Marco et Paulo, alioquin manifesta esset pugnantia inter Mattheum et eos.

Bucer in chap. xxxiii (*Scr. Angl.*, p. 109) writes: Ista qui pie & religiose ponderauerit, is quonam pacto queat dubitare, Dominum existente causa stupri, diuortium duobus apud Matthaeum locis planissime concessisse: eamque ob rem, istam causae stupri exceptionem, debere ex Matthaeo, verbis & responsis eisdem Domini apud Marcum & Lucam adiungi . . .

[2] cf. Eells, Hastings: *The Attitude of Martin Bucer . . . the Bigamy* . . ., p. 20, n. 4; and 'Metaphrasis et enarratio in epist. D. Pauli apostoli ad Romanos'. (Ed. 1562, p. 344; ed. 1536, p. 307.)

[3] See preceding note.

himself granted by giving authority to divorce. (Chap. xxxv, Milton's trans., op. cit., p. 300).

The passage in S. Paul's Epistle is very doubtful evidence, for its meaning is obscure and presents a textual difficulty. Modern scholars, like Dr. K. E. Kirk in his *Marriage and Divorce*, come to the same conclusion as regards the textual difficulty of this passage.[1]

Although a comparison between Bucer's references to the Fathers and to Scripture, and between those references of the *Collectiones*, shows that the opinion of the compiler of the *Collectiones* was against the permissibility of divorce (save in case of adultery) and re-marriage, the section on divorce in the *Reformatio Legum* breathes undoubtedly Bucer's spirit.[2] Bucer, of course, did not belong to the drafting Committee of the *Reformatio Legum*, as he had died in February 1551. But his judgement on the question was well-known at least to Peter Martyr and Bishop Hooper, who belonged to the Committee.[3] Bishop Hooper sent to Bucer his own treatise on the subject (October 17th, 1550):

> I send also what I wrote three years ago on the Decalogue, that your Excellency may know what is my opinion on Divorce: be kind enough to read this also, that, if through human frailty I have erred in this matter, I may correct it, being admonished by your learning and fraternal admonition.[4]

Although the *De Regno Christi* may not have been widely known at the time of the draft of the *Reformatio Legum*, Bucer's teaching was known from his commentaries on the Gospels and on the Epistle to the Romans, and from his controversy on celibacy with Stephen Gardiner, the Bishop of Winchester. The part he had played in the divorce case of Henry VIII and in the bigamy of the Landgrave of

[1] K. E. Kirk: *Marriage and Divorce* (London, 1933); note 3 in extenso, pp. 92-93: 'A difficulty is created here by the fact that S. Paul says that the indissoluble tie which binds the wife to the husband till death is *by law*, and the fact that he is speaking *to men that know the law*, implies that he means the Jewish law . . . But while the Jewish law prohibited a wife from divorcing her husband, she was perfectly free if divorced . . . to marry again . . . etc.'

[2] cf. Dibdin, op. cit., p. 25.

[3] ibid., p. 10 ff. cf. also Peter Martyr on celibacy: 'Quique de his plura loca Patrum colligere voluerit, is legat D. Buceri luculentam, piam, ac sanctam responsionem, ad episcopum Vintoniensem.' (Petris Martyris Vermilii Locorum Communium . . . Tomus Primus, Basileae MDXXC, p. 1094.)

[4] cf. C. Gorham, op. cit., p. 186, nr. LII. cf. also Bucer's letter (extract) to Hooper; Glocester Ridley, op. cit., p. 209, note a. Peter Martyr, to whom Hooper also had sent that statement, answers Hooper (November 4th, 1550; Gorham, op. cit., p. 196, nr. LIII): 'Concerning Divorce I do not reply to you; partly because you yourself put off the matter for another time; partly because I very well know that you understand what I think, together with the Church of Strassburg and all the other brethren in Christ.' On Hooper's treatise on Divorce see: *Early Writings* (Parker Society), pp. 382-387.

Hesse was also known to Archbishop Cranmer and others.[1]

The revolutionary suggestion in the *Reformatio Legum* of divorce *a vinculo* and re-marriage found thus a strong support in ideas put forth by Martin Bucer.

The fundamental difference in the conception of marriage between Catholicism and Protestantism explains the interest of the opposing parties in interpreting passages of Scripture and of the Fathers to an extent which often seems to obscure the principal idea behind the controversy. To the *sacramental* idea of matrimony Bucer is opposed, saying plainly and without reluctance:

> Constat autem, matrimonium et divortium esse res civiles . . . Quod nemo sanctorum et verorum Episcoporum unquam damnavit . . . (*Scripta Anglicana*, p. 101, *De Regno Christi*, chap. xxviii.)

From that statement with its implications contradictory to the prevalent teaching by the Church on Marriage, Bucer attempts to draw his conclusions, which, to a certain degree, seem to have paved the way for the article on Divorce in the *Reformatio Legum*.

[1] John Burcher (June 8th, 1550) writes to Henry Bullinger: 'Bucer is more than licentious on the subject of marriage. I heard him once disputing at table upon this question, when he asserted that a divorce should be allowed for any reason, however trifling; so that he is considered, not without cause, by our bishop of Winchester as the author of the book published in defence of the Landgrave . . .' (*Original Letters* (Parker Society), vol. II, pp. 665-666.)

cf. Cranmer's letter to Osiander (December 27th, 1540), '*Remains of* . . .', pp. 404-408. cf. *Original Letters*, vol. II, pp. 551-557, various letters relating to the Divorce of Henry VIII, referring to Bucer's opinion. cf. H. Eells: *Martin Bucer and the Bigamy of Philip of Hesse*, pp. 30-43, historical account of Bucer's dealings in the divorce affair of Henry VIII. cf. also Bucer's Letter; our work, pp. 251-252.

§ 11

BUCER'S SUGGESTIONS IN 'DE REGNO CHRISTI' CONCERNING THE LAWS FOR RELIEF OF THE POOR

> BEcause in these days, lyke as not manie yeres sithe, manie lustie and sturdie persones be suffred to begge, men counterfaitinge horrible deseases and infirmities, sitte by the commen ways crauinge Almose: dyuerse go about Westminster Haulle, and other places, with gloues, under pretence to gather for the mariage of poore Maidens, but in deade to haue wherwith to coople with Harlottes, or to riotte at Dice: And some craftie Hypocrites, no Friers in coates, but more subtil then Friers in maners, under colour to relieue and mayntain Orphanes, poore wydowes, poore Scolers, and other, gather muche, but put all into their owne purses . . . I thought it uery necessarie, to set forthe in Englishe the mynde and opinion of the Reuerende Father, and Excellent clerke Master Martyne Bucer, touchinge the right geuinge and distribution of Almose, and prouision for the poore, declared in his boke entitled *De regno Christi*, made for the *Moste Blissed King Edwarde*. . . . (To the Reader, p. 3.)[1]

These prefatory words to the English translation of two chapters of Bucer's *De Regno Christi* on the Relief of the Poor might seem to justify us in regarding Bucer's proposals as suggestive for the legislation of that time. They certainly met the need for an elaborate scheme on the subject and they bear most striking similarity to the Elizabethan Poor Laws. But to attribute to Bucer's draft much influence on those laws under Elizabeth may seem, on the other hand, to be jumping too hastily to a conclusion, if one considers the fact that the Elizabethan laws as regards relief of the poor, are based on the preceding laws of Henry VIII and Edward VI, and that those laws were drafted before Bucer wrote his work.[2] However that may be, there are none the less important links of connection with English thought and the English provisions in Bucer's chapters which show his intimate knowledge of the social condition in England and in certain passages indicate distinct characteristics of the Elizabethan law which were not provided for in either the legislation of Henry VIII or of Edward VI.

[1] *A Treatise, How by the Worde of God,* Christian mens Almose ought to Be distributed. Math. vi. WHen thou geuest thyne Almose, let not the Trompettes be blowne before the: as Hypochrites do in their Sinagoges, and Streates, to haue Praise of Men. (No year, no place.)

[2] Karl Holl: *Gesammelte Aufsätze*, vol. I, p. 515 4.5. (ed. Tübingen, 1927) writes, after having given a short account of the characteristic of Bucer's proposals: 'In diesem Geist hat Elisabeth nach sorgfältiger Vorbereitung durch die Gesetze vom Jahre 1597 und 1601 das Armenwesen neugeregelt.' But cf. W. Pauck, op. cit., p. 92.

The law under Henry VIII (1530-31), '*An Acte* concernyng punysshement of Beggers & Vacabunds' (22 Hen. VIII, ch. 12) was the first in a series dealing with beggars and poor, on which all subsequent laws were based. But as the provisions made in this law are 'chiefly repressive: designed to limit the number of beggars rather than to provide relief', preventing 'those who were not really impotent from begging, and punishing more effectively the able-bodied vagrant',[1] the law was soon amended and corrected by the following statute 27 Hen. VIII, ch. 25. 5 Eliz. ch. 3, although it has certain additions and variations, is modelled on 22 Hen. VIII, ch. 12. Only 14 Eliz. ch. 5 repeals it as well as it repeals 3 & 4 Edw. VI, which had followed 27 Hen. VIII, ch. 25. Four laws during the reign of Elizabeth are important: 5 Eliz. ch. 3; 14 Eliz. ch. 5; 39 Eliz. ch. 3; 43 Eliz. ch. 2. The Elizabethan law has, in common with the Henrician Law (27 Hen. VIII, ch. 25), the sharp distinction drawn between the able-bodied beggars and the impotent. The chiefly repressive law of Henry VIII had not yet the distinct provision for organized relief work, which it got under Elizabeth, when the relief work was made compulsory and formed a legal part of the organization of public welfare.[2]

The number of beggars and vagabonds had increased to such an extent as to threaten to become a menace to the community, if the State did not take legal action by regulation. To administer relief was not a mere charitable philanthropic idea but served also to deter from vice and anarchy, a danger of which the State was largely aware. That the relief work for the poor is a public affair, to be organized by the laws of the State and the Church, and not left to the private means of individuals, is the main characteristic which binds together the Henrician laws with those of Edward VI and Elizabeth and is also the principal idea of Bucer. By making the birthplace or place of living responsible for the upkeep of its poor, a certain restriction was laid upon the movements of beggars and vagabonds. They could be traced and settled.[3] Other characteristics are prohibition of any begging. The poor have to be divided into two classes, those able-bodied, who can work, and the impotent and aged,

[1] Leonard, E. M.: *The Early History of English Poor Relief* (Cambridge, 1900), pp. 53, 54 ff.

[2] Our references to the various laws are taken from: *Statutes of the Realm* (1547-1584-85), vol. IV, part I (1819).

[3] cf. Bucer, op. cit., p. 21: 'And therfore Christian Magistrates ought to make this lawe, First, that no man bee suffred to beg: but that euerie man do maynteyne, and kepe his owne householde, kynred, and allies, if he be able to do it: the iudgement wherof, ought to perteigne to the ordynarie Magistrat. And that such as be destitute off such helpe, be mayteyned by the Citie, towne, uilage, or Congregation where they dwell.'

who cannot work. The first class has to be put to work in workhouses and other institutions, thus making its members earn their living and preventing them from loitering and begging. The other group has to be maintained by relief-funds, collected by the Church, by the district or parish. Hospitals, orphanages, houses for the destitute and aged have to be built. No private alms are allowed as indiscriminate giving may fail to reach the real poor and seems only to support pretenders and evil elements in this community which take advantage of the situation. The poor-box, or the chest for alms, in the Churches is meant to provide funds for distributing the alms later with official supervision, and to prevent the indiscriminate giving by the individual. The office of the deacon as prescribed already in the Ordinal is, to take a careful account of the number and condition of the poor in the parish. By thus ascertaining the real state of affairs in the parish, it is hoped to make possible the distribution of the money to those who really need it. Specially appointed 'officers' guarantee for the State the settlement of the poor, supervision of them and provision for them. The parishes, to which the poor belong, which are not able to provide for their maintenance, may be relieved by being allowed to send the poor to a neighbouring district, which is able to support them. All these characteristics of the poor-law legislation can be traced in Bucer's chapters in his *De Regno Christi*.

(1) All begging is prohibited. Bucer distinguishes between the able-bodied poor and the poor unfit for work, and thus suggests the twofold system for their maintenance. The able-bodied may, by work given to him, be enabled to earn his living; the other class who have to be provided for by means of money legally and officially collected, may be sent to a hospital or an institution for old-aged people. This distinction is also characteristic of the Elizabethan law, but was first introduced by 27 Hen. VIII, ch. 25.

(2) Bucer suggests the appointment of 'officers' who are to regulate the settlement of the poor in their respective districts. This regulation is characteristic only of the Elizabethan law.

(3) Bucer proposes the interchangeable scheme of housing the poor in different districts, if one district cannot provide for its own destitute.

(4) Bucer wishes to enforce the official and legal distribution of the alms thus preventing private alms-giving.

(5) Bucer knows the *poor man's chest*, as means to prevent indiscriminate giving.

(6) Bucer gives a special account of the duties of the office of a deacon, which is mainly intended for obtaining information about the social and economic condition of the parish: he suggests visiting, careful taking account of the number of impotent and poor and the keeping of a book in which to enter such information.[1]

To these special suggestions have to be added some more general remarks of his. Like Calvin, he regards labour as the means for an able-bodied person to earn his living, thus distinguishing between two classes of poor. A person who shrinks from labour has thus no right to food and support: the biblical locus classicus, so frequently used by Calvin as well as by Bucer is 'if any would not work, neither should he eat' (2 Thess. iii. 10).[2]

The reasons Bucer gives for his stress on the point, that no indiscriminate giving should be allowed are that:

(1) It is against the Holy Ghost;

(2) It is against the Communion of Saints;

(3) The unworthy more often receives the money than the really needy;

(4) It is often done out of an hypocritical attitude and self-pride to receive the due thanks of the poor.

Another feature is his constant reference to the 'godly and christian Emperors' like Valentinian, etc., who built hospitals and provided money for the poor. He mentions also the 'fourth part' of all revenues, which at one time was taken from the Church for the relief of the poor.

All these references to Bucer's *De Regno Christi* in relation with the

[1] cf. Bucer, op. cit., p. 12: 'Suche as the Deacons shall fynde, that neither can gette their owne lyuinge, nor haue off their neighbours, that doo relieue theim: their Names, with the maner off their neade and behauiour, thei ought to write in A particular boke, And certayn tymes to uisite theim, and to call theim unto theim, that thei may the more certanlie knowe, how well and uertouslie they use thalmose of Good People, and what thinges from tyme to tyme, thei neade.'

cf. also: 1552 Ordinal (fifth question): And furthermore, it is his office *where prouision is so made*, to searche for the sicke, poore, & impotente people of the parishe, & to intimate theyr estates, names and places where thei dwel, to the Curate, that by his exhortacion they maye bee relieued by the parishe, or other conueniēt almose . . . (cf. Brightman, F. E., op. cit., pp. 951 and 953.)

Bucer, op. cit., p. 12. (*Scr. Angl.*, p. 81); cf. also Harrison, B.: *An Historical Inquiry* . . . (London, 1845; pp. 315 ff.). The fyrst poynt then off the Office of the Deacōs of the poore, is, that thei make diligēt serche, who lacke in deade, and be not able to relieue their owe lacke . . .

[2] cf. R. H. Tawney, *Religion and the Rise of Capitalism*, p. 113. Bucer mentions the passage in these chapters (*Scr. Angl.*, pp. 50 and 81); also *De Regno Christi*, p. 62; also in a letter to W. Bill (cf. Harvey, op. cit., p. 155); in his letter to Cranmer (December 1550; Gorham, op. cit., p. 219).

p. 6: 'For those that may gette their lyuinge by their labour and trauayl, and wil not, ought to be put out of the Churche: *He that dothe not labour, let him not eate*, saith the Apostell.'

legislation for the poor, are not only evidence that his views had much in common with the provision made and the proposed schemes at the time of Henry VIII and Edward VI, but that it can be said that some special features of the Elizabethan law, which are not to be found in the preceding laws, at least suggest the possibility that his elaborate scheme was helpful for the Elizabethan lawgivers. Some extracts of Bucer's chapters in the contemporary English translation may even better illustrate this conclusion, specially if compared with the laws under Elizabeth.

The translation of the chapters, often not verbatim, well brings out the essentials.

(1) *Distinction between the able-bodied and the unfit*; and the necessity that the work done officially by public authorities
. . . Morouer lest those, that be not worthie to haue the Almose of the Churche, and of good men, shoulde take it from those that be worthie, and in deade neadie: Good Magistrates ought to renue and put in execution, that lawe off God, and off the Emperour Valentynyan, whiche forbiddeth, that any man be suffred to begge: and commaundeth, that those that be able to labour, shoulde be forced to labour: and that suche as be not able to labour, sholde be kept as our Brethern, and membres, eueryе one in the Congregation where he dwelleth. And that this may bee the better doon, commaundement ought to be gyuen, that euerye man maintaine such as be of his one howsolde, or otherwise properlie ioyned to him, if he be able: . . . (pp. 16-17).

(2) *Appointed officers for settling the poor*
And because it may be, that some Towne, or uilage is so poore, that it is not able to relieue al the Poore therof: that suche also be not left unprouided, it is uery requysite, that in euerie Shire, certayne godlie, and spirituallie wise men, be appoynted: who may sende suche poore people from the places where thei cannot be relieued, to such Congregations, where thei may be sufficientlie relieued (p. 17).

(3) *Interchangeable scheme of settling the poor in different districts, if one district is unable to maintain them*
. . . And that euery Citie, Towne, and uillage, doo mayntain suche poore people, as their friendes be not able to keepe, and not suffer theim to wander abrode . . . (p. 17) . . . If any citie, towne, uilage or congregation, be not able to, maintaine the pouertie therof, that then, by the discretion of the chief Gouernour of the contreye, such poore people be sent to some richer Congregation, where thei may be relieued (p. 22).

Numbers 2 and 3 ought to be closely compared with 14 Eliz. ch. 5, xvi:

> ... And when the number of the said poore People forced to lyve uppon Almes be by that meanes truely knowen, then the said Justices Maiors Sheryffes Baylyffes and other Offycers shall within lyke convenient tyme devise and appointe, within evrye there said severall Divisions, meete and convenient places by their dyscretions to settle the same poore People for thire Habitacõns and Abydynges, yf the ꝑishe within the whiche they shalbee founde shall not or wyll not provide for them.

cf. also xxvii:

> *Provyded* also, That forasmuche as yt ys thought that the Inhabytauntes of divers Countyes Cytyes and Townes within this Realme be not able to releve the poore lame and ympotent ꝑsons with Money to be collected in manner and fourme aforesaid, and that yt were over greate a burden to the Collectours for to geather ... And that the Inhabitauntes of every suche ishe or Ꝑishes to the whiche suche poore or ympotent ꝑsons shalbee so appoineted ...

cf. also xxviii.

A similar provision was already made in 5 Eliz. ch. 3, xii, 27. Henry VIII, ch. 25, xxiii orders the surplus of rich and wealthy parishes to be distributed for the poor parishes in the neighbourhood.

(4) *The poor man's chest* mentioned in the Royal Injunctions of Edward VI (1547) and in the Elizabethan Injunctions (1559)[1] is named by Bucer with the Greek term *gazophylakion* (pp. 7-8, *Scripta Anglicana*, p. 51). He writes (p.18):
... ther wilbe som, that, not withstandyng this most holy prouysion for the poore, will not put their Almose in to the comen cheste, or boxe off the lorde, but will rather geue their Almose with ther owne handes, if they be mynded to geue any at all. Such mens pride must be mette with, not onely by a lawe off the Magistrat, but also by the discipline off the Churche.

(5) The '*Fourth Part*' of all revenues meant for hospitals and other charitable institutions: Bucer writes (pp.15-16):
In tyme longe past, the Fourth parte of all Reuenues, that either belonged to the Spiritualtie, by their Possessions, or cam to hit by good mens gysts, and oblations, was taken for the relief of the poore. Besydes, manie uertuous Princes, and good Men made Hospitals, and howses for the Relief off the poore: Some for suche as were Hole of bodye, and some for suche as were

[1] Frere and Kennedy, op. cit., vol. II, pp. 126-127, n. 29.
Frere, W. H., op. cit., vol. III, pp. 16-17, n. 25, and p. 3, n. 17.

> sicke: Some to keepe Infantes, and some to comforte Straungers, and Banissħed men: But all these in contynuannce of tyme, through the wycked Monkes, and Pryestes, were conuerted from those godlie uses, and turned to the mayntenaunce of their owne bellies, Pleasures, and pryde.

The *fourth* part is mentioned (Frere and Kennedy, *Visitation Articles and Injunctions* . . . (1910), vol. II, p. 305, n. 67) in Bishop Hooper's Interrogatories of 1551-52. But it is the *fortieth* part (Frere and Kennedy, op. cit., vol. II, p. 121, n. 14) in the Royal Injunctions of Edward VI (1547).

§ III

BUCER'S TEACHING ON USURY

Although Bucer does not deal with the subject of usury in his *De Regno Christi*, references to his conception of usury cannot be omitted in this section of our work since it is too vital and *modern*, when contrasted with the teaching on the subject by his contemporaries, to be passed over silently. And as Bucer, while engaged on the draft of his *De Regno Christi*, was also involved in a heated controversy on usury with Young at Cambridge, his teaching forms almost an additional chapter to his *Kingdom of Christ*.

His contemporaries were shocked at his attitude towards that 'vice', criticizing him as severely as they had done on his 'lax' views regarding marriage. Andrew Perne, a violent antagonist of Bucer at Cambridge, accuses Bucer after his death of having taught that usury was allowed among Christians.[1]

It has usually been stated that it was Calvin who for the first time put forward a theory breaking away from the medieval doctrine of the Church. It is true that Calvin has influenced by his elaborate studies on the question religious bodies revolutionizing the economic aspects of the time. But it is also true that in Bucer's writing, beginning with his commentary on the Gospels and his commentary on the Psalms, we find expressed the same line of thought often using the same arguments.[2] The question even arises whether Calvin got his

[1] *Scr. Angl.*, p. 931: '. . . de mordacibus item vsuris quasi is eas licere inter Christianos sentiret . . .'

[2] Bossuet, J. B., in his 'Traité de l'usure' (ed. *Oeuvres complètes de Bossuet* . . . Paris, 1866, vol. XXXI, p. 43) writes: 'Aussi n'y a-t-il que ceux qui ont méprisé la tradition et les décrets de l'Eglise qui on combattu cette doctrine. Bucer est le premier auteur que je sache, qui ait écrit que l'usure n'étoit pas défendue dans la loi nouvelle. Calvin a suivi . . .'

conception from Bucer. That matter lies outside the scope of this work, but it may remind the student of the fact, that what has been said of Calvin's teaching on the subject can easily be applied to Bucer as well. Klingenburg's study of the question[1] is most relevant and revealing by giving a comparison of the views of the two Reformers.

We are not concerned with Bucer's statements in his earlier writings (as they do not differ from the teaching of his last years) but our task will be to deal, if only summarily, with his controversy with Young at Cambridge in 1550.

It can be said in general that since Bucer's aim as regards a Reformation was to exercise a decisive and radical influence by way of criticism of the real social as well as economic conditions of the public life of the nation, he did not ignore the fact that the question of taking interest had to be considered as a particular case of the general problem of the social relations of a Christian community, which must be solved in the light of existing circumstances, and which cannot be confined to a theoretical treatment of the subject by the Church.

In the course of his lectures on the Epistle to the Ephesians at Cambridge,[2] Bucer enlarged on the subject of covetousness (πλεονεξία) and expressed his views as regards usury. This he did especially to meet the anxieties of certain of his students, whose consciences were struck by the fact that they were only able to pursue their study at the university, if they lent their capital on interest. He had warned against 'foenerationem iniquam' and 'mordentes usuras', but had added that any human and Christian communication and mutual relationship makes it necessary to create various contracts. The use of money in such circumstances might be 'aliquando vitiose, aliquando sine vitio'. The view held by Bucer in his lecture alarmed many persons and led to the subsequent attack by Young to which Bucer's tract 'De usuris' (*Scripta Anglicana*, pp. 789-796) is the reply. Here in referring to his lecture and explaining the circumstances which had induced him to lecture on 'interest', he gives an explicit account of his teaching. By commenting on the passages of Scripture in question (Old Testament as well as New Testament) he had stated Matt. vii. 12 to be the text from which all directions as regards usury had to be taken:

> '. . . whatsoever ye would that men should do to you, do ye even so to them . . .'.

[1] Klingenburg, G., *Das Verhältnis Calvins zu Butzer* (Born, 1912), pp. 22-41.
[2] cf. *Praelectiones in Ephesios* . . . pp. 168-169.

Any mutual contract means mutual responsibility, and thus excludes the danger that the one party takes too great advantage of the other party — provided that they act according to the general rules as expressed in the Gospel. If a person by lending money takes interest and thus takes advantage of the pressing situation of the borrowing party and gains, he mutually ought also to share any loss in which the borrowing party might be involved by being unable to turn the money he borrowed into profit. Also, as the person who lends money enters a risk of losing the money, so the person who gains by borrowing has to make the person from whom he borrowed share in his gain. Bucer explains the word *usury* by tracing it back to its original meaning and by attempting to clear the term from any wrong implication. The original Hebrew term נשך means the *abuse* of usury and is prohibited; for multiplying too much is an abuse. The word originally means *excessive* interest, which is forbidden, but not *any* interest is forbidden. The interest by which the other party is involved in loss and not helped, that is the meaning of the Hebrew term and is prohibited: 'usura mordens, qua proximus afficitur damno, non iuvatur' (*Scripta Anglicana*, p. 792). But the meaning attached to the term *usury* as such is usually confined to that prohibited kind of usury, and leads to wrong implications.

The Latin term *usura* by rightly describing that which is received by the *use* of money, does not necessarily imply that it is sin:

> Adieci, agnoscere me, vsurae nomen abusu eo esse pertractum, vt tantum illicita vsura hac voce significetur. id autem dicebam factum esse, praeter sermonis latini proprietatem (p. 789).

Thus it is wrong, according to Bucer, to say that our Lord (Luke vi. 35 . . . lend, hoping for nothing again) prohibited any kind of taking interest:

> Item ex non vero intellectu dicti Domini, Mutuum dantes, & nihil inde sperantes, dogmati inesse vsuram a *Christo* prohibitam, pecuniam accipere pro pecuniae vsu, quocunque modo accipiatur (p. 789).

He then refers to other Latin terms such as *interesse*, *cessans lucrum*, *emergens damnum* . . . Bucer's views do not seem to have convinced Young who advises him, if he should lecture again on the precarious question, to make it perfectly clear, that he was not in favour of the vice of extortion, because already Bucer's views seem to have led students to usury. To which Bucer replies, that he always had spoken against the abuse of usury, but the fact that usury was abused, was no reason why the right use of usury might not be allowed, as any other kind of commercial transaction or financial contract was allowed. Usury, rightly used, the taking of interest on a legal scale (Bucer refers to the practices on which money is lent in other countries (*Scripta Anglicana*, p. 792)) may even be profitable to the life of the community. Thus in denouncing the obvious and scandalous practices of money-lending, he does not see why the taking of interest, if legally controlled and accepted in the right Christian spirit, could not be turned into another useful institution for the community. Thus — in the same spirit — he had denounced in his *De Regno Christi* the frauds and avarice of merchants, and yet urged the Government to undertake the development of the woollen industry on mercantile lines. That a system was wrong did not mean to Bucer abandoning the principal and true idea behind the system. In the controversy with Young he seems to have had the final word in his tract:

> Cum itaque Iungus non posset illud vsurae genus, quod ego admitto, peccati conuincere, hortabatur me, vt cum rursus de hac re agerem, bene explicarem, eum qui pro vsu pecuniae suae partem lucri accipiat, quod Dei beneficio innoxium obueniat, communicet etiam damno, si quod ille qui pecunia vtitur, contraxerit (*Scripta Anglicana*, p. 796).

Yet his teaching was revolutionary in a time when usury was regarded as a kind of heresy. The medieval doctrine that usury *per se* was to be prohibited stands in absolute contrast to Bucer's and Calvin's teaching which differentiates between the abuse of usury and usury lawful *per se*, not taking it for granted that the taking of interest, which is only another term for usury, implies a sinful action. Their 'quantitative' distinction of what is lawful usury and what is extortion, is the typical appeal of the Reformers to the Christian conscience and attitude to God and fellow-men. Where this conscience and mutual fellowship is disturbed by a covetous and selfish reasoning of the person, the Reformers pass as severe a judgement on those unscrupulous men as the medieval Church's doctrine could pass by its principal and fundamental statement about usury. The question of discipline and freedom of conscience tries to break through the rigid laws of an ecclesiastical system, which prevent men acting according to their consciences. Bucer's judgement on Divorce, his judgement on the wearing of ecclesiastical vestments, and here on usury, can all be traced back to this his main doctrine: Anything is lawful and allowed as long as it does not stand in absolute contrast to God's commandment. The Roman Catholic conception is thus to Bucer avoiding the issues at stake, when formulating precepts which take from the person the responsibility of deciding.

Thus Bucer's 'shocking' new teaching can be explained as his constant and often indirect attack against Romanism. Here lies the explanation why his teaching on the subjects mentioned leads to terms so opposite to the teaching of Roman Catholicism: just because the Roman Church has a definite doctrine on a matter it is wrong for Bucer, and must be superseded by a new doctrine which even may appear to be absurd or too far reaching.

Bucer never hesitated to criticize and to demand punishment for those who took advantage of the social position of their neighbours by fraud or subtle manipulation of money, and here he differs in no wise from the teaching of the Roman Church. But he does not find the remedy for those evils in passing or adhering to rigid laws but by appealing to man's obedience to God's law.

When Laud in 1621 (70 years after Bucer wrote his treatise) said in a sermon:

> If any man be so addicted to his private, that he neglect the common, state, he is void of the sense of piety, and wisheth peace and happiness to himself in vain. For, whoever he be, he must live in the body of the Commonwealth and in the body of the Church,

he did not say anything different from what Bucer had written, although Laud may have still adhered to the medieval conception of usury, and although on the other side Bucer was in favour of taking interest.

Bucer wrote:

> Neither the Church of Christ, nor a Christian Commonwealth, ought to tolerate such as prefer private gain to the public weal, or seek it to the hurt of their neighbours.[1]

[1] Quotations from Tawney, R. H.: *Religion and the Rise of Capitalism* (Pelican Books, publ. 1938), pp. 72 and 129.

‘DE REGNO CHRISTI’

§ IV

APPENDIX

Letter of Martin Bucer to Edward VI

(MS. Smith 67, n. 22, fol. 63-66, at the Bodleian Library; cf. here pp. 16; 100).

R. Edwardo VI Martin Bucerus.
Ex autographo.

Serenissime atque Religiosissime Rex. Amplissimae Regiae Majestati tuae perpetua precor divinae benevolentiae atque beneficentiae incrementa in subeuntem novum annum et omne aevum. Libros hos duos de eterni filij Dei et unici servatoris regno apud nos restituendo, conscribere occasione, quam in praefatione indicavj, et nunc Sacrae Majestati tuae sero satis exhibere tamen visum est. Studium hoc qualecunque meum S.M.T. in meliorem velit partem accipere etiam atque etiam oro. Nam etsi res, quas tractavi, sanctae sunt, ac salutares cumprimis: eas tamen sine arte et sermonis venustate, quae decebat, et res ipsas et tuam Sacram Majestatem congessi: deinde putide sunt omnia descripta. Confido autem S. Majestatem tuam rerum his Libris contentarum amore quo flagrat maximo patientiam sibi facile confirmaturam inconcinnae et injucundae cum tractationis tum descriptionis. Habet quidem S. Majestas tua pleraque omnia his meis prodita commentarijs, pridem non modo celebrata: tam assidua Scripturarum lectione quam crebris pijsque concionibus: verum etiam plane perspecta et meditata religiose: quemadmodum a Christi regno et doctrina omnino alienum est, quicquid non est antiquum apud Dei filios duntaxat, et pervulgatum: attamen dum ea tam paucis adhuc sunt ad veritatem persuasa, reque ipsa recepta, haud vereor fastidiosam S.M.T. fore harum rerum etiam ex hac mea admonitione recognitionem. Magis metuo, non defuturos, qui minime [p. 64] pauca ex his, qui ad recipiendum solide Christi Regnum confirmo, ut sunt, esse necessaria, judicaturi sint, nimis insolentia: receptuque tantum non impossibilia. Sacra vero Majestas tua, qua sedulitate et pia judicij perspicacia, divinas versat scripturas, agnoscit, nihil horum non contineri praecepto illo primo, a quo pendent caetera omnia: *Diliges Dominum Deum tuum ex toto corde tuo ex tota anima tua et cunctis viribus tuis*; nec dubitabit credenti et in nomine omnipotentis filij Dei molienti, atque conanti non possibilia modo verum etiam esse factu facilia, quaecunque ipse mandavit: *mandata enim eius gravia non sunt.* Virtute itaque accinta celesti Sacra Majestas tua curabit efficietque quam primum, ut populis suis Evangelium regni Christi ubique pure ac plene adnuncietur per idoneos et fideles ministros: talesque singulis quoque praefici parochijs operam dabit: quod utrumque, quo citius queat praestare, non differet, quam severissimi[?] Academiarum suarum, in quibus Evangelistas illos, et Ecclesiarum curatores erudire formarique oportet instituere ac perficere. Atque ne desint fidis regni Christi administris sua necessaria stipendia, sacrilegia illa summo studio, et quamprimum coercebit, quibus parochiae tam miserae vitae aeternae destituuntur ministerijs: dum illae vel committuntur non indignis modo hominibus et ineptis: verum ijs etiam qui se tantum inde, non Christi populum pascere student: vel alijs vijs, suis immo [p. 65] Christi patrimonijs sic spoliantur, ut ministros sibi necessarios parare et sustentare non valeant. Cum vero dominus sacrae Majestati tuae hoc dederit, ut subditis suis justam regni sui restituerit administrationem, aderit ei quoque magnifice, ut et caetera omnia in suo regno uti oportet, ad ejusdem aeterni Regis et Servatoris nostri salvifica decreta corrigat et componat. Haec ut idem Sospitator noster Sacrae Majestati tuae det cum mature ac fortiter aggredi, tum plene ac feliciter conficere, assidue orabo, idque cum omnibus sanctis, qui in hoc et in alijs regnis atque populis nomen Christi invocant, ut qui a Sacra Majestate tua pro ea, quam dat de se, expectatione ex initijs tam optatis nihil expectent vulgare, nihil mediocre, sed qualia praestitit Dominus per Davidem, Jehizkiam, Josiam et similes heroas, absolutam quandam ut doctrinae ita et disciplinae totius Christi restitutionem: reiquepublicae ad hanc exactam conformationem, ut Regnum filij Dei vel alicubi et in hoc maximae Sacrae Majestatis tuae regno; priusquam veniat dies ejus terribilis et gloriosus, plane obtineat: ad sanctorum omnium, quam late hic orbis patet, mirificam consolationem, et salutarem regni atque populorum multorum imitationem, ad gloriosissimi denique nominis Dei et Patris nostri coelestis sanctificationem cum divina quadam et Sacrae Majestatis tuae laude et gloria. Gratia et Spiritus ejusdem Dei Patris et Redemptoris, Regisque nostri summi S.M.T. semper et confirmetur et augeatur Amen Meque [p. 66] illa inutilem servum suum habere dignetur ut facit commendatum.

Cantab: IIII Cal: January M.D.L.

Serenissimae ac religiosissimae
Regiae Majestatis tuae
Adictissimus minister
Martinus Bucerus.

The text of Bucer's letter to Edward VI, printed by Harvey, op. cit., pp. 159 ff. (from MS. C.C.C.C. 119, 2) differs from the text here reproduced (MS. Smith 67, pp. 63-66, n. 22, at the Bodleian, Oxford) as follows:

in line		
3-4		words after 'incrementa' from 'in' to 'aevum' do not occur in H(arvey)
5	H	'nostri' after 'servatoris'
6	H	'occasionem' instead of 'occasione'
6-8	H	'occasionem quam in praefatione indicavi, conscribere & nunc sero satis S.M.T. exhibere vi sum est'
9-10		'etiam atque etiam oro' not in H
10	H	'sint' for 'sunt'
12	H	'venustati' for 'venustate'
14-15	H	'commemoratarum' for 'contentarum'
15	H	'amorem' for 'amore'
15	H	'flagret maxime' for 'flagrat maximo'
15-17	H	'patientia, facile confirmatum iri, inconcinnae, etiam iniucundae tractationis, atque descriptionis'
19	H	'cum assidua D. scripturarum lectione: tum'
21	H	'uti' for 'quemadmodum'
21	H	'religione' for 'religiose'
22	H	'omnino est alienum' 'non antiquum est' '&' before 'apud'
25	H	'fastidiosam fore S.M.T.'
27	H	'pauca ex his, quae'

31	H	'M.T. qua & sedulitati'
32	H	'agnoscet'
34		'tuum' after 'Dominum Deum' not in H
37-38	H	'facta facilia'
38	H	'etiam' for 'enim'
41	H	'populis eius evangelium'
44	H	'mature' for 'citius'
44	H	'quod verumque' for 'utrumque'
45	H	'securissimam Academiarum'
46-47	H	'institui formarique oportet, instituere ac perficere'
49	H	'etiam quamprimum'
50	H	'parochia tam misere'
51	H	'illa'
55-56	H	'ut necessarios ministros sustentare non valeant'
57	H	'regni ipsius'
62-66	H	'cum mature tum foeliciter adgredi et conficere, orabo, cum innumeris sanctis, et in his aliis regnis atque populis: qui omnes a S.M.T. pro ea, quam dat de se'
69-70	H	'heroes' 'ita quoque disciplinae'
70	H	'Christi totius'
72-73		from 'et in hoc' to 'tuae regno' not in H
75-78	H	'consolationem: cum divina quadam S.M.T. laude: & salutarem multorum imitationem, cum gloriosissima nominis Dei & patris nostri coelestis sanctificatione'
80		'Dei' before 'Patris' not in H
81-88	H	'semper confirmetur, etiam augeatur. Amen, habeatque ipsa me suum inutilem servum, ut facit commendatum. Cantabrigiae, XII. Cal. Nov. MDL. Deditissimus in Domino servulus Martinus Bucerus'.

CHAPTER IV

BUCER'S CORRESPONDENCE CONCERNING THE VESTMENT CONTROVERSY

. . . At the Begynninge, it was but a Capp and a Surplice, and a Typett; but now it is growen to Bishopps, Archbishopps and Cathedrall Churches, and the overthrow of Order established, and (to speake Plaine) to the Quenes Maiestie's Authoritie in Causes ecclesiasticall.

(Matthew Hutton, Dean of York, to Burghley, October 6th, 1573.)[1]

There emerge clearly the two pre-suppositions which lie at the root of all puritan argumentation and give a deep import to divisions which at first sight seem to be nothing but petty squabbles. The first is the contention that there must be scriptural warrant for everything that is done in public worship; this involves a denial of the authority of the Church to decree rites and ceremonies. When it is pointed out that such a demand for scriptural warrant must not be pressed so as to include small matters of indifferent detail, then recourse is had to the second pre-supposition, viz. that the matters in dispute are not indifferent, being popish, and therefore superstitious, idolatrous, antichristian.[2]

I

We learn from a letter of the Polish Reformer, Iohn à Lasco, to Bucer (October 12th, 1550) that à Lasco had been consulted by Hooper when he was contending for the abolition of the episcopal vestments. To this letter of à Lasco Bucer replied in a lengthy epistle (presumably October 20th, 1550) which has played an important part in all further discussions on the subject. Hooper, too, had written to Bucer (October 17th, 1550) and to Martyr, enclosing a summary of his opinions asking them to state their views on the controversy.[3] Bucer in replying to Hooper (November 1550) observes: 'But I have written

[1] p. 262: in William Murdin: *A Collection of State Papers relating to affairs in the Reign of Queen Elizabeth* . . . (London, 1759).

[2] W. H. Frere: *The English Church in the Reigns of Elizabeth and James I* . . . (London, 1904), p. 114.

[3] cf. Gorham, op. cit., pp. 185-186, and P. Martyr's letter to Hooper (November 4th, 1550), ibid., pp. 187 ff., p. 188: '. . . I could not keep your Manuscript longer than one night. For the messenger, by whom I received it, departed hence the following day, very early in the morning, to Cambridge, whither you had desired that by that person I should send what I had read to Master Bucer, which I did diligently and without delay.'

more fully on these points to Master Iohn à Lasco.'[1] Peter Martyr himself had written to Hooper (November 4th, 1550) and had clearly been made cognizant by Bucer of his correspondence with à Lasco since he writes to Bucer from Oxford (November 11th, 1550): 'I send back also, as you desired, that which you wrote to à Lasco, and also that which you received from him.'[2]

When Archbishop Cranmer, in a letter from Lambeth (December 2nd, 1550), asked for Bucer's opinion and judgement on the vestment controversy in connection with Hooper's own case, he knew already, as his letter shows, of the various discussions of the subject, in which Bucer, Ridley, à Lasco, Peter Martyr and Hooper had been engaged.[3] Cranmer's own anxiety to obtain a clear statement was due to the personal difficulty that had arisen in the case of Hooper himself. In April 1550 he had been offered the vacant bishopric of Gloucester. But he objected strongly against the use of episcopal vestments, as being 'Aaronical, anti-christian habits and vestures'. His refusal to accept the bishopric by referring to the use of vestments, aroused a wide and furious discussion. Ridley, then Bishop of London, was most severely opposed to Hooper's standpoint. The controversy, which excited much interest, wore on for months and ended in Hooper's consent to consecration to the bishopric in March of the following year.[4]

Hooper was strongly backed by à Lasco's Stranger's Church in London. À Lasco's intervention was made for the sake of his own Church, since he was anxious to be allowed to discard the use of vestments, and to enjoy complete immunity and freedom from intervention from the side of the Anglican Bishop in London. The correspondence between Bucer and à Lasco reveals the interesting fact that Bucer could not and did not want to take the line of Hooper

[1] cf. Gorham, op. cit., p. 208.

[2] ibid., p. 197.

[3] cf. Appendix to this chapter, n. 7.

[4] He was consecrated at Lambeth on March 8th, 1551, by Cranmer, assisted by Nicolas Ridley, Bishop of London, and Iohn Poynet, Bishop of Rochester (Stubbs, *Regist. Sacr.* (Oxford, 1897), p. 103, from *Reg. Cranmer*, 332). In a letter of February 15th he had written to Cranmer from the Fleet prison: 'I now acknowledge the liberty of the sons of God in all external things: which I affirm and believe neither that they are impious in themselves, . . . only the abuse, which can be pernicious to all, of those who use them superstitiously or otherwise evilly do I blame, together with Dr. Bucer, Dr. Martyr, and all godly and learned men . . .' (The original Latin is printed in: *Later Writings of Bishop Hooper* . . . (Parker Society, 1852), pp. xv-xvi; Gorham, op. cit., n. LXV, p. 233, gives a translation of the letter. Our English translation is taken from C. H. Smyth, op. cit., p. 218, which seems to be more correct in regard to this special passage of the letter.)

On Hooper's case see also pp. xii ff. in *Later Writings of Bishop Hooper*.

On the controversy between Hooper and Ridley see my 'Note' in *J.T.S.*, July-October 1943 (vol. XLIV, No. 175-6, pp. 194-199): *Bishop Hooper's 'Notes' to the King's Council, October 3rd*, 1550. Ridley's answer to Hooper in: *The Writings of John Bradford . . . Letters, Treatises* . . . (Parker Society, 1853), pp. 375 ff.

and à Lasco, but was on the side of the bishops, who were opposed to Hooper.[1] This fact that Bucer more or less seemed to voice thoughts akin to those of the English Church most probably induced Cranmer to write to him. If this judgement is correct we are justified in seeing Bucer as one who took the part of the Church, which believed in continuity and tradition, even at the risk of alienating himself from those who, in disregarding the external functions of the Church and her ancient traditions, favoured arguments for the future rigidity and intolerance of Puritanism.

Cranmer, who seems to have scented the larger issues of this controversy, which was to recur again and again in English Church history, clearly wanted to get Bucer's support. He puts two questions before him. From the second question it becomes evident that he was most anxious to widen the scope of the problem, by introducing the question of offence against Church and State by those who refused to wear the apparel.

Cranmer — knowing of Bucer's part already played in the affair — addressed with wise anticipation his letter to one whom he knew to be on his side. Bucer's letter to Hooper and to à Lasco must have been valuable information for Cranmer. Thus those letters of Bucer to Hooper and à Lasco, being the prelude to the correspondence with Cranmer, are as important as his letter to Cranmer.[2]

The two questions put before Bucer by Cranmer were:

(1) Whether without the offence of God, it may be lawful to the ministers of the Church of England to use those vestures which at these days they wear, and so be prescribed of the magistrate?

(2) Whether he that shall affirm that it is unlawful, or shall refuse to wear this apparel, offendeth against God, for that he sayeth that thing to be unclean that God hath sanctified; and offend against the magistrate, for that he disturbeth the politic order?[3]

Bucer's reply is written in a lengthy style, although Cranmer had expressly asked for a short answer, and is written with great reluctance to intervene in the controversy. Both questions are answered in the affirmative, with slight reservations: he thinks that

(1) They that be such ministers of the Churches of England, may (as I think), wear with God's pleasure, those vestures which be

[1] cf. also Burcher's remark in his letter to Bullinger (December 28th, 1550), *Original Letters*, vol. II, p. 675.

[2] cf. Martyr's letter (January 28th, 1551) to Bullinger, where Martyr gives an account of the story, and the part his own and Bucer's letters played in it. (*Original Letters*, vol. II, pp. 486 ff., and footnote on p. 488.)

[3] The English is that of the translation, which was published in the 'briefe examination' in modern spelling, fol. A.1.

Latin cf. appendix to this chapter, n. 7.

at this day in use . . . [It should, however, be explained by the minister that the vestments is a 'signification' and has nothing to do with the 'Roman Rite'.][1]

(2) They[2] which do say that it is not lawful to use the apparel that is in question, in any manner, . . . which I have described: I say, that they be at the least in error, for that they deny all things to be holy to them that be sanctified . . . I must needs say, that they take from the godly Magistrates their due honour, which doth deny that their judgment ought to be followed in these matters. Rom. xiv. for that they do declare the use of these garments to be observed of that consideration, which I have a little before described . . . [3]

The reservation as regards this second question is significant, as it characterizes the way by which Bucer approaches this and similar problems, and the words of this reservation occur — often in the same connection and sequence of thought — in other letters dealing with the same subject. He writes to Cranmer (December 8th, 1550)[3]:

. . . since undoubtedly at this day these Vestments have given rise to superstition in some, and to pernicious contention in others — it would be far better to abolish them: nevertheless, in this order, and on this condition; that we should first abolish all sacrileges; false and impious doctrines; perverse, superstitious, and profane disciplines, and rites; and all spoliation of Churches; and that we should restore the whole doctrine and discipline of Christ . . . I perceive, how Satan struggles to sow contentions about religious dogmas and rites, lest the whole of the religion of Christ should be restored, as it ought to be . . . Indeed, unless such horrid and manifest sacrileges, and contempt of God be taken out of the way . . .

Bucer stresses the fact that this question cannot be dealt with singly and separated from the principal issues behind it. It has to be seen in the synopsis of doctrine, discipline, order and rite, which only will guarantee a wholesome and satisfactory Reformation. Thus he cannot disconnect from this problem the other manifold and apparent deficiencies of the Church. He enlarges on lack of ministers, on spoliation of churches, and other ecclesiastical conditions, which need first to be reformed. The question of vestments is only a minor issue of the far greater and urgent need for Reformation. It is

[1] Bucer brings the plural 'those, who say' whereas Cranmer's question was 'he who shall . . .' 'A briefe examination . . .', fol. A.2, verso ff. Bucer's reply cf. *Scripta Anglicana*, pp. 681 ff.

[2] Cranmer's Latin cf. appendix to this chapter, n. 7.

[3] cf. Gorham, op. cit., pp. 218-219, and p. 220.

only an outcome of a system which is bad in its roots. Unless those roots of abuses in doctrine and church order are torn out, it is no use to concentrate on this particular question, as if by its solution every thing would become straight and successfully restored.

Thus he had written on similar lines to Hooper:[1]

> But when I observe that, in England, an abuse of these Vestments prevails, alas, in many places, up to this moment, most willingly would I suffer much in my own person if I could bring about their salutary abolition; — accompanied, however, by the abrogation of, not only the marks and signs, but the nerves and joints of Antichristianism . . .

This he enlarges, giving examples of ministry, church administration, etc., which need adjustment. He continues:

> We know . . . that these evils, which I have just mentioned, are the primary members of Antichrist, — are his flesh, and his nerves, of which he entirely consists. If we could but fight against these evils, with united forces . . . then the abuse of Vestments and of all other things would easily be abolished, and all the marks and shadows of Antichrist would vanish. But if, in the very first place, these principal members of Antichrist, his substance and his very body, be not cut off altogether . . . we shall labour in vain in our endeavours to dissipate the marks and shadows of Antichrist . . .

And in a letter to William Bill, then Master of Pembroke Hall, Cambridge, who had asked his advice on similar questions, Bucer enlarges again on the present problem and explains that those in favour of the abolition of vestments, supporting their claims by referring to the 'Aaronical and Papistical abuses', do not see the real issues at stake: it is wrong — he writes — to say, because those things have been abused, that they cannot be used piously by Christians. For the abuse does not depend on those things, but depends on the attitude of those who abuse them:

> Et falsa est illa: Quibuscunque rebus usum est sacerdotium Aharonicum et abusum Papisticum, iis Christiani uti pie non possunt. Rerum enim abusus non in rebus, sed in animis haeret abutentium.[2]

And therefore, because Hooper and his followers approach the problem from a wrong angle, he cannot agree with them, although he would like to have the use of those vestments reduced as liable to

[1] cf. Gorham, op. cit., pp. 200, 202.
cf. also Bucer's letter on the abolition of altars, extract in Gasquet, op. cit., pp. 231-232, n. 3; the entire letter in Harvey, op. cit., pp. 131 ff.; in English translation, Gorham, op. cit., pp. 209-212.

[2] Bucer to Bill (November 17th, 1550), cf. Harvey, op. cit., p. 152.

misinterpretation. But to aim at their abolition only, without at the same time aiming at the abolition of more serious abuses, will never do. At the same time, Bucer cannot follow the doctrinal conclusions of Hooper and his friends, who say that because there is no explicit reference in Scripture to those vestments, the Church, which is founded on the Scriptures only, has no right to advocate rites and uses not accounted for in Scripture. Here the main difference of Bucer and the English bishops from Hooper's party is clearly indicated: the Puritan contention was always to allow only those rites and doctrines for the Church, which could be traced back to Scripture, not allowing for the individual development of liturgy and worship of the Church. Tradition was only justifiable in their eyes in so far as it was ordained by the Scriptures. Bucer and his English friends on the other side knew too much of the history of the Church to ignore the fact that rites and ceremonies, which had belonged to the Church since ancient times, even if not prescribed by the Bible, could not be abandoned, because they formed an integral part of Christian worship and Church-order. He argues that while, for instance, it was not indicated in the Gospels in what attitude we should approach the Lord's Table, nor at what time of the day we ought to celebrate the Eucharist, etc.,[1] nevertheless, customs had developed, which were not objectionable to Christian church life. Christ had not given explicit rules for our churches, in order that Christians might in perfect freedom order those things according to their Christian conscience.

> Constat praeterea Dominum . . . substantiam [as regards sacraments] tantum instituisse, et commendasse propriis praeceptis; caetera vero omnia reliquisse ordinanda Ecclesiis . . .

And

> Falsum enim est nihil licere nobis adhibere in sacris ceremoniis, nisi quod proprio mandato sit nobis iniunctum.[2]

Here already the main argument of all future Puritan controversies was contradicted by Bucer. As Hooper voiced to a certain extent opinions of the Swiss Party, among whom he had many friends, his support by à Lasco, finds easy explanation: à Lasco saw the opportunity for the Swiss, whom he also favoured, to get a stronger hold in England, if only Hooper succeeded.

[1] Bucer to à Lasco (October 20th, 1550), cf. Strype, op. cit., p. 449. Latin here p. 156.
[2] Bucer to Bill (November 17th, 1550), cf. Harvey, op. cit., pp. 150, 151.
Almost verbatim he had written the same to Hooper (November 1550): 'Constat etiam Dominum nostrum Iesum *Christvm* substantiam tantum ministerij, cum verbi, tum sacramentorum, suis verbis nobis praescripsisse, & caetera omnia quae ad decentem & vtilem administrationem mysteriorum eius pertinent, ordinanda permisisse Ecclesiae.' (*Scr. Angl.*, p. 708.)

Thomas Bell, in his 'anti-Brownist' pamphlet *The Regiment of the Church*, after having given extracts from Bucer's letter to Hooper, sums up Bucer's views by bringing them under seven heads:[1]

(1) that *Christ* hath onely prescribed in his word, the substance of his holy worship.

(2) that hee hath giuen power to his Church, to dispose and order all other things, which concerne the decent and profitable government and administration of his holy Mysteries.

(3) that the Church may appoint her Ministers to weare speciall garments, euen in the time of the holy Ministerie.

(4) that such garments may bee ordained, for decencie and for edification.

(5) that the vse of such garments, cannot be condemned by any Text of Scripture: nor yet they iustly accused of any sinne, who appoint them to be worne.

(6) that no abuse of man, Antichrist, or the maister-divell of hell, can so pollute them, but they may this day be lawfully vsed of the faithfull.

(7) that the Church may ordaine ceremonies, for honest and godly significations.

The more important was it for Cranmer to secure the judgement of the Continental Reformer, Martin Bucer, in order to show that the Church of England did not differ in this question from the views of the Continental Reformers on it. À Lasco, who had also been eager to persuade Bucer to join the group of the Polish Reformer, who tried to back up Hooper, had soon to realize that his efforts were in vain.

Bucer's stand on the side of the archbishop and in favour of his contention that the vestments in themselves were not anti-Christian, was too valuable a fact not to be employed by churchmen against Puritans in the next scene of the drama, which had its vigorous revival in the first years of the reign of Queen Elizabeth.

II

The correspondence of Bucer relating to the controversy (Cranmer's letter to Bucer, Bucer's reply to Cranmer, Hooper's letter to Bucer, Bucer's letter to à Lasco) had, at that time, been extant only in manuscript form. Now in the reign of Elizabeth, when the Puritans renewed their claims for abolition of the vestments, men like

[1] Bell, Thomas: *The Regiment of the Church* . . . (London, 1606), chap. viii: 'Of things indifferent in particular' (pp. 77-82), pp. 81-82.

Archbishop Parker and Whitgift were keen to publish Bucer's correspondence and circulate it as a vindication of the rightness of the Church's policy under Elizabeth against the Puritans. But when those letters together with others were printed in the 'briefe examination' as an appendix, they had been already translated into English, thus serving the purpose of the bishops in an even better way, for they could now be read by anybody. The print of the original Latin version of those manuscript letters was not any longer regarded as important, as they were now translated into English. That accounts for the fact that some of the letters in their original version were not printed even up to the nineteenth century. The Latin original of Bucer's letter to à Lasco is now for the first time edited in this work. And as certain passages of the original had been omitted by the English translators, passages which had no straight relation to Elizabethan conditions of church life, it is of importance to get the original Latin version published. Three letters of à Lasco (à Lasco's letters were, of course, not included in the collection of the letters translated into English, as not being of first-hand importance like those of Hooper, Cranmer, Martyr or Bucer) escaped the notice of à Lasco's bibliographer, Kuyper, and are also brought here for the first time.

The story of the letters, employed as evidence against the Puritans under Elizabeth, can be briefly stated. John Strype writes:

> The whole letter [of Bucer to à Lasco] was translated into English, and set forth not far from the beginning of Queen Elizabeth's reign, for the use of the Church, that then was exercised afresh with the same controversy; . . .[1]

And Walter Haddon writes to Matthew Parker, the archbishop, who had to give the authoritative statement against the Puritans:

> . . . Hoc etiam rectissime factum est, quod *Buceri* sententiam & *Petri Martyris* apponi curavisti; quorum auctoritas licet sola plebeiorum istorum, & novitiorum commenta frangere posset: tamen perfectissimi Theologi tam graviter in his caussis argumentati sunt, ut ipsis rationem momentis omnibus satisfieri possit, qui secum aures sinceras, & nullis errorem praejudiciis occupatas afferre volunt. Quapropter in doctrina satis arbitror esse processum; in disciplina reliquum esse debet, ut illorum importunitas poena divinciatur, qui contra Principis edictum, & publicas Ecclesiae constitutiones in rebus arbitrariis vociferantur . . . (June, 1566).[2]

[1] John Strype: *Ecclesiast. Memorials*, vol. II, part I, p. 352 (ed., Oxford, 1822).
[2] Roger Ascham: *Epist.*, op. cit., p. 445; n. 8 in the appendix of letters to this chapter.

A small book was edited by the Queen's printer (presumably in 1566): 'a briefe examination for the tyme of a certain declaration . . .' It was published anonymously, but by official authority. It was the answer to a certain Puritan writing, 'A briefe Discourse against the outwarde Apparell and Ministring Garmentes of the Popishe Church'. The 'briefe examination' was a reply, as it states on the title-page, against

> a certaine declaration, lately put in print in the name and defence of certaine Ministers in London, refusyng to weare the apparell prescribed by the lawes and orders of the Realme. In the ende is reported the iudgement of . . . M. doctour Bucer . . .

As the vestment rubric of the Prayer Book was not abolished under Elizabeth, as had been attempted by the Swiss Party under Edward VI, all the clergy had to submit to it. On those grounds the new controversy arose, since many ministers at London refused to obey. The struggle was fierce and Parker had not an easy stand, but tried rigorously to proceed against the disobedient ministers.[1] At that time their 'Discourse' was hurriedly printed. Steps were taken against the circulation of the illegally printed work. The 'briefe examination' was the answer, whether or not its production was due to Parker's influence. Frequent use of Bucer's testimony as regards those questions, was made by the writer of this pamphlet:

> J shall wyshe them to haue a respecte to theyr former callyng and profession of the Gospell . . . Trustyng that they wyll so aduisedly expende the earnest counsell of these two notable Fathers, Maister Bucer, and maister Martir, in this their purposed discussyng of the cause, that they wyll finally rest in quiet . . .[2]

The Puritans were not in the least satisfied by this work. Their tendency was to claim Bucer as being on their side, and they accused their opponents of having not only misinterpreted him, but having ignored the fact that he could not be said to be their authority. They replied to the 'examination' by another pamphlet:

> An answere for the tyme, to the examination put in print, without the authours name, pretending to mayntayne the apparrell prescribed against the declaration of the mynisters of London . . . answering point for point the statements of the examination.[3]

[1] W. H. Frere's account ('Grappling with Puritanism', pp. 111-128, in: *The English Church in the Reigns of Elizabeth & James I*) of the controversy in the time of Elizabeth is an excellent study, which ought to be read in conjunction with this chapter.

[2] fol. ++1 in 'a briefe examination' (to the Christian reader).

[3] 1566. With special reference to Bucer on pp. 18, 36 and 38, 125-129.

Apart from their 'answer' to the 'Examination' there exist letters and writings, which illustrate the Puritan reaction to the claim of the 'Examination', to employ Bucer's writings in the warfare against the Puritans. Thus L. Humphrey and Thomas Sampson write to Henry Bullinger (July 1566):

> That the prescribing habits [to the clergy] is inconsistent with christian liberty, we have the testimony of Bucer, who was of opinion that the distinction of dress should be entirely done away with, as well on account of the present abuse of it in the English churches, as for a more decided declaration of our abhorrence of antichrist, a more full assertion of our christian liberty, and the removal of dissensions amongst brethren. These words he made use of in his letter to master à Lasco, who was altogether on our side . . .[1]

In the same letter they complain that their opponents had translated Bucer's letters into English and published them for their own purpose. In the controversy with Whitgift, a few years later (about 1573), Cartwright, who had been reminded by Whitgift of Bucer's views on these special points in his letters, blames him, that he had withheld the letters by not printing them. A similar accusation he had already made against Whitgift as regards the print of Bucer's *Censura*. Cartwright writes:

> But, if this epistle [i.e. Bucer's letter to à Lasco], and others of M. Bucer's, with his notes upon the book of common prayer, which are so often cited, . . . were never printed (as I cannot understand they were); then, besides that you do us injury, which go about to prejudice our cause by the testimonies of them, which we can neither hear nor see, being kept close in your study, you also do your cause much more injury, whilst you betray the poverty and nakedness of it, being fain to ransack and ruffle up every dark corner, to find something to cover it with. Therefore it were good, before you took any benefit of them, to let them come forth, and speak their own testimonies, in their own language, and full out. For now you give men occasion to think that there are some other things in their epistles which you would be loth the world should know, for fear of fall of that which you would gladly keep.

To which Whitgift answers:

> The place of M. Bucer maketh directly for my purpose; and therefore, in giving place unto it, you grant as much as I hitherto

[1] *Zurich Letters*, 1558-1579 (Parker Society, 1842), pp. 157 ff., 161, 162; cf. also *Zurich Letters*, 1558-1602, 2nd Series (Parker Society, 1845), p. 120: John Abel to H. Bullinger, June 6th, 1566.

> have required. For M. Bucer used the example of apparel, which is one thing in controversy betwixt us, and saith plainly that the church hath authority to appoint such things, as have neither commandment nor example in the scripture. These epistles of M. Bucer, and of M. Martyr, with the epistles of other learned men, be printed and published wholly and fully, and it cannot be that the same should be unknown unto you, the books being so common: your pleading of ignorance in this is but a colour.[1]

Whitgift's surprise that Cartwright had not seen the pamphlet containing the letters is sincere and justified. The book was printed at the time of Cartwright's objections and accessible to everybody. The original Latin version of the letters, of course, was still only known in manuscript form.

But the Puritans were not content with criticizing only, they aimed higher. They attempted to unearth writings of Bucer of an earlier period which they thought would serve their purpose. Thus they turned to Bucer's Commentary on the Gospels, where they supposed to find easily a statement relating to the question of rites and ceremonies.

The 'briefe discourse' quotes Bucer in his exposition on S. Matthew, ch. xviii, in order to maintain that the Strassburg reformer was on the side of those who were opposed to the use of the ornaments. But in reply to this claim the 'briefe examination' does not find it difficult to discharge the statement made by the 'briefe discourse'. The 'briefe discourse' had written:

> And in such case as we are nowe, he [i.e. Bucer] willeth, that in no case they should be receyued: as doth most plainly appeare in that which he wrote vpon the xviij chapter of S. Mathewes gospel, and vpon these wordes: *Vae mundo ob offendiculis*, Woo to the worlde by the reason of offences or occasions of fallings: wherafter manye wordes to this effecte, he sayth: That no man will earnestlye stryue to maintayne these superstitious ceremonies, but such as be eyther open enimies of Christ, or else backeslyders from Christ. *Hostes aut desertores* . . . (fol. C, verso).

That part of his commentary to the Gospel of S. Matthew (ch. xviii) which they thought made for their purpose, was translated and edited as a special small pamphlet:

> The mynd and exposition of that excellente learned man Martyn Bucer/ vppon these wordes of S. Mathew: woo be to the wordle

[1] Whitgift, op. cit., vol. I, p. 259; ibid., p. 261. cf. also vol. II, pp. 38 ff., pp. 56 f., p. 584.

[*sic*] bycause of offences. Math. XVIII. Faythfully translated into Englishe, by a faythfull brother, with certayne objections & answeres to the same.[1]

It contains a passage of Bucer's Commentary on the Gospel. By this the editor of the 'briefe examination', quoting the passage in extenso, attempts to establish proof against the Puritans' claims. The 'briefe examination' argues thus:

> But you (peraduenture) fearyng leste this his saying [i.e. Bucer's] were not so strong vpon your part as you wyshed, you farther say, that he wylleth in suche case as ye are nowe, in no wyse to receyue them. Wherevnto you cite his exposition vpon the. xviii. Chapter of Saint Mathew. This place yf you would haue indifferently rehearsed, you should haue opened to the worlde, that his mynde was, that some ceremonies abused, might be styl retained. His wordes are these, in the begynning almost of that his exposition: *Fateor equidem, licet ab Antichristis inuectum sit. &c.* Though whatsoeuer thing is decreed, contrary to the libertie of externe matters, it hath ben brought in by Antichristes, as the difference of persons, meates, dayes, places, and very many moe: yet because commonly men were perswaded that all those thynges were the commaundementes of the Churche directed by the spirite of God, so receyued all those thynges as comming from the wyll of God: I acknowledge in deede, that reason it is, we vse circumspectly euen now the libertie obtayned by Christ, and with Paule sometyme circumcise Timothy, that is, that we vse well some ceremonies, whiche others abused, takyng occasion thereby to teach Christ purely, although by no meanes these inuentions of man can be compared with circumcision, or the lyke ordinaunces of God. Thus farre Doctour Bucer. In this sentence though many thinges may be noted: as that the false opinion of men dyd not perswade hym to caste all these thinges away: as that these thinges were not to be refused, because they were the deuises of man: . . . yet it shall suffise to put you in mynde, that he thynketh godly men may well vse some rites whiche were abused before tyme. So that if you take one peece of his exposition with another, you shal not neede to terme your betters and felowe seruauntes in Christ that receiue this apparell, to be enemies or shrinkers.[2]

The writer of the 'Examination' reveals clearly the methods by which the Puritans tried to convince, and where Bucer actually stood. And yet, here in the small pamphlet published by the Puritans in the same year (1566) as the 'discourse', they bring the

[1] Printed at Emden, 1566.
[2] 'Briefe examination', pp. ++++++1 verso ++++++2.

same passage of Bucer,[1] which was so obviously proved by their opponents as speaking in favour of those rites, and against those, who by publishing it, tended to make Bucer their ally.

Although the bishops' party had to admit that Bucer, in his letter to Hooper, wrote

> that he woulde haue ben at some great coste, so that this controuersie eyther had neuer ben moued, or very speedyly repressed and extinct,[2]

they are yet entitled to claim him on their side, as his other writings prove. And although Bucer's words are sometimes ambiguous, and as apparently he would prefer a reduction of the use of vestments, yet he would never have put forth those arguments, which Hooper and now again the Puritans employed. The fact that both parties used Bucer's writings for their argumentation, might lead to the conclusion that Bucer had avoided committing himself on either side. But it is quite obvious from his writings, that the Puritans were not justified of claiming him as on their side. That both parties attempted to get his support is strong evidence for the assertion that his opinion was regarded as authority. If they say 'Preceptes of men must not be receyued' the bishops, like Parker or Whitgift are entitled to quote Bucer against them, as the 'Examination' does.[3]

And if they are accused by the writer of the 'Examination' 'to disturbe politicall order lawfully taken', Bucer as stated in his letter to Cranmer, would never have objected to laws which had been approved by the Government.

[1] The translation of that passage in the Emden copy 1566 'The mynd and exposition . . .' runs thus: (fol. B.ii. verso to B.iij): 'In dede I confesse y[t] what so euer hath ben ordeyned against the libertie of externall thynges, as difference of persons, meates, dayes, places, & other like thinges innumerable, hath ben alltogether brought in by the rable of Antichrist: yet because the comon people were persuaded that all suche thinges were commaundementes of the Church, ruled and guyded by goddes spirite: therfore they receaued them generally as thynges procedinge from godes will and appoyntmente. And for this cause we muste euen in these oure dayes be circumspect in vsynge the libertie purchased for vs by Christ, and with Paul somtymes circumcise Timothy: that is to say, for oure partes, vse well some ceremonyes which other men abuse: sekyng (as it were) an occasion by that meanes, to preache Christ syncerely and purely. Albeit thes inuentions of men can by no meanes be compared to circumcision and such like ordinances of God . . .'

[2] 'Examination', fol. ++++++1 verso.

[3] Doctour Bucer vpon this place may teache you the same, who most godly pronounceth thus: *Quicquid homo statuerit, quod quomodocunque ad vsum proximorum faciat. &c.* Whatsoeuer man shall decree, whiche by any meanes may make to the vse of his neighboures, for that the same is deriued from the rule of charitie, as be lawes ciuill, domesticall statutes, ceremonies and rytes whiche Christian men vse, thereby to teache or heare Goddes worde more commodiouslye, or to praye, and about the Lordes Supper and Baptisme, yea, & whatsoeuer shalbe a furtheraunce to passe our lyfe here more profitablye and decently: that thing ought not to be esteemed as a tradition or precept of man, though by men it be commaunded, but as the tradition or precept of god. Thus farre Doctour Bucer. (The author then quotes Calvin as in accordance with Bucer's teaching: Inst. lib. 4, cp. 10, par. 30). (fol. +++3).

The special reference of the 'Examination' to the first clause of Article 34 of the Thirty-Nine Articles:

> Whosoever through his private judgement, willingly and purposely, doth openly break the traditions and ceremonies of the Church, which be not repugnant to the Word of God, and be ordained and approved by common authority, ought to be rebuked openly . . .

is meant as a warning.[1]

And here again it is stressed that if Bucer would have liked the repression of vestments, he would have desired that only as done 'not by priuate auctoritie' but 'that they were orderly put away'.[2]

The passage in his *Censura* referring to the problem, was not known to the Puritans, as the *Censura* was not printed up to 1577. And although he advocates there the abolition of vestments, the Puritans would hardly have gained anything by referring to this passage. For his argument is not, as they argued, that the vestments were 'in themselves' anti-Christian, or that 'pious men' could not use them 'piously'.[3] In this connection another attempt by one of the Puritans to show Bucer as their ally should be mentioned: the author[4] of 'A petition directed to her most excellent Maiestie . . .' refers to a passage in a letter of Bishop Pilkington to the Earl of Leicester, in which it is said that Bucer, when he was asked why he did not use a square cap answered, 'Because my head is not square'. To make use

[1] 'Examination', fol. +++++++2.

[2] ibid., fol. +++++++1 verso, fol. ++++++2.

[3] Quartum in hac praescriptione est, de vestibus quibus vti debeant ministri in ministrando. Has opto vestes tolli, non quod credam in ipsis quicquam esse impij per se, vt pij homines illis non possint pie vti: sed quia video illas nimis multis esse superstitioni (desunt enim passim Ecclesijs idonei Doctores) tum nunc quoque raptas etiam ad materiam contentionis nocentioris multo quam quisquam satis explicauerit. Ad haec consentaneum est contentionis crucis Christi, adspirare nos, vt exteris rebus omnibus, ita & externo ministrorum cultu ad simplicitatem Christi seruatoris & Apostolorum; tum testari modis omnibus, nihil esse nobis cõmune cum illis, ac ideo minime omnium cum Romanensibus Antichristis, libertatem denique Christianam, quibusuis in rebus praeclare tueri & prae nobis ferre. *Scr. Angl.*, p. 458: *Censura*.

[4] F. J. Powicke: *Henry Barrow* . . . (London, 1900), disavows that Henry Barrow is the author of the 'petition', usually ascribed to him. 'A petition directed to her most excellent Maiestie, wherein is deliuered . . .' (anonym. no place, no date), claims, on p. 74, Bucer on his side, by referring to a passage in a letter of Bishop Pilkington to the Earl of Leicester, where Bucer is stated to have said: 'Bucer, when he was asked why he did not wear "quadrato pileo", made answer, "Quia caput non est quadratum".'

cf. *The Works of James Pilkington* (Parker Society), Cambridge, vol. MDCCCXLII, p. 662, letter of October 25th, 1564.

Peter Heylyn (*Ecclesia Restaurata, or The History of the Reformation of the Church of England:* . . . London, MDCLXI, p. 92) refers to the same incident but claims David Calderwood's *Altare Damascenum* as the author of this 'calumnious' statement: 'And by this Passage we may rectifie a Mistake, or a Calumny rather, in the *Altare Damascenum*. The *Authour* whereof makes *Martin Bucer* Peremptory, in refusing to wear the *Square Cap*, when he lived in *Cambridg;* and to give this simple Reason for it: *That he could not wear a Square Cap, since his Head was Round.*'

of this rather legendary remark of Bucer, which seems scarcely to bear any relation to the question at stake, characterizes the mentality of men, who in order to achieve their purposes, did not even shrink from having recourse to absurd gossip.

In conclusion it can be said that Cranmer's anticipation of the course Bucer would take in the controversy proved to be right. Bucer, who had already, before he was asked by the archbishop, taken his firm stand against the 'Father of Nonconformity', Hooper, in spite of all the efforts made by the Puritans to interpret his writings as in their favour, did stick to his points. The question of order, the question of obedience to the authorities, the question of continuity and tradition for the Church, the question of authorization of rites and ceremonies which had no scriptural warrant, were all answered in the affirmative. The argument of Hooper and his partisans, that the vestments in themselves were anti-Christian and not things indifferent, and their approach to the problem was regarded by Bucer as besides the mark. The use of vestments can turn into abuse, as the Lord's Supper was still abused and celebrated by some ministers in the way of the Mass. There, in the mentality towards rites and ceremonies, lies the root of the problem. If that mentality was reverent and free from 'Popish and superstitious' interpretations, there would be no need for waging war against the outcomes of a conception which in itself was wrong. That is Bucer's real conviction. And therefore for him Hooper and his circle deceived themselves, as they did not understand the means by which a real Reformation could be aimed at. His final judgement may be seen from a passage in his letter to William Bill:

> Absit enim, ut ego meam onerem conscientiam eo horrendo abusu, quo his vestibus nimis multi sacrificuli, ut etiam cunctis, quamvis sanctissimis verbis et ritibus, quae ad sacram communionem sint proscripta in libro publicorum sacrorum Angliae, abutuntur, ad commendandum tam quantum possunt abominationem Missae suae, quam palam dicunt se in administratione coenae facere. Atque utinam, qui usum vestium istarum oppugnant, eum ex hoc manifesto abusu oppugnarent, et non ex eo quamsi per se impium sit, quo modo liber uti rebus, quae fuerunt vel in usu Aharonico, vel in abusu sacerdotii Papistici . . .[1]

We have seen the way in which Bucer approached the problem; how firmly he had answered the questions put before him by Cranmer; the manner in which he spoke against Hooper, and by what means

[1] cf. Harvey, op. cit., p. 153.

his letters were used as evidence against the Puritans by the Elizabethan divines. It is surely not unreasonable to ascribe in part to this influence the retention of the custom of using vestments in the Church of England.

We annex to this chapter correspondence of Bucer relating to the controversy, correspondence which to a great extent has not yet been published:

(a) cf. *J.T.S.*, July-October 1943; pp. 194-199.
(1) à Lasco's Letter to Bucer, October 12th, 1550.
MS. Rawlinson D.346.
(2) Bucer's Letter to à Lasco, October 20th(?), 1550.
MS. Rawlinson D.346.
MS. New College D.343.
(Cambridge Univ. Libr.) MS. Mm. IV, 14.
(British Museum) Add. MSS. 28571.
(3) Peter Martyr's Letter to Bucer, October 25th, 1550.
MS. New College 343.
(4) à Lasco's Letter to Bucer, October 26th, 1550.
MS. New College 343.
MS. Rawlinson D.346.
(5) à Lasco's Letter to Bucer, November 15th, 1550.
MS. New College 343.
(6) William Bill's Letter to Bucer, November 5th, 1550.
MS. Rawlinson D.346.
MS. New College 343.
Harvey, op. cit., n. IX, pp. 141-143.
(7) Cranmer's Letter to Bucer, December 2nd, 1550.
MS. New College 343 (autograph).
MS. Rawlinson D.346.
cf. Pocock, op. cit., pp. 130-131.
(8) W. Haddon's Letter to Matthew Parker, June 1566.
Roger Ascham, *Epist.* (ed. 1703), p. 445.

In order to have a quicker survey of the chronology of the correspondence the following table of dates might prove useful, to which is added the order of the pamphlets of the Elizabethan divines and the Puritans, in which partly letters of Bucer were also printed.[1]

[1] To this table the letter of William Bill to Bucer (November 5th, 1550) and Bucer's reply to W. Bill (November 17th, 1550) ought to be added, as dealing with similar questions and referring to the vestment controversy (Bill's letter to Bucer is now for the first time published in extenso). The greater part is printed by Harvey, op. cit., n. IX, pp. 141 ff. Bucer's reply to Bill, see Harvey, op. cit., n. X, pp. 143 ff.

October 12th, 1550, à Lasco's Letter to Bucer (now for the first time published).

October 17th, 1550, Hooper's Letter to Bucer, cf. Gorham, op. cit., n. LII, pp. 185 f.[1]
Latin: Hooper's Works, op. cit., vol. II, p. xiv.

October 20th(?), 1550, Bucer's Letter to à Lasco (now for the first time published in its Latin Original).

October 25th, 1550, Peter Martyr's Letter to Bucer (now for the first time published).

October 26th, 1550, à Lasco's Letter to Bucer (now for the first time published).

November 4th, 1550, Peter Martyr's Letter to Hooper, cf. Gorham, op. cit., n. LIII, pp. 187 ff.

November (?), 1550, Bucer's Letter to Hooper, cf. Gorham, op. cit., n. LV, pp. 200 ff.
Latin: *Scripta Anglicana*, pp. 705 ff.

November 11th, 1550, P. Martyr's Letter to Bucer, cf. Gorham, op. cit., n. LIV, pp. 196 ff.

November 15th, 1550, à Lasco's Letter to Bucer (now for the first time published).

December 2nd, 1550, Cranmer's Letter to Bucer, see appendix, n. 7, and Pocock, op. cit., pp. 130-131.

December 8th, 1550, Bucer's Letter to Cranmer, cf. Gorham, op. cit., n. LVIII, pp. 214 ff.
Latin: *Scripta Anglicana*, pp. 681 ff.

Chronological order of the Elizabethan pamphlets relative to the controversy:

A briefe discourse against the outwarde apparell and Ministring garmentes of the popishe church.
psalme. 31.
I haue hated all those, that holde of superstitious vanities.
Robert Crowley. 1566.

The mynd and exposition of that excellente learned man Martyn Bucer/ vppon these wordes of S. Mathew: woo be to the wordle [*sic*] bycause of offences. Math. XVIII. Faythfully translated into Englishe, by a faythfull brother, with certayne objections & answeres to the same. Printed at Emden 1566.

A briefe examination for the tyme, of a certaine declaration, lately put in print in the name and defence of certaine Ministers in London, refusying to weare the apparell prescribed by the lawes and orders of the Realme.

[1] Our references to C. Gorham are made, as there the letters are translated already into English.

In the ende is reported, the iudgement of two notable learned fathers, M. doctour Bucer, and M. doctour Martir, sometyme in eyther vniuersities here of England the kynges readers and professours of diuinitie, translated out of the originals, written by theyr owne handes, purposely debatyng this controuersie.

col. Imprinted at London in Powles Churchyarde by Richarde Iugge, Printer to the Queenes Maiestie.
Cum priuilegio Regiae Maiestatis.

VVhether it be mortall sinne to transgresse ciuil lawes, which be the commaundementes of ciuill Magistrates.

The iudgement of Philip Melancton in his Epitome of morall Philosophie. The resolution of D. Hen. Bullinger, and. D. Rod. Gualter, of D. Martin Bucer, and. D. Peter Martyr, concernyng thapparrel of Ministers, and other indifferent thinges.

page 101 *verso*:
Imprinted at London in Powles Churchyarde by Richarde Iugge, Printer to the Queenes Maiestie.
Cum priuilegio Regiae Maiestatis.

An ansvvere *for the tyme, to the* Examination put in print, vvith out the authours name, pretending to mayntayne the apparrell prescribed against the declaration of the mynisters of London.

Phillip. III.

As many as be perfect, let vs be thus mynded but if you be othervvise mynded, god shall reuele euen the same to you.

M.D.LXVI. [1]

§ I

APPENDIX OF LETTERS

(1)

à Lasco's Letter to Bucer, October 12th, 1550.
MS. Rawlinson D.346, fol. 4.

Post meum huc reditum totus eram hactenus in transferenda suppellectilj mea et migratione e Lambeto huc Londinum, vir doctissime, necdum plane mea hic Londinj composui omnia. Deinde in causa nostrarum Ecclesiarum perpetuus prope modum esse cogor. itaque

[1] The following letters are contained in the 'Examination' as well as in 'whether it be mortall sinne . . .': (in contemporary English):
1 Cranmer to Bucer, December 2nd, 1550.
2 Bucer to Cranmer, December 8th, 1550.
3 Hooper to Bucer, October 17th, 1550.
4 Martyr to Hooper, November 4th, 1550.
5 Bucer to à Lasco, October 20th, 1550.

dabis ueniam, quod interea ad te nihil literarum dedi. Hoperum [*Hoperus?*] re salutarij uerbis tuis agit gratias & se tibi[1] uicissim uoluit diligenter commendarj. Magnum illi certamen de uestibus illis Epālibus imminere uidetur. rogatus quam cum ipso sentirent, catalogum omnium conscripsit. atque inter alios te quoque nominauit. adiecit Petrum Martyrem, Bernardinum, et me atque inter Anglos complures. Summa uero sententiae suae est, Vestes illas, per se quidem, ut creaturas Dej non esse malas: sed usum illarum relatiue esse impium. hoc est quatenus & Papistici sacerdotij reliquiae ac notae sunt, atque etiamnum habentur in Papatu. discrimenque illud Papisticum clerj a reliqua ecclesia alit: non sine contumelia sacerdotij clerj. Et quod de singularj ministrorum in Ecclesia apparatu uestiario neque mandatum neque exemplum ullum extare uideamus. Imo uideamus Patronos istiusmodj uestium fateri, hoc genus uestium ad imitationem Aaronici sacerdotij inuecta esse. quod suum peculiarem olim uestium apparatum habebat. Itaque hanc talem uestium istarum usum damnat Hoperus: Et medium atque indifferentem esse negat. Hic uero meam quoque sententiam rogat: Sed ego utilius fore putarem, si omnes nos, hoc est, tu, Petrus Martyr, Bernardinus et ego eandem sententiam daremus. Atque ego quidem, id quod te alioque nosse puto, ab Hopero hac in parte non dissentio. sed libenter tuam quoque sententiam haberem. Quare te oro ne graueres [graueris?] paucis quod his [hic?] sentias indicare. Nos his[?] iam quattuor seniores Ecclesiae nostrae uiros, gratia[s] Deo, probos pios gre-[?] & non indoctos eligimus.[2] Et totidem Diaconos q. curam egenorum habeant. Ad octauum diem ego me ipse coram Ecclesia sistam[?]ut audiam num me pro suo ministro habere uelit. ibidem faciet et Martinus Flander collega formam ceremoniarum nondum licuit [?] absoluere. ubj absoluero[?] ad te mittetur formam disciplinae abs te expecto. Et oro ut illam accelerius[?] capita tua de Eucharistia legi: & quae me offendant per otium indicabo. Vale uir sanctiss. et ministerium nostrum quod orsi sumus Deo tuis precibus quaeso commendare[?]. Ego et uxor mea optamus, tibi et tuae toti familiae fausta et felicia uosque saluica[?] cupimus.

Londinj 12 Octob. 1550. Joannes a.Lasco

(original)

Peter Martyr in a letter to Bucer (November 11th, 1550, from Oxford) refers probably to this letter:

> Possibly Master à Lasco may have signified to you, as he has to me, his earnest desire that some Confession on the Sacramentarian Question should be drawn up and set forth, in such a way that you,

[1] se tibi (?) (*or:* scribi (?)).

[2] elegimus (?).

Bernardine, he, and myself might consent to it. I answered, that I did not disapprove his design; and I advised him to talk the matter over with you. I took this course, because I feel assured that, if both of you should subscribe to the same opinion, it would be easy for me also to accede to it. Now, if this intimation has not been made from himself, you have from me what is in his mind. (cf. Gorham, op. cit. n. LIV, pp. 198-199.)

(2)

Bucer's Letter to à Lasco, October 20th(?), 1550.

(1) The original Latin draft in Bucer's own handwriting is to be found in the Rawlinson collection of manuscripts (MS. Rawlinson D.346, fol. 9-15, in the Bodleian Library).
(2) A contemporary copy, presumably by Bucer's amanuensis, with corrections in Bucer's own handwriting is preserved in the Bodleian in MS. New College, CCCXLIII.
(3) Another copy written by an English hand, is at the Cambridge University Library (MS. Mm. IV, 14(3), fol. 6-8), which omits certain passages, also omitted later in the English translation of the letter.
(4) Still another Latin copy of the letter is to be found in the 'Additions to the MSS. in the British Museum, 1854-1875', p. 510, Add. MS. 28571 n. 5, fol. 27. In the Catalogue of the Additions the date is given as '(October 20th, 1550)'. English Translations of the letter in:

(1) 'a briefe examination for the tyme, of a certaine declaration . . .' Imprinted at London in Powles Churchyarde by Richarde Iugge, Printer to the Queenes Maiestie. Cum priuilegio Regiae Maiestatis. fol. C3-D4, v.
(2) VVhether it be mortall sinne to transgresse ciuil lawes, which be the commaundementes of ciuill Magistrates. The iudgement of Philip Melancton in his Epitome of morall Philosophie. The resolution of D. Hen. Bullinger, and. D. Rod. Gualter, of D. Martin Bucer, and. D. Peter Martyr, concernyng thapparrel of Ministers, and other indifferent thinges. – Imprinted at London in Powles Churchyarde by Richarde Iugge, Printer to the Queenes Maiestie. Cum priuilegio Regiae Maiestatis. pp. 81-101.
(3) Strype, John: *Ecclesiastical Memorials* . . . (ed. Oxford, 1822), vol. II, part II, pp. 444 ff. n. LL.

The manuscript volumes of Cambridge, the Bodleian, New College and British Museum contain the letter among other contemporary letters related to the controversy, which seems to suggest that a collection of letters was intended as a combined statement. Thus in the 'briefe examination' Bucer's letter to à Lasco appears among an equivalent collection of letters related to the controversy:

(1) Cranmer to Bucer
(2) Bucer to Cranmer
(3) Hooper to Bucer
(4) Martyr to Hooper
(5) Bucer to à Lasco

Bucer's own original manuscript draft provides the basic text for that here reproduced. As Bucer's handwriting is — to say the least — difficult to read, it is not surprising to find many discrepancies and deviations between the various copies of the letter. The English copyist (C)[1] has most variants in his copy, finding it hard, apparently, to decipher the original. The copy with corrections in Bucer's own hand (NC)[2] — although in small points occasionally differing from the original — serves well as guide to Bucer's original draft. We have not indicated all variations in the various copies. Passages in brackets (indicated by a line in the margin) are only to be found in the original draft (Rawlinson) and in the NC copy, and are omitted in C and in the English translation. The page numbers in the margin (pp. 444 ff.) refer to the English translation in Strype's *Memorials*.

A few quotations from the letter are printed in Glocester Ridley: *The Life of Dr. Nicholas Ridley* (London, 1763):

here:		
p. 153: Quid enim vetet — officii sui	cf. Ridley,	op. cit., p. 320, note
p. 155: Aharonicas — significaret	cf. ,,	p. 317, note
p. 155: Si enim nullo liceat . . .		p. 318, note g
p. 155: Usus tintin. — sacras act.		p. 317, note b
p. 155: Ita quid — deserviat		p. 317, note f
pp. 155-156: Distribut. — cultui Christi		p. 318, note
pp. 158-159: Summa itaque — salutaris obtin.		pp. 320-1, note l
p. 160: res multas quas — pl. alia		p. 318, note g.

MS. Rawlinson, D.346, fol. 9-15.[3]

444 Amplissime Domine & colendissime symmysta.

S.D. Det nobis Dominus, ut his Ecclesiae eius difficilibus temporibus sic instituamus, atque peragamus omnia, ne scandala

[1] Cambridge—copy.
[2] New College—copy.
[3] C (= Cambridge Copy): Domino Joanni à Lasco, M. Bucerus,

illi augeantur & pericula, Amen. Equidem quo diligentius circumspicio et considero quid fructum praecipiamus[1] de illa controversia vestium, quid etiam adhuc per eam Satan moliatur: optarim coram Domino, ne verbo quidem esse motam: omnes vero interim nostri ministerij homines in docenda poenitentia salutarique rerum omnium usu, adeoque in commendandis sumendisque vestibus salutis, consentienter atque strenue percepisse[2] ac pergere. Video enim, vir ornatissime, apud non paucos, proh dolor, video mirum studium in abolendo Amaleko, in lapidibus, ligno, vestibus et his rebus, quae extra nos sunt, qui interim in suis studijs vitaque (sua)[3] universa totum Amalek tenacissime retinent. Novi etiam qui hanc rixam adiuvant: ut interea minus curentur & vigeantur [*vrgeantur?*] illa prima & summe necessaria de submovendis ab Ecclesiarum spolijs sacrilegis de parandis singulis parochijs indoneis ministris de restitutione disciplinae.

Mihi, si ceremoniae & vestes illae per se impiae[4] haberentur, donec tollerentur ab ordinaria potestate, Episcopalem procurationem in me nunquam susciperem.

|| Et ut ego illum nostrum novi existimarim eum ad Evangelistae quam Episcopi munus esse aptiorem. Donum Τῆς γυβερνήσεως late patet atque per amplam sapientiam nullumque (vitae) usum requirit. Sed novit ille humeros suos. ||

Verum rerum humanarum ad rem quamquam putem haudquaquam alienum esse ab hac [f. 9v] quaestione moneri nos ut probe observemus solitas illas Satanae artes quibus nos a cura necessariarum rerum ad solicitudinem abducit earum, quae possint differri ab inquisitione certae doctrinae Christi ad ea, de quibus pauci idem videre possunt: quibus denique mirum
445 zelum plerisque hominibus incendit purgandi quae extra nos sunt: ut intestinas sordes negligamus. Cum enim quicquid faciamus, verbo aut opere, tam privatim quam publice, facere debeamus in nomine D.n. Jesu, gratias agentes per ipsum Deo & patri, non minus profecto accurate debemus cavere, nequid vel usurpemus vel negligamus, cuius nobis non certa constet ratio ex ipso Dei verbo in actionibus atque rebus domesticis, atque in Ecclesiasticis. Semper & in rebus omnibus peccatum est, quod ex fide non est certi verbi Dei.

[5] Sed ad propositam quaestionem in se ipsa considerandam.

[1] percipiamus. [2] C and NC (= New College Copy): perrexisse.
[3] Words in brackets to be found in one of the other MS.—copies.
[4] C: impurae. [5] C: Sed redeamus ad propositam . . .

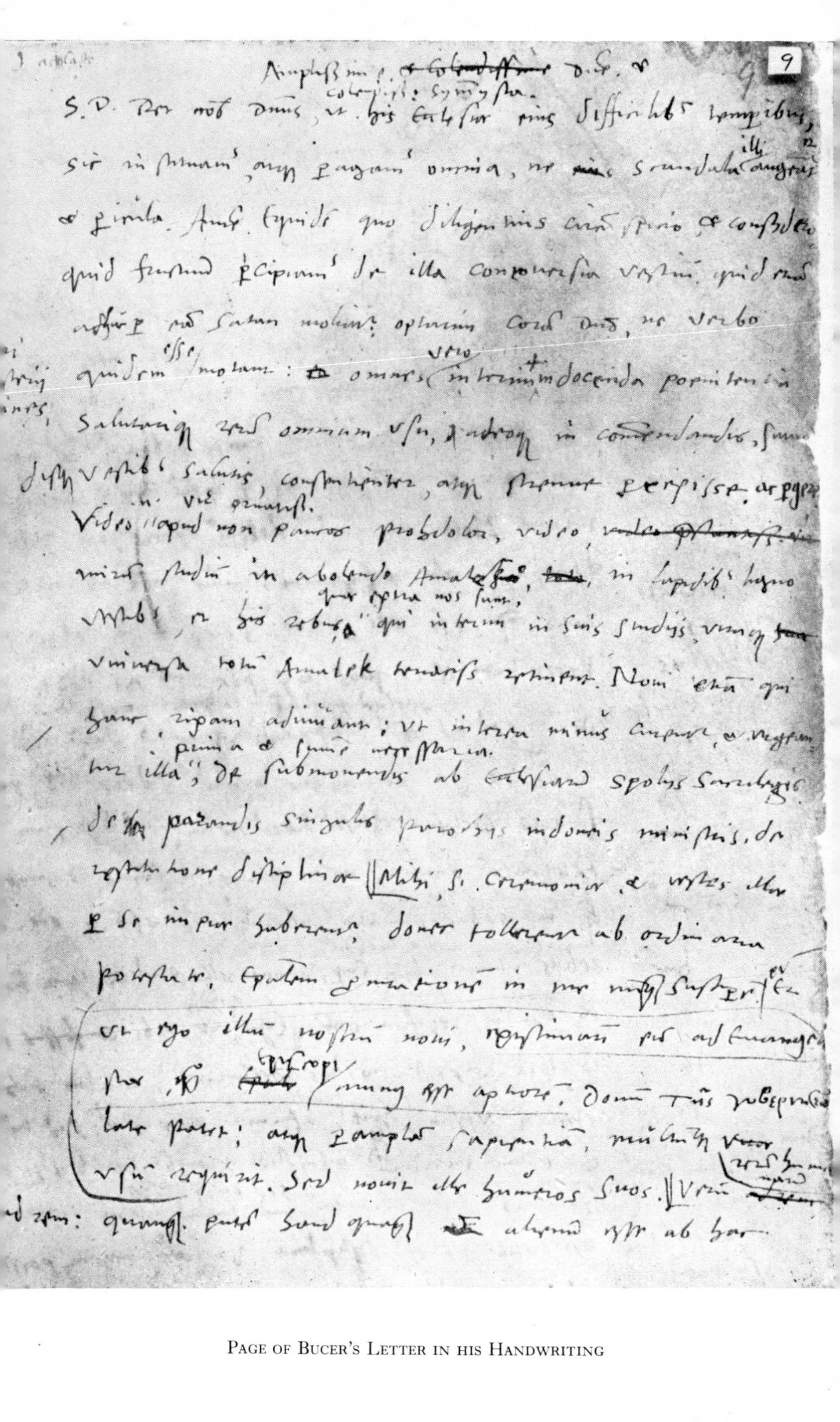

9

Page of Bucer's Letter in his Handwriting

41

Salve plurimum D. Bucere charissime. Legi librum
quem ad D. Petrum Alexandrum misisti de controversia
inter D. Hoperum et D. Londinensem, in quo multa
a te et docte explicata, et fuse disputata sunt.
Quare nunc oro ut sententiam tuam quanta poteris
verborum brevitate constrictam, de his quaestionibus
ad me mittas. An sine offensa Dei liceat ministris
ecclesiae Anglicanae, illis uti vestibus quibus
hodie utuntur, atque a magistratu praescriptae sunt.
An is qui affirmaverit nephas esse aut renu-
erit his vestibus uti, peccet in Deum, quia immundum esse dicit quod Deus sanctificavit, et in magistratus, quia violet ordinem politicum. Ad haec
si brevissime respondeas, et quid sentias, primo
quoque tempore ad me miseris, gratissimum mihi
facturus es. Meis omnibus tibi tuisque omnibus
plurimam salutem et prospera omnia de animo opto.
Vale. Lambethi 2o Decembris.

Tuae paternitatis studiosissimus
T. Cant.

Original of Cranmer's Letter to Bucer

(cf. pp. 169-170)

Expendi quantum datum est, tuas rationes, et tamen adhuc aliud videre non possum quam esse Ecclesijs Christi liberum relinquendum usum rerum externarum omnium nec minus in sacris ceremonijs quam in rebus privatis. Liberum autem usum, voco, quo pij homines rebus utuntur a deo conditis absque superstitione ulla & ad certam fidei in Christum aedificationem. Ego, quidem, ut tibi confessus sum, & re ipsa apud nostros declaravi, malim nihil a nostris retineri vestium quibus utuntur papistae: idque propter tum pleniorem Antichristiani sacerdotij detestationem, tum clariorem Christianae libertatis attestationem, denique etiam propter evitandas[1] noxias inter fratres contentiones. Sed tamen vestibus uti velim Ecclesiarum ministros gravibus, quibusque ab alijs hominibus discernerentur. Sed in primis velim vigere inter eos totam Christi disciplinam. Ut vero negem, posse ab Ecclesijs ac ministris veris Christi aliquid de vestibus quibus abutuntur Antichristi[2] usurpari absque superstitione et ad [fol. 10] certam fidei in Christum aedificationem, nullis certe me adhuc video scripturis adduci. Quid enim vetet Ecclesias Christi albam illam vestem, vel plures etiam usurpare praecise ad commonefactionem beneficij divini quod nobis praestat per sacrum Ecclesiae ministerium, beneficium lucis & dignitatis doctrinae celestis, per quod et ministri magis memores sint officij sui: & habeantur cum propter hoc
446 ipsum tum ex admonitu insignis istius in maiore a vulgo Ecclesiae veneratione. Velimus enim nolimus, fateri cogimur, insignia gerentium publica munera, conferre aliquid ad retinendam, augendamque magistratuum, publicaeque potestatis authoritatem, si caetera non desint, quibus vera reverentia his per se subsistit. Nam si haec non adsint, insignia illa, ingerunt non venerationem sed singularem potius detestationem eorum, qui his indigne utuntur virtutum notis. Signa quidem sunt signa non res. quantum tamen valeant ad monendum ac etiam movendum animos, dante incrementum Deo, qui observet, mirabitur.

Proinde, ubi caetera constet ministrorum vera dignitas, et consentiat Ecclesia aliqua publico iudicio, de vestibus quibusdam retinendis, et tantum ad quandam donorum Dei, quae Deus per Ecclesiae ministerium nobis praestat ad iuniorum[3] & rudiorum[4] commonefactionem, submota omni superstitione, equidem videre non possum cur non usus eiusmodi[5] vestium, in tali Ecclesia deseruire possit ad aliquam sacri ministerij commenda-

[1] C: evertendas. [2] C: sacerdotes. [3] NC: iuniores. [4] rudiores. [5] C: huiusmodi.

tionem ac proinde et ad aedificationem fidei. Nam quid prohibeat, ut eodem fidei spiritu praediti, non possint & hodie tam paucis signis, eadem pietate uti, qua veteres sancti usi sunt adeo multis. Habebant illi expressum de usu suorum signorum praeceptum[1] fateor, & hoc permultum [f. 10v.] ad pium eorum signorum usum valuisse non nego. At ex eo ipso, quod deus horum et tot signorum usum praecepit certo discimus posse ipso dante eorum signorum usum deservire promovendae purae religioni. Nec quicꝗ habere in se impuri aut superstitiosi nec posse etiam eum [*cum?*] abusu vitiari impiorum ut minus salutaris sit pijs hominibus pie usurpatis.[2] Iam cum nobis verbo suo, ad preces nostras sanctificet[3] Deus omnia, faciatque puris omnia pura, quid causae dicamus ex Dei verbo, ut negemus, Deum tali signorum, de quibus agimus, usui, in tali Ecclesia, non bene-
447 dicturum, ut ei Ecclesiae valeat ad nonnullam ministerij commendationem, atque proinde et ad aedificationem aliquam fidei. Qui enim promisit se benedicturum cunctis operibus manuum nostrarum, quae in eius nomine suscipimus, quomodo suam his signis benedictionem negaret, cum usum eorum talem qualem nos exposuimus, nusquam prohibuerit dominosque nos constituerit sabbathi ac rerum huius seculi omnium?

At si demus, haec ita uti commemoravi de talium signorum usu, fieri posse, fraternae prorsus et a Deo mandatae charitatis est, ut talium signorum, talem usum, in tali Ecclesia, liberum relinquamus talis Ecclesiae iudicio, & conscientiae: nisi apertum videamus abusum: vel superstitionis ut si res istae usurpentur tamque aliquid in se contineant cultus divini per se vel contemptionis ut si maiori, & saniori Ecclesiae parti displiceant: vel captatae male gratiae hominum, quibus non his rebus sit gratificandum quoque hoc illi ad quandam rapiant indignam Christianis servitutem.

Constabat D. Pauli sane tempore ex clarissimis Dei Scripturis Christianis liberum esse factum usum dierum, ciborum atque aliarum rerum externarum omnium: atque indubitatae infirmitatis in fide de hoc dubitare: tamen spiritus sanctus pronuntiat, infirmos huiusmodi suscipiendos esse, & non ad dijudicationem cogitationum, non debere contemni a robustioribus fide in his rebus unicuique concedendum ut de suo certus sensu sit: Dominum enim assumpsisse & hos infirmos. Si iam tantum vult spiritus sanctus deferre ijs, qui omnino in manifesto sunt errore, dum ab ipso pendent, in primarijs ac necessarijs partibus

[1] C: scriptum. [2] C: usurpantibus. [3] C: ad patres nostros significet . . . fecitque.

religionis syncerae, quid concedendum sit ijs, de rerum externarum libero usu, quos teneri errore convincere [fol. 11] ex Dei verbo non possumus? Nam,[1] quomodocunque versem & expendam duo illa vestra argumenta. Imitationes sunt Aharonici & notae sacerdotij Antichristiani, ideo defugiendae sunt amantibus Christum, non tamen apparet his concludi, id quod tu
448 instituisti. Aharonicas enim ceremonias imitari per se vitiosum non est, vitiosum tantum est, si quis eas usurparet tanquam ad salutem necessarias, aut ut Christum adhuc futurum in carnem significaret. Si enim nullo liceat modo ea quae fuerunt sacers dotij Aharonici ac etiam ethnici[2] neque templa fas est nohabere, nec ferias sacras observare. Nihil enim praecepti expressum verbis est in divinis Scripturis his de rebus. Colligitur tantum ab exemplo veteris populi, eas & nobis ad aedificandam pietatem esse utiles; idque comprobat experientia. Iam aliquid esse notam Antichristi, in nulla inest re in hoc enim nullae res conditae sunt a Deo: Sed pendet totum a consensu atque in Antichristianismum, et eius professione: quo consensu quaque professione commutatis consensu ac professione Christianismi, nihil potest in rebus ipsis haerere notae Antichristianismi. Usus tintinnabulorum erat nota Antichristianismi in nostris Ecclesijs, cum illis populus vocabatur ad Missas: cumque pulsarentur contra tempestates. nunc nota est Christianismi: cum illis congregatur populus ad Evangelium Christi et alias sacras actiones. Ita quid vetat ut eadem vestis apud impios impietatis notae, apud pios pietati deserviat? Novi equidem quam plurimos sanctissimos Christi ministros, qui tali veste sic pie usi sunt, et etiamnum utuntur, ut mihi profecto religio sit, ullum eis ob hanc rem peccatum adscribere, nedum peccatum tam atrox, communicationis cum Antichristo: ob quod renuncianda sit omnino Christi communio omnibus qui satis moniti eam communicationem cum Antichristis nolint deserere. Distributionem panis & calicis & sacrificuli daemonum in sacris Mithrae celebraverunt, ut Justinus Martyr[3] & Tertullianus[4] [fol. 11v]

[1] NC: Nam cum Deus res omnes mundi in hoc condiderit, ut illis utantur ad ipsius gloriam, quanta possim diligentia duo tua versem, e. expendam argumenta.

[2] NC adds: vsurpare.

[3] Justin Martyr: *Apologia* I, 66, 4: *Ὅπερ καὶ ἐν τοῖς τοῦ Μίθρα μυστηρίοις παρέδωκαν γίνεσθαι μιμησάμενοι οἱ πονηροὶ δαίμονες· ὅτι γὰρ ἄρτος καὶ ποτήριον ὕδατος τίθεται ἐν ταῖς τοῦ μυουμένου τελεταῖς μετ' ἐπιλόγων τινῶν, ἢ ἐπίστασθε ἢ μαθεῖν δύνασθε.*

[4] Tertullian: *De praescriptione haereticorum* XL, 1-4: . . . 2. A diabolo scilicet, cujus sunt partes intervertendi veritatem, qui ipsas quoque res sacramentorum divinorum idolorum mysteriis aemulatur . . . 4. et si adhuc memini Mithrae, . . . celebrat et panis oblationem . . . Also referred to in: 'A briefe examination', fol. +++++3.
cf. also Whitgift, op. cit., II, p. 39, notes 2 and 3.

meminerunt; quid autem id obstat, quo minus & nos eandem ceremoniam pie usurpemus? De hac vero ceremonia dicetis, habemus Domini praeceptum. Recte. Ex hoc ipso autem liquet, eandem rem, qua impij ad cultum abutuntur daemonum posse, apud filios Dei deservire cultui Christi, si Christi praeceptum
449 accedat. Christi autem praeceptum est, uti in sacris nostris omnia sic instituamus atque usurpemus, ut decorum & ordo servetur & fides aedificetur. Si qua iam Ecclesia indicet & experiatur etiam quales per multas esse hodie per Germaniam non dubito, vestis talis usum, apud suos nonnullam afferre commendationem sacri ministerij; atque ideo & ad decori, ordinisque rationem atque fidei instaurationem aliquid conferre, quid quaeso afferre ex Scripturis possim, cur ea Ecclesia non sit suo hac de re iudicio relinquenda nec ob id contemnenda, aut ad ullam iudicij sui disceptationem protrahenda. Servabit enim talis Ecclesia modum in his rebus cruci Christi congruentem & ne quis obrepat abusus, advigilabit. Si itaque talem vestium libertatem, usumque piae sanctaeque Ecclesiae non admittes, propterea quod mandatum de eo Domini & exemplum nullum habeat, non video, quomodo possis ulli Ecclesiae concedere ut coenam Domini celebret mane, & in aede publica, Dominoque singulariter consecrata: dispensentque[?][1] sacramenta genua flectentibus, aut etiam stantibus; ac mulieribus perinde atque viris. Nec enim mandatum Domini de his nec exemplum accepimus. Imo exemplum dedit Dominus contrarium: nam vesperi & in privata domo, coenam suam exhibuit, & sacramenta distribuit tantum viris & discumbentibus. Sed dicetur in Anglia plerique vestibus utuntur cum manifesta superstitione, & ad fovendum corroborandumque in populo superstitionem. Ita toto hoc sacramento abutuntur quam plurimi uti et Baptismate [fol. 12] atque ceremoniis universis. Huic itaque malo occurramus, totumque profligamus: eo autem ut ademptio vestium conferat aliquid; tamen ad depellendam hanc perniciem omnem haudquaquam sufficiet, ipsos oportebit sacrificulos submovere fidisque atque ad regnum
450 Christi & vere doctis & probe animatis commutare. In hoc ergo, in hoc, est nobis cum primis incumbendum fide enim purificantur omnia quia corda: fides vero tum gignitur tum augetur auditu verbi Dei: hic auditus affertur per Evangelij praedicatores. Hos itaque requiramus: atque ut copia eorum sit, urgeamus reformationem. Academiarum visitatio[2] sit unde quam

[1] C: dispensenturque. [2] vtque [?].

plurimi idonei Ecclesijs ministri parentur et ad ipsa aeternae salutis ministeria sustententur commode: clamare nunquam cessemus, contra sacrilegia illa, quod indignis & impijs hominibus pigniora[?] sacerdotia produntur carnalium obsequiorum causa, quod parochiae omnino papisticis artificijs, atque violentia tam misere acciduntur:[1] || nam & Episcopi & nobiles mercedem hinc reddunt oeconomis suis, & alijs ministris: & uni tria, aut quatuor tradunt sacerdotia, qui ne uni seruiat: ut illi collatores eo maiorem de prouentibus Ecclesiasticis partem sibi retineant. Cuius enim quaeso inuentum, poscere primi anni fructus & decimas? Vel tum[?] quarum exactione sic vigilant, ut contingat toties per mortem, vel alias vacantibus sacerdotijs illos, ex uno sacerdotio, in uno anno ter primos fructus, adeoque trium annorum fructus percipere. Cuius iam, quod hodie uendunt in aula facultatem sacerdotia plura occupandi? Et quibus hanc uendunt facultatem, nisi sceleratissimis, nemo enim alius emeret. Cuius quod Episcopi dant dilationem suscipiendi muneris Ecclesiastici ad annos decem, aut duodecim, hominibus qui nunquam Ecclesiae uolunt ministrare, ut interim tamen fruantur (hi) bonis sacerdotiorum? Cuius, quod pueris nobilium, Archidiaconatus conferuntur, prouentum ducentarum librarum.|| Haec (igitur), haec sunt vere papistica facta: quae cunctis opibus & viribus oppugnare debemus: || his enim id efficitur, ut frequentes inuenias in Anglia Ecclesias, quae in sex & septem annis nullam audierunt concionem.[2] || In lapides, ligna, vestes, & res istiusmodi, quae per se nihil adferunt quaestus, nihil conferunt ad voluptates & honores esse severis perfacile est hominibus maxime qui soluti sunt superstitione papistica, & a quibus sublata sit potentiorum ex submotione harum rerum offensio, at depellere sacrilegos (istos) a spolijs Ecclesiarum, [fol. 12v.] & nihil omnino praetermittere, quod eo collaturum aliquid videatur ut singulis queant parochijs idonei & parari & sustentari curatores: hisque adesse ad plenam disciplinae Christi restitutionem: hoc vero impossibile etiam est nedum difficile omnibus illis, qui dicere nondum possunt, mori mihi lucrum est, Christus vivere. Et: absit mihi gloriari nisi in cruce Domini nostri Jesu Christi: in quo mihi mundus crucifixus est, & ego mundo. Perplacet, ut longissime submoveantur cuncta Antichristi non insignia tantum & notae; sed quaevis etiam eius vestigia atque

[1] C: tam miserae accisae sunt.

[2] Originally in B (Rawlinson Copy): Haec, haec sunt vere papistica facta, quibus id efficitur, ut frequentes inuenias in Anglia Ecclesias, quae in sex & septem annis nullam audierunt concionem. Contra ista ergo in primis nobis dimicandum est.

umbrae, in quibuscunque illae demum rebus haerere videantur, sive in lignis, lapidibus, vestibus, ac quicquid tandem illud sit: Sed corpus prius, & substantiam Antichristi tum eius insignia, vestigia & umbras eius profligare studeamus. Corpus autem
451 Antichristi & substantia consistit in impijs Ecclesiarum vastatoribus & spoliatoribus: per quos non disciplina tantum Christi, sed et doctrina tota opprimitur, & exterminatur. Haec cum considero, & respicio, ut debeo, in praecepta Domini, & exempla opto, ut quicunque Christi esse volumus, ita regni eius restitutionem moliamur, sicut Dominus ipse eius molitus est, institutionem. Quaeramus ante omnia probeque instruamus[1] omni Christi doctrina & disciplina Evangelistas, qui propter Christum Dominum & Evangelij praedicationem relinquant omnia: perque horum ministerium populos regno Christi adducamus ac singulis[2] [fol. 13] suos pastores fideles adiungamus, qui non minus laborent, ut quae sunt insignia & notae Christianismi, revocent & extare recte faciant, quam ut insignia & notas aboleant Antichristianismi: quaeque[?] & has ita velim aboleri,[3] ut ne ulla quidem eorum haereat memoria in ullorum hominum cordibus. Hoc autem cum fieri nequeat nisi Christi regnum plene recipiatur, in hoc ipsum optarim nos omnes totis viribus incumbere; cumque ad id opus sit quam plurimis *συνεργοις*, optarim nobis cum omnibus, qui amant vere D. Jesum, facere qualem omnino liceat in Domino syncretismum, tot enim iam annorum experientia docti videmus, Dominum perpaucis dare, ut a sententia discedant, quam semel sibi obfirmaverunt: maxime vero si etiam pro ea pugnauerint: ut plane necesse sit, aut Christianam dissolvere communionem cum multis, quos omnino assumpsit Dominus: aut alterum alteri concedere ut utrique suum pulchrum sit, etiam si alteri non ita videatur. Difficillimum certe & sanctissimis viris est, plane suos non esse raroque[?] et inter hos reperitur qui non res quaslibet potius
452 quam inventa cedere sustineat sui ingenij. Hanc vero infirmitatem cum cernamus Deum ferre in nobis tam indulgenter, vae duritiae nostrae si ad eandem nos indulgentiam non flectat, emolliatque exemplum Domini & Dei nostri. Summa itaque religione cavendum non dubito primum, ne obortas quaestiones suscipiamus statim definiendas: ipsique nullam moveamus non ad regnum Christi prorsus necessariam. Agnoscamus iudicij nostri imbecillitatem; metuamus innatam arrogantiam; & in proprijs inventis peruicatiam: [fol. 13v.] Quae sunt ad salutem

[1] NC: instituamus. [2] C: singulos. [3] NC: velim autem & has ita aboleri,

cognitu necessaria, dilucide, clareque ac copiose tradita sunt nobis in divinis scripturis omnia & de harum rerum studio atque perfectione deest omnibus nobis quam plurimum id studij & perfectionis implere aliquando absolvereque elaboremus. De caeteris rebus disputemus cautissime: definiamus tarde, aut nunquam, nihil pugnemus. Si autem Satanae astu et negligentia nostra orta pugna de his rebus fuerit: ab ea, qua liceat ratione quam primum discedamus: aut constituamus inducias. Victoria enim raro aliqua: nunquam vera [*vero?*] admodum salutaris obtinetur.

Hic [*hinc?*] vides vir sanctissime indubie, quid optem[1] fieri, & de vestium controversia, & libertate ceremoniarum aliarum. Vellem magno redimere non esse motam: postquam autem est mota, discedi ab ea opto, & reijci illam in alia tempora quam primum. || Vobis Germanis, & Gallis velim suam concedi in ceremonijs consuetam simplicitatem: & hanc uos omni uindicare calumnia & amabilem reddere, commendatione solidae in Christo Domino consensionis, officiosae communionis: disciplinae efficacis: alijs quoque pijs ac prudentibus pastoribus concedi optem, si id nondum possit fieri, per publicum regni Dei decretum, saltem per piam conniuentiam eam in omni ceremoniarum usu libertatem, ut eas possint, quisque pro sui populi captu ad fidei aedificationem moderari, nec cogantur praescriptis rationibus per omnia inhaerere. Vtile enim est, Christianam libertatem, etiam aliqua rerum istarum varietate commendari.

Caeterum suspendi velim totam hanc controversiam, an plane Antichristianum sit, quouis animo & modo usurpare aliquid in Christi ceremonijs, praeter expressum Christi praeceptum, quod notam Antichristus fecerit suae impietatis; & omnes nos totis viribus hoc agere atque urgere, ut statim emittantur per omne regnum Evangelistae quotquot idonei queant inueniri, diligentissime inquisiti per vniversum regnum: & mittantur cum religiosissime explorati, examinatique ad regulam Spiritus S.: tum etiam instructi certa, & solide explicata universae & doctrinae, & disciplinae Christi ratione, atque descriptione: simulque ut [fol. 14] cottidie parochijs idonei praeficiantur curatores, quotquot Dominus dederit.

Quo vero citius obtineri tot queant, quot opus fuerit, & Evangelistae & pastores, ut quam primum Academiae seuerissime reformentur, tum a sacrilegijs arceantur, & parochiarum &

[1] C: optimum.

collegiorum in Academijs omnes fuci: 1. quicunque nec reipsa Ecclesijs sua praestant ministeria: nec se ueris in studijs progressibus, ad haec ministeria instituunt, ac praeparant: liberentur quoque Ecclesiae & collegia omnia cunctis & exactionibus Papisticis, & largitionibus in homines, Ecclesijs nihil commodantibus: Constituatur denique atque consecretur & Christo crucifixo certum aerarium: & quod sit omnibus sacrosanctum. Vnde in primis ea procurentur, quae ad religionis requiruntur salutarem administrationem: tum Christi pauperibus suppeditetur, vnde [*ut*?] bene pieque viuant: remoueatur mendacitas: instituatur ea rerum communicatio inter sanctos, qua cuique quantum cuique satis sit ad viuendum Deo praebeatur: vti exemplum habemus primae Ecclesiae.

Habes vir colendissime quas ego optarim questiones, aut non moueri aut quam primum opprimi motas: aut certe in alia reijci tempora: Vtilem enim earum decisionem non audeo mihi polliceri: habes item in quae uelim nos omnes eodem spiritu & ore, cunctisque cuiusque viribus incumbere. || Argumenta tua illa duo Aharonici sacerdotij est ideo exhibito iam Christo contumeliosum est, ut erat exhibendo gloriosum. Res istae notae sunt Antichristianismi, non igitur usurpandae deditis Christianismo, apud me omnino id non concludunt quod tu instituisti. Multa enim ad gloriam exhibiti Christi ex institutis sacerdotij Aharonici mutuavimus pie: ita res multas[1], quas Antichristi
453 notas fecerunt suae [fol. 14 v.] impietatis, possunt etiam notae esse regni Christi, sicut symbola panis & vini, Aqua Baptismatis, impositio manuum, conciones, Sacra loca, feriae, & quam plurima alia. Iam patent illa longissime, Domini est terra & plenitudo eius, non diaboli, non Antichristi, non impiorum. Filius hominis est Dominus Sabbathi: Sabbathum est propter hominum: non homo propter Sabbathum. Pura omnia puris. omnis creatura Dei bona, nec vitari potest bonis hominibus, per abusum malorum. Aeque verbum Domini per omnia sequendum est in actionibus privatis atque publicis, omnia enim facienda sunt in nomine Domini Jesu & ad gloriam Dei: quam igitur concedimus nobis in usu privato rerum externarum libertatem: ne cui negemus in publico Spiritus Christi verus oppugnans Antichristum, oppugnat quae Antichristi sunt prima, & propria primum, Spiritus Christi moliens regni Christi restitutionem, quae regni Christi prima & propria sunt, primum restituit: doctrinam & disciplinam.

[1] C. multae.

Cavendum est, & illud Satanae artificium, quo efficit plerumque, ut peccata faciamus, quae peccata non sunt: ut quae sunt peccata revera in nos minus observemus: aut ut contra ea, quae peccata esse definimus, non eam exeramus quam oportebat, severitatem. || Vti in praesenti questione, ego non video, qui possit quisquam bona conscientia Christi communionem praestare ijs, qui vestibus illis vtantur; dumtaxat satis moniti quicunque statuerit, esse aliquam in harum vestium usu, cum Antichristo communicationem. || Haec det Dominus ut religiose expendas, vir amplissime, || mihique oro, rescribas libere, quicquid habere tibi videberis: siue pro tuis argumentis confirmandis: siue pro meis infirmandis. ||

Scio, te quaerere Christi gloriam: audivique ex te, de quo tibi permultum gratulor: te de iudicio tuo esse solicitum: nec illud audere statim confirmare, etiam videaris tibi plane verbum Dei sequi, cogitare enim & te hominem esse, labique posse. Te itaque per crucem filij Dei, per salutem Ecclesiarum, quae tantum hodie premuntur calamitatibus per quaerendam omnibus nobis Ecclesiarum consensionem & pacem in Christo, te, oro & obsecro, nequid praepropere in ista de ceremonijs quaes-
454 tione. Vidisti infirma multa in Ecclesijs Saxonicis: vidisti autem etiam multa, de quibus agis gratias Deo: ne igitur sine summa necessitate abijciamus illas, quas Dominus tam praeclare assumpsit. O, si eo res Ecclesiarum Gallicarum, Italicarum, Polonicarum prouectae essent: In hoc regno quam religiosissime caveamus, [fol. 15] ne conatus Satanae adiuuemus imprudentes, qui quasvis inijcit quaestiones atque controversias: ne quaestionem suscipiamus tractandam de propaganda doctrina Evangelij & restituenda disciplina: eaque de causa de remotione fucorum, a ministerijs & Ecclesiasticis & scholasticis: qui etiam ordinem Episcoporum cum nequit sibi retinere totum seruum, abolendum satagit. et ea occasione sic spoliare Ecclesias, ut, cum desint stipendia, sacra ministeria committantur cuique novissimo de plebe. Has Satanae cogitationes obseruemus, eisque quantum dabitur a Domino, obsistamus: nulla ex parte, vel inscientes eas adiuvemus. Pauci sumus Christum Dominum qui quaerimus ipsum et nemo nostrum non multa premitur infirmitate: suscipiamus igitur nosmet ipsos invicem ut nos Dominus suscepit: Condonemus nobis mutuo, quae condonat Dominus: quo vrgente inter nos charitate sincera & officiosa, possimus uno spiritu, uno ore, et summis omnium opibus Antichristi ita corpus & substantiam profligare: ut nulla bonorum

offensione, certa autem apud filios Dei fidei aedificatione, queamus abolere etiam cuncta Antichristi signa, vestigia, umbras.

Domine Jesu, unice nostri, ut cum patre, ita et inter nos conciliator, depelle a mentibus nostris, quicquid nos distrahit, quicquid serenitatem iudicij de nobis invicem obscurat: quicquid denique absolutam in tuis ministerijs conspirationem, coniunctamque atque acerrimam & adserendi regni tui, & profligandae tyrannidis Antichristi contentionem ulla ex parte removantur: adspiraque mentibus nostris spiritum s. tuum, qui in omnem nos inducat veritatem: det videre eadem, & moliri primaque primum quibus tui regni nobis vis omnis restituatur; et Antichristi omnia, ex omnium hominum deleantur cordibus & memoria. Haec, pro infinita tua in nos charitate: bonitas ipsa & charitas fili Dei proque gloria nominis tui. proque salute electorum tuorum largiri ne nobis dignare ne impij usque dicant: ubi est Christus eorum. Amen.

(3)

Peter Martyr's Letter to Bucer, Oxford, October 25th, 1550.
MS. New College 343, fol. 14-15 recto. (Autograph).

Clarissimo viro D.D. Martino Bucero Theologiae Regio professori
Domino suo plurimum observando
Cantabrigiae.[1]

S.D. Litterae quas ad me dedisti, partim laetitiam ingentem attulerunt, quod tuos ad te incolumes peruenisse, dei gratia, intellexerim, nam id uehementer cognoscere optabam. Deo itaque gratias, qui te in isto communi exilio dignatus est consolari. Partim etiam, non nihil tristitiae apportarunt, quod Hopperus nos duos ita uoluerit suae opinionis testes habere. Memini ante duos menses, a quodam nobili me super hac re fuisse consultum, et in eandem ad unguem sententiam, quam modo tuam esse significas, rescripsisse. unde miror quid illi uenerit in mentem quod secum faciam. Imo superiori hebdomada, hic in disputationibus publicis disceptatum est, an ceremoniae Aharonicae ab ecclesia christiana[2] reuocari, aut retineri possent, ubi ego distinxi ceremonias ueteres, quod aliquae illarum sacramenta proprie fuisset, ut circumcisio, sacrificia, et huiusmodi quae Christum[3] ut uenturum, et representabat, et credentibus exhibebat, alias

[1] This is the address written on the back of the letter (fol. 15 verso), to which is added in Bucer's handwriting: '28. Octob. 1550 De Causa Hupperi.'
[2] In the MS.: xpīana.
[3] In the MS.: xp̄s.

uero fuisse actiones, et ritus, quod ad decorum ministerij, et ad aliquam aedificationem facerent, primum genus inuocari, aut retineri posse, negaui, at in alio genere nostram ecclesiam liberam feci,atque illam inductionem quadam ostendi. modo aliquos ex illis ritibus accepisse, modo contra illos non nihil statuisse, prout nostris temporibus aut commodum aut utile uidebat esse.

Atque ut uno uerbo dicam, cum his quae tu ad me scripsisti, per omnia consentio. Et licet huic libertati ecclesiae faueam tecum nihilominus opto, ut ea simplicitas qua utebamur Argentorati, reuocetur, nam istum ceremoniarum apparatum, nihil prodesse animaduerto. populus enim totus papisticus adhuc domini coenam ut nunc habetur, nihil uult a missa differre. atque cum non erudiatur, in dies res abitur in deterius, quod homini pio acerbissime dolendum est. Per illum eundem quo tuas litteras hodie accepi, et ab Hoppero mihi redita est epistola, qua orabat, ut hoc suum scriptum legerem, atque ad ipsum de mea sententia rescriberem, ut lectum ad te statim mitterem. Itaque legi duabus his aut tribus horis, et cum ad te redeat nuntius, per ipsum eundem ad te Hopperi libellum transmitto. Ex quo tu nihil aliud deprehendes, quam quod ex tuis litteris iam uidi te nosse, imo quod prius legerem tuam epistolam, potissimum me iuuit, ut quod ab isto diceretur expedite intellexerim.

D. Johannes à Lasco ut uides manu sua subscripsit, ego id facere nolui, sed per litteras quid sentiam, intra unum aut alterum diem ei significabo. In ista questione ut paucis dicam, id me tantum non nihil mouet, quod Paulum uideo priori ad corinthios circa finem, duo potissimum spectare in ritibus uel traditionibus ecclesiae. primum est, ut aedificet, alterum ut servetur ευταξία et in his uestibus, nil mihi se offert, quod ad ευταξίαν aedificatur solide faciat. Video sane ministros decoro uel ornamento non nihil inseruiri. sed cum decorum et ornamentum eius possit aliunde peti, ratio ista non multum apparet habere momenti. sic tamen responsionis meae summam temperandam esse cogitaui, ut ostendam me quidem cum illis cupere simplicem, castamque sacramentorum administrationem, et ut uestes huiusmodi quamprimum facta fuerit potestas, remoueatur non tamen adduci posse ut haec pernitiosa utentibus, ut esse ut fuisse statuam. Nam inter ἀδιάφορα numeranda omnino censeo, quorum interdum bonus, interdum malus usus esse possit et quo modo adhiberi, modo remoueri liceat, & ut opportunitas & mouendi regni dei sese obtulerit. consilium meum in negocio Hopperi erat, ut episcopatum sibi oblatum ab initio suscepisset, ad suam ecclesiam inisset, eamque concionibus, disciplina, et diligenti cura sic instituisset, ut omnibus aliis dioecesibus exemplo haberetur, at nihil horum perfectum est, contentio eo exarsit, ut postac non facile sperem, Dominum Londinensem, R^{ssm} Cantuariensem adducendos, ut has ceremonias fortasse parum utiles aboleri sinat, cum se & illis tantopere opposuerit, quod si ad tantum contentionem uentum non esset, aliquid potuisset fortasse impetrari. Caeterum ego de his rebus nunquam fui consultus, et res est eo loco, ut uix absque aliquo damno sperem explicari posse. Practicis ut italice dicitur, administranda est res publica et eisdem opus est inter ministros ecclesiae. nam si prius res inter collegas tractaretur, non sic arderet ignis concionum, ut restingui non posset. Audio tamen Hopperum ab Aula, non parum fauoris in hac causa sibi conciliasse. ita ut multi putent, ei quod ita pugnauerit, non male casurum. Quod autem mihi nunc dum scribo in mentem uenit non tacebo. Quando cogito illum nos duos, ut scribis, sibi testes aduocasse suspicor ne id sit fortasse quo ad aliam contentionem de diuortio, quam cum eodem Londinensi habet. Atque hoc ideo mihi se offert quod existimare non possum, illum ignorare, quidnam de ista quaestione uestium a nobis iudicetur. Scripsissem libenter fusius, uerum nuntius sua festinatione admodum urget, quare te uehementer oro, ut uxori ac omnibus tuis meo, coniugis, et Julij nomine salutem plurimam dicas, eisque significes nobis omnibus maxime uoluptati esse, quod tecum et uiuat, et ualeat. Deus uos omnes sospitet. 25. Octobris. Oxonij. Himanuelum quoque si eum uideris salutari uelim.

Totus tuus.
Pet^{o} Martyr.

(4)

À Lasco's Letter to Bucer, October 26th, 1550[1]
(1) MS. New College 343, fol. 4;
(2) MS. Rawlinson D.346, fol. 5-6.

Habeo tibi gratiam, vir sanctissime, quod de disciplinae rationibus ad me scripsisti. Placet ordo illius, & dabo operam ut illum sequamur. Quod ad vestium controuersiam attinet: earum praesertim, quas Papistici sacerdotij fulcra, atque ornamenta esse constat: desumptas alioqui ex Judaismo, id quod libri ipsi Papistarum manifeste testantur: Et inductas non aliam ob causam, quam ut Papae sacerdotium ornent, Christi uero Domini sacerdotium eleuent, atque obscurent: aliud sane iudicare non possum, quam ut illas haudquaquam admittendas esse credam, ijs, qui sacerdotij Papistici impie-

[1] A quotation from this letter is printed in Glocester Ridley, op. cit., p. 314, n. a; cf. here, p. 165: Et plane – sententias rogare posset. – But Ridley has not the words after *fiducia* (potius – proferretur).

tatem ex uerbo Dei perspectam, exploratamque habent: hoc potissimum tempore, quo vestes istiusmodi tanta sanguinis Christiani profusione, prorsusque Antichristiana tyrannide, urgeri, imperari, atque instaurari uidemus. proque notis quibusdam societatis Antichristianae passim reputari, sicubi adhuc in pretio habeantur. *Quare D. Hoperi consilium, si rem dextre agat, improbare hic non possum. Et plane ego ipse Domino Hopero suasi, cum ex illo quaeri audirem, quemnam sibi hac in parte assentientem haberet: ut te non praetermitteret, sed nos vna omnes nominaret,* qui hic peregrini sumus: eo quod nos omnes hic consensuros esse non dubitarem. Si quid hic est peccatum igitur per me peccatum est. Sed non tam est peccatum ulla malitia, quam Christiana fiducia potius: quam profecto certam esse putabam. Quod non prius tibi res sit indicata, quam nomen tuum proferretur: factum est temporis inopia: constitutum enim erat D. Hopero tempus breuius ad respondendum, quam ut omnium sententias rogare posset. Sed mox ut ea, quae ad aulam transmisit, describi potuerunt: ad D. Petrum Martyrem transmisit omnia. curauitque ut ad te demum etiam perferrentur, putoque te illa, aut habere iam, aut prope diem habiturum esse. Doleo vero & ego, tantum pro hisce uestibus certamen exortum esse. Sed non uideo, Dominum Hoperum huic dissidio occasionem praebuisse. Si enim alij illum sine uestibus istiusmodi ferre uoluissent,[1] *quas se tuta conscientia sua gestare non posse credit*: quemadmodum alios ille ferre non recusat, posteaquam aliud persuadere non potest, nihil fuisset dissidij. Sed cum pro Episcopo illum alij habere nollent, nisi cum uestium istiusmodi, & nonnullarum aliarum ceremoniarum apparata: iussus est, scripto, consilij hac in parte sui reddere rationem, quod & fecit, atque hinc lachrymae istae omnes, quod aiunt. Responsum est enim scripto ipsius: & additae obiectiones quaedam, quae ille rursum omnia altero scripto refutauit. Ad extremum responsum est etiam ipsius refutationi scripto, ut audio, prolixo: sed cuius exemplar haberi nondum potuit, ut a me legi posset. Interim res pendet adhuc: sunt tamen qui rem compositam iri cupiunt. Ad quam sane rem non inutilem fore putarem D. Cziechi praesentiam: quem nunc istic apud vos esse puto. Ego sane omnia Papistica, e Christi Ecclesia sublata prorsus, abolitaque esse optarim. Papistica autem uoco omnia, quae ad ornandum, muniendumque Regnum, & sacerdotium Papae, quocunque tempore, ac praetextu, per quoscunque item extra verbum Dei, inuecta sunt. Neque enim ista[2] sola pro Papisticis habenda esse puto: quae sub Regno iam Papae per ipsius tyrannidem imperantur, sed illa etiam, quae ante reuelatam mundo ipsius impietatem, ab ipso usque

[1] ? noluissent. [2] NC: ea.

Apostolorum tempore ad ornandum impietatis suae, tametsi mundo tum incognitae mysterium (iam tum alioqui meditatum) praeter Verbi Diuini regulam constituebantur, quantumuis speciosa nostrae rationi esse uideantur. Imo uero ipsum quoque Euangelium, quatenus Papisticum est, hoc est, falso, ac maliciose ad confirmandam ipsius tyrannidem detortum, a Christi Ecclesia quam longissime abesse uelim. tantum abest, ut mihi libertatem ullam permittam retinendi quidque in Ecclesia, eorum, quae Papa ad ornandum confirmandumque Regnum, ac sacerdotium ipsius quocunque o͂o praetextu, tempore, atque authore usurpauit. Et quidem potissimum hoc tempore facere id non auderem: quo Ecclesias utcunque iam restitui coeptas, inaudita tyrannide cogi rursum ad Papismum uidemus. Hic si tu aliter sentis: optarim sane audire petitas ex verbo Dei consilij tui rationes: idque in charitate, atque libertate christiana. Caetera ex Martino tuo cognosces. Vale mi pater: & libertatem nostram boni consule. Sic sum compositus, ut in causa religionis nihil mihi dissimulandum apud amicos esse putem. Saluere iubeo tuam, cum tota familia quam officiosissime reliquosque fratres in Domino omnes. Uxor mea quoque tibi, & tuae, reliquaeque toti familiae salutem adscribi iussit. Seque tuis, ac tuorum precibus commendat, expectat enim iam horam suam intra dies paucos, ut pariat, quod illi Dominus faustum & felix (ad salutem ipsius) esse uelit. Iterum uale Londini 26. Octobris. Anno 1550. Tuus ex animo quantus est Joannes à Lasco, manu propria.[1]

(5)

À Lasco's Letter to Bucer, November 15th, 1550.
MS. New College 343, fol. 40.

S. Pensionem tuam mitto ut uolebas per D. Sans. decisis. 40. coronatis, quos te ex tradita tibi per me pridem[?] Fagij Junioris pecunia insumpsisse scribis. His vero totidem denuo addidi, ac Domino Richardo Hilsio nostro tradidi: ut eorum nomine censum annuum Fagio Juniori constituat, quem tu indicaueris aequum fore. itaque tibi ad illum ea de re scribendum erit. quae ad D. Hoperum de uestium controuersia scripsisti, nondum ut oportet, perlegi. sed in ijs quae ad me scripsisti, adfers multa quae mihi quidem extra causae nostrae fines ac scopum adducta esse uidentur. Non agitur de uestibus ipsis, ut rebus a Deo conditis: quas in se bonas esse ut omnia

[1] This letter is extant in two MS. copies:
(1) The original autograph in: New College MS. 343, fol. 4.
(2) A contemporary copy in: Rawlinson MS. D. 346, fol. 5-6. This copy bears at the beginning in another handwriting: 'Ad bucerum.'

quae a Deo sunt condita nemo negat. sed de certo quodam illarum usu ac modo agitur. quem ego abusum & corruptionem bonarum rerum esse puto. Nam & res optimas non raro corrumpimus, & male illis utimur. Finis uero ac scopus causae est, An uestium eiusmodi usus ac modus ministro Ecclesiae Christi conueniat: quem ministrorum Ecclesiae Antichristi in blasphemo ipsorum sacerdotio fulcra atque ornamenta esse constat. Et quem Deus, typici, non autem ueri Christi sacerdotij rerum item futurarum umbras, non rei exhibitae testimonia in sua Ecclesia esse uoluit. cum nos iam in Christo Domino vero nostro atque unico sacerdote omnia exhibita nobis esse credamus et doceamus. Quare quae inter fulcra atque ornamenta ministrorum Antichristi numerari non possunt: quae item Deus umbras rerum futurarum esse uoluit, quas iam in Christo exhibitas habemus: ea ad causam nostram existimo non ita multum pertinere. Sed nunc non possum plura de his, nam Dominus me paululum manu sua prona tangere uoluit in adimendo mihi filiolo, Paulo, quem mihi ante diem sedecimum dederat. nam hac nocte ante diluculum e vivis excessit. Et uxor puerpera grauiter laborat. Vale, Et Deum pro nobis ora, tuosque omnes saluta.

Londini 15. Novemb. Anno 1550.

Tuus quantus est ex animo
Jo à Lasco manu propria.

Scripta mea quaeso remittas quae apud te reliqui.

Cover: Doctissimo Et Sanctissimo viro
D Martino Bucero . . .

Accep. 20 Nouemb.
Nondum . . .

At the bottom of folio 15 of Bucer's letter to à Lasco in the Rawlinson MS. (D.346): Hijs literis respondetur infra per. d. J. à Lasco fol. 5. But the letter is not extant there in that collection and is probably this letter of the New College MSS.

(6)

William Bill's Letter to Bucer, November 8th, 1550.
MS. New College 343, fol. 28-28 verso.
MS. Rawlinson, D.346, fol. 25-25 verso.
Extracts printed by Harvey, op. cit., pp. 141 ff.

'Clarissimo doctissimoque Theologo D. Martino Bucero sacrarum Scripturarum praelectori publico, Cantabrigiae.'

'Doctissimo theologo D. M. Bucero
Guilielmus Billus salutem et pacem
in Christo seruatore precatur.'

Quum graves lites de autoritate Magistratuum nuper ortae sunt inter pios aliqui viros, quae nisi mature ac prudenter dirimantur, periculum est ne magnam iacturam nuper emendatae religioni sint allaturae: ausus sum hoc tempore ad tuam humanitatem venire optime Bucere vt tuum in hijs controversijs auxilium solidumque iudicium expetam. Vna controversia est, An liceat Magistratibus politica autoritate statuere aut retinere in emendata religione consuetas Romanae ecclesiae caeremonias in ministrandis sacramentis, et ordinandis ecclesiae ministris? Vt albam, capam, vestimentum, superpellicium, baculum episcopalem (sic opinor vocant) et id genus reliqua? Quaestio non est vtrum expediat, vtrum melius sit? sed an omnino liceat? Quidam impium esse serio credunt, quia Aaronicum sacerdotium olent, quod abrogatum est. deinde etiam et Papisticum, quod deterius est. Nec licitum esse in ecclesiam talia introducere. quia cum Christi simplex institutum obscurant, non adornant: tum veteres vmbras, impios errores, ac vanas superstitiones fouent non tollunt. Alij contra a parte legum Anglicarum stant, tribuentes Magistratubus autoritatem in istiusmodi rebus indifferentibus ad aedificationem aut ad publicum ordinem conseruandum in ecclesia, ceremonias tales vel instituendi vel retinendi.

Altera controuersia est, An bona et possessiones quae olim corrupto iudicio aut supersticioso animo donabantur Coenobijs Collegijs alijsue ecclesijs, possint publica autoritate et consensu, conuerti denuo in priuatos vsus Regis aut aliorum?

Alij sic putant quemadmodum autoritas legum ratum facit quod priuatum est vt id publicum fiat: ita ex publico priuatum reddere possit. Justum enim est quod lex iubet in rebus externis. nec potest esse ἀνομίαῄ αδικία iniquitas aut iniuria vbi nulla legis praeuaricatio. Terram autem dedit filijs hominum, quisque suam inde portionem possideat iuxta regni decreta. Item, In quibus corrupta superstitio et principium et medium et finem dedit, in hijs abusus corrigi non potest nisi et res ipsa tollatur. At pleraque coenobia tali superstitione ditata sunt. ergo prorsus tolli debent. Alij contra. Quod deprauata natura et amor sui fecit priuatum, id Christiana charitas fecit publicum, etsi animo interdum superstitioso. ergo contra legem charitas fit. quod semel publicum est id rursum priuatum facere. Haec pauca in vtranque partem propterea memoraui vt Dominationi tuae controuersias istas aliquousque aperirem. Nunc igitur quaeso a te optime Bucere qui semper omnibus iuuandis teipsum dedere soles, obsecroque per amorem tuum quem geris erga sanctam veritatem et pacem promouendam, si tantum otij tibi a rebus tuis sit, Judicium et censuram tuam iuxta verbi Dei regulam in hijs caussis libere digneris exponere. fieri potest vt diuina bonitas has lites tua opera omnino componat, piam concordiam conciliet. Equidem enitar quantum Dominus dederit, tuis argumentis fretus, vt idipsum efficiam sedulo. Dominus Jesus conatus tuos omnes foeliciter dirigat. Vale et per otium quaeso rescribe.

Ex Aula Westminster. 8. Idus Nouembris.
D. tuae obseruantissimus
Guil. Billus.[1]

(7)

Cranmer's Letter to Bucer, December 2nd, 1550.[2]
Original: MS. New College 343, fol. 41.
Another Copy: MS. Rawlinson D.346, fol. 41.
Printed by N. Pocock, op. cit., from MS. Copy at British Museum.

Doctissimo viro D. Martino Bucero, theologiae in Academia Cantabrigiensi professori Regio.

Salve plurimum, D. Bucere charissime,[3] Legi libellum quem ad D. Petrum Alexandrum misisti de controversia inter D. Hoperum et D. Londinensem, in quo multa a te et docte explicata et fuse[4] disputata sunt. Quare nunc oro ut sententiam tuam quanta poteris verborum brevitate constrictam de hiis quaestionibus ad me mittas. An sine offensa Dei liceat ministris ecclesiae Anglicanae illis uti vestibus quibus hodie utuntur atque a magistratu praescripta sunt. An is qui affirmaverit nephas esse aut recusaverit hiis vestibus uti peccet in Deum quia immundum esse dicit quod Deus sanctificavit et in magistratus qui violet ordinem politicum. Ad haec, si brevissime respondeas,[5] et quid sentias primo quoque tempore ad me miseris,

[1] Bucer's reply (November 17th, 1550), cf. Harvey, op. cit., n. x, pp. 143 ff.

[2] This letter has been printed by Nicholas Pocock in *Troubles connected with the Prayer Book of 1549* (pp. 130-131, n. LXVIII, Camden Society, 1884, New Series XXXVII). Pocock states that it was printed from a manuscript copy of the Br. Mus. Add. MSS. 28571, fol. 46.

The original Latin in Cranmer's handwriting is preserved in the New College MS. 343, fol. 41. It differs only in three places from that printed by Pocock.

[3] MS. New College has 'charissime' where Pocock prints 'clarissime'.

[4] MS. New College has 'fuse', where Pocock prints 'pure'.

[5] MS. New College has 'respondeas', where Pocock prints 'responderis'.

The English translation (in the 'briefe examination', p. Ai) has accordingly: '*ryght welbeloued* Master Bucer' and 'are learnedly declared, and *largely* disputed'.

At the back of the letter MS. New College has: 'Doctissimo viro D. Martino Bucero. Theologiae in Achademia [*sic*] Cantabrigiensi professori Regio', to which is added by

gratissimum mihi facturus es. Mei omnes tibi tuisque omnibus plurimam salutem et prospera omnia ex animo optant.

Vale. Lambethi 2° Decembris. [1550] Tuae paternitatis studiosus T. Cant.

(8)

Walter Haddon's Letter to Matthew Parker, June 1566[1].

Reverendissimo in Christo patri, D.D. Matthaeo Parkero, Archiepiscopo Cantuariensi.

ACcepi literas tuas, & libellum una missum; & utrumque mihi gratissimum fuit, quoniam fuit te dignissimum. Hoc etiam rectissime factum est, quod Buceri sententiam & Petri Martyris apponi curavisti; quorum auctoritas licet sola plebeiorum istorum, & novitiorum commenta frangere posset: tamen perfectissimi Theologi tam graviter in his caussis argumentati sunt, ut ipsis rationem momentis omnibus satisfieri possit, qui secum aures sinceras, & nullis errorem praejudiciis occupatas afferre volunt. Quapropter in doctrina satis arbitror esse processum; in disciplina reliquum esse debet, ut illorum importunitas poena divinciatur, qui contra Principis edictum, & publicas Ecclesiae constitutiones in rebus arbitrariis vociferantur. Tua maximam commendationem providentia debet habere, qui prius istos errores exploras, quam se in Rempublicam insinuent: & illorum Magistros eo ablegas, ubi ipsi sibi prodesse possunt si velint, aliis obesse, si velint, non possint. Deus tibi Spiritum suum continenter impertiat, ut ejus Ecclesiam diu & feliciter administres. Vale. Brugis Idibus Junii 1566 . . .

Gualterus Haddon.

[1] Letter in: *Rogeri Aschami Epistolarum, Libri Quatuor* . . . Editio Novissima, Prioribus auctior . . . *Oxoniae* . . . MDCCIII, p. 445.
cf. also Parker's Letter to Haddon in *Correspondence of Abp. Parker* (Parker Society, 1853), pp. 284 f., n. CCXIX.

another hand, presumably Bucer's amanuensis (as it is the hand by which several letters of Bucer were copied with corrections by Bucer's own hand): 'Accep: 7. Decemb. Nondum responsum.' (Bucer's reply is dated December 8th, 1550. cf. *Scr. Angl.*, pp. 681 ff.)

The letter of which up to the print by N. Pocock only the English translation was known, could not be traced (according to the statement in the edition of the *Remains of Archbishop Cranmer*, p. 428, n. CCXCII), in its Latin original. The *Remains* print only the English translation which was taken from 'a briefe examination'.

CHAPTER V

STEPHEN GARDINER AND MARTIN BUCER

The matter of justificatyon, wyth 'onlye faythe justifieth', and whether faith excludeth charitye in justification, perteineth no more to the use and practise of oure Churche of Englande, althoughe in knowledge it be a grave matter, then the triflinge question I rehearsed perteined to the hearers edification in good livinge. I beseche your Grace to know howe I put a difference betwene use and knowledge. The knowledge of justification, as I have said, is, in learninge, of more waighte, and such as, for the entreating of it, manye have wepte even here at home, besides those that have wepte in Germanye; but the use and practise of it is no more necessary in the state of the Church of England then is the handlinge of the other question. . . .

Gardiner to Somerset from the Fleet (October 27th, 1547.)
Muller, J. A.: *The Letters of Stephen Gardiner* (Cambridge, 1933), p. 407.

. . . the principle maintained in this our most difficult and dangerous struggle is, that salvation is obtained for us by Christ alone, and therefore that nothing is to be imposed upon men beyond what Christ himself has imposed; . . . The Lord grant in the mean time, that you may faithfully retain and rightly explain that chief head of christian doctrine, namely, the article of justification. For as long as that is retained in the churches, even in any degree, the kingdom of Christ will yet remain amongst you . . .

Bucer to Cranmer (October 29th, 1539), *Original Letters*, Vol. II, pp. 527+529.

NEITHER Henry VIII nor Protestantism could be made responsible for the failure of the mission of the German emissaries to England in 1538. That was the view of Bucer. The inefficiency of the emissaries themselves was one of the reasons which caused the breaking off of the negotiations. This is the first point stressed by Bucer in his letter to Landgrave Philip of Hesse, on September 16th, 1539. The second factor, responsible for the failure, was, in the eyes of Bucer, even stronger: the policy of the Bishop of Winchester, Stephen Gardiner, seemed to him the chief reason for the unfavourable reception of Protestantism in England. In the same letter to Philip, Bucer states that Gardiner might have persuaded the king, that from the political point of view a friendship or alliance with the German princes might prove to be unwise. Winchester, the politician, is the destroyer of the

English churches. That is Bucer's opinion.[1] Henry VIII could be accused only in so far as he was the executor of plans and suggestions made to him by Gardiner. Only since about 1539 did Bucer criticize Gardiner so severely. Before 1539 he had even thought the bishop as one on his side and a fervent champion for the course of the Reformation. He knew Gardiner's *De Vera Obedientia*, praising it highly in the preface to it written by him, Capito and Hedio (cf. App. to this chapter).[2] But soon Bucer had to realize that Gardiner's opposition to Rome was caused by political reasoning and not by the desire of a Protestant Reformation. The 'Henrician' Gardiner could never conform to Protestant doctrine. The bishop's anti-Rome attitude deceived Bucer, who believed in Gardiner's doctrinal and ecclesiastical opposition against Rome:

> . . . seing the King our late soveraigne lord hath in his boke determined this mattier, and there reproved the teaching of 'onelie faith' or 'faith alone' as a vertue separate, it is soroful to me to se eny homelies made after this sort to be sent furth in the name of oure soveraigne lord that now is, with suche a vehemencie to call hym no trew Christen man that denieth that doctrine.[3]

The predominant place given to the State by men like Gardiner soon caused Bucer and the Continental reformers to accuse English churchmen of a mere dependency on the State. They accused them of lacking responsibility towards the demands of the Church. Bucer even goes so far as accusing Gardiner of insincere motives. He says, that the loyalty claimed by Gardiner and the theological principle defended by Gardiner on grounds of strict obedience to the Sovereign, were a mere pretence in order to achieve his ambitious aims of governing affairs of State and international concern: the 'fervent desire to retain their tyranny and licentious liberty into all the fylthy excess of life'.[4] The desire for power, for unlimited liberty, is con-

[1] cf. Bucer in his letter to Landgrave Philip (September 16th, 1539), Lenz, Max: *Briefwechsel Landgraf Philipp's . . .* (Leipzig, 1880), part I, pp. 103 and 104.

cf. Bucer in his letter to the Landgrave (October 16th, 1539), Lenz, op. cit., part I, p. 110.

cf. Bucer in his letter to the Landgrave (November 26th, 1540), Lenz, op. cit., part I, p. 244.

cf. Bucer in his letter to the Landgrave (December 13th, 1544), Lenz, op. cit., part II, p. 273.

[2] Bucer sends a copy of Gardiner's *De Vera Obedientia* to Vadian on January 17th, 1536. Mentioned by Pierre Janelle in *Obedience in Church and State*, p. xxviii. cf. here, p. 6, n. 3.

[3] In Gardiner's letter to the Privy Council, August 1547, in Muller, J., op. cit., p. 364.

[4] cf. Bucer: *Gratulatio . . . ad Ecclesiam Anglicanam* (1548), p. 54.

Bucer accuses Gardiner in his letter to the Landgrave (September 16th, 1539) by saying that the bishop's policy is only meant to retain his luxury and to replace the Pope by the King and by men like Gardiner. Letter in Lenz, op. cit., part I, pp. 99 ff., n. 29. The same letter in extract in *Letters & Papers Henry VIII*, 1539, vol. XIV, part II, p. 54, n. 186.

cealed behind the religious claims of men like Gardiner, such is his suspicion. In various letters to Landgrave Philip, Bucer criticizes Gardiner most unfavourably, and yet seems to have felt always that here in their diverse opinion on the power granted to princes the main difficulty lies and remains in the negotiations between the Catholic Party in England and the Protestant Party of the Continent. Gardiner is regarded by Bucer in those letters as the chief instigator of that hostile attitude against Protestantism. Bucer feels and understands that the king is persuaded by Gardiner's political reasoning that an inclination towards Protestantism will: (*a*) arouse public disturbances in England and cause revolts and (*b*) hinder any advancing and friendly alliance with France, an alliance which will certainly be of greater importance for England than that with the politically less strong Protestant Party.

It is almost coincidental that Bucer at this stage in 1538, when he tries to explain to himself and to the Landgrave the reasons why negotiations with England had to fail, has become the political adviser of the Landgrave on other matters. Bucer was called to Hesse by Philip to deal with the Anabaptists, who had become a disturbing element in the Landgrave's district. Bucer's presence in Hesse made it possible for him to come in closer contact with Philip. The acquaintance became even more friendly in autumn 1539, when Bucer took a favourable attitude towards the bigamy of the Landgrave and achieved the consent to the bigamy by Luther, Melanchthon and the 'Kurfürst'. Since then Bucer was one of the most intimate friends and advisers of the Landgrave. He almost superseded his private secretary. The numerous letters from Philip to Bucer and vice versa on most secret political topics reveal the fact that Bucer had gained a deep insight into political affairs and negotiations with other countries. It was a most opportune moment at which Bucer was chosen by the Landgrave as his adviser. He could see that questions on ecclesiastical affairs were concerned with international policy, with political negotiations going on between countries such as England, Germany, France, Italy, and the Emperor. Here he found the explanation of the attitude of England towards Protestantism; here he saw Gardiner as the man who was mainly concerned with the protection of peace and order for England. By his influence on Philip, it was possible to contribute indirectly to Philip's conferences with England. In Philip and in Gardiner the two parties met each other. The Landgrave was regarded by Gardiner as the spokesman of the Continental Protestant Party, a man who ought not to be underestimated. He is to Gardiner 'chief captayne of the Protestantes' or 'a goodly champion of Christes Gospel'.[1]

Confronting the Act of the 6 Articles in 1539, on Celibacy of the Clergy, Justification by Faith only, the doctrine of the Sacrament of the Altar, etc., Bucer and his partisans felt religious principles attacked, on which for them an agreement had to be reached between English divines and those of the Continent. If no consent would be gained on the doctrine of justification all other negotiations and agreement on smaller points would be useless:

> The Lord grant in the meantime, that you may faithfully retain and rightly explain that chief head of christian doctrine, namely, the article of justification . . .[2]

writes Bucer to Cranmer from Strassburg on October 29th, 1539.[3] It is interesting to compare Bucer's letters of the same period, the one to Cranmer on October 29th, with that to Philip on September 16th, on the same topics. In his letter to the Landgrave, Bucer accuses Gardiner of the sudden change of Henry in issuing the 6 Articles: in his letter to Cranmer the name of Gardiner is not mentioned, although Cranmer must have felt whom Bucer means when writing:

> . . . and it appeared that antichrist had evidently gained the victory; for whatever may yet remain of christian doctrine, those decrees seemed so likely to empty the kingdom of all duly qualified ministers of Christ, as that all the churches would be for the future entirely in the hands of the followers of antichrist, who had thus found their opportunity for restoring the Roman pontiff without any great difficulty.[4]

In the attempt to trace the main reason of dissent between English Church doctrine and that of the Continental Protestants, Bucer on the Protestant side and Gardiner on that of conservative Catholicism in England seem to agree that the doctrine of justification and the problem of obedience in Church and State are the decisive points of disagreement. It is interesting to state that even before the controversy in 1541, when they met at Ratisbon, between Gardiner and Bucer, both men developed apart from each other their true con-

[1] Gardiner in his letter to Paget, November 5th, 1545; Muller, p. 161.
" " Paget, November 13th, 1545; ibid., p. 185.

[2] *Original Letters* (Parker Society), vol. II, p. 529.

[3] Letter in: (1) *Politische Correspondenz der Stadt Strassburg im Zeitalter der Reformation* (ZweiterBand, 1877 . . . Strassburg, pp. 634-635); (2) *Epistolae Tigurinae* (Parker Society), pp. 344 ff. Note several variants in the text between the Strassburg edition and that of the Parker Society.

[4] *Original Letters*, vol. II, pp. 527-528.

ception, that those two problems have to be overcome if ever one were to reach a basis for successful discussion. Bucer insisted from the beginning on the doctrine of justification, Gardiner objected to it at all times. Bucer was so insistent on it as being the essential and vital part of Protestantism, Gardiner objected to it because his king had objected to it, and as it might involve England in civil war and revolution, the 'new learning' being a source of anarchism. As it is the life question for Protestantism, so it is the most dangerous doctrine for England:

> The knowlege of justification, as I have said, is, in learninge, of more waighte, and such as, for the entreating of it, manye have wepte even here at home, besides those that have wepte in Germanye; but the use and practise of it is no more necessary in the state of the Church of England . . .

writes Gardiner to Somerset, from the Fleet on October 27th, 1547.[1] Even in prison he still keeps his political argument, that the doctrine has to be opposed, as endangering the realm, whilst Bucer argues as the theologian.

The very point of Bucer's accusation against Gardiner that the bishop argues as a politician in church affairs, is made by Gardiner his chief argument against the indifferent or better against the anarchic attitude of the Protestants against any State authority. Bucer's theological accusation is met by a political accusation of Gardiner, that the new doctrine of Protestantism endangers the order of the realm and creates even for the Church a State, where the Church forfeits that secular order, which only makes it possible for churchmen to live, to act and to work.

Bucer's suspicion of the sincerity of Gardiner's theological conceptions is met by an equal suspicion by Gardiner of the sincerity of Protestantism, which also seems to Gardiner a mere pretence to overthrow established religion and government. The opposition against the Emperor by the Protestants makes Gardiner argue against the soundness of their religion, which will cause disturbance or anarchy. Protestants in England, men like Joseph or Barnes, proclaiming Protestant doctrines as e.g. that of *justificatio sola fide* work 'every engine of warfare' that they 'may gain admittance [i.e. for Protestant doctrine]; nor is there an easier entering passage than by the preaching of "only faith" '; nor do they 'doubt that that plant, if it shall have struck root in our soil, at length by continual watering and diligent culture, will some time bring forth those bitter fruits

[1] Muller, op. cit., p. 407.

which, tasted but once, will readily effect the miscarriage of all other religion'.[1]

To be on the alert against the danger of the New Doctrine, which, given a chance to enter will overflood the whole country, is even more important to Gardiner after the death of Henry. The young king, Edward VI, has to be guided and advised by wise men so long as he is not of age. At this moment, when the country has not a ruler who can decide how to act, it is even more important not to involve the country in more disturbances by adding religious problems and changes of obviously dangerous character. Gardiner repeats that again and again in his letter to Cranmer of June 1547, in entreating him to be careful in publishing the Homilies, which will cause with their innovations unnecessary disturbances, and to retain the old traditions,

> tyll owr sovereyn lord that now is, cum to his perfect age, whom God graunt then to fynd suche people as his father left, not altered with any innovation.[2]

As long as religion is not changed by innovations, there remains for Gardiner the hope that Protestantism will not advance in England and that he can retain the course indicated by Henry VIII. The dangerous moment might be overcome and the young king might become the heir of Henry's ecclesiastical policy. It is Gardiner's duty to watch just now

> those especially who are not too well disposed toward royalty, against whom it has been proclaimed not once only, nor ambiguously, not in some riddle by which fools are deceived, but with clear and evident testimony by which thoughtful men are moved, that we must be on our guard and use great foresight.[3]

The Anabaptists and other sects of the new learning are the danger for the Commonwealth, as recent discovered plots have proved.[4]

The troubled statesman, fearful, prophesying, foreseeing, suspicious against any change in religion, tries to keep at all cost his Catholic conception which he had managed so easily to bring in accordance with the policy of Henry VIII, but which he saw now after the death

[1] Muller, op. cit., pp. 334-335. Gardiner to Cranmer, July 1547. The original Latin runs: 'qui omnem movet machinam qua intromittatur, nec commodior est transitus quam ut sola fides predicetur. Neque non dubitat eam plantam, si solo nostro coaluerit, continua tandem irrigatione et cultura dilligenti, acerbos illos fructus producturam aliquando, qui vell semel gustati omnis relique religionis abortum facile sint effecturi.'

[2] ibid., pp. 310, 312, 313.

[3] ibid., p. 318.

[4] ibid., pp. 319, 320.

of Henry and under the government of men like Somerset endangered. Gardiner, the bishop and churchman, argues against Protestantism as statesman, and yet as the churchman, who hopes to save his Catholic belief, which agreed so well with his principle of loyalty towards a king who had not forced him to abandon his doctrine and church practice. The oath of supremacy to Henry had never changed his churchmanship. His opposition against the doctrine of justification by faith only although learnedly elaborated with theological arguments and testimonies from the Fathers, is always connected with that political concern of his, will it not cause the same secular troubles as it did in Germany? With it goes the other argument, that the doctrine cannot be accepted, as it leads to consequences, which mean also giving up the sacramental teaching of the Real Presence in the Catholic conception. It shows again how inseparably arguments of political and theological character are bound together for Gardiner: If disturbances are caused by the teaching of the new doctrine for the realm, it means the same to him, as if by that new doctrine the Catholic dogma will be attacked. Both arguments are for Gardiner of vital importance:

> Do the German examples move us not at all? Those men, hitherto unconquered, now, unwilling and reluctant, have been overthrown by that foolish sophism [i.e. justification by faith alone], which they could maintain neither by pen nor sword. If they had been willing to withdraw at the proper season from their fatuous persistence in this opinion, long since would they have had their affairs settled, to the greatest disgrace and harm of the bishop of Rome. But the force of that sophism drove Luther, for the sake of defending his consistency, to pervert the mysteries of the sacraments and fall away to the insane assertion of necessity. When he halted at the Sacrament of the Eucharist, there rose up not a few who assailed the timidity of the man because he did not dare to follow out the full force of that proposition to the end; viz., that he utterly abolish the Eucharist also, which cannot stand with that doctrine; a thing which Zwingli and others so clearly handle, that it is evident to anyone that these things are so joined and interdependent that whoever has admitted the doctrine of 'only faith' in justification is compelled to reject the Sacrament of the Eucharist in the way we profess it.[1]

The very fact, that in the bishop's eyes the peasant revolt and other inner disturbances in Germany had broken out, that the imminent danger of war between the Protestant princes and the Emperor was always menacing, made him suspicious of any change

[1] Muller, op. cit., p. 335.

of more decisive character in religion. Their religious claim of reforming abuses and false doctrines of the Church meant to him throwing the State in a position of war or revolution:

> . . . but this I take to be trewe, that if the [walle of auctorite, which I accompted established in our last agrement, be oones broken, and newe water] lett in [at] a lytel gappe, the vehemence of noveltie wyl floo further thenne your Grace wold admitte. And whenne men here of newe gere, every man makith his request, sum newe hose, sum newe cotes, sum newe cappes, sum newe shirtes; like as in religion we have seen attempted where the people thought they might prevayle; which caused the commotion in Germanye, *in bello civili rusticorum*, and hath made the s[ame] styrre there nowe *in bello civili nobilium*. It was a notable acte of our late souverain lord to reforme and thenne moderate religion as he did, which he did not without al trouble. And we be [in a time] whenne al quietnes is required, . . . our late souverain lord was wont to saye, [which I shal] never forget, speking of hymself, [if the ol]d man had not loked to the pacificacion, he sawe men desirous to set forth ther owne fansyes, which [he th] ought to have excluded by his pacification . . .

writes Gardiner to Cranmer in June 1547.[1]

The king provides that safety even for the Church, which enables the clergy to live a life undisturbed. The deepest obligation Gardiner owes is to the king and his country, as his fortune and life are inseparably connected with those of his sovereign:

> . . . for this I owe to the father, the dead prince, to whom I am under the deepest obligations; this I owe to the son, whom I hold as my prince; this I owe to my country and all good men whose safety I share, since I sail in the same ship . . .' (Gardiner in his letter to Cranmer, July 1547).[2]
>
> His king is the 'staye' and 'Father of Christendom'[3] and his 'amitie bytwen your Majestie and thEmperour' is 'the very meane to extincte the light enterprises of Fraunce, and to expelle the Turke, and to quiet Germanye; and that without your Majestie there canne be nothing stable' (Gardiner to Henry VIII, on May 12th, 1542).[4]

Gardiner is always anxious to express his loyalty to the king and to make it the one reason of all his actions. The king 'hath, by the

[1] Muller, p. 308.

[2] ibid., p. 349. The original Latin ibid.

[3] ibid., pp. 94, 97. The whole letter is of interest. Letter to Russell, Browne and Sadler, May 17th, 1542. Gardiner quotes to them his conversation with the Imperial Ambassador Chapuys.

[4] Muller, op. cit., p. 94. Gardiner quotes to Henry his conversation with Chapuys, and Chapuys' opinion on Henry is reported in the words above noted.

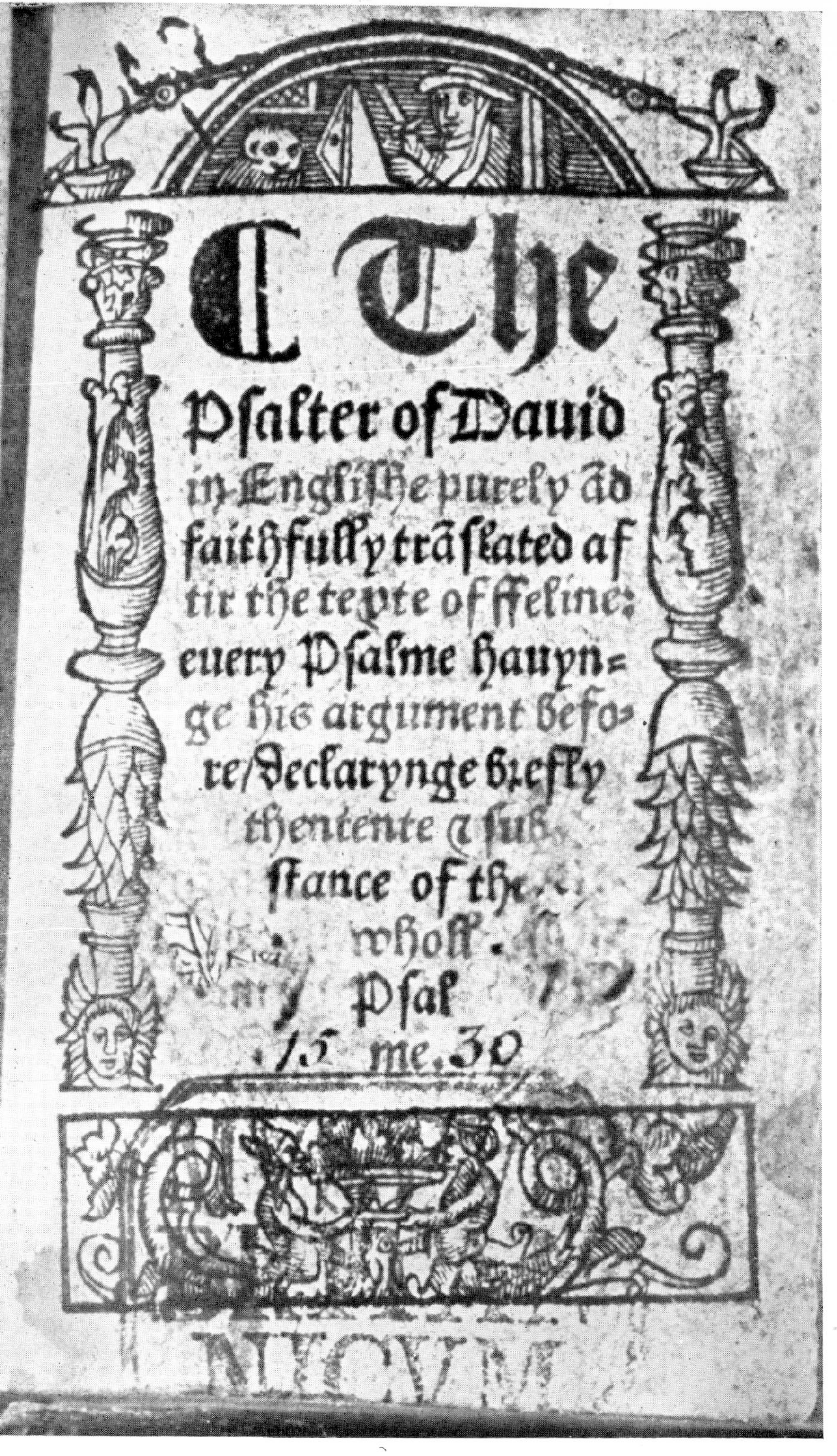

¶ The
Psalter of Dauid
in Englishe purely ād
faithfully trāslated af
tir the texte of Feline:
euery Psalme hauyn=
ge his argument befo=
re/declarynge brefly
thentente & sub
stance of the
whole.
Psal
15 me. 30

TITLE PAGE OF BUCER'S PSALTER IN ENGLISH
(Strassburg, 1530; enlarged. cf. p. 219)

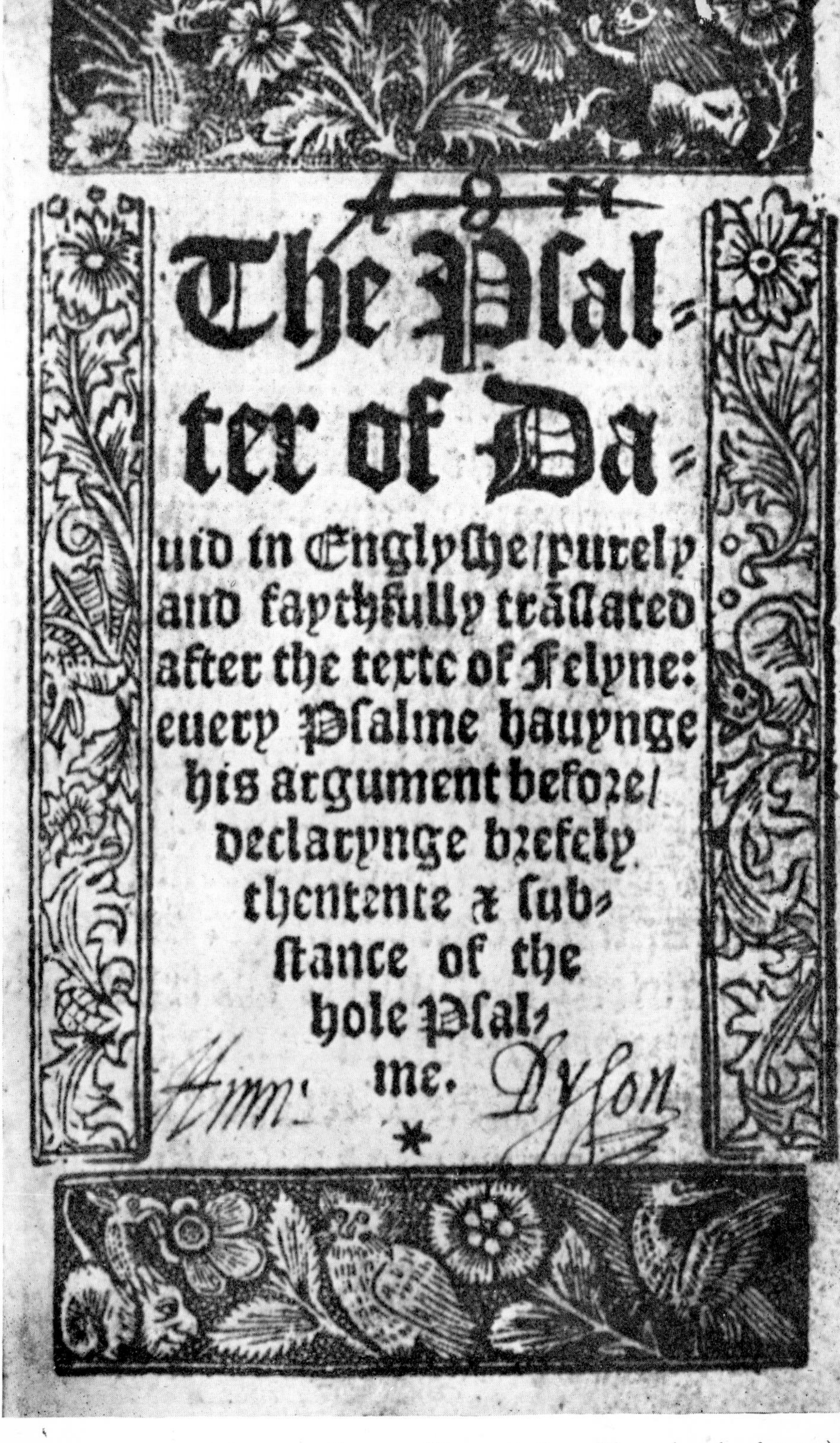
The Psal=
ter of Da=
uid in Englyshe/purely
and faythfully trãslated
after the texte of Felyne:
euery Psalme hauynge
his argument before/
declarynge brefely
thentente & sub=
stance of the
hole Psal=
me.

TITLE PAGE OF BUCER'S PSALTER IN ENGLISH (Thomas Godfray edition; enlarged. cf. p. 220)

inspiration of the Holy Goost, componed al matiers of religion'.[1] The supremacy of the king is incompatible with any other form of government, and gives the king power to protect his country. This argument of Gardiner makes him audaciously state that the Protestant princes should listen to the king, accept his proposals in political and ecclesiastical matters, and should not try to impose their policy and religion upon England. The inconvincible conviction of Gardiner of the Divine right of his king explains his attitude in negotiations with the Protestant Party. The Articles proposed by the Protestant princes at Schmalkald presented to Edward Fox on Christmas Day 1535 as the basis for a league with England, make Gardiner state his disapproval to Cromwell. Gardiner was asked by Cromwell to give his opinion on the proposal to the king, and did so, strongly expressing his feeling of superiority over the German Party. In his statement the reason of his dislike of Protestantism is well illustrated. Here also an answer is given to the question, why any Protestant mission to England had to fail, so long as Gardiner was in power and could raise his disapproval officially:

> . . . inasmoch as the Kinges Highnes, being of thastate of a king, and, in his realme, an emperour, and hed of the Church of England; and among the prynces of Germany oonly dukes and lower degrees; such also as knowlege thEmperour for ther supreme lord; . . . howe shal they, without the consent of the hed of ther Church, which is thEmperour, establish with us the agrement upon ther religion? Or howe shal we, without derogating the Kinges cause of his prerogative and supremite, convenaunt with them in that behaulf; whom we knowe as noo hedes of their Church, but inferiour membres, . . . ? Me semeth the worde 'association' soundith not wel. Ne it were convenient that the Kinges Highnes shuld have any lower place thenne to be chief, principal, and hed of the leage, and the rest not to be associate, but adherent and dependaunt therunto, as contrahentes . . .[2]

All considerations and actions by Gardiner in ecclesiastical or theological matters can be traced to his simple principle *Rex dixit*. True as the saying *Roma locuta causa finita* as true it is for Gardiner, that everything rests on the word of his sovereign. The king as pater patriae has to be obeyed, his main concern of protecting his

[1] op. cit., p. 122.

[2] Muller, op. cit., pp. 72-73, 74: 'For so shal they obteyne the glorye, that they shal thenne send unto us, not to lerne of us, but to instructe and tech us; not to sue to us, but to directe our Church in such ceremonyes as by ther deliberacion shuld be commened of and concluded.' This statement to Cromwell has most probably to be dated, middle of February 1536 from Lyons, when Gardiner was ambassador at the French Court.

realm has to be the main concern of any citizen, the main duty of the Church in collaborating with the king. Without that co-operation the Church does not only endanger the secular safety of sovereign and realm but brings herself in danger, as being in the same boat ('qui in eadem nave navigo'). Gardiner's main anxiety has always been that the Church by being not obedient to this essential demand will involve the realm in serious controversies. For that reason the Church has to be careful and on the alert in considering reform schemes and in listening to new teaching. The Church has to guard the interests of the realm, which are endangered by throwing open the gates to revolutionary new learning. The assumption of the Protestants, to send their emissaries to instruct and teach England, to direct the Church, is met by Gardiner's assumption, that the Protestants were too inferior as to be able to influence English affairs. Their machinations had to be stopped, or at least to be minimized. They had to be moved to agree to the supremacy of Henry VIII, for 'the King our master hath a special case, bicause he is emperour in himself and hath noo superior'.[1]

The Germans' dislike of the Emperor Charles V, and the fact that Protestantism had not acknowledged a supreme head, but was governed by various smaller princes and dukes, proves to Gardiner that conservative Catholicism can never meet on equal grounds with Protestantism. The attitude of the Church towards sovereigns becomes to Gardiner the touchstone of the rightness of religious claims. If Protestantism should ever be acceptable to Gardiner and his party, they had to be convinced that Protestantism would never object against any kind of supremacy of the Regent:

> If [in] Germanye such as have been brought up in those opinions had in ther behavour a more perfite reverence, and obedience to thEmperour, who whatsoever he be, he is ther superiour, thenne wolde I thinke the lernyng might be good to tech obedience to princes; but I see it is not soo. If I sawe that parte more civile, more honest, more reasonable thenne they wer wont to be, I might thinke the lernyng good for sumwhat in this worlde; . . .[2]

The lines of arguing here developed by Gardiner do not only throw a new light on the problem of the relations between England and the Continental Reformers under Henry VIII, but are the best indications to show where the main difference comes out in the arguments between Gardiner and Bucer on doctrinal topics in their

[1] Muller, op. cit., p. 75.
[2] ibid., op. cit., p. 161 (to Paget, November 5th, 1545).

various controversies. Bucer's arguments circle round his theological conception, whilst Gardiner mainly reflects on those doctrinal problems as the politician and statesman, who looks to their practical effect on the affairs of the realm. It shows also why Bucer was fortunate in gaining influence with his doctrine in England, because at that moment, the politician Gardiner was replaced by Cranmer, who was more conciliatory and did not force those strict consequences on matters of Church doctrine and discipline as Gardiner did.

The flood, so extremely feared by Gardiner, cannot be stemmed by him, as Cranmer and other churchmen have already opened some small gate for it to enter. The Homilies are the opportunity for the new learning to flood the country. The safety of the realm is in danger, but still more important to Gardiner, his so long and strongly-guarded church principles are going to die with the death of his sovereign, Henry VIII.

At this time, when Protestantism gains hold in England, Gardiner is not any longer an authoritative person in political or ecclesiastical affairs in England. His imprisonment and later his retiring to the country make him realize that the opportune hour has come for Protestantism. Gardiner has stepped into the background at a moment when the authority he had under Henry VIII might have changed the religious issues in England.

When Gardiner got again into power under Mary, even when he returned to Roman Catholicism, it was too late to turn down Protestantism, which had become in those few years under Edward VI an unconquerable movement in spite of persecution under Mary.

His doctrine of obedience to the State authority was perhaps unconsciously stressed so much by him, as still believing that his sovereign would never attempt to reform the Church decisively by listening to Protestant doctrine, would try to protect Roman Catholicism detached from the Papal supremacy, which was, for Gardiner, the only safeguard against any innovation.[1]

Against this background of the two main conceptions of Gardiner and Bucer, their controversy on theological problems and those of the relation between State and Church has to be set, if we will understand the force of their arguments. Their attitude was already developed apart from their actual controversy, and when they met in 1541 at Ratisbon, two fundamentally different conceptions are

[1] p. 460: 'Peut-être croyait-il [Gardiner], ou du moins voulait-il croire et donner à croire, que l'Eglise henricienne ne s'éloignait pas trop, en certains points, de l'idéal des réformateurs catholiques.' Pierre Janelle: 'La Controverse Entre Etienne Gardiner et Martin Bucer sur la Discipline Ecclésiastique' (1541-48): pp. 452-466 in *Revue Des Sciences Religieuses*. Université de Strasbourg. Tome VII, 1927.

seen which could only be overcome by the defeat of one of the opponents. Bucer was the fortunate one, who, helped by political events and by support of men equal to him in England, could finally gain access to the discipline and learning in the Church in England.

It was at the Colloquy of Ratisbon in spring 1541 that the 'Henrician' Bishop of Winchester, Stephen Gardiner, and the 'Théologien-diplomate par excellence',[1] Martin Bucer, met for the first and last time. The story of that Colloquy and of the attempts of Charles V to reunite the opposing Church parties on the Continent, has often been written by sixteenth-century theologians of both camps. The meeting and discussion between Gardiner and Bucer is only a minor incident in the story of the great conference of eminent theologians. But the discussion started there caused a years-long war of pamphlets between the two men. An account of their discussion is given by Gardiner as well as by Bucer in their various writings. William Turner, in his anti-Gardiner pamphlets,[2] refers also to the controversy.

Although Gardiner accuses Bucer as well as Turner of having given an incorrect account of the actual order of their discussion, and although the accounts as given by Gardiner and Bucer are divergent as regards the order in which the theological topics at their meeting were discussed, it can be said that the discussion revolved round the questions of obedience to the sovereign and celibacy. In connection with 1 Cor. vii. 37 the question of the authority of a sovereign over his subjects was discussed. That is also not denied by Gardiner. But he accuses Bucer of having reversed the order. The Scripture passage seems to have served Gardiner to illustrate his argument, that the article on celibacy for the clergy, issued by Henry VIII, might have a scriptural warrant in the verse referred

[1] Constant, G.: *La Réforme En Angleterre* (*Le Schisme Anglican*) . . . Paris, 1930, p. 231.

[2] *The huntyng and fyndyng out of the Romyshe foxe, which more then seuen yeares . . . MDXLIII.* col. *Jmprynted at Basyll* . . . September 14th, 1543, fol. E vij: '. . . when he was requyred of Martyn Bucer what scripture he had to proue that prestes myght not mary, lyke a perfit canonist for lacke of scripture made thys reson. The same autorite hathe the kynge ouer all the prestes of hys realme and hys other subiectes that a father hath ouer hys chylderne. But a kynge may forbyd the prestes of hys realme to mary.' – *The Rescvynge of the Romishe Fox Othervvyse called the examination of the hunter deuised by steuen gardiner. The Seconde Covrse of the Hvnter At the romishe fox & hys aduocate, & sworne patrone steuen gardiner doctor & defender of the popis canonlaw & hys ungodly ceremonies . . . col; Jmprynted haue at winchester Anno Domini* 1545. 4. *nonas Martij. By me Hanse hit prik.*, fol. Kviij, ff.

cf. also Muller, James: *The Letters of Stephen Gardiner* . . . pp. 478 ff., and Janelle, Pierre: *Obedience in Church and State* . . . pp. xlvi-xlvii. (Janelle in this work gives an excellent account of the controversy between Gardiner and Bucer, pp. xli-li.)

to. It seems obvious that Bucer, who, since the publication of the 6 Articles in 1539, felt uneasy about the course of the English churches, and who seems to have thought to have an opportunity for achieving a better understanding with the English churches through Gardiner at Ratisbon, began the discussion by asking the bishop how the law for celibacy of the clergy could be justified. Gardiner, in trying to answer, then seems to have turned to 1 Cor. vii as illustration.

Bucer in his *Responsio* to Latomus (1544) refers to this particular point of the discussion with Gardiner.[1]

Bucer's reference in his work against Latomus caused Gardiner, in his *Conquestio* (fol. Aiij, ff. and L verso, ff.)[2] to give his account of the discussion and to 'correct' Bucer's report.

Another subject on which the two men seem to have conversed was that of justification. Bucer writes in his *Gratulatio*:

> I thowght mete here to declare, esspeciallye seing in the reueylinge and disclosinge of oure disputation begone at Ratisbona about the nature & disposition of faithe which iustifieth (that is to say) which attacheth so perfectly the mercy of god that iustifyeth vs in Christe our Lord, that it maketh vs assuraunt of euerlastynge helth, I disclosed and confuted certayne of hys deceytfull argumentes, wherwith he wēt about to disproue oure right confessiō & verie apostolike doctrine.[3]

Judging from the language and accusations used in their controversial writings following their meeting, the conversation between Gardiner and Bucer confirmed their mutual suspicion and dislike.[4]

To Bucer's allusion to the discussion in his anti-Latomus work, Gardiner had answered by two Epistles (1544 and 1545-46).[5] The Epistles were written in a strongly invective and unbalanced tone. Paget writes to Sir Petre (April 23rd, 1546):

[1] *Scripta Duo Adversaria D. Bartholomaei Latomi . . . Et Martini Buceri . . .* 1544, pp. 70-71. cf. also Bucer's *Gratulatio*, op. cit., pp. 55 f., where he recalls his meeting with Gardiner and their discussion. Gardiner's 'horrible dogma that the human transgression of human laws is rightly to be punished more heavily than that of divine laws' is specially remembered by Bucer at that occasion. cf. Gardiner's MS. *Contemptum humanae legis* . . . (now printed by P. Janelle, op. cit., pp. 174 ff.; cf. ibid., pp. xlviii ff.). cf. Gardiner's *Exetasis* . . . pp. 155 ff.

[2] Stephani VVinton: *Episcopi Angli, ad Martinvm Bvcerum*, De Impudenti eiusdem Pseudologia Conquestio . . . *Lovanii*, . . . Anno 1544.

[3] fol. B and B verso in Hoby's translation of the *Gratulatio*.

[4] cf. Gardiner's *Epistola* (fol. Ciij verso): 'Ita porro conturbatis, . . . figitis . . . omnia . . . illotis pedibus conculcata, & a porcis, luto coenoque conspersa & oblita . . .' cf. also fols. Aij, Bij, D verso, and passim. cf. Bucer's hard criticisms of Gardiner's life and character, in *Gratulatio*, pp. 39, 53, 54.

[5] *Conquestio* (op. cit.), 1544, and *Episcopi Angli ad Martinvm Bvcervm Epistola* . . . (1546).

> ... I send you a book of my lord of Wynchester's making against Bucer in manner of an epistle, wherein if he had contained himself *a maledicentia* it had been well done. For the matter therein I find me much satisfied.[1]

And Richard Hilles writes to Bullinger (April 30th, 1546):

> ... the bishop of Winchester has very lately republished a book against Bucer, altogether full of bitterness and invective, in which he professes his contempt of him on every account, attacks his learning ...[2]

And Thomas Hoby in the prefatory letter to his translation of Bucer's *Gratulatio* refers to Gardiner's Epistles by saying:

> My Lord of Winchester (far unsemely for a sober bishop) has expressed and set forth in his two most contumelious and railing epistles against him, winking at, and overhipping his well most innumerable opprobrius words, checks, taunts, rebukes, quarrelings scoffings revilings and scoldings railings, wherwith they are filled as full as they may be heaped together.[3]

Bucer's answer was eagerly expected by his friends.[4] But not before 1547-48 did Bucer reply. His reply is not directly addressed to Gardiner.

His *Gratulatio*, which was soon translated into English, as already mentioned, by Thomas Hoby, who was at that time staying with Bucer, was addressed to the English Church, congratulating her for the definite Protestant course and for the excellent quality and soundness in doctrine of the leaders of this Church, men like Cranmer. And then Bucer refers to the attack made by Gardiner in his *Conquestio* against him and his teaching on celibacy. Bucer then exclusively deals with that question by frequently referring to his dispute with Gardiner and to the bishop's published Epistle. The passage of 1 Cor. vii which had only served at their discussion as an illustration in connection with the question of the rights of a sovereign is now made subject to an exclusive investigation on celibacy bearing no longer any relation to the subject of the authority of a sovereign. Controversy on celibacy is now the central problem dis-

[1] *Letters & Papers, Foreign and Domestic, Henry VIII*, vol. XXI, part I, 1546; p. 329, no. 661.

[2] *Original Letters*, vol. I, p. 254.

[3] cf. the letter in extenso in the Appendix to this chapter. This passage fol. Aiij in modern spelling.

[4] cf. letter of Bradford (op. cit., Letter VI, pp. 17 ff.) to Traves (May 12th, 1548): 'I have sent you a book of Bucer against Winchester, in English, lately translated, which I never read; therefore I cannot praise it ...' (p. 19).

cf. Letters of Myles Coverdale to Hubert (op. cit., pp. 512-513 and 519-520) from Bergzabern.

cussed by Bucer and Gardiner. Bucer attempts to prove his interpretation of I Cor. vii as being correct by referring to the Church Fathers. Gardiner by examining the passages quoted by Bucer from the Fathers, tries to show that Bucer could not claim them on his side. But it is of interest to note that the particular verse (vii. 37) of the chapter in S. Paul's Epistle so hotly disputed by the two opponents, was understood by Gardiner as well as by Bucer as referring to the father's authority over his daughter, an interpretation which is at least doubtful.

When Bucer answers Gardiner's accusations in the *Conquestio*, he enlarges on the question of celibacy in his *Gratulation*, Bucer's reply to Gardiner's *Epistola* is contained in his *Disputata Ratisbonae*. And here it is even more difficult to conceive at first sight this writing as an answer to Gardiner's other Epistle. For Bucer's reply is most ingeniously woven into that comprehensive account of the History of the Colloquies at Ratisbon. Here the problem is not that of celibacy or of the rights of a sovereign, but mainly and exclusively that of justification and faith. As that question had been the main issue between the Protestants and Roman Catholics at Ratisbon, he not only feels justified in including the similar controversy between himself and Gardiner in his treatise on justification, but also considers it serving Gardiner well, to place his arguments beside those of Bucer's other Roman Catholic opponents. Thus, by not indulging in a special work as reply to Gardiner's Epistles, Bucer intended to show that he did not pay too much importance to Gardiner's attacks, attacks which demanded not a special reply, but could be dealt with in passing.

The reply of Bucer in his *Disputata* to Gardiner's *Epistola* deserves special attention, for it not only seems to be unknown to research on the relation between Gardiner and Bucer, but also contains a most interesting contribution to the controversy on justification between Gardiner, the Roman Catholic in his doctrinal outlook, and the Protestant, Bucer. It furnishes a further illustration to Gardiner's repeated complaints to Somerset and Cranmer, in which he thoroughly opposes the doctrine of justification as expressed in the Homilies and as held by Cranmer and his friends.[1] It shows also that the general trend of the Homilies as regards justification and faith was almost equal to that of Bucer in his arguments against Gardiner and the Roman Catholics.

[1] cf. *Letters of Stephen Gardiner* (in Muller, J., op. cit.)
to Cranmer (July 1547), op. cit., pp. 336 ff.;
to Somerset (October 14th, 1547), op. cit., pp. 382 ff.;
to the Privy Council (August 1547), op. cit., pp. 362 ff. and passim.

A study of the vast problem of celibacy is not in the scope of this work, but a few remarks on the special discussion between Gardiner and Bucer about the term *digamos* seems to be justified in connection with this chapter.

§ I

'DISPUTATA RATISBONAE'

(Bucer's Reply in his *Disputata Ratisbonae* to Gardiner's *Epistola* of December 1545[1])

The *Disputata* of Bucer provide an excellent source of information on one of the main controversial subjects between him and Gardiner.

In including in his *Disputata* his reply to Gardiner Bucer shows that the bishop's arguments and objections to *justification by faith only* contained in his *Epistola* against the Reformer form part of the History of the Colloquies at Ratisbon (1541 and 1546) between the Catholic and Protestant Parties. Seen in relation with the discussion at Ratisbon, Gardiner's 'cavillations' express some of the main objections of the Catholics against the Protestant doctrine, and will not be understood merely as his personal opinions and insults in a private dispute with Bucer, entirely separate from the main subject of discussion at the Colloquies.

It is worth while to insist on this fact, that Bucer's *Disputata* contains his answer on the special subject of *justification*, a fact which was overlooked by research since the title-page of the *Disputata* refers to Bucer's response to the Bishop of Winchester's tenet of celibacy of the clergy opposing that of Bucer. This reference by itself is misleading since the reply to those questions raised by Gardiner in his

[1] The full title of Bucer's Disputata runs: *Dispvtata Ratisbonae, in Altero Colloquio* Anno XLVI. *ET* Collocutorum Augustanae Confessionis *Responsa*, quae ibi coeperant, completa, De Iustificatione, & locis doctrinae Euangelicae omnibus, quos doctrina de Iustificatione complectitur.

Tractata et Decreta De Concilianda Religione, in Comitijs, Ratisbonensi, Anno 41. Spirensi, Anno 44. Vuormaciēsi Anno 45. & Augustano, Anno 48. *Responsio ad Stephanvm*, Episcopum Vintoniensem, Anglum, De coelibatu sacerdotum & coenobitarum . . . *Per Martinvm Bvcervm*. 1548. On p. 692: Argentorati, Mense Nouembri, anno M.D.LVII.

The title of Gardiner's letter is as follows: Stephani VVinTON. *Episcopi Angli, ad Martinvm Bvcervm Epistola*, qua cessantem hactenus & cunctantem, ac frustratoria responsionis pollicitatione, orbis de se iudicia callide sustinentem, vrget ad respondendū de impudētissima eiusdē pseudologia iustissimę conquestioni ante annū aeditę. Louanii, Ex officina Seruatii Zasseni. Anno M.D.XLVI. Men. Martio. On last page: XII. Decembris. Anno Incarnationis M.D.XLXV.

previous letter (*Conquestio . . .*)[1] are contained in Bucer's *Gratulatio.*[2]

None of those historical surveys of the Colloquies at Ratisbon was so entirely dedicated to the controversy on *justification* as the *Disputata* with its statement:

> . . . de iustificatione, et locis doctrinae Euangelicae omnibus, quos doctrina de iustificatione complectitur.

The desired conciliation between Protestants and Catholics was dependent on an agreement on that doctrine, all other articles were of secondary importance in view of this fundamental dogma, all other articles were more or less the outcome of it. 'Celibacy, discipline,

[1] *Stephani VVinton. Episcopi Angli, ad Martinvm Bvcer*um, De Impudenti eiusdem Pseudologia Conquestio. *Lovanii*, Ex officina Rutgeri Rescij, Anno 1544. Men. August. (Col. VI. Calen. Augusti 1544.)

[2] The Gratulation of the mooste famous Clerke M. Martin Bucer, a man of no lesse learninge and lyterature, then Godlye studie and example of lyuing, vnto the churche of Englande for the restitucion of Christes religion. And Hys answere vnto the two raylinge epistles of Steuē, Bisshoppe of Winchester, concerninge the vnmaried state of preestes and cloysterars, wherin is euidently declared, that it is against the lawes of God, and of his churche to require of all suche as be and must be admitted to preesthood, to refrain from holye matrimonie.

> Translated out of Latin in to Englishe.
> Hebru. xiij.
> Wedlocke is to be had in price emonge al men, & is a chamber vndefyled. As for hoore keapers, & adulterers, God wyll iudge them.

It is the translation by Hoby of Gratulatio Martini Buceri Ad Ecclesiam Anglicanam, de Religionis Christi restitutione: Et, Responsio Eiusdem Ad Duas Stephani Episcopi Vintoniensis Angli conviciatrices Epistolas, De coelibatu sacerdotum & coenobitarum: in qua demonstratur, S. coniugij abstinentiam contra Dei & Ecclesiae leges exigi ab omnibus ad sacerdotium & admissis & admittendis.

> Hebr. XI. [*sic*]
> Honorabile est inter omnes coniugium, & cubile impollutum. Scortatores autem & adulteros iudicabit Deus.

1548

last page: Anno Christi MDXLVII Mense Novembri.

Martinus Bucerus.

Note: Janelle in his article on the controversy between Gardiner and Bucer gives an account of all writings of both men relating to that controversy.

J. A. Muller in his *Stephen Gardiner and the Tudor Reaction* refers also to the various writings (p. 311).

Neither Janelle nor Muller mentions Bucer's reply, contained in his *Disputata* to Gardiner's *Epistola.*

Janelle only states that there is another edition of the *Gratulatio* of Bucer annexed to the *Disputata*, without referring to the relation of the *Disputata*, which contains the reply to Gardiner's *Epistola*, to the controversy: Janelle writes (pp. 462-463 under no. 15): 'Même opuscule [*Gratulatio . . .*], imprimé à la suite de *Dispvtata . . .* Bien que la pagination de la *Gratulatio* soit indépendante, et la typographie exactement semblable à celle de [no.] 14 [*Gratulatio*, separate print], il s'agit bien d'une édition distincte, et sans doute postérieure, une erreur de détail se trouvant rectifiée . . . Il est significatif que Bucer ait choisi, pour le joindre à un recueil rétrospectif de pièces relatives aux colloques, son opuscule contre Gardiner.' (Jannelle, Pierre: 'La Controverse . . .' op. cit.).

The two copies, that of the *Gratulatio* in separate print, and that annexed to the *Disputata*, mentioned by Janelle, are according to his statement the copies of the Bibl., Nat. B.U.R. Strasb. and of the Bibl. Nat., Sainte-Geniève. Janelle gives only the year of print, which is in both cases 1548. A copy of the *Gratulatio* annexed to the *Disputata* is also at the Bodleian. The *Disputata* gives, on p. 692, exact date and place: Argentorati,

authority of Church and State' had to be seen and answered from that 'articulus stantis et cadentis ecclesiae'[1].

Bucer's reply to Gardiner's *Epistola* on that topic is contained in the '*Secunda Realis Controversia De* natura & certitudine fidei' (op. cit., pp. 441-555) of the *Disputata* and thus forms part of the discussion at stake between the Protestants and the Catholics at the second Colloquy at Ratisbon in 1546, which is there recorded by Bucer. That gives the impression as if Gardiner had been one of the discussing parties, whereas Gardiner's and Bucer's controversy is connected with the Colloquy of 1541, when both men met for the first time. In 1546 the main opponents to Bucer and his Protestant friends were the Roman Catholics Eberhard Billick and Malvenda,[2] whereas Gardiner himself was only present at Ratisbon in 1541. To Bucer the objections of the Catholics in 1546 were on the same line as Gardiner's in 1541 and in his *Epistola*, to be equally dealt with. At the point when the discussion in 1546 reached the same or similar line of argument to that of Gardiner, Bucer incorporates Gardiner's remarks made in his *Epistola* (1545) into his own continuous report

[1] This ought to be said in view of Janelle's statement (op. cit., p. 452), who, disregarding Bucer's reply in the *Disputata*, considers 'celibacy . . .' as the principal point of the discussion.

[2] D. Petrus Maluenda Hispanus, theologus Sorbonicus, cf. op. cit., p. 8.

Mense Novembri, anno M.D.LVII. The same date is found on p. 84 of the annexed *Gratulatio*, without reference to Strassburg: that fact may seem to contradict Janelle's statement that the *Gratulatio* is an edition 'sans doute postérieure'.

H. Eells writes: 'He [Bucer] also included a defense of the doctrine of justification against the attacks of Stephen Gardiner, and a reply to his opinions on sacerdotal celibacy and monasticism' (*Bucer*, op. cit., p. 390), and '. . . Bucer found it necessary to attack Gardiner's ideas on justification in the *Disputata Ratisbonae*. So he determined to complete the task by including in the book a *Response* to the *Epistola*. After that Stephen could no longer say that he did not dare to reply to his statements on celibacy' (*Bucer*, p. 391). These statements made by Eells need some correction. Bucer, in the *Disputata*, included only his defence on the doctrine of justification against Gardiner's attack. The misleading statement made by Bucer on the title-page of the *Disputata*, that it also contains his response on celibacy (cf. note 1, p. 186) seems to have caused Eells to state that it also contains 'a reply to his opinions on sacerdotal celibacy and monasticism'. Bucer's reply on celibacy contained in his *Gratulatio* has nothing to do with his reply concerning *justification* in his *Disputata*.

But apart from the *Disputata*, dated by Bucer: Argentorati, Mense Novembri, anno M.D. LVII (p. 692), there exists the *Gratulatio ad ecclesiam Anglicanam*, which bears on its title-page: 'Responsio Eiusdem Ad duas Stephani Episcopi Vintoniensis Angli conuiciatrices Epistolas, De coelibatu sacerdotum & coenobitarum: in qua demonstratur, S. coniugij abstinentiam contra Dei & Ecclesiae leges exigi ab omnibus ad sacerdotium & admissis, & admittendis.' Here the note on the title-page is justified as the *Gratulatio* contains the reply on celibacy. As the *Gratulatio* is also dated November 1547 (p. 84) and also published at Strassburg with the *Disputata* in 1548, it seems to be evident that Bucer intended to publish the *Disputata* and the *Gratulatio* in one edition, so that the reference made on the title-page of the *Disputata* would actually refer to the reply in the *Gratulatio*. A copy of the *Disputata* and a copy of the *Gratulatio* are actually bound together in one volume at the Bodleian. Both tracts have on the title-page the year 1548.

of the discussion at Ratisbon in 1546. He quotes on several occasions selected passages of that Epistle and fits them into the discussion between himself and his 'adversaries' in 1546. While Bucer states occasionally that statements cited from Gardiner belong to his *Epistola* or bear relation to the Colloquy of 1541, it is hardly unjust to conclude that he intended to make Gardiner's arguments form part of the discussion between himself, Billick and Malvenda.[1]

Under special headings Bucer deals with objections brought forth by Gardiner in his *Epistola*. By comparing the order in which Bucer replies to Gardiner's Epistle with the order in which the controversial points raised by Gardiner appear in his Epistle, it is proved again that Bucer did not intend to reply to Gardiner's work taking up point for point of that letter. But by incorporating points of Gardiner's Epistle, which bear resemblance to the problems which the discussion in 1546 has just reached, it becomes clear, that Gardiner's objections are nothing original but take the same line as those objections by Malvenda or Billick. The other point which has to be observed, is that Bucer writes also not a straightforward continuous reply, but scatters his observations here and there among his story of the Colloquies at Ratisbon:

pp. 453-454: *Responsio ad Cavilla Vintoniensis*, contra id quod dicimus, Charitatem nasci ex fide, fideique semper cohaerere. (refers to Gardiner's Epistola G ij verso).

p. 471: *Excvssio Loci II Pet. i. Stvdete* firmam facere uocationem uestram: quem obiecit Vintoniensis. (refers to Gardiner's Epistola G).

pp. 481-483: *Reiectio Calvmniae Vintoniensis*, in eandem confictam ab aduersarijs in dictis nostris pugnantiam, de securitate fidei & trepidatione conscientiae, quae simul in sanctis deprehenduntur. (refers to Epistola E ij).

pp. 490-494: *Reiicitvr Cavillatio Vintoniensis* contra hanc de certitudine salutis doctrinam, qua calumniatur ea doceri & peccandi securitatẽ, & neglectum bonorum operum. (refers to Epistola G verso).

pp. 494 ff.: *Reiicitvr Altera Vintoniensis Calu*mnia criminantis, ueram fidei certitudinem in dogmatis necessarijs euerti a nobis, per confictam fidei certitudinem.

pp. 511-518: *Obiectio ex D. Avgvstino, contra* certitudinem salutis:

[1] In summing up his reply to Gardiner's objections on the subject of faith, Bucer draws the attention of his reader also to his answer to Malvenda: 'Item quae de eadem re dicta a nobis sunt supra in responsione nostra ad scripturas, quibus Maluenda probare conatus est, iustificationem perfici per bona opera' (op. cit., p. 502), and 'Hac de re diximus etiam supra, in responsione nostra ad scripturas per Maluendam adductas, pro suo nouo dogmate, iustificationem bonis nostris operibus perfici & consummari' (op. cit., p. 475).

	eiusque solutio, & solutionis eius, contra Vintoniensem assertio. (refers to Epistola E ii — E ii f.).
pp. 523-530:	*Refellvntvr Calvmniae Vintonien*sis, contra id quod dicimus iustificationem sola fide apprehendi. (refers to Epistola E iiij verso — F verso).
p. 531:	*Caui*llatur praeterea Vintoniensis de uita aeterna admodum irreligiose. (refers to Epistola G verso).
pp. 536-537:	Cum ergo Vintoniensis rogat, quam vim habeat ea sententia . . . (refers to Epistola G ij).
pp. 538-544:	*Defenditvr oratio Articvli Con*ciliati Ratisbonae, . . . anni XLI. Iustificare nos fide, quatenus illa apprehenderit misericordiam Dei in Christo, & non quatenus habet cha[ri]tatem sibi adiunctam. (refers to Epistola Giij-H).
pp. 544-546:	*Qvae in Doctrina Vintoniensis De* iustificatione, cum Euangelio Christi sunt consentanea, quae secus. (Epistola Hij).

Apart from these sections, in which Bucer deals specially with Gardiner's arguments, the Bishop is mentioned on pp. 518 and 523.

The *Disputata*, intended to be the vindication for the right course of Protestant doctrine against growing Imperial and Catholic influences, could supply suitable illustration of the kind of argumentation used by Catholics, by incorporating certain passages of the *Epistola*. And the violent and unbalanced way of writing certainly showed the Bishop of Winchester in an unfavourable light in those selected passages. The opportunity given to the *Disputata* to compare Gardiner's arguments with those of continental Roman Catholics, made Bucer also realize that the reconciliation between both parties was practically impossible so long as they would not agree on the main doctrinal issue. Without that agreement the keenness of Bucer and the political desire of Charles V for conciliation would prove useless.

Gardiner, on the other side, became more and more assured by these negotiations, that the teaching of the Reformers was repugnant to that of the Church he represented, whereas Bucer was sure that his Protestant doctrine was not only wholesome but also apostolic, and that Gardiner's objections and those of his partisans were opposed to the *right confession and very apostolic doctrine.*[1]

In the *Epistola* of 1545 Gardiner had taken the line of argument initiated at Ratisbon to reveal the dangers of the 'erroneous doctrine' of the Protestants. His introductory pages are intended to show why this doctrine must be wrong and to what consequences it would lead:

[1] cf. *Gratulatio* (Eng. trans. by Hoby), fol. B to B verso.

The Protestants had separated themselves from the Catholic Church and her teaching, from the 'Pillar of Truth'. The disunity among their own groups was sufficient evidence to him that this disunity among themselves was a consequence of having fallen from the Church and of having disobeyed the authority of the *one* Church.[1] Gardiner, the emissary of his sovereign at the Colloquy in 1541, writes in his *Epistola*: In those articles to be agreed upon, one can discern the Reformers' contention on *justification, original sin and free will*, which is the seat of all their errors.[2] He believes Bucer to be at the bottom of all dissent, he is the 'corypheus' of all those who disturb and ruin anything not in accordance with their doctrine.[3] Bucer is to Gardiner the chief instigator for the Emperor's plan, although for Gardiner Bucer's scope and aim is different from that of Charles V, Bucer's intention being merely dissent.[4] And yet, although he speaks of Bucer as that 'manikin' (*homuntio*, fol. A), he must have seen in Bucer an opponent not to be underrated.

Bucer insists in his *Disputata* on the fact that the teaching of the Protestants at Ratisbon was in conformity with that of the *Confessio Augustana*, and that thus Gardiner cannot maintain that his teaching is different from that of the other Reformers.[5]

As can be seen from the respective headings under which Bucer deals in his *Disputata* with Gardiner's arguments, the controversy revolves round the topics of faith, salvation and justification. The relation of faith to charity needs to be clearly worked out, in order to show on the one side (that of Gardiner) that faith joined to charity is essential for salvation, and on the other side (that of Bucer), that faith alone, by apprehending the mercy of God, is necessary for salvation, but that no part can be ascribed to charity in working out justification or to apprehend remission of sins.[6] By faith men are justified, means that in faith men apprehend the mercy of God only.

Faith and charity as joined together, had always been the assertion of Gardiner. He objects to the doctrine of the Reformers of a *fides specialis* as it makes people too certain of their salvation, so that they neglect their perseverance and patience in good works for life eternal: it makes them also neglect their observance of God's commandments, weakening their efforts and zeal to work out their salvation.

[1] cf. *Epistola*, fol. Cii, Biij verso—Biiij, Eiiij verso, Cij verso—Ciij.
[2] cf. ibid., fol. D verso.
[3] cf. ibid., fol. Aii and fol. Bii.
[4] ibid., fol. D verso—Dii.
[5] cf. *Disputata*, pp. 61 ff., 481, 482, 544.
[6] cf. *Disputata*, pp. 538 ff.; *Epistola*, fol. Giii—H verso and passim.

Thus Gardiner objects also against the same doctrine as expressed in the Homilies, when in 1547 he writes to Protector Somerset:

> The booke of homilies in the sermon of salvation teacheth the clere contrar[ye] to the doctrine established by thacte of Parliament; even as contrarye as *includethe* is contrarie to *excludethe* . . . &c.[1]

Connected with this question of faith and charity is that of the certainty (*certitudo*) of our salvation. Quotations from the Fathers are employed by Gardiner as well as by Bucer in order to establish their case. A passage of S. Augustine's *De Civitate* (Lib. XI, chap. 12) made them start a special discussion in connection with the question of the certainty we have by faith of our salvation. S. Augustine wrote:

> . . . for we call them happy whom we see live well in this life, in hope of the immortality to come, without terror of conscience, and with true attainment of pardon for the crimes of our natural imperfection. These, though they be assured of reward for their perseverance, yet they are not sure to persevere. For what man knows that he shall continue to the end in action and increase of justice, unless he have it by revelation from Him, that by His secret providence instructs few (yet fails none), herein?[2]

Bucer states that his adversaries say that Augustine obviously denies in this passage that the saints are as certain about their perseverance, as they are about the reward for their perseverance. Then by referring to one of his former writings (*De Vera Ecclesiarum in Doctrina Caeremoniis . . .*) Bucer says that he has there already expounded the passage of S. Augustine and had written there that Augustine denies that we can be certain about our perseverance. Bucer writes:

> . . . D. Augustinum negare nos certos esse de perseverantia nostra, indeque de salute nostra certitudine scientiae, non autem certitudine fidei . . .' (*Disputata*, p. 511).

To this subtle distinction made by Bucer, *certitudo scientiae* and *certitudo fidei*, Gardiner objects. Faith, justification, charity, good works, are here the main controversial subjects. The same topics in the respective Homilies were objected to by the same arguments of Gardiner as he objects to them in his controversy with Bucer. And

[1] cf. his letter (October 14th, 1547) in Muller, J., op. cit., p. 382.

[2] Bucer brings this passage on p. 511 of the *Disputata*. Bucer differs from Augustine's text in two instances: Bu. 'non imprudenter', Aug. 'non impudenter'. Bu. 'cum spe futura', Aug. 'cum spe futurae'. The English translation is from Healey, John: *The City of God* . . . (London, 1931), Book X, chap. xii, pp. 190-191; cf. Gardiner's *Epistola*, fol. Eii—fol. Eiii.

the line taken by Bucer is very similar to that of the Homilies. Thus for instance, the Homily on Salvation states:

> ... we must renounce the merit of all our said virtues, of faith, hope, charity, ... and trust only in God's mercy, and that sacrifice which our ... Saviour Christ Jesus ... once offered for us ...[1]

Similarly Bucer had written in his *Disputata*:

> ... quod ea in nulla nostra fide, poenitentia, charitate, aut ullis nostris virtutibus, sed in sola Dei misericordia, & meritis Christi, eiusque pollicitatione nititur & consistit.[2]

Or in the Homily it is said:

> ... by faith ... we embrace the promise of God's mercy ...

and Bucer:

> Dicimus quidem nos per fidem iustificari, quatenus fide misericordiam Dei ... apprehendimus ...[3]

And again:

> That faith doth not shut out repentance, hope, love ...

And Bucer:

> ... fides viva [by which people believing in Christ are certain about their salvation and life eternal has necessarily adjoined to it] ... veram peccatorum poenitentiam, & Dei dilectionem, ...[4]

The Homily defines faith:

> true and lively faith, which nevertheless is the gift of God, and not man's only work.[5]

Bucer stated also as regards that faith, that it is not our but God's work:

> faith, that worketh by charity ... the which faith hath charity always joined unto it,

which is expressed by Bucer:

> Qui enim vere in Deum credit nunquam illam [sc. charitatem] dimittere sustinet.[6]

It is the faith which worketh by charity (fidem operari per charitatem).[7] This faith is certain and confident of salvation. And the

[1] 'A Sermon of the Salvation ...' *Certain Sermons or Homilies* (New ed., London, S.P.C.K., 1843), p. 27.

[2] *Disputata*, op. cit., p. 500.

[3] Homilies, op. cit., p. 29. *Disputata*, op. cit., p. 539.

[4] ibid., pp. 22-23. ibid., pp. 492-493.

[5] ibid., p. 22. ibid., p. 525.

[6] Homilies, op. cit., p. 37. *Disputata*, op. cit., p. 455.

[7] Homilies, op. cit., p. 34. *Disputata*, op. cit., p. 538, and passim.
cf. also particularly *Disputata*, pp. 453-454 and pp. 538-544, where Bucer deals exclusively with the question of the relation of faith and charity.

passages referred to by the Homilies (Hebrews xi. 1; xi. 6; 1 John v. 13; John xiv. 21; 2 Pet. i. 10, etc.) are also typical for Bucer's *Disputata*.

These examples are inadequate illustrations for the similar doctrinal outlook between the Homilies and Bucer's teaching in his *Disputata* in so far as they merely convey an impression of a few selected passages. But it is difficult to show otherwise consistent similarities, because for that reason one would have to compare the general tone of the Homilies with the general trend of thought to be found in Bucer's work. The argumentation, the approach to the doctrine as given by Bucer in his controversy with Gardiner is in its characteristic features shared — although not copied from or depending on Bucer — with the Reformer's writing.

Gardiner tried to contradict Bucer's arguments by a new work, the *Exetasis*, in which he attempted to neutralize the strength of Bucer's reply (in the *Gratulatio*) by examining his quotations from the Fathers, of which he says that Bucer had 'profanely misused' them. But the *Exetasis* is only a reply to the question on celibacy as discussed in Bucer's *Gratulatio*, and does not contain an answer to the *Disputata*. This writing of Gardiner, which was sent to the printer in 1548, was, however, owing to Gardiner's imprisonment, not printed until 1554, three years after Bucer's death.[1]

The controversy thus, between Gardiner and Bucer, started in 1541 and, continued in their various writings, lasted almost thirteen years, though actually after seven years in 1548 with Bucer's reply in the *Disputata* the end had been reached.[2]

Bucer's reply to Gardiner in the *Disputata*, the reply so impatiently expected by Gardiner, settled the matter on the dogma of justification in a way neither Bucer nor Gardiner could have anticipated: Article XI of the Thirty-nine Articles and the relative Homilies expressed the authoritative teaching of the Church of England on that doctrine, so strongly defended by Bucer against Gardiner and so strongly attacked by Gardiner.

[1] Exetasis testimoniorum, quae Martinus Bucerus ex Sanctis Patribus non sancte edidit, ut patrocinetur opinioni de caelibatus dono, quam sine dono spiritus, contra Ecclesiam defendit orthodoxam. Louvain, 1554.
cf. Muller, J., op. cit., pp. 437-438.

[2] cf. Janelle's article 'La Controverse Entre Étienne Gardiner et Martin Bucer . . .' pp. 452 ff. in *Revue Des Sciences Religieuses* . . . Tome VII, 1927 (Strassbourg).

§ 11

ON THE TERM 'DIGAMOS'

Since the divorce case of Henry VIII,[1] since the bigamy case of the Landgrave of Hesse, since his controversy with his Roman Catholic opponent Latomus on celibacy, Bucer's interest had never ceased on the problems of marriage, divorce and celibacy.

In his Response to Latomus (1544)[2] Bucer gives in the section De Coelibatu, inter alia an exposition of 1 Tim. iii. 2 and Titus i. 6 (a bishop must be husband of one wife) and gives in this connection his exegesis on the word *digamos*. He refers to the Fathers (especially to S. Chrysostom) as being of his opinion.

This exposition aroused Gardiner's opposition in his *Conquestio* (1544). He scorns Bucer's explanation as not being scholarly and finds it entirely irreconcilable with the common usage of the Greek word. His arguments on that word are taken up by Robert, Bishop of Avranches, in his *Pro Tuendo Sacro Coelibatu* of 1545;[3] (Sequitur Responsio ad Buceri calumnias, pp. 120-145).

Bucer's conception of the Greek term and that of his opponents, Gardiner and the Bishop of Avranches, throw some light on the study and classical knowledge of those men, which is relevant in order to show the immense care taken by them to support their claims.

The argument is: Do the passages in the Epistles of S. Paul prohibit polygamy or bigamy or do they mean that it is prohibited to

[1] cf. Simon Grynaeus' letter to Martin Bucer (September 1531) on the matter of Henry's divorce from Catherine of Aragon. (*Original Letters*, vol. II, pp. 552-554) cf. also Bucer's letter, here p. 251 f. Also the letters from Grynaeus to Henry VIII (September 1531) and from Melanchthon to Bucer (November 8th, 1531), op. cit., pp. 554-557. H. Eells in his *The Attitude of Martin Bucer toward the Bigamy* . . . pp. 30-43, gives an excellent account of Bucer's judgement in the matter of Henry's divorce.

[2] Responsio altera et solida, Martini Buceri ad D. Bartholomaeum Latomum . . . pp. 74 ff. (De coelibatu) in Scripta Duo Adversaria D. B. . . . Latomi . . . et Martini Buceri (Strassburg, 1544).

[3] Robert II, Cenalis, Bishop of Avranches, one of the many eminent Roman Catholics on the Continent opposed to Bucer (others were: Eck, Cochlaeus, Latomus, Pighius, Gropper, Billick, Malvenda), had already attacked Bucer once on his Eucharistic teaching. To this Bucer had answered in 1534 in his *Defensio Adversus Axioma Catholicum, id est Criminationem R. P. Roberti Episcopi Abrincensis* . . . Cenalis disliked Bucer profoundly and calls him: 'mali corvi ovum pessimum' (p. 322 in: Cenalis, R.: *De utriusque gladii facultate* . . . Paris, 1546). It is also of interest to note that the bon mot among theologians of the sixteenth century: 'Erasmus laid the eggs and Luther hatched them' (cf. Gardiner to Somerset, October 27th, 1547, in Muller, J.: *The Letters of Stephen Gardiner* . . . p. 403) was converted by Cenalis into: '. . . nemo est qui ignoret, quod vbi Erasmus innuit, Bucerus irruit: & quae ille oua fouit, genimen istud viperae exclusit, vt nescias vtrum verius sit, seu quod Bucerus erasmizat, an quod Erasmus bucerizat.' (cf. Cenalis, Robert: *Pro Tuendo Sacro Coelibatu* . . . Paris, 1545, p. 139).

marry again after the death of the first wife; and is that statement only confined to a Bishop? Bucer, by relying on S. Chrysostom, states: Husband of one wife is:

> qui unam tantum uxorem habet, non cum uxore concubinam, nec repudiata priore duxerit alteram . . . (cf. *Responsio* . . . op. cit., p. 77).

The Bishop of Avranches states:

> S. Paul does not mean by 'husband of one wife' that a Bishop is reminded here not to live polygamous. For Bigamy and Polygamy are also prohibited to all men, not especially to bishops only. It means here: 'semel atque iterum nuptiator.' Bigamus or digamos has to be understood in that way: as example he alludes to *δις κραμβη θανατος*=semel & iterum crambe, mors:[1] The *δις κραμβη* stands not for double crambe. S. Paul means (with reference to the word bigamia) not 'plures uno tempore ductas uxores' but 'repetitas succisivis temporibus nuptias . . . non plures aut habere, aut habuisse uxores. Polygamus enim est, qui aut pluribus simul, aut aliquoties repetitis fruitur nuptiis'. (*Pro Tuendo*, . . . op. cit., pp. 144-145).

As on the same line Gardiner had argued before against Bucer, the Bishop of Avranches makes explicit use of Gardiner's arguments.[2] Gardiner writes in his *Conquestio*:

> . . . Certe quidem in digami uocabulo detorquendo, quod inter prima ille argumenta ponit, consentitis ambo. Ita enim scribis, eum qui alteram uxorem duxerit priore mortua, a recentioribus uocari digamum, contra omnem Graecae linguae usum & scripturam, & ueteres canones. De linguae usu Bucere, quam falsus sis, spero me palam facturum, ut tuam arrogantiam omnes intelligant. Primum illud in confesso sit (δὶς) aduerbium Graecum, & Numeri & ordinis esse, ac seorsum & in compositione, semel & iterum succedenter numerata, & quod (Latinum bis) exprimit significare, ut

[1] cf. Juvenalis, Satire VII, 154: occidit miseros crambe repetita magistros.

[2] cf. the passage in the work of the Bishop of Avranches (*Pro Tuendo* . . . pp. 144-145): 'Puderet & hoc vanissimum repellere commentum, nisi scirem insignioris notae viros in hac ipsa arena fuisse versatos (Vintoniensem intelligo & Campensem) quo fingis verba Pauli dicentis, Oportet episcopum esse vnius vxoris virum, non bigamum, hoc est, non habere plures simul vxores. Quasi vero hoc genus bigamiae non sit etiam iure diuino omnibus vetitum, aut adulterium solis prohibeatur episcopis. Est igitur bigamus semel atque iterum nuptiator: sicut dicere solemus, *Δὶς κράμβη θάνατος* i. crambe non gemina sed repetita, mors: & *δίστοκον* mulierem appellant, quae bis peperit, non quae geminos foetus ediderit. Qua ratione bis iterumve consulem dicimus, qui succesiue duos gessit consulatus. Sic polygamus hoc loco dicendus est, qui nuptias non semel contraxit. Cui intelligentiae subseruiunt Epiphanius, Chrysostomus. Denique quis non? Falso igitur detorques bigamiam in verbis Pauli ad plures vno tempore ductas vxores, quae verius ad repetitas succisiuis temporibus nuptias referenda est. Sic ergo est intelligendum istud, Oportet episcopum esse vnius vxoris virum, hoc est, non plures aut habere, aut etiam habuisse vxores. Polygamus enim est, qui aut pluribus simul, aut aliquoties repetitis fruitur nuptiis.'

> Δὶς κράμβη θάνατος semel & iterum Crambe, mors. ad quam formam dicimus Latine, bis Crambe mors, δίγλωσσον autem δίλογον Graeci appellant, qui duas calleat linguas, unam uidelicet & item alteram, & δίστεγον quod duplex habeat tectum, in qua compositione horum trium uerborum fateor uno eodemque tempore utramque numeri partem consistere, ut Δίστεγος non dicatur, quod olim unum, nunc aliud habeat tectum, sed in quo duo tecta eodem tempore numeres, quod quoniam in aliquibus uerbis obtinet, in quibus rerum significatarum natura patiatur . . . (fol. Hij ff.).

Gardiner thought that Bucer's interpretation of the term *digamos* was similar to that in the anonymous *Dialogus Neobuli*, the publication which defended the Bigamy of the Landgrave of Hesse. Thus Gardiner concludes, the suspicion that Bucer was the author of the *Dialogus*, was almost justified.[1]

Hastings Eells in his work *The Attitude of Martin Bucer* . . . (op. cit., p. 173), writes:

> Four years later, in January 1546, Cochläus, who was engaged in a controversy with Bucer over celibacy said, 'A year ago I read a libel brought from Germany'.

Eells when referring to W. W. Rockwell (*Die Doppelehe des Landgrafen* . . . Marburg, 1904, p. 124, note 1), for this statement about Cochlaeus, ought to have verified Rockwell's source. Rockwell writes (op. cit.):

> In der Januar 1546 erschienenen Schrift, In xviii Articulos Mar. Buceri . . . Responsio Jo. Cochlaei schrieb dieser, indem er Bucer wegen Aeusserungen über den Cölibat angriff: 'Et ante annum legi libellum ex Germania allatum, in quo pluralitas uxorum similibus rationibus astruitur.' etc.

If Rockwell could have read the passage he ascribes to Cochlaeus in its context, he would have observed that Cochlaeus[2] quotes this passage and the preceding text from Gardiner's *Conquestio*. The quotation of Cochlaeus from Gardiner's *Conquestio* begins on fol. 61 verso, indicated by the marginal remark: 'Verba Episcopi Vin-

[1] cf. Gardiner, *Conquestio*, op. cit., fol. H verso—H ij: '. . . ante annum legi libellum ex Germania allatum, in quo pluralitas uxorum similibus rationibus astruitur. Huius te authorem aliqui suspicati sunt. quum uero ista tradas, causam illam haud poteris improbare. Certe quidem in digami uocabulo detorquendo, quo inter prima ille argumenta ponit, consentitis ambo. Ita enim scribis . . .' cf. also Letter of John Burcher to Henry Bullinger (June 8th, 1550): '. . . so that he [sc. Bucer] is considered, not without cause, by our bishop of Winchester as the author of the book published in defence of the Landgrave.' (*Original Letters*, op. cit., vol. II, p. 666). On the *Dialogus Neobuli*, cf. chap. vii (pp. 154 ff.) in H. Eells: *The Attitude of Martin Bucer towards the Bigamy of Philip of Hesse* (1924).

[2] *In XVIII. Articvlos Mar. Bvceri* . . . Responsio Jo. Cochlaei . . . M.D. xlvi, fol. 61—fol. 62 verso.

toniensis. G.4.' The marginal reference is made to the page of Gardiner's *Conquestio*. The quotation from Gardiner begins with:

> Et quemadmodum ex uerbis Euangelij colligit Chrysostomus, omnes esse doni coelibatus capaces . . . (fol. H).

And thus the reference to the 'libellum ex Germania allatum' is contained in the quotation of Cochlaeus from Gardiner's *Conquestio*, which should also have been noticed by Rockwell, if only he would have read on immediately after the passage referred to, where Cochlaeus says:

> Haec Anglicus iste Episcopus, quem Cels. uestrae Ratisbonae in proxime ibi habitis Comitijs uiderunt, ubi Regis sui apud Caes. Maiestatem legatum agebat. Libenter profecto uidebo, quid solide ad ista respondere possit Bucerus, aut ullus complicum eius . . .

Thus the words ascribed to Cochlaeus by Rockwell and Eells are those of Gardiner.

§ III

APPENDIX I

Preface of Bucer, Capito and Hedio to Gardiner's *De Vera Obedientia*

PIO LECTORI S.D.

NActi nuper orationem, de vera obedientia R.P. Stephani Episcopi Wintoniensis, committere non potuimus, quin eam tibi communicaremus. Sic docet in hac verus hic Episcopus non minus solide & religiose, quam erudite & eleganter, veram obedientiam esse sequi in omnibus verbum Domini, & hanc Deo in Principibus & Magistratibus, qui gladium gestant, primam praestandam. Horum quoque munus esse, se Deos, patres & pastores exhibere iis, quos illorum fidei commisit Deus, cuius omnes per omnia sumus. Et ideo potissimum, quod illos veram doceri religionem, & in omnibus ad Dei placita institui pro virili sua curent, vera se nimirum Ecclesiarum post Christum capita praestantes. Cum Episcoporum partes sint, gregem domini sacra Euangelii dispensatione pascere, vitaeque exemplo ad Christum in omnibus dirigere: & hoc Principibus iuxta Dei verbum parendo, non imperando. Inter quos is demum vere primatum obtinet, qui fide & sedulitate in hoc sacro munere alios antecellit.

Hic denique videbis mirum & iucundum sane artificem, in detegendo exitiosissimo illo fuco, quem Romani Pontifices adeo diu iam faciunt toti prope occidenti, se penes esse regni coelestis & terreni gubernacula: sed vt primos in terris [p. 717] Christi vicarios habere summam & absolutam potestatem in Ecclesias & principes illarum vniuersos.

O vero memorandam Dei benignitatem in Serenis. hunc Regem, omneque regnum Britanniae, cui tales dedit episc. Nam non hunc solum habet Anglia, qui cum vera pietate, eruditionem certam, & vere Episcopalem pro grege dominico solicitudinem coniunxit. Est illi & Thomas Cranmerus Archiepiscopus Cantuariensis, totius Anglicanae Ecclesiae primas, vir sanctimonia vitae, doctrina, constantia & sedulitate in administratione Ecclesiae eximia. Vidimus & ipsi hic & allocuti sumus, idque non vulgari cum fructu pietatis R. Patrem Edoardum Foxeum Episcopum Herenfordensem, Serenissimi Regis Britanniae, ad eos Germaniae Principes & Respu. legatum, qui instaurandis iuxta verbum Domini Ecclesiis student, virum profecto multis nominibus amabilem & suspiciendum. Tanta praeditus est modestia, comitate, doctrina, iudicii acrimonia, & quod vere Episcopale est, in regnum Christi ardore praecipuo. Nec dissimilis huic est, collega eius D. Nicolaus Haeteus Archidiaconus Eboracensis. Qui Angliam habent cognitam, ii praedicant & alios non paucos hisce virtutibus ornatos, quos pientissimus Rex Ecclesiis suis praefecit, praestans scilicet id, quod ei Dominus iniunxit, pastorem & patrem populi sui, quo videas, illum non impia dominandi libidine, aut impatientia iusti & sancti imperii inductum, vt imperium Ro. Episcopo in Ecclesia Anglica lege curiata, omnibus scilicet ordinibus suffragantibus, & legem hanc scientibus, abrogarit.

Agnouit quod res est, suo periculo Ecclesiam Christi a pseudoepiscoepis [*sic*] vastari, & impium esse commentum, illos Principum animaduersioni esse exemptos, *Omnem siquidem animam Deus potestatibus supremis, quae gladium gestant, subiecit,* hoc est, vt D. Chrysostomus hunc locum enarrat, *non solum saeculares,* quos vocant, *sed sacerdotes etiam & monachos,* imo addit, *& si Apostolus sis, & si Euangelista, & si Propheta aut quisquam alius, nec enim euertit pietatem subiectio. Nec dixit Apostolus* (addit) *simpliciter, omnis anima obediat, sed subiecta sit.* Haec ille. Sacerdotes cunctis quidem mortalibus praepositi sunt administratione verbi Dei, omnes enim verbo Dei parere debent. at quia nec doctrina, nec vita semper id praestant. quod est in eorum officio, voluit Deus omnibus saeculis esse eos sub iurisdictione & coercitione Principum & Magistratuum, qui gladii potestate funguntur. Desunt & Principes proh dolor plus nimio muneri suo, verum quoniam multitudo Principum mala, voluit Deus hos suo iudicio relinqui, esseque cunctis mortalibus sacrosanctos.

Moueat vero nos praeclarum hoc & amplissimum Dei donum in Ecclesiam Anglicanam, quod eius Principi talem mentem inspirauit, vt eundem ardentius iam & nostris Principibus oremus, quo & illi tandem inducant animum, quod gerunt munus & rite cognoscere, & digne obire. In primis vero vt a gubernaculis Ecclesiae remoueant eos, qui in Ecclesia vere non sunt, vtpote qui palam impie & viuunt & docent, cum quibus Apostolus vetat cibum sumere, quod sint adulteri, Scortatores, idololatrae, raptores, ebrii, & aliis summis flagitiis & sceleribus contaminati, quorum denique si sacris communices, ipsae te Pontificum leges sacra communione excludunt: Et praeficiant Ecclesiis quales Apostolus[?] & omnes piorum Principum leges, tum sanctorum pontificum canones requirunt, qui Christo cum ipsi credant & viuant, tum praedicando idonei sint intenti.

Hodie namque quotumquemque Episcopi nomine & loco habes, qui quid Episcopi munus sit vnquam serio quaesierit cognoscere, nedum implere. In hoc potius totis viribus incumbunt, vt Euangelium Domini Iesu Christi modis omnibus oppugnent, & suis nephariam illam licentiam, impia doctrina & vita flagitiosa omnem religionem vitaeque sanctimoniam auertendi & prorsus extinguendi tueantur. In deligendis pastoribus gregis dominici id potissimum requirunt, vt sint in doctrinam puram Euangelii, illi vocant Lutheranam, maxime meledici, caeterum nihil pensi habent, quid sciant, aut quid viuant, excepto, ne habeant vxores legitimo connubio sibi coniunctas. Nam si quis *κοιλιολάτρης*, ad eos e castris Euangelii transfugiat, qui vxorem legitimam duxit, eam ipsi relinquunt, tantum ne habeat loco honestae coniugis. Ordinem dicunt non ferre, vt quis sancti thori maritus sit, meretricium vero cubile, & grauiora pro ridiculo habent. Sic obseruant Canonem illum Concilii Neocaesarien. *Presbyter, si vxorem duxerit ab ordine illum deponi debere, quod si fornicatus fuerit, vel adulterium commiserit, extra Ecclesiam abiici, & ad poenitentiam inter laicos redigi oportet.*

Quos leges Dei & sanctorum Principum nullo modo ferunt in Ecclesia, incestos, adulteros & scortatores, hos nostri Episcopi scientes & prudentes Ecclesiis praeficiunt. At si quis suae fragilitatis conscius propter vitandam fornicationem, iuxta praeceptum Dei per Apostolum expositum, 2 Corinth. 7. vxorem ducat, & meditetur vnius vxoris vir absque crimine viuere, qualem Episcopum requirit lex Dei, is in sacro ministerio tolerari non potest. At conculcare legem Dei, propter hominum traditiones, quid est, si hoc non est? Interim autem dum perditos adeo & deploratos homines Episcopi nostri sacro muneri praeficiunt, in hac luce veritatis Euangelicae vbique potentissime effulgentis, nec admittunt, qui sanam Christi doctrinam dissipato nimium & exitiose erranti gregi Christi administrarent, soluuntur passim homines religione, intercidit omnis respectus honestatis, profligatur cunctus pudor, ruitur in vniuersa scelera & flagitia furore summo.

Istuc autem quid nobis adferre possit quam certum & sempiternum exitium, idque perbreui? Nec enim potest Deus ferre suam tanto furore oppugnari misericordiam, quam nobis hoc saeculo exhibit tam splendide & magnifice. Vere itaque orandus Deus est indesinenter & precibus flagrantissimis, vt aperiat Principibus nostris oculos, donet eos agnoscere quo sint ab ipso loco constituti, [p. 718] praestent veros pastores, patres, & Deos populo suo. Contemnant tandem ementitam istam pseudoecclesiasticorum immunitatem, & in omnes potestatem, quam illi aliquot Principibus partim superstitione, partim vi oppressis extorserunt. Sequantur potius verbum Dei & exempla pientissimorum Principum Mose, Iehosua, Piorum Iudicum & Regum populi veteris, tum Constantini, Theodosii & aliorum qui in Christiano quoque populo, legibus quae adhuc nobis extant, & imperio in omnes Episcopos & totum Ecclesiasticum ordinem, in primis curarunt, vt religio sarta fecta esset. Nemo potuit potestatem concedere Ecclesiam Dei euertendi: & quam immunitatem pii Principes sanctis olim Episcopis donarunt, ea tam nihil pertinet ad plaerosque, qui hodie Episcoporum titulos sibi venditant, quam nihil ipsi cum sanctis illis patribus habent commune. Quam quae pii Principes ordini Ecclesiastico contulerunt immunitatem, eam, nullis vnquam Episcopis eo valere voluerunt vt sua essent exempti iurisdictione. Id quod aperto apertius testantur sacrae leges, quae de Episcopis & Ecclesiasticis rebus extant in Codice, & Nouellis Iustiniani. Vel vna illa de his rebus *constitutio summaria.* 123. abunde docet, sed cum multis aliis, vt & religiosi Principes, curam religionis sibi in primis competere iudicarint, suaeque animaduersioni subiectos habuerint, ordinem Ecclesiasticum vniuersum. A posterioribus Principibus qui nomine potius quam re ipsa imperium Romanum tenuerunt, dolo & vi istam licentiam extorserunt Romani Pontifices.

Vera sacerdotum libertas & immunitas est, verbum Domini libere & & intrepide, sermone & facto praedicare omni carni, summis Regibus aeque, atque infimis ex plebe. Vt impune doceant impie, & viuant scelerate, tyrannis est, non libertas aut immunitas Ecclesiae. Quā si Pseudo Episcopis nostris vlla potest Principum iurisiurandi religio cofirmare, est iusiurandum vinculum impietatis extremae. Et si potuerunt abiurare Principes potestatem in istos qui

Reipub. Christianae tantum inferunt exitium, abiurare potest pater curam & defensionem filiorum, maritus vxoris, imperator exercitus, gubernator nauis & eorum quos naui venit. O vero grauissimam in nos iram Dei, putare Principibus & Magistratibus nephas esse Reipubl. Christianae summas auertere pestes, aut vllis hominibus derasum verticem, & praescriptis verbis factam vnctionem, huc valere, vt soli impune pietatem omnem profligent, & inuicem confessam inuehant & tueantur idololatriam, vitaeque peruersitatem incomparabilem, idque freti potestate & opibus Ecclesiae, patrimonio crucifixi. Vere igitur maxima instantia orandus Deus, vt donet nobis, qui plane sumus, vt oues dispersae & absque pastore, Principes secundum cor suum, qui nos gregem suum, & opera manuum suarum pascant, regantquae in iudicio & iustitia, qui curent ante omnia doctrinae & Ecclesiasticae administrationis synceritatem. tum & vitam reliquam omnem, quo tandem vere populus Dei simus, liberatique ab omnibus internis & externis hostibus, seruiamus ipsi Domino & seruatori nostro, in sanctitate & iustitia, coram ipso omnibus diebus vitae nostrae. Quam foelicitatem regno Christi propriam esse S.S. in D. Zacharia & omnibus piis vatibus testatus est. Interim fruere pie lector spiritu & studio hoc vere Episcopali, quae tibi ista Wintonensis oratio praeclare exhibet. Disce hinc quae sit vera obedientia, omnium ordinum in Ecclesia Christi, oraque Dominum, vt similes Doctores obedientiae vbique plurimos excitet, incrementumque doctrinae eorum eiusmodi largiatur, quo illa vbique obtineat, & coeamus tandem, vereque vniamur, & omnes foeliciter ad omnem sanctimoniam & pietatem proficiamus, sub vno capite & Rege atque Episcopo nostro supremo, domino nostro Iesu Christo, quem Dominum confiteri debet omnis lingua. Ipsi sit gloria in saecula. Vale.

V. F. Capito.
C. Hedio.
M. Bucerus & caeteri Ecclesiastae Argentoratenses.

(from: Goldast, Melchior, 'Monarchia Sancti . . . Imperii . . .' (Hanoviae, . . . 1612), vol. I, pp. 716-718.)

§ IV

APPENDIX II

Letter of Sir Thomas Hoby to his brother Sir Philip Hoby (prefixed to Hoby's translation of Bucer's *Gratulatio ad Ecclesiam Anglicanam*).

(fol. Aij—Aiiij) cf. here: pp. 9; 184.

To his right worshypfull Brother Syr Philyppe Hobye knight, M. of y[e] Kinges maiesties ordinaunce, Thomas Hobye wishethe grace and peace throught our lorde Jesus Christe.

*Em*onge the sundrye and manifolde benifittes, whiche from my tender childhod I haue fou̅de in yow, and receaued at your handes (most especiall good brother) thys is not the leaste: that ye haue now of late dayes, of the good zeale ye beare to Gods worde (which at all tymes hath byn moste feruent in you) caused me to be sent not only in to such a regiō where as florissheth Gods worde, all good letters bothe holye and prophane, all honestie, & puritie of lyfe, & men in all artes and sciences moste cunning and experte: But also to such a man who is of no lesse wisdom, knouledge, & godlines, then of fame, reporte & renoune, & be by all godly mens iudgementes, one of the perfectest, and greatest Clerkes nowe lyuinge namelye M. Martyne Bucer, in whose daylye conuersation and companye, and by whose wisdome learninge, and documētes, I shoulde receaue and learne, that shoulde belonge not onlie to myne owne furtherance & profyt, but also to the consolation and comfort of you, & all my frendes, whō hytherto I haue founde moste beneficyall towardes me. Sythe therfore it hath thus chaunced by your most godly procurement & prouision, that I should for a season here remaine with this profounde and famous Clerke, ye myght not vnworthelye & in dede, with iuste cause, impute vnto me, either the vyce of ignauie, or els obliuion and forgetfulnes of your moste large and ample benefittes, if I should let slippe suche a mete, apt, and necessarye epistle of his, and especiallie beinge writtē and indited to the whole churche, or congregation of Englande, bothe learned & vnlearned, & in the which he expresseth not only the assured and vnfained loue that he beareth, & at all tymes hathe borne towardes this realme, and rulars and ministers of the same, but also very euidentlye declareth, and with moste manifeste testimonies of scripture, setteth furthe at large suche thinges as maye be to the profitt and furtherance of many, and wherin he hath confuted (not al, for it were in maner an infinite worke to stande aboute all, but) as many sophisticall & wranglinge schoolishe reasons, as are of any probabilitie or likehoode, whiche my lorde of Vvynchester (farre vnsemely for a sober Bisshoppe) hath expressed & set forthe in his two moste cõtumelious & railing epistles agaĩst him, winkĩg at, & ouerhippĩg his wel most innumerable opprobrious wordes, checkes, tauntes, rebukes, quarellinges scoffinges, reuilĩges & scoldinges railinges, wherwith they are filled as full, as they may be heaped to gether. In the which are so fewe argumẽtes or reasons of any probabilitie: that had not the vrgẽt and instant requeste of his frendes, certain of oure coũtraymen bien, he wold neuer once haue put penn to the paper, nor yet haue made ànye a do about them, but wolde haue left them to the iudgemẽt & arbitrimẽt of the reader, notwithstanding now of late dayes it chaunced that he gate a litle vacant tyme to do the same (seing he promised it to certaine) from his manifolde impedimentes, & necessarie ecclesiastical busines (wher with we knowe such men are no smale dele let) & to reconcile him selfe (which the Bisshoppe scornfullye, after his olde wõte, casteth in his tethe) to his brother, before he lay his offringe vpon the altare. The whiche thoughe it be brefe, and cõpendious & not set forth to the largeste, yet is it verye dilucidious, pithie, & full of argumentes concluded not onlye vpon ye holy gostes vnfained decrees, apoĩtmentes and ordinaunces, but also the olde and holye doctores of the church, and for the brefnes of tyme sufficient inough. The which when he had finisshed, I furthe with toke in hande acording to my childishe talent, to translate into our vulgare and cõmune speache, and haue sent it vnto yow to thentent some well disposed and better learned which purchaunce wyll not bestowe so moch tym as the translation therof requireth, maye yet at the least wyse peruse it acording as he thinketh beste, so that at lengthe it may be worthy to come abroade for the profit and instruction of the ignoraunt, whiche haue not receaued the knowledge of the Latin tonge, because it is written to them, as wel as to the other. Wherin I will desyre yow to accept my good wyll, as thought it colde extende farther and do moch better, which yf ye do, it shalbe a great incourage and vrgent cause vnto me to employ and bestowe the reste of my studie, dilygence and laboure herafter in other affayres, which I truste shalbe no lesse acceptable vnto yowe, then great furtherance to myne oune profyt & vtilitie. The spirite of treuthe be with yow, who guide yow in all your pathes, acording to his will, and lead yow into all gostlye knowlege. Amen.

At Argentyne, Kalendis Februarij.

CHAPTER VI

MARTIN BUCER'S COMMENTARY ON THE PSALMS AND THE ENGLISH PSALTER[1]

Calvin to the Reader (At Geneua, the xxiij of Julij 1557): '... And before J went in hand with the exposition at the entreatance of my brethren, J said (as truth was) that J therfore surceased, bycause that most faithfull Doctor of the Church *Martin Bucer* had by the singuler lerning, diligence, and faithfulnesse, which he hath performed in this work, at leastwyse atteyned thus much, that there shoold not be so greate neede of this my trauell.[2]
... habere videlicet eos [sc. commentarios in D. Pauli epistolam ad Rom. & in Dauidis hymnos] in se tam plenam & perfectam vndique doctrinam Christianae religionis, interpretationemque tam luculentam & perspicuam, vt cum illorum veterum augustissimorum hominum & virorum doctissimorum monumentis, quorum iam multis seculis consecratae literae atque artes fuerunt, quosque religionis & sacrorum interpretes cuncti hos mille annos amplius asciuerunt, omnibus ex partibus conferri compararique posse existimaret.

John Redman on Bucer's Commentaries on the Epistle to the Romans and on the Psalter. (*Scripta Anglicana*, p. 880.)

§ I

BUCER'S COMMENTARY ON THE PSALMS[3]

FIVE years before the first Bible in English was edited by Coverdale in 1535, Bucer's Latin Psalter of 1529 had been translated into English and was printed at Strassburg in 1530.[3]

To draw the inference from this fact that Bucer's Commentary played some part in the story of the English Bible seems premature. Any attempt to draw such a conclusion seems even more unjustified in the light of the wide research done on the subject of the History of the English Bible. For scholars like Anderson, Westcott, Driver — to name only a few outstanding authorities on the subject — find no

[1] The numbering of the verses of the Psalms used in this chapter is that of the Prayer Book version.

[2] The Psalmes of Dauid and others. With M. John Caluins Commentaries. ANNO DO. M.D. LXXI *back page*: Jmprinted at London by Thomas East and Henry Middelton: for Lucas Harison, and Gorge Byshop. Anno Do. M.D.LXXI.

[3] S. Psalmorvm Libri Qvinque Ad Ebraicam Veritatem Versi, Et Familiari Explanatione Elvcidati. Per Aretium Felinum. Theologum. On the last page: Argentorati, Georgio Vlrichero Andlano Chalcographo, Mense Septembri, Anno M.D.XXIX. Engl. transl. cf. here: pp. 218 ff.

place for Bucer's Psalter in their research on the sources for the English Bible. The recent collective work on *The Bible in its Ancient and English Versions* edited by H. Wheeler Robinson (Oxford, 1940) also makes no reference to Bucer's Psalter. Clapton's parallel Print of Coverdale's Psalter of 1535 and that of the Great Bible of 1539-41, brings many references to Munster, Luther and the Swiss-German version as sources for Coverdale, but no quotation from Bucer's work.

It has been clearly indicated that the 'Douche and Latyn' versions mentioned on the title-page of Coverdale's Bible, from which he translated his Bible into English and the 'fyue sundry interpreters' were the Vulgate and Pagninus, Luther and the German-Swiss of Zwingli and Leo Juda, and the published Pentateuch, Jonah and the New Testament by Tyndale; and that for his revised version for the Great Bible Coverdale employed the Latin Bible of Sebastian Munster of 1534-35.[1] Thus any attempt to rank Bucer's work among the sources employed by Coverdale will be met with suspicion and will need some excuse if it cannot be established by convincing evidence. The result of research for external historical evidence is discouraging.

The two Psalms printed as examples of the English Version of Bucer's Commentary also seem not to have encouraged Waterland and Cotton to carry out further research or to see any connection between the version of the English Bible and that of Bucer.[2]

But our discovery that Bucer's Commentary furnished large textual material for the notes in the Psalter of 'Matthew's Bible' and that the Superscriptions (Arguments) of the Psalms in that Bible are those from Bucer, and the other fact, that the English Version of the Psalms in the Primer commonly known as 'Marshall's Primer' (in various editions) is that of Bucer's translated Psalter, seems to justify our claim that Bucer's work has some relation with the History of the English Bible.

The five versions mentioned provided undoubtedly the material for the bulk of the English Bible. But that does not exclude the

[1] Westcott, Brooke Foss: *A General View of the History of the English Bible* (3rd ed. revised, London, 1905), pp. 161-163, 181 ff.

Driver, S. R.: *The Parallel Psalter* . . . (2nd ed., Oxford, 1904), pp. xii-xiv.

The Bible in its Ancient and English Versions (Ed. by H. Wheeler Robinson), Oxford, 1940, pp. 167 ff. & 176. Clapton, Ernest: *Our Prayer Book Psalter, containing Coverdale's Version* . . . (S.P.C.K., London, 1934), pp. ix–x. Anderson, Christopher: *The Annals of the English Bible*, 2 vol. (London, 1845).

[2] Waterland, Daniel: *The Works of the Rev. Daniel Waterland* (Oxford, 1823), vol. X, pp. 300-302: Psalm xcv.

Cotton, Henry: *Editions of the Bible and Parts thereof . . . with an Appendix* (Oxford, 1852), pp. 353, 354 (Appendix) Psalm xix; cf. also, pp. 134-135.

possibility that Coverdale for special parts of the Bible relied also on other sources. He writes:

> . . . And to help me herein, I have had sundry translations, not only in Latin, but also of the Dutch interpreters, whom because of their singular gifts and special diligence in the Bible, I have been the more glad to follow for the most part, according as I was required . . .[1]

The assumption, therefore, that Coverdale for his English Version of the Psalter read also Bucer's Commentary seems not to be without foundation, for Bucer's Commentary was a work of 'special diligence', widely known and praised and containing exegetical material collected from Hebrew, Greek and Latin authorities, which made it easily compete with any other commentary. That Coverdale in later years met Bucer personally, admiring him deeply, is also known from existing correspondence.[2] The Psalter, which formed an essential part of Church-worship needed special attention and care if, translated into the vernacular, it was to be of lasting value. It had to be in 'such a Language and Order as is most easy and plain for the understanding both of the Readers and Hearers'.[3]

Psalms in the vernacular were already sung and read by congregations who used the Primer, and who thus were acquainted with the English translation of Bucer's Latin Psalter. This seems to be a further indication that Coverdale not only knew that translation but also drew from it, being the first printed Psalms in English, which also was actually a book of worship for use in Church. Coverdale's gift of adaptation and of choosing and selecting the right text for his English Bible, displays itself here again, for he never fell for one version, but took here a passage and there an expression from the source before him, never becoming entirely dependent on it. We shall see that there are striking similarities between Coverdale's Version and that of Bucer, and yet the fact that he never took over an entire Psalm from it makes it difficult to state exactly when and where he used it. Proof of our claim can be made only by collecting material of internal evidence. Thus our task in this chapter will be concerned, after having given a description of Bucer's Latin Commentary and its character, with investigating in special sections its relation with English Versions. The English translation of the Commentary has to be brought into relation with Coverdale's Version, with Matthew's Psalter and with the Psalms of the Primer.

[1] p. 12, *Myles Coverdale unto the Christian Reader* (*Works of Bp. Coverdale, Remains* . . . (Parker Society, Cambridge, 1846)).

[2] *Remains of Bp. Coverdale*, op. cit., p. 510, n. XVIII and passim.

[3] '*Concerning the Service of the Church*', at the beginning of the Book of Common Prayer.

When this chapter was finished in 1941 we found our claim confirmed by the recent publication of the American, Mr. Charles C. Butterworth, *The Literary Lineage of the King James Bible* 1340-1611 (Philadelphia, 1941).[1] Mr. Butterworth for the first time connects also the fact of the existence of the English Version of Bucer's Psalter with the story of the English Bible. He also draws attention to the fact that the English Version of the Psalms in 'Marshall's Primer' is that of Bucer's Psalter in English. As we had finished the chapter before the American publication was accessible in England, and before we knew that Mr. Butterworth had come to similar conclusions we had hoped to add something entirely new to research. Now we can only claim the discovery that the notes in the Psalter in 'Matthew's Bible' are largely dependent on Bucer's Commentary.

In September of 1529 Bucer's Latin Commentary on the Psalms was published. For some obvious reasons it was printed under the pseudonym of *Aretius Felinus* (not Aretinus Felinus, as in the article on George Joye in the *D.N.B.*). In a letter from Strassburg (beginning of July 1529) to Zwingli, Bucer himself states three reasons for the choice of the nom de plume:

> I am employed . . . in an exposition of the Psalms, which, at the urgent request of our brethren in France and Lower Germany, I propose to publish under a foreign name, that the work may be bought by their booksellers. For it is a capital crime to import into these countries books which bear our names. I therefore pretend that I am a Frenchman, and, if I do not change my mind, will send forth the book as the production of *Aretius Felinus*, which, indeed, is my name and surname, the former in Greek, and the latter in Latin.[2]

[1] Butterworth, Charles C., op. cit., pp. 64 ff.: *The English Psalter of 1530*, pp. 76 ff. *Joye's Psalter of 1534*, pp. 101 ff. *The English Primers*, pp. 281 ff. and passim.

[2] English translation by Thomas McCrie (History of the Progress and Suppression of the Reformation in Italy . . . Edinburgh, London, 1827, p. 36). When he wrote that letter his Commentary was not yet finished.

'. . . sed pro mea facultatula in Psalmis, quorum enarrationem, impulsus a fratribus *Galliae et inferioris Germaniae*, statui edere sub alieno nomine, quo a Bibliopolis illorum libri emantur. Capitale enim est nostris nominibus praenotatos libros regionibus illis inferre. Simulo itaque me Gallum, et veritatem in locis illis communibus Patrum autoritate obtrudere studeo, multa non suis locis infulcio. *Aretii Felini*, quod meum nomen et cognomen est; sed illud Graece, hoc Latine; librum, nisi consilium mutavero, faciam. Tria specto hac impostura. Primum, si quo modo captivis illis fratribus sincerior tractandi Scripturas ratio commendari possit. *Alterum*, si tolli in dogmatis religionis nostrae intempestiva peregrinitas, et Scythica illa a *Lutheranis* invecta debacchandi rabies. Tertium, ut tutius hinc sacris possent consolationibus, in persecutione, quam ferunt, confirmari. Quare etiam in priore parte operis verbosius omnia explicare annisus sum, quo reliqua liceret adstrictius. Obsecro te, dum per otium licuerit, unum et alterum Psalmum degustare digneris, et monere quam primum licuerit, eorum quibus possim hoc opus magis frugiferum reddere. Viginti duo tantum adhuc excusi sunt, quos tibi mitto. Supersunt multi eorundem argumentorum. Quare sarcire et emendare licebit, quicquid peccatum est in parte jam impressa. Item si

His intention to avoid by the choice of a pseudonym Catholic as well as Lutheran attention, seems to have been successful at first. The disguise was even carried a step further by dedicating his work to the Dauphin Francis and dating the dedicatory letter from Lyons.[1] His frequent references to French proverbs and sayings in his Commentary, his quotations from Rashi, were other means of deceiving the reader about the author. Nobody would have suspected a German as the author of a work which was so obviously of French character.

At first sight his fear of the Lutherans seems difficult to understand. But not only Roman Catholics were opposed to him at that period. About that time, the *Supper-Strife* was raging; it was the year before the Colloquy at Marburg (1530). Bucer was strongly suspected and accused by the Lutherans of being a Zwinglian, a Sacramentarian. The suspicion was justified by the fact that in translating Bugenhagen's Latin Psalter into German in 1526,[2] Bucer had introduced his own conception of the Eucharist into the explanation of Psalm cxi. He had taken advantage of Bugenhagen's offer, to allow him to alter and correct as much as he liked in translating it into German. Obviously Bugenhagen did not suggest that Bucer ought to introduce into the commentary of a Lutheran his, at that time, Zwinglian conception of the Sacrament. The position became even more awkward for the Lutherans, as Melanchthon and Luther, whose letters of praise to the Commentary were prefixed to Bugenhagen's work, and Bugenhagen as well were believed of taking the

[1] Before the preface stands the letter to: 'Clarissimo Ac Pientissimo Principi, Francisco Valesio, Christianissimi Galliarum Regis primogenito, & Delphino, Aretius Felinus, Salutem precatur.' Date: 'Lugduni, iii. Idus Julias, Anno M.D.XXIX.'

[2] *Psalter* wol verteutscht auss der heyligen sprach. Verklerung des Psalters | fast klar vnd nutzlich | Durch Johann Bugenhag aus Pomern | Von dem Latein inn Teutsch | an vil orten durch jn selbs gebessert . . . Gedruckt zu Basel durch Adam Petri | im iar. M.D.xxvi [in January]. Preface to the Christian reader by Martin Bucer (Strassburg, iii. October 1525), where on fol. aiij and aiij verso he gives an account, how it came that he translated Bugenhagen's Commentary.

---

consilium meum parum tibi probaretur in extrudendo opere, simul mihi indices. Nihil enim aliud specto, quam ut prosim. Jam novi quantum tibi Dominus dederit, quid tale sit, despiciendi. Audio te jam in Psalmis versari; quare ut non erit a tuo jam exercitio mihi de enarrandis Psalmis praecipere alienum, ita minus quoque negotiosum . . .' (Letter in *Huldrici Zuinglii Opera*, vol. VIII, Zurich, 1842, p. 316, no. LXII. cf. also, pp. 319, 340-341). Passage of the Letter quoted by A. L. Herminjard: *Correspondance des Réformateurs, Genève-Paris*, 1868, Tome II, 1527-1532, p. 194, note 2. Herminjard dates the letter: du commencement de juillet 1529. As in another letter to Zwingli from July 10th, 1529 (cf. p. 319), Bucer refers to the same matter, Herminjard's dating seems to be correct. (The note given by Herminjard with the reference to Bucer's letter, stands as note to a French translation of certain passages of Bucer's dedicatory letter to the Dauphin, in his Commentary on the Psalms.) cf. also Bucer's letter to Ambrosius Blaurer (October 18th, 1529) (Schiess, T.: *Briefwechsel der Brüder Blaurer* . . . vol. I, p. 198, n. 154).

same doctrinal line as the Zwinglians.[1] When a separate edition of Psalm cxi of Bugenhagen's Psalter in Bucer's translation was published, the title to it suggested that it was the work of Bugenhagen. No reference was made to the fact that the passage concerning the Lord's Supper in that Psalm was Bucer's comment and not Bugenhagen's. The reader was completely deceived about the authorship when reading at the end of that separate print: 'Who likes to get further comment on the Lord's Supper by the same author [Lehrer], may turn to his exposition of the cx. psalm.'[2]

In those circumstances it seems to have been advisable to Bucer not to publish his Commentary under his own name. When it was discovered, however, that Aretius Felinus was the name for Bucer, he had to listen to strong accusations,[3] as he had been accused already in the affair of Bugenhagen's Psalter. In a letter to his friend Blaurer (January 26th, 1530) Bucer makes mention of those attacks for having used a pseudonym: 'id nunc tanquam inexpiabile scelus detestatur . . .'[4] The name Felinus was from now onward inseparably connected with Bucer, often used in his correspondence.[5]

Bucer, in compiling his work, used commentaries of Hebrew

[1] On the subject cf. correspondence of Luther, Bucer and Bugenhagen, see vol. XVII, n. XIV-XVI, pp. 1962-2007 in Walch, J. G.: *D. Martin Luther, Sämtliche Schriften . . .* (Halle, 1745).

[2] Der CXI. psalm Dauidis | mit der exposition vnd verklerung des Hochgelertē Johannis Bugenhagij Pomerani Pfarrherren zu Wittenberg. 1526.

Dariñ ain rechter Christlicher bericht des Nachtmals Christi vnnsers herren | ainem yegklichen verstendigklich gegeben wirdt . . . fol. B iiij: . . . Wer fernern bericht des Nachtmals halben | dises leerers haben will | der mag seyn erklerung über den hundert vnd zehnden Psalm lesen. Finis.

[3] Joh. Eck in his *Replica* . . . (1543) fol. 10 & 10 verso and fol. 12 makes special reference to Bucer using that fictitious name. Cf. also passage in Erasmus' letter of Nov. or Dec. 1529 (quoted by Eells, Hastings: *Martin Bucer* (Yale University, 1931), pp. 127-128).

[4] Schiess, T., op. cit., p. 204, n.158.

[5] A most entertaining and elucidating explanation of Bucer's name and nom de guerre is given by Verpoortenn, Albert Menon: *Commentatio Historica, De Martino Bucero* . . . (Coburg, 1709), pp. 115-116. cf. also Clement, D.: *Bibliotheque Curieuse* (Han. 1754), vol. V, p. 356-357. cf. also Bucer's letter to the 'Italian Brethren' (December 23rd, 1541), *Scripta Anglicana*, pp. 689-691, 'Aretius Felinus' (p. 691). cf. also Letter to 'Aretium Felinum' (December 23rd, 1549), in qua dat ei consilium de valetudine curanda. C.C.C.C. MS. 119/107. cf. also Letter of Utenhove to Dryander:

Utenhovius Dryandro: Strassburg January 3rd, 1584 postscript . . . D. Phalesius quoque habet ex meis [libris] Aretium Felinum in Psalmos . . . (pp. vi-vii Append. Epistola II in: F. Pijper: *Jan Utenhove*. Leiden, 1883). Pijper adds the following note to the name Felinus mentioned by Utenhove (p. 22, note 3): *Benedictus Aretius*, destijds professor te Marburg, was schrijver van Commentarii in Pentateuchum et Psalmos. Meer bekend en herhaaldelijk gedrukt zijn zijne 'Theologiae problemata', en 'Examen Theologicum'. This reference is evidently wrong, as the Commentary mentioned is certainly that of Bucer under his pseudonym. The Commentary of Benedictus Aretius was a rather unknown work at that time, and seems even to have been published at a much later date. There is no proof in any case that Benedictus Aretius is identical with Aretius Felinus, whereas the Commentary of Aretius Felinus will certainly have been of value to Utenhove, who admired Bucer.

scholars and the *Targum* of the Psalms ('Paraphrastes Chaldeus Rabbi Ioseph', or 'Paraphrases Chaldaea'). His own knowledge of Hebrew gave thus far-reaching importance to his Psalter. These Jewish commentators, whom he employed were mainly three: Rabbi Kimchi, Rabbi A. Ezra and Rabbi Solomon ben Isaac (Rashi). Rashi's Commentary on the Psalms written at the end of the eleventh century furnished, besides the two other Rabbinic sources, a most reliable source for the Hebrew text at that time, and was also used by Luther. Rashi has about 61 Glosses in French written in Hebrew characters contained in his Commentary on the Psalter. Bucer refers to some of those French Glosses.[1] The Rabbinic commentaries of Kimchi and Rashi on the Psalms were contained in the Rabbinic Bible of 1516-17, which was edited by Felix Pratensis. That Rabbinic Bible was an epoch-making edition of the Old Testament.

When Bucer wrote his work, many commentaries on the Psalms were compiled. Besides the Rabbinic commentaries known and used at that time, also Christian theologians like Pagninus, Luther, Bugenhagen, Pellican, Leo Juda, Zwingli and Munster, Lefèvre and Olivétan (to name only a few) were engaged on exegetical works. The editor of the Rabbinic Bible (which he had dedicated to Pope Leo X), Felix Pratensis, a Jewish Anastat, who had become an Augustinian Friar, wrote also a paraphrasis on the Psalms, also dedicated to Pope Leo X. This Paraphrasis was used by Bugenhagen, who, himself probably ignorant of Hebrew, relied entirely on it as his authority. It was also known to Bucer, and 'Matthew's Bible' in its Psalter of 1537 refers to it as well.

How much Bucer was indebted to Kimchi can be seen from his own confession in his 'Praefatio ad pium lectorem',[2] and also from George Joye's statement in his *Apology* against Tyndale (February 27th, 1536). Bucer knew of course Luther's Psalter.

With those works at hand, his Commentary became an important work of reference. It was a collective work on the Psalter, containing the views, translations and comments of the most eminent interpreters of the time. It enabled anybody, who wanted to get acquainted with the various textual problems, to form his opinion on

[1] Arsène Darmesteter in: *Les Gloses Françaises de Raschi dans la Bible*, Paris, 1909 (Extrait de la Revue des Études Juives Annees 1907-1908) quotes those 61 Glosses to the Psalms (Psaumes, pp. 106-113). In comparing the Glosses quoted with the Glosses referred to by Bucer, we found out that Bucer quotes Glosses which are not mentioned by Darmesteter, but are actually standing in Rashi. The Glosses mentioned by Bucer are those to: Psalm xv. 3, xxii. 15, xxv. 4, xxix. 7, xlviii. 4, lxxxiii. 15, civ. 25, cxxix. 7, cxl. 3. French expressions used by Bucer on Psalm i. 1, iv, v. 12, vi. 6, xi. 7, xiv. 1, xxxviii. 10, xxxix. 3, xli. 13, xlvi. 2, li. 1, lviii. 8, lxxiv. 12, lxxvi. 12, lxxxi. 11, cxxvii. 3, cxxxvii. 8, cxli. 8.

[2] cf. his Commentary (editio 1529), p. 7 verso (numbered at the foot of the page).

the most suitable translation. Bucer's critical attitude and objective treatment of all the other commentators quoted by him, reassured the reader, and made him choose that rendering which seemed most plausible to him. A work like that of Pratensis, for instance, did not give the various readings and comments of other authorities, and yet was regarded by Bugenhagen, as most reliable source. But here in Bucer's work a new start was made, a handbook was given to the student of the Bible.

Bucer's linguistic excursions are not limited to the various Rabbinic versions. He knew Hebrew, Greek and Latin well, which enabled him to apply towards all the various texts a superior critical attitude, thus securing a text most likely to be correct. He took a certain passage, examined the various possibilities of interpretation as given by Rabbinic and other commentators, compared them with the text of the Vulgate or Septuagint, consulted Jerome, Augustine or other Fathers, and then gave his rendering from his own knowledge of Hebrew, Greek or Latin, being independent enough to state his own opinion. This opinion might sometimes contradict interpretations which were still approved at his time by other scholars. But he values Augustine, Aquinas, Kimchi, or Pratensis, the Vulgate or the Septuagint, only in so far as they contribute to the right understanding of the original text. Where they hinder a right understanding, he prefers an interpretation gained by textual investigation. The text is not correct to him for the mere reason that it is the reading of the Vulgate, or because an Hebrew expert advocates a certain reading, or because the authority Pratensis has spoken. Thus, in Psalm xxii. 17 he is for instance in favour of Pratensis' text, which reads *karu* in spite of all Hebrew authorities. He is not in favour of Pratensis because of his Christian interpretation or because he is in accordance with the Vulgate in this passage, but because Pratensis claims in the name of God that this his reading exists in one of the manuscripts and because it is entitled to compete with all other interpretations. On the other hand, Bucer criticizes Pratensis when his reading is misleading and due to a misunderstanding of the Hebrew as in Psalm xlv. 9. The Vulgate and Septuagint are quoted as the traditional interpretations, but have to be altered when necessary. He is opposed to the Vulgate version of Psalm i. 6: *resurgent*, which he regards an inappropriate rendering of the Hebrew term, and which bears a doctrinal implication. He also corrects the Vulgate, e.g. in Psalm civ. 25, by stating that *iadaim* has been wrongly rendered by 'spatiosum manibus'.

The index of names given in the 1547 edition of Bucer's Psalter shows the wide range of authorities which had been consulted for his work. There are the classics, Greek as well as Latin, Aristotle and Plato, Homer and Herodotus, Cicero, Virgil, Ovid, Horace, Tacitus and Pliny. There are the Church Fathers Tertullian and Cyprian and Chrysostom or Augustine, to name only a few. Pliny provides Bucer with that knowledge of Natural History which scholars at the time usually derived from Pliny.[1]

Bucer's work underwent several editions on the Continent.[2] He himself improved it by adding and correcting material. The strange rendering of the name *Jahwe* in the original edition by *Autophyes* is altered by him. The explanation to the note *Selah* as given in the 1529 and 1547 editions by Bucer is of interest, as he refers to Kimchi, and as the marginal note in 'Matthew's Bible' bears some striking similarity.

A posthumous edition of Bucer's Commentary was done by Robert Stephan at Geneva in 1554. That edition aroused some controversy between Vossius, Grotius and Rivet, as the Genevan Press was accused of having altered doctrinal statements of Bucer for the sake of Calvinistic interpretation.[3]

The work was also translated into French.[4] And in 1530 an English translation was published at Strassburg, which was followed by another English edition by Thomas Godfray. Another English edition was later printed by Edward Whitchurch, the printer of the *Great English Bible*. The work was highly praised by Calvin in his Commentary to the Psalms, which was also later translated into English.[5]

It is not surprising that a Commentary of such quality found its way into England at a time when English theologians were engaged on the work of rendering the Bible into English. From external evidence it seems at first sight difficult to find out the exact rôle Bucer's Commentary did play in the history of the English Bible and how far — if at all — it was used by English theologians.

Richard Bayfield seems to have introduced Bucer's Latin Commen-

[1] cf. Bucer's Commentary on Psalm xxii. 21 (the unicorn). cf. also Bucer's Commentary on Psalm ciii. 5 (the eagle renewing its youth), where he refers to various stories about the eagle as given by *Saadiah*, *Aristotle* and *Pliny*.

[2] 1529, 1547, 1554. A copy of the 1529 edition at Christ Church, Oxford, bears the signature of Robert Burton, the author of the *Anatomy of Melancholy*. A copy of the 1547 edition belonged to John Barcham (Barkham) of Corpus Christi (at the Bodleian).

[3] cf. the letter of Vossius to Hugo Grotius (Amsterdam, June 17th, 1642): Vossius, Gerhard, J.: *Gerardi Joan Vossii et Clarorum Virorum ad eum Epistolae* (London, 1690), pp. 402(2) f. cf. also *Hugonis Grotii Votum pro pace Ecclesiastica* . . . 1642, pp. 31-32. cf. also *Andreae Riveti Apologeticus, pro suo de verae & sincerae pacis Ecclesiae propositio, Contra Hugonis Grotii Votum* . . . (Lugd. Batavor . . . 1643), pp. 65 ff.

[4] *Declaration Familiere* sur le second liure des Pseaumes. Par M. Martin Bucer. Par Philbert Hamelin. 1553.

[5] cf. here p. 205.

tary as well as the English translation into England among other 'heretical' books. That was in 1530-31.[1]

It is self-evident that if the Latin Commentary was banned, the English translation as well had to be banned. And, as we shall see later, Psalms of Bucer occur in the English Primer — known as 'Marshall's Primer' — that Primer with its other Protestant tendencies had as well to be prohibited.

The first fact derived from lists of prohibited books is a negative one, for, although Bucer's Psalter was known and forbidden in England, we derive no knowledge by whom and to what extent it was used, and how it influenced work on the English Bible. But it provides us also with the fact — on which we shall dwell in a later section of this chapter — that some of its Psalms, as contained in the Primer, were read and sung in Church services by people in England, being the first printed English Version of the Psalter.

Next mention of the Psalter is made by George Joye in his controversy with Tyndale, February 1535. Here Joye employs Bucer's rendering of Psalm i. 6 as an argument against Tyndale's accusation, that Joye, by editing Tyndale's New Testament, somehow revised in 1534, had rendered the word *Resurrection* used by Tyndale, by *the life after this life*, or *very life*. Joye's rendering had a tendentious meaning. The term Resurrection might imply the Roman Catholic conception of the state of departed souls between death and resurrection. To strengthen his argument that he was perfectly entitled to translate the Latin term with a different English word, he refers to Bucer's Commentary. He states that Bucer in Psalm i. 6[2] interprets the Hebrew *iakumu*, translated by the Vulgate with *resurgent*, as *to be*

[1] In the Royal Proclamation [of June 22nd, 1530] we find mentioned in the list of Books prohibited: 'David's psalter, in English'. cf. Wilkins, D.: *Concilia* . . . (London, 1737), vol. III, p. 739. (The date given by Steele, R.: *A Bibliography of Royal Proclamations* . . . (Oxford, 1910), vol. I, p. 13, n. 114: 'before March 6th, 1528-29', disagrees, however, with Wilkins' statement.

In the list of 'heretical books' by Stokesley, Bishop of London (December 1531), 'The psalter in English' is mentioned. cf. Letters and Papers, Foreign and Domestic, Henry VIII, vol. V, 1531-32, pp. 768-769, App. 18, Heretical Books. cf. also Thomas More: *The cōfutacyon of Tyndale's answere* . . . (London, 1532), fol. B b.2.

The 'Provincial Council' (1532?) mentions 'Felinus super psalterium' as among the heretical books. cf. Wilkins, op cit., vol. III, p. 720; and Steele, Robert: 'Notes on English Books printed abroad' (*Transactions of the Biographical Society*, vol. XI, London, March, 1912), pp. 214, ff. cf. also Foxe, John: *Acts and Monuments* (Ed. Townsend, London, 1846), vol. IV, p. 685 (sentence on Richard Bayfield), 'Felinus upon the Psalter . . . The Primer in English . . . The Psalter in English . . .'

[2] cf. Bucer's Commentary (ed. 1529) ad locum, p. 8 verso: *Lo Iakumu*, quod uerti, non consistent, plerique uerterunt, non surgent, & de resurrectione mortuorū disputarunt, significat autē id uerbi, proprie, stare, consistere, nonnunquā se statuere uel erigere, eoque & surgere. At hic, cum per illationem, hoc, ei (tanquā quisquiliae &c.) subijcitur, quis non uideat Vatem dicere uoluisse, improbos & flagitiosos, qui ijdem sunt, in iudicio, et magno illo sanctorum concilio, quod aderit uenienti in maiestate patris, ad iudicandum minime staturos, id est, iri condemnatū. Caeterum resurgent,

able to stand (which is also the version of the Prayer Book Psalter). The usual Latin translation (Vulgate)[1] had often aroused a disputation on the resurrection, which was admitted by Bucer, who thus furnished Joye with a welcome argument against Tyndale. Joye, who had been at Strassburg, must have known Bucer's Commentary intimately in referring to that special passage of his Commentary and by stating that Bucer for his translation of the Hebrew term uses Rabbi Kimchi. Joye writes:

> If T[indale]. will englisshe thys verbe *Resurgo* euery where to ryse agayne in bodye | so shal he translate it falsely | corruppe the text and bringe the reder in to no small errour | as once did one preacher in a sermon | expownyng this verse of the first psalm. *Ideo non resurgent impij in iudicio &c.* englysshing yt thus: wherfore the vngodly shal not ryse agayn in the iugement. wherat many were offended and astonied | and some beleued that the vngodly shulde not ryse agen at the generall iugement. which worde in that place Philip melanchton | Martyne Bucere | Conradus Pellicanus | zwinglius | Campensis | (men of greter knowleg | higher lerning | and more excellent iugement in holy scripture | in the hebrew | greke and latyne then Tindal is or euer lykely to be) translate it into these verbis: *consistunt* | *constant* | *perstant* | *durant* | *viuunt*: rendering the verse thus. *Ideo non constant non consistunt non durant* | *or non viuunt impii in iudicio* &c. that is to saye the vngodlye abyde not | nor endure | nor lyue in the company of the iust at the iugement: whether it be in the generall or partic[u]lare iugement of euery soule departed | as Rabbi Kimhy cyted of Bucere vpon that same verse taketh *Judicium* in that place: . . .[2]

Another evidence is given in the fact that 'Matthew's Bible' not only adopts the superscriptions or 'arguments' from the English version of Bucer's Psalter, but that a great part of the marginal material in the Psalter of 'Matthew's Bible' has its origin in Bucer's Latin Commentary, which must have been carefully studied by the compiler of

[1] It is interesting to note that Felix Pratensis, in his paraphrasis on the Psalter, does neither dare to alter the text (*resurgent*) nor refer in a marginal note to another interpretation of that term. He, the Augustinian Friar, who had dedicated his work to Pope Leo X, was still too orthodox a Roman Catholic to render such a vital passage into a new meaning.

[2] cf. George Joye: 'An apology made by George Joy, to satisfy, if it may be, W. Tindale.' 1535 (February 27th). Edited by Edward Arber, Birmingham, August 15th, 1882 (*The English Scholar's Library*, n.13), p. 11.

cf. on the doctrinal statement, Mozley, J. F.: *William Tyndale* (London, 1937), pp. 271 ff.

---

sed non in resurrectionē uitae, astabunt tribunali Christi, sed ut pronunciata sententia, mox se recipiant in ignem aeternū, paratum diabolo & angelis eius. R. Kim. Iudicium hic diem mortis cuiusque intelligit, & concilium iustorum, coetum sanctarum animarum, in quem sancti post hanc uitam admittentur, reprobi excludentur, ut qui pereant animo & corpore, ideoque non habeant stationem, & ut uerbum uerbo reddam, non surgant, consistant, ac permaneant inter iustos.

those notes for the Psalter of 'Matthew's Bible', since notes derived from Bucer are well selected from the bulk of his Commentary. A special section of this chapter will show in detail the dependence of 'Matthew's Psalter' on that of Bucer.

In this connection of providing evidence for the relation of Bucer's Commentary to the English Psalter, reference has to be made to Sebastian Munster's Latin Bible of 1534-35, which Coverdale employed for the second edition of the English Bible. For many examples adduced as evidence stating that Coverdale employed Munster,[1] if compared with Bucer's Commentary show that Munster and Bucer render certain passages very similarly and give the same linguistic or grammatic reasons for their interpretation. Munster, as well as Bucer, relies on Rabbinic authorities, mainly Rabbi Kimchi, which explains a great deal of their agreement in the version of certain passages. Munster's Bible is about five years younger than Bucer's Latin Commentary. But before Munster's Bible was issued, already his Hebrew-Chaldee Dictionary had been published.[2] By bringing a certain Hebrew-term in its biblical context, an explanation of the Hebrew passage is made easier. That dictionary forms the basis for Munster's Bible. Here in the dictionary already we find words occurring in the Psalter rendered as later in his Latin Bible. As Munster's Bible as well as his Dictionary rely on Hebrew authorities it is thus not surprising that Bucer's Commentary favouring the same sources comes to the same conclusions in translating certain passages. Thus sources for Munster, Bucer and Coverdale, were Hebrew authorities, and Coverdale employing Munster for his second edition of the English Bible, thus introduces indirectly Kimchi and other Rabbinic authors through the agency of Munster.[3]

A number of instances quoted by Walter[4] as illustrating the dependence of the English Version on Munster if compared with Bucer's Commentary, show that Bucer gave the same explanation and translation:

e.g. Psalm cxl. 10 in English has: Into deep pits
Bucer and Munster have: In foveas (which is different from the Vulgate).

[1] cf. Clapton, Ernest, op. cit., pp. xvii ff. and in parallel text passim.
Driver, S. R.: *The Parallel Psalter* . . . (2nd ed., Oxford, 1904), pp. xiv. ff.
Westcott, B. F.: *A General View* . . . (3rd revis. ed., London, 1905), pp. 183 ff.
Walter, Henry: *A Letter to the Right Reverend Herbert, Lord Bishop of Peterborough* . . . (London, 1823). *A Second Letter* . . . (1828), pp. 39 ff. and passim.
S. Munster's Latin Version of the Psalms is printed in *The Latin Elizabethan Prayer Book* (London, Vautrollerius 1574).

[2] *Aruch: Dictionarium Chaldaicum* . . . several editions, 1523, 1525, 1527.

[3] Box, G. H.: Introduction to Finch, R. G., *The Longer Commentary of R. David Kimhi*, S.P.C.K. (London, 1919), pp. vii, xx.

[4] Walter, Henry: *A Second Letter to the* . . . (London, 1828), pp. 39 ff.

Psalm lxxxiv. 6 in English has: Rain
Bucer and Munster have: pluvia (different from the Vulgate).
Psalm cii. 3 in English has: hearth
Bucer and Munster have: focus (different from the Vulgate).
Psalm ciii. 5: in English has: Thy mouth
Munster (Dictionary) 'significat etiam *adi* i.q. *pi* Psl. 103.
Bucer in his comment to the verse 'maxillas . . . os'.

(Those four illustrations are examples taken at random from Walter, who of course does not include Bucer, as he claims Munster as source for Coverdale.)

The fact that the Scottish Reformer, Alexander Alesius, in his Commentary on the Psalms (1554) refers to Bucer's Commentary,[1] and the fact that John Boys (1571-1625), Dean of Canterbury, employed to a large extent Bucer's Commentary in his *Exposition*,[2] shows only that Bucer's work was well known in a period when the English Bible had still not reached its completion in the edition of the Authorized Version.

It is also noteworthy that Dr. Thomas Holland (one of the translators of the Authorized Version (see Westcott, op. cit., pp. 113, 346)) possessed Bucer's Latin Commentary (1529), as the signature of the copy at Cambridge University Library indicates.

But special research claims that there exists an even closer relationship between Bucer's Psalter and that of the English Bible, than could be realized from the meagre external evidence. A close study of the English translation of Bucer's Commentary and of its various links with the English Primer and English Bible attempts to provide the material of internal evidence for this yet unconfirmed statement.

[1] cf. *Primvs liber Psalmorvm et divi Hieronymi* . . . Expositus ab Alexandro Alesio D. in celebri Academia Lipsensi. 1554, fol. Lij, verso, exposition to Psalm xi. 3.

[2] cf. Boys, John: *An Exposition of the Proper Psalmes, used in our English Liturgie* . . . At London 1616: second part, London 1617.

An Exposition of al the principall Scriptures used in our English Liturgie, London, 1610 (3 parts).

Reference to Bucer's Commentary: in the *Exposition of Proper Psalms*: Pt. I, pp. 20, 22, 26, 57, 68-69, 79, 82, 84, 94, 96, 106, 114, 122, 139, 143, 159, 169-170.

Pt. II, pp. 17, 18-20, 90, 92, 100, 138, 144, 147-148, 152, 168.

By referring to Bucer Boys quotes also Kimchi, to whom Bucer had made reference (e.g. Pt. I, p. 96 to Psalm ii). It is not surprising that Boys, who employed all great contemporary theological authorities for his Exposition, and of whom it is said that 'no writer of the seventeenth century quotes so widely and frequently from contemporary literature, as Boys' (*D.N.B.*) should have made use of Bucer's work. It is the more interesting as Boys lived in the period of work on the Authorized Version of the Bible, which is evidence that among theologians of the period Bucer's work was well known.

Peter Martyr became also early acquainted with Bucer's Commentary, which influenced Martyr, still in Italy, greatly. cf. Schmidt, C.: *Peter Martyr Vermigli* (Elberfeld, 1858), p. 20.

§ 11

THE ENGLISH TRANSLATION OF BUCER'S PSALTER

Soon after Bucer's Latin Commentary had been published in 1529, an English translation of it was printed at Strassburg by Francis Foxe in 1530. It was followed by another edition, printed at London by Thomas Godfray (no date). The translator is unknown.

The opening words of the short preface to the reader 'John Aleph greteth the English nacion' do not occur in the Godfray edition, which otherwise agrees verbatim with the preface of the Strassburg edition. Was John Aleph a pseudonym for the translator? The translation has been attributed to George Joye.[1] In supporting this we may note that Thomas More writes in his *Confutation* of 1532: 'The Psalter was translated by George Jay, the preste, that is wedded now . . .'[2]

It may be noted also:

(1) Joye escaped from England in 1527. From Strassburg he published several of his works, and seems to have been there till 1532. He must have come into contact with Bucer, whose Commentary was printed at Strassburg in 1529, and its English translation in 1530.

(2) Joye's statement in his *Apology* against Tyndale (February 1535) quotes a special passage of Bucer's Commentary, which means that he must have known the Psalter well.

(3) Joye prefixes to his *Apology* of February 1535 on the title-page Psalm cxx. 2: 'Lorde, delyver me from lyinge lyppes, and from a deceatfull tongue.' This is the rendering in Joye's translation of the Psalter of August 1534. But it is also that of the English version of Bucer's Commentary. The version of August 1534 by Joye transmits no reference to the author of the Latin original. Cotton (vol. I, p. 135) ascribed it in brackets to 'Friar Felix, an Augustinian Eremite'

[1] cf. Anderson: *Annals of Engl. Bible*, vol. I, p. 393, note 2. The article on George Joye in the *D.N.B.* (by Sir Sidney Lee) states that the Bishop of London, Stokesley, had added to the list of heretical books on Advent Sunday (December 3rd) 1531 'The psalter in English by Joye'. A similar statement is made by Anderson (op. cit., vol. I, p. 306). Source for Anderson is the MS. Lambeth, 306 f. 65. But the MS. has simply 'The Psalter in English', without making any reference to George Joye.

cf. MS. Lambeth 306, fol. 65, and: Letters & Papers, Foreign and Domestic, Henry VIII, vol. V, 1531-32, pp. 768-769, App. 18: *Heretical Books* (p. 769, n. 29) where an extract from the MS. is given. cf. also Furnivall, Frederick J.: *Political, Religious and Love Poems* (Early English Text Society, Original Series 15, London 1866, re-edit. 1903), pp. 62-63, also printing a section of the MS.

[2] More, Thomas: *The cōfutacyon of Tyndales answere made by syr Thomas More* . . . Prentyd at London . . . 1532, in: 'the preface to the crysten reader', fol. B b.ii.

(sc. Felix Pratensis). The same suggestion appears in a modern pencil note on the front leaf of the Cambridge copy.

The differences between the English version generally in this edition of August 1534 and the English version of Bucer's work 1530 (Strassburg and Godfray edition) is so considerable as to suggest that the two are made from different Latin versions. The explanation in the *D.N.B.* article, that Joye employed for the 1534 edition 'the Latin version, which Martin Bucer issued under the pseudonym of Aretinus[!] Felinus in 1529' ('There can be no doubt, that Joye completed his work some years before it was published') can hardly be regarded as satisfactory. The summaries before each Psalm in the 1534 edition bear resemblance neither to the Latin summaries of Bucer's work, nor to the English translation of the summaries of Bucer, nor to those of Felix Pratensis.

(4) Some additional confirmation may be found in the fact that the English of the Psalms in 'Marshall's Primer' is generally verbatim the same as that of the English version of Bucer's work. Now there are reasons for ascribing 'Marshall's Primer' to George Joye (cf. here pp. 224 ff.).

The Editions of the Psalter

I

The Psalter of Dauid in Englishe purely ād faithfully trāslated aftir the texte of ffeline: euery Psalme hauynge his argument before declarynge brefly thentente & substance of the wholl Psalme.

On the reverse:

Johan Aleph greteth the Englishe nacion. Be glad in ye Lorde (dere brothern) & geve him thankes: which nowe as ye laste of his merciable goodnes hath sente ye his Psalter in Englishe, faithfully & purely translated: which ye may not mesure and Juge aftir the comē texte. For the trowth of ye Psalmes muste be fetched more nyghe ye Ebrue veritie, in the which tonge Dauid, with the other syngers of ye Psalmes firste sunge them. Let ye gostly lerned in ye holy tonge be iuges. It is ye spirituall man (saith Paule) which hath the spirit of god y^t^ muste de-rne [decerne] & iuge all thynges. And ye men quietly sittynge (if the truth be shewed them) muste iuge and stand vp and speke (the firste interpret^r^ holdynge his pease) god geve ye true spirituall & quiete sittynge iuges Amē.

col:

Emprinted at Argentine in the yeare of oure lorde 1530. the 16. daye of January by me Francis foxe. Praise ye the lorde.

(Henry Cotton: *Editions of the Bible and parts thereof in England from the year MDV. to MD.CCCL. with an Appendix* . . . Oxford MDCCCLII. Appendix: Cotton, II, p. 390. Appendix F: Descriptions of Editions of the Psalms.)

(This edition, now at the British Museum, belonged once to Charles Combe (1743-1817) (*D.N.B.*), but beyond that date it is difficult to find out to whose library it belonged originally.)

2

The Psalter of Dauid in Englyshe | purely and faythfully trãslated after the texte of Felyne: euery Psalme hauynge his argument before | declarynge brefely thentente & substance of the hole Psalme.

To the reder. BE glad in the lorde (dere brethern) & gyue hī thākes | whiche nowe at the last | of his merciable goodnes hath sent you his Psalter in Englysshe | faithfully & purely translated: which ye may nat mesure & iuge after the comē texte. For the trouth of the Psalmes muste be fetched more nygh the Hebrue verite | in the which tonge Dauid with the other sīgers of ye Psalmes first songe them. Let the gostly lerned in the holy tonge be iuges. It is the spirituall man (saith Paule) which hath the spirite of god that must decerne and iuge all thynges. And the men quietly sytting (if the truth be shewed them) must iuge and stande vp & speke (the first īterpretour holdynge his peace) god giue you true spirituall and quiete syttynge iuges. Amen.

col:

Printed at London by Thomas Godfray. Cum priuilegio Regali. Praise ye the lorde. Amen.

(This edition belonged to Humphrey Dyson.)

3

Later still another edition was printed by Edward Whitchurch (1540?). There is no date to this edition. But it was printed after the English Bibles of Coverdale and of 'Matthew', thus showing that Bucer's Psalter was still ranked next to the version of the English Bible and also showing that the version of the English Bible was not regarded as an authorized or standard version. Whitchurch, who had also printed the English Bible, by editing anew Bucer's Psalter in English, prints the Psalter now 'Cum priuilegio ad imprimendum solum'. Thus Bucer's Psalter, once banned in England, gains a legal position. The title is[1]

[1] The italicized words are printed in red letters in that copy.

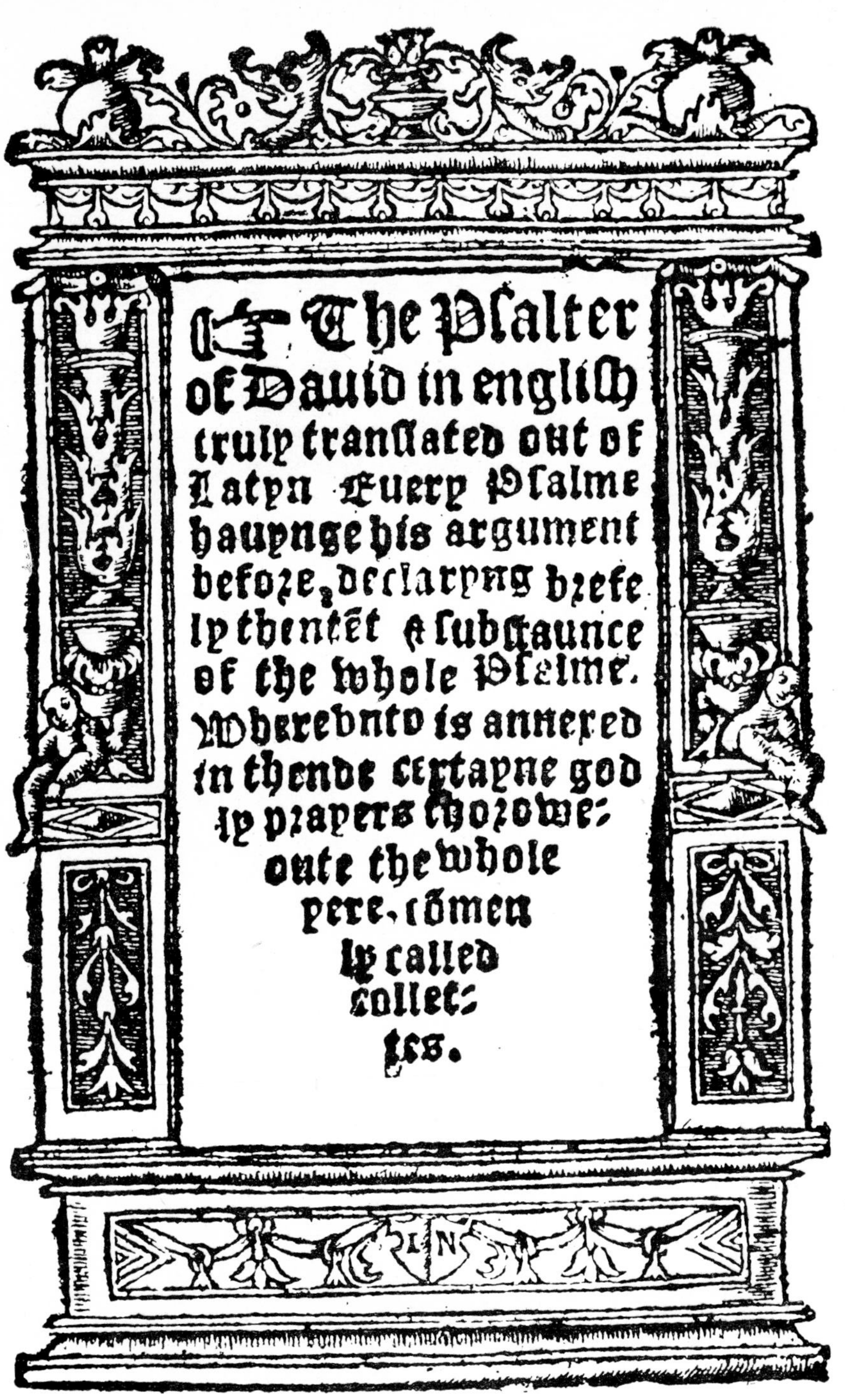

☞ The Psalter
of Dauid in englissh
truly translated out of
Latyn Euery Psalme
hauynge his argument
before, declaryng brefe
ly thentēt & substaunce
of the whole Psalme.
Whereunto is annexed
in thende certayne god
ly prayers thorowe-
oute the whole
yere, cōmen
ly called
collec-
tes.

Title Page of Bucer's Psalter in English
(Whitchurch edition; enlarged)
(cf. p. 221)

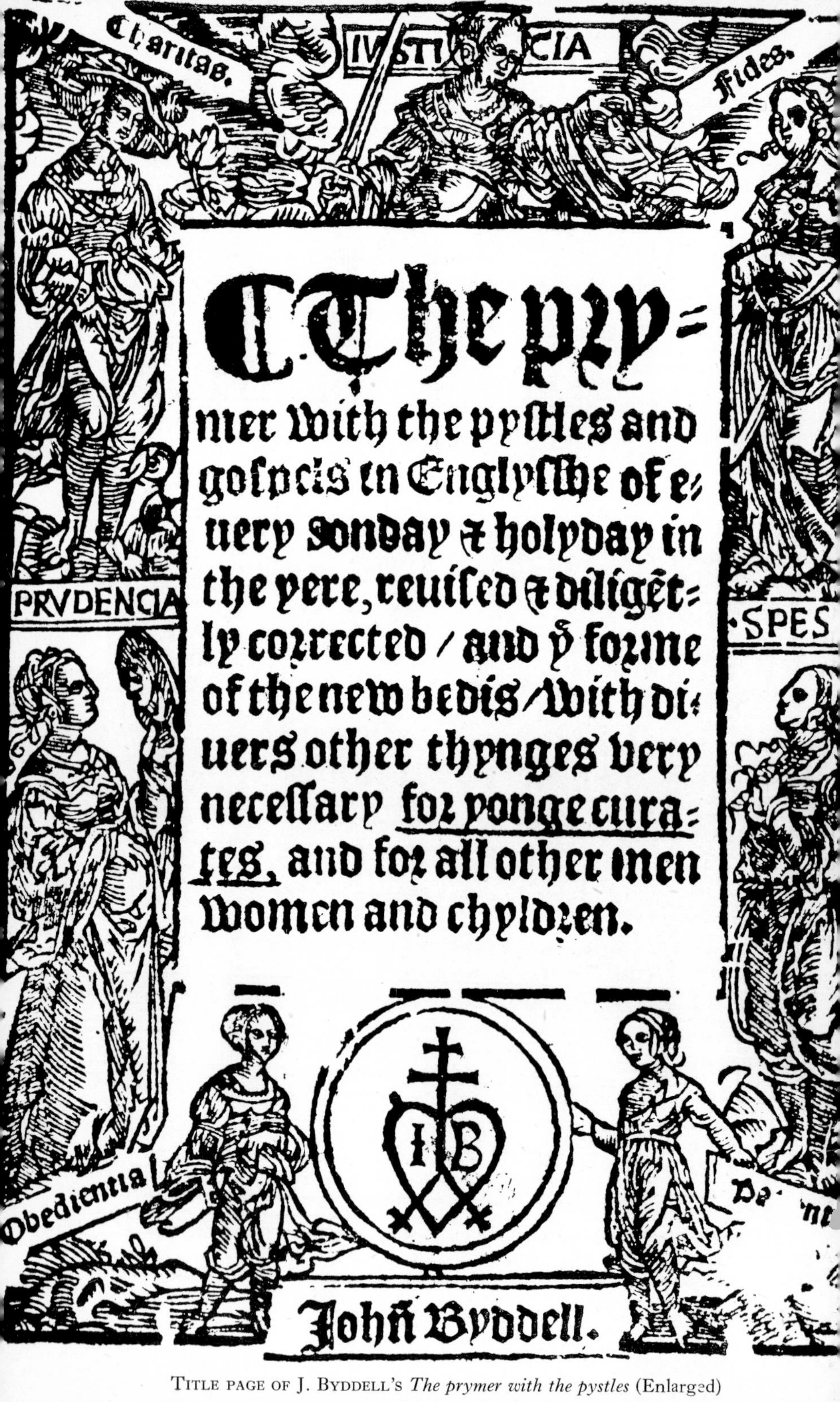

¶ The pry=
ner with the pystles and
gospels in Englysshe of e=
uery sonday & holyday in
the yere, reuised & diligēt=
ly corrected / and yͤ forme
of the new bedis / with di=
uers other thynges very
necessary for yonge cura=
tes, and for all other men
women and chyldren.

John Byddell.

TITLE PAGE OF J. BYDDELL'S *The prymer with the pystles* (Enlarged)
(cf. p. 226)

The Psalter of *Dauid in english* truly translated out of *Latyn* Euery *Psalme* hauynge his *argument* before, *declaryng* brefely *thentēt* & substaunce of the whole *Psalme*. *Wherevnto* is annexed in thende certayne godly *prayers thorowe*-oute the *whole yere*, cōmenly called *collettes*.

On Fol. cxxviii verso:

Jmprynted by *Edwarde* Whytchurch Cum priuilegio ad imprimendum *solum*.

The fact that the Psalter contains at the end the collects for the year even shows that it was used as a book of worship in the Church. A curious misprint occurs in the 'argument' to Psalm i. Whitchurch's edition has: '... They that forsake theyr counseyls, ye wayes, the earnynge, ...' whereas the former editions (Strassburg and Godfray) have:

They that forsake theyr coūseyls | the waies | the lernyng | ...

Two copies of this edition are kept at the British Museum.[1] The edition is a well-printed small volume in red and black letter print. On the reverse of the title-page is a small woodcut of David and Bathseba, which appears also in the *Great Bible* of 1539 (printed by Whitchurch and Grafton) to 2 Samuel xi.

4

David's Psalter, diligently and faithfully trāslated by George Joye, with brief Arguments before every Psalme, declaringe the effecte therof. Psalme cxx. Lorde, delyver me from lyinge lippes ād from a deceaitful tong. — *on. fol.* 221: Thus endeth the text of the Psalmes, translated oute of Latyne by George Joye. The year of our Lorde M.D.xxxiiii, ye monethe of Auguste — Martyne Emperowr. 1534. (There is no dedication nor preface — quoted from Cotton: II, p. 390 n. 2.)[2]

In the English version (Strassburg, Godfray and Whitchurch edition) all Bucer's exegetical work has been omitted. The Psalms only are translated with the summaries which form the headings of

[1] One of the two British Museum copies is bound together with: 'The bokes of Salomon, namely: Prouerbia. Ecclesiastes. Sapientia, and Ecclesiasticus, or Jesus the sonne of Syrach. Cum priuilegio, ad Jmprimendum solum.' *fol. clii, verso*: 'Jmprynted in London in the olde Jury, by Edwarde Whytchurch.'

[2] Cotton, I, p. 135: *David's Psalter*, translated from the Latin (of Friar Felix, an Augustinian Eremite) with brief arguments, by Geo. Joye; Antwerp, by Martin Emperowre.

the Psalms in Bucer's original version. The English of those summaries is, however, sometimes only an abstract or inaccurate rendering of the Latin. The same summaries (in English) occur later in the Psalter of the 'Matthew Bible' of 1537.

In rendering the text itself into English some eminent departures must be noted:

In Psalm xix. 5, for instance, the translator renders Bucer's 'umbraculum' by 'clouds', misunderstanding the Latin term, although Bucer in his note in the Commentary to the passage makes it clear, what he meant by it.[1] In Psalm xxiii. 2: 'He made me to feed in a full plenteous *battleground*', whereas Bucer's Latin has: In conseptis soli herbidi facit me accubare. Psalm xli. 9 Bucer's Latin has: . . . struxit mihi insidias, which is rendered by: 'supplanted me'[2] Psalm lxxvi. 6 Bucer has: Ab increpatione tua Deus Iaaecob, consopitus est currus & equus, rendered by: For thorowe thy fearfull thretenynge rebuke | o God of Jacob | their horse and cartes went all to hauoke.[3]

The number of characteristic words and expressions in the English version is worth mention. In Psalm xci. 5 the word 'bugges' (i.e. bogies), as later in Coverdale's version of 1535, occurs in the English version of Bucer's Commentary and does not seem to be a term characteristic of the 'first modern translation' of Coverdale as stated.[4] Thus also 'The universally known phrase, "Three score years and ten" in Psalm xc. 10, is an English expression' which is not 'introduced here by Coverdale, where the Hebrew, and even Wyclif, has plain "seventy",' as stated by Isaacs,[5] but is already to be found in the English version of Bucer's Commentary.

Coverdale never used one special or individual version (Latin, Greek, German or English) exclusively for his translation. He also did not translate from the Hebrew directly, but his knowledge of the languages mentioned and the opportunity of having before him already contemporary versions from the Original Hebrew or Greek text of the Bible, enabled him 'to select and adapt, according to his

[1] Bucer, Commentary, p. 110 v.: Quoque magis haec illustret, Solem similem sponso facit egredienti ex umbraculo suo. Mos Ebraeis fuit, ac etiamnum obseruatur, ut sub expanso uelo, sponso sponsam tradant, e quo cum progreditur, cunctos exhilarat, e. nuptiarum festum incipitur.—cf. marg. note in Geneva Bible to the same passage—cf. also Forcellini's references to Cicero on the term umbraculum. cf. umbraculum in Vulgat. Isai xxv. 4: LXX: σκέπη Hebr. zēl umbraculum ab aestu.
Ezek. xxxi. 17: LXX: σκέπη Heb. zēl sub umbraculo.

[2] cf. Bucer's commentary ad locum.

[3] Bucer comments to the passage: Versu septimo currum & equum, pro curribus & equis utentibus dixit, quos Deus consopit, eripiendo illis vitam.

[4] cf. Isaacs, J., p. 171, in: *The Bible in its Ancient and English Versions*, Ed. by H. Wheeler Robinson (Oxford, 1940).

[5] Isaacs, J., op. cit., p. 210.

own judgment, what appeared to him to be the right meaning of each verse from the different versions of other translators' (Clapton, op. cit., p. xxi). The similarity of certain passages between the English version of Bucer's Latin and Coverdale's versions of the Psalter in the 1535 and 1539 Bibles is so striking, that it seems definitely to suggest that Coverdale knew Bucer's work in Latin and in English and employed it for his English Bible.

As Coverdale knew Latin and Greek but not Hebrew sufficiently, a work like that of Bucer would be invaluable, if available. It was a compendium of all important text variants with references to Hebrew authorities (such as Rashi, Kimchi and A. Ezra), it was made from the Hebrew text and not a rendering of the Vulgate.

Bucer's Psalter in English provides the version of the Psalms in 'Marshall's Primer', which appeared before Coverdale's Bible was published. The Primer in conjunction with the English editions of Bucer's work acquainted English people with the beauty of the Psalter in English and those Psalms were sung and read before Coverdale gave the Bible to his nation. The summaries so characteristic of Bucer's Commentary and a great deal of exegetical and explanatory material provide the summaries and some marginal glosses for 'Matthew's Bible' of 1537. The Psalter in 'Matthew's Bible' is Coverdale's rendering of 1535. 'Matthew's Bible' is the link between Coverdale's Bible of 1535 and 1539 and its Psalter is closely related to Bucer's Commentary.

The Appendixes to this chapter, I. select list of characteristic words and expressions in the English version of Bucer's Psalter; II. some Psalms given as examples from Bucer's English version, together with the examples given from the Primer and 'Matthew's Bible'; III. Marginal and textual notes in 'Matthew's Bible'; IV. Descriptive Arguments, are intended to provide some internal evidence and illustration for our claim that Bucer's Commentary has to be included in an account of the History of the English Bible as a source employed by its compilers.

§ III

'MARSHALL'S PRIMER' AND MARTIN BUCER'S COMMENTARY ON THE PSALMS

The Psalms contained in 'Marshall's Primer' in English were printed before Coverdale's Bible was published. The first printed Psalter in English was a translation of Bucer's Commentary of 1530 (Strassburg, another edition by Thomas Godfray, London).

A comparison of both versions shows conclusively that 'Marshall's Primer' employed the English version of Bucer's Psalter. The Psalms contained in the various offices of the Primer are taken over from Bucer's work. Edward Burton's statement,[1] that the psalms which appear in the Primer do not follow the English translation of Bucer's Psalter, needs correction, for even the most superficial comparison of the two versions shows Bucer's version as the source for the Primer.

It has been claimed, as we have mentioned already, that George Joye was the translator of Bucer's Latin Psalter into English. 'Marshall's Primer' has also been ascribed to George Joye. The editor of 'Marshall's Primer', by employing the English version of Bucer's work for the Psalms of his Primer, must certainly have been well acquainted with the latter work. If Joye was the translator of Bucer's Commentary, it would be easy to suggest that he quite naturally turned to his own translation of the Psalms for the provision of Psalms for the Primer.

That Joye can be said to be the translator of the Primer becomes evident from Thomas More's statement in the *Confutation* (1532):

> For the Prymer and Psalter, prayours & all | were trãslated and made in this maner, by none other but heretykes. The Psalter was translated by George Jay the preste, y^t is wedded now | and I here say the Prymer to, wherein the seuen psalmes be set in wythout the lateny, leste folke shold pray to sayntes. And ye Dirige is lefte out clene | leste a man myght happe to pray theron for hys fathers soule.[2]

[1] Burton, Edward: *Three Primers* . . . (Oxford, 1834), preface, pp. xliv-xlv.

[2] More, Thomas: *The cõfutacyon* . . . op. cit., fol. Bb. ii. cf. also The Bishops declaration, May 24th, 1530: 'Owt of the Prymar' (Wilkins, David: *Concilia Magnae Britanniae* . . . vol. III, p. 733 (London, 1737)).

The Primer is also mentioned in the List of heretical books issued by the Bishop of London on December 3rd, 1531 (cf. MS. Lambeth 306, f. 65, in Letters & Papers, Foreign and Domestic, Henry VIII, vol. V, 1531-32, pp. 768-769. App. 18: *Heretical Books*, p. 769, n.27).

The summaries or 'arguments' from Bucer's work are only used for the Psalms contained in the Dirige, for Psalms cxix and cxxxix and for the 'Psalms of the Passion'. All

The Litany and the Dirige were omitted in the undated edition of 'Marshall's Primer' printed by J. Byddell.[1] The translator of the Primer in the following edition printed by Byddell in 1535, answers More's accusation by stating in the preface (to the Litany):

> FOrasmoche good christen reder, as I am certeynly perswaded, that diuerse ꝑsones of small iudgemēt and knowlege in holy scripture haue ben offended, for that y^t in the englyshe prymer, whiche I lately set forthe, I dyd omitte & leaue out the letany, whiche I take god to witnes, I dyd not of any ꝑuerse mynde or opinion . . . (fol. lij verso).

This statement seems to be intended to meet More's criticism. The statement does not say that the translator was not George Joye.

The translator of the English Primer reprinted with only slight text-alterations the Psalms from the English Version of Bucer's Psalter. He made use also of some of the short summaries before each Psalm (which occur again in the Psalter of the 'Matthew's Bible' of 1537), characteristic of Bucer's Psalter, by transplanting them into the Primer before the Psalm concerned.[2] He writes in the Preface to the Dirige (in the 1535 edition, fol. K iv f.):

> An admonition or warnyng to the reder | necessarie to be hadde and redde | for the true vnderstandinge and meanynge of ye Dirige | hereafter folowynge . . . For a more manifest and clere sight wherof, as touchynge the psalmes, bicause fyrste y^u shalte not

[1] Butterworth's statement (op. cit., p. 104) needs here some correction, when he writes: 'It is of course, possible that these English Primers of Marshall represent the translation that Joye had made. According to More's report, however, Joye's Primer had the Seven Psalms 'sette in without the Letanye'; whereas these editions of Marshall's are found to include both the Litany and the Seven Penitential Psalms.'

[2] The summaries occurring in the Primer (to Psalms: 5-7, 22-31, 40-43, 45, 51, 116, 119, 120, 121, 130, 138, 139, 146, 148-150) have verbatim the same English text as those in Bucer's Psalter in English. The English of the summaries in 'Matthew's Bible' differs from that of the Primer and that of Bucer's Psalter in English, as he apparently translated from Bucer's Latin and seems not to have used the already extant English translation.—cf. here p. 229. It is of interest to note that the summary to Psalm cxix in the Primer of Henry VIII, 1543 (cf. Burton, op. cit., p. 493) has definitely as its source that of Bucer.

---

other Psalms of the Primer appear without the summary. The undated edition of the Primer has only two summaries (to Psalms xxii, cxix).

The Psalms as they occur in the order of the Primer:
The Matins: Psalms xcv, viii, xix, xxiv, xciii, c, lxiii, lxvii, cxlviii-cl.
The Prime and Hours: liv, cxvii-cxviii, cxx-cxxviii.
Evensong: i-iii, cxv, xiii, xliii, cxxix, cxxxi.
Seven Psalms: vi, xxxii, xxxvii (but xxxviii is printed), li, cii, cxxx, cxliii.
Dirige: cxvi, cxx, cxxi, cxxx, cxxxviii, cxlvi, v-vii, xxiii, xxv, xxvii, xl-xlii, li, xlv (but lxvi is printed), xliii, cxlviii-cl, xxx.
Commendations: cxix, cxxxix.
Psalms of the Passion of Christ: xxii-xxxi (verses 1-6).

The English version of Psalm xcv (in Matins) differs widely from that in Bucer's Psalter in English and has apparently another source.

be ignoraunt of the effecte of the mater conteyned in them, I haue put a lytle shorte argumēt before euery psalme of the same. wherin breuely I haue declared, expouned [*sic*], and set forthe theffecte, entent, & meanӯg of the whole psalme folowynge, the whiche lytle shorte argument and exposition, I beseche the gentle reder, diligently to apply and compare euer vnto the psalme therunto annexed, and than tel me whether I be a lyer or no, or els whether they be blynde teachers, that haue broughte the in suche a fonde folyshe trade . . .

There is another edition of the Primer printed by John Byddell in which Psalms of Bucer's Psalter occur.[1] The significant feature of this Primer as different from those other editions mentioned is that in the margins to the English text of the Psalms a parallel Latin text is printed. This seems obviously to suggest at first, seeing both texts side by side, that the Latin text should be the text from which the English translation was made. But the Latin is the Vulgate version (the Gallican version of S. Jerome), whereas the English is the translation from Bucer's Latin Psalter: to give two passages for example:

Psalm cxxxviii:

THE PRIMER (Bucer's version of the Psalms)	THE MARGIN OF THE PRIMER (Gallican version of S. Jerome)
I Shall magnifye the w^t all my hert: & before the princys of the worlde I shall prayse the.[2] I shal fall downe vpon my knees at thy holy tēple, & shal magnifie thy name for thy mercy and trouthes sake. For y^u hast extolled thy name & thy worde aboue all things. In what tyme so euer I called vpon the, thou gracyously . . .	Confitebor tibi dñe in toto corde meo: qm̄ audisti v̄ba oris mei. In cōspectu angelorum psallam tibi: adorabo ad templū sanctum tuum | et confitebor nomini tuo. Suꝑ mīa tua et veritate tua: qm̄ magnificasti suꝑ oē nomen sctm̄ tuū. In quacūq; die inuocauero te: exaudi . . .

Psalm cxvi. 5

The lord is our rightous god, he is prone vnto fauour: he is redy and	O dñe libera animā meā misericors dñs & iustus: & deus noster misere-

[1] The prymer with the pystles and gospels in Englysshe of euery sonday and holyday in the yere, reuised & diligētly corrected | and ye forme of the new bedis | with diuers other thynges very necessary *for yonge curates* and for all other men women and chyldren.

. . . Johñ Byddell.

col: . . . Jmprynted at London in Fletestrete, at the sygne of the Sonne, by me Johan Byddell. (Balliol copy: Arch. c. 12. 13).

[2] Bucer's Latin text to verse 1 has: 'coram dijs . . .' The English version of Bucer's Latin (the Strassburg edition of 1530) has: 'I shall magnifie the with all my harte: and shall prayse y^e in the presens of the goddis.'

bent to mercy. The lorde kepeth the poore symple ones. I was full poore, and full of care, & he saued me. Turne the (oh my soule) vnto thy rest for y[e] lorde hath rewarded the. For thou hast delyuered my soule from deth, myn eyen frō teares, & my fete frō slydinge. I shal continue and dwel before y[e] lord amonge the lyuing men.

tur. Custodiens paruulos dn̄s hūiliat' sū: & liberauit me. Conuertere anima mea in requiē tuam: quia dn̄s benefecit tibi. Quia eripuit animā meā de morte | oculos meos a lachrymis: pedes meos a lapsu. Placebo dn̄o in regione viuorū.

EDITIONS OF THE PRIMER

In the Bodleian Library:

(1) A Prymer in Englyshe, with certeyn prayers & godly meditations, very necessary for all people that vnderstonde not the Latyne tongue. Cum priuilegio Regali.

col: (*before exposition on Psalm li*):

Thus endeth the prymer in Englysshe with many goodly and godly praiers. Imprented at London in Fletstrete by Johan Byddell. Dwellyng next to Flete Brydge at the signe of our Lady of pytye. for wyllyam Marshall . . . (no date) (*Shelfmark:* Douce B.B. 67).

(2) *Primer* [Imperfect edition]: *col:*

Be it knowen to all men by these presentes, that it is prohibited by our soueraigne lorde the kynge, by his letters patentes, to all printers, boke sellers, and marchauntes, & all others that (without licence had of hym, that at his costes and charges printed this boke) they in no wyse do printe, or vtter in sale, or otherwyse, at any place with in our sayde soueraigne lordes dominions, this booke, entitled and called thenglyshe primer, at any tyme within sixe yeres nexte after the printynge hereof, as they wyll answere at theyr perylles, and auoyde the penalties mentioned in the priuilege here-unto grraunted.

Jmprynted at London in Fletestrete by Johñ Byddell | dwellynge at the signe of the Sonne | nexte to the cundite | for wylliam Marshall | the yere of our lorde god M.D.xxxv. the. xvi. day of June. (*Shelfmark:* Clar. Press suppl. e. 29[h]).

This dated edition of the Primer (June 16th, 1535) has an interesting manuscript entry in its Calendar (fol. C ii verso) on the date of October 29th:

This day the xxix day of Octob. disseasyd Elysabethe Lucar a dowghter of powle wythpoll in the yere of our lorde 1537.

Elizabeth Lucar was the wife of Emanuel Lucar, a member of the Merchant Taylors' Company and was buried in the church of S.

Lawrence Pountney (London). In John Stow's *A Survey of the Cities of London and Westminster* (Ed. by John Strype . . . London 1720) the eulogistic poem inscribed on Elizabeth Lucar's grave-stone is printed. (Book III, p. 189). We read in Strype's edition: 'The said *Elizabeth* deceased the 29. day of October, An. Dom. 1537. Of yeeres not fully 27. This Stone, and all hereon contained, made at the cost of the said *Emmanuel*, Merchant-Taylor.' According to the long poem inscribed, Elizabeth Lucar must have been an outstanding personality, highly educated and pious. The entry in the Primer seems to indicate being made by someone related to the family of the Lucars (cf. also, article on Lucar, Cyprian in *D.N.B.*, and Metcalfe, Walter C.: *The Visitation of Suffolk* (Exeter, 1882), p. 82).

Cambridge University Library:

(1) 'A goodly prymer in Englysshe' (about 1535).

This edition was translated by George Joye, and edited by William Marshall. Without printer's name. (Vol. I. p. 113, n. 576 in Sayle's Cambr. Univ. Libr. Catalogue of Early English Printed Books.)

(2) The Primer printed by Thomas Godfray:

A primer in Englysshe | with dyuers prayers & godly meditations. The contentes . . . || Cum priuilegio regali. *Col*: Printed at London by Thomas Godfray. Cum priuilegio Rygali [sic]: (Sayle: Vol. I. p. 111, n. 562.)

Oxford Edition:

Three Primers put forth in the Reign of Henry VIII . . . second edition. Oxford at the University Press M.Dccc.xlviii.

§ IV

THE PSALTER IN 'MATTHEW'S BIBLE' AND MARTIN BUCER'S COMMENTARY ON THE PSALMS

The Psalter in 'Matthew's Bible'[1] is taken over from Coverdale's Bible of 1535 with only slight and unimportant alterations in the text. The numbering of the Psalms is corrected to agree with the

[1] For convenience sake we speak of 'Matthew's Bible', although the name of the editor, John Rogers, ought to be mentioned. The controversy on the names *Matthew* and *Rogers*, however, does not concern us here in our study. cf. on the controversy J. Isaacs, pp. 172 ff. in *The Bible in its Ancient and English Versions*, Ed. by H. Wheeler Robinson (Oxford, 1940) and J. F. Mozley: *William Tyndale* (1937), App. E.

original Hebrew numbering, not with that of the Vulgate. The *Alleluia* finds its English rendering. The note on *Selah* is different from that of Coverdale at the end of his Psalter. In Psalm cxix the divisions are headed by the Hebrew characters א, ב, not only by the English *Aleph*, *Beth* . . . of Coverdale. The Psalter is divided into five sections: 'Treatyses' (1. Psalms i-xli; 2. Psalms xlii-lxxii; 3. Psalms lxxiii-lxxxix; 4. Psalms xc-cvi; 5. Psalms cvii-cl). The divisions are in accordance with those of ancient Scripture tradition. Luther, Bucer and Olivétan use them for their Psalters. But in 'Matthew's Bible' they appear for the first time in English.

The most distinguishing feature, however, of the Psalter in 'Matthew's Bible' from that in Coverdale's Bible is the extensive commentary (consisting of notes in the margin as well as in the text). The notes are of explanatory, 'edifying' and linguistic character. They try to explain difficult passages, they appeal to the reader by quotations of similar passages in the Old and New Testaments, and they interpret difficult Hebrew terms, like *Iduthun*, *Neginoth*, etc., in the superscriptions of the Psalms. They also interpret other terms occurring in the text. Each Psalm is introduced by a summary, describing the content. These descriptions are often of christological character, indicating that the particular Psalm is to be regarded as a *Typos* or *Figure* of Christ or *His Church*.

The main and only source for these summaries has been Bucer's Psalter, an observation which has hitherto completely escaped any attention. Bucer in his Latin edition (1529) gave a descriptive note to each Psalm, as a summary or 'argument' at the beginning. Those 'arguments' were translated together with the Psalms into English in the English edition of Bucer's Psalter in 1530. They form the material for the summaries of Matthew's Psalter, occurring almost verbatim in it. If the wording by Matthew differs from the English version (1530) of Bucer's Psalter, Matthew used the original Latin of Bucer. That was done when the translator of Bucer's Psalter did not closely follow the original.[1]

As regards the notes it can also be stated that Matthew had at hand Bucer's Latin Psalter and not only the English version. Some of Matthew's notes bear the closest resemblance with those in Bucer's Latin copy, which were of course omitted in the English version of Bucer's Psalter, which gives only the text and the summaries. Matthew, when quoting in his notes Hebrew authorities, like Rabbi Kimchi and A. Ezra, copies them with Bucer's context.

As main sources for the notes to Matthew's Psalter have been

[1] cf. also here p. 225, note 2.

claimed Lefèvre and Olivétan.[1] But as the following illustrations will show, Bucer has to be ranked among them as well.

The subsequent examples attempt to show that technical terms of the superscriptions, summaries and text-notes were taken over by 'Matthew's Bible' from Bucer's Commentary. The dramatic conception of Psalm ii, as if different persons were in conversation (God, the Prophet, the King and the Enemy), which is expressed in Matthew's Psalter by introducing the names of the persons in the margin, has also Bucer as source, and is to be found in Olivétan as well.

Some notes in Matthew's Psalter, which come from Lefèvre and Olivétan bear striking similarity to those in Bucer's Latin Commentary. As Olivétan had been at Strassburg (staying with Capito, Bucer's friend),[2] and as Lefèvre also once took refuge at Strassburg

[1] cf. Westcott: *History of the English Bible*, pp. 71, note 1, and 177 and notes. Two notes from Lefèvre are given by Westcott as examples (pp. 338-339). We give at random some more references to be found in Matthew's Psalter: To Psalms xvi. 9, xxxiii. 13, xxxvi. 9, xxxvii. 3+11, xli. 1. Lefèvre's Bible is dated 1534, Olivétan's Bible, 1535. Matthew's Psalter provides another source from which he took his notes. The note in the text to Psalm ix (description of the Psalm) states: 'Felix readeth the tytle thus: vnto the victour or ouercomer of the death of a fole . . .' The reference is made to Felix Pratensis' Psalter, which reads: 'Vincenti super morte insipientis . . .'

[2] *Note on Olivétan.* The affinity between the notes of Olivétan with those of Matthew and Bucer may find its explanation in the fact that Olivétan (in 1528 refugee in Strassburg) was not only known to Bucer, but seems also most probably to have been his pupil in Greek and Hebrew. He will certainly have known his Commentary, not to say, even have employed it. At the same time it remains a controversial point whether the 'youth of Noyon' mentioned in a letter by Bucer of May 1st, 1528 to Farel, is Olivétan, as maintained by Herminjard and Négrier, or whether it is only 'as good a guess as can be made' (Eells). The acquaintance between Olivétan and Bucer as stated by Herminjard and Négrier, and Olivétan's studying under Bucer, rests entirely on the hypothesis, that the youth of Noyon is Olivétan. Another letter to Bucer by Andronicus (April 29th, 1533) provides some more support to the assumption that Bucer and Olivétan were well acquainted. cf. Négrier, Charles-Abel: *Pierre Robert dit Olivétan.* (Montauban, 1891), p. 15 and p. 25. The letters mentioned in Herminjard tom. II, n. 232, p. 131 and tom. III, n. 415, p. 44 and note 20 on the same page. Eells, Hastings: *Martin Bucer and the conversion of John Calvin*, pp. 404 ff., end of 406. In the *Apologie du translateur* of the French Bible (Olivétan, 1535, fol. iiij verso col. ii), the translator, by explaining the various interpretations of the Hebrew *Jahwe*, says inter alia: 'Les autres *Autophyes* | cestadire existent de soymesme.'

Bucer, in the first edition (1529) of his Latin Psalter, renders the Hebrew *Jahwe* throughout by *Autophyes*, and tries to justify his translation by referring (in his *Ad Lectorem*) to Lactantius (Divin. Institut. lib. I, c.7). Bucer's rendering is so unusual, that even he himself in the later edition (1547) abandons it. The French translator thus seems to have referred to Bucer's Commentary, as no contemporary translator otherwise, as far as known to me, used the peculiar term Autophyes.

The following note on Job xxxix. 12 (quoted by Laune) in Lefèvre's Bible of 1534 compared with a similar note by Bucer on Psalm xxii. 21, is of interest: the source for Bucer as well as for Lefèvre is Pliny:

Lefèvre: Rhinoceros est une beste laquelle aucunement ne se peult dombter ne faire domestique ayant une corne en la narine, ennemie de l'elephant et en aguisant sa corne a quelque pierre se appareille a la bataille, regardant tousjours de frapper au ventre pour ce que cest la partie plus tendre. (cf. Laune, op. cit., pp. 44-45.)

Bucer: Haec ut Plinius scribit, & nomen ipsum indicat, in nare cornu unum habet, alter genitus hostis Elephanto . . . ad usus hominis mansuefieri non posse . . . (Bucer refers also to Iob. xxxix.)

Plinius: . . . rhinoceros unius in nare cornus, qualis saepe, visus. alter hic genitus

in 1525,[1] it is not unreasonable to suggest that they made contact with Bucer. They will even have known his Commentary and might have used it for their editions of the French Bible of 1534 and 1535. Matthew, by employing their notes, does also indirectly — apart from his direct use of Bucer's Commentary — draw from Bucer's notes.

(1) BUCER — OLIVÉTAN — MATTHEW

Psalm xiii. 2:

Bucer: in animo suo consilia ponebat, id est, anxie, quid sibi facto opus esset, deliberabat.

Olivét.: cest | prendray ie deliberation.

Matth.: That is | how longe shal I take deliberacyon.

Psalm lviii. 1:

Bucer: . . . Num vere mutam iustitiam loquimini . . .

Olivét.: ou | la iustice est elle vrayemēt muette | q̃ deuez pronōcer? & les choses droictes q̃ deuez iuger | o filz des hōes.

Matth.: Or | Is the iustyce in dede domme | that ye ought to pronoūce: & ye rightwes thynges that ye ought to iudge | O ye sonnes of men.

Other passages to Psalm lxxxvii. 3, to Psalm vii (superscription), lxv. 12, lxxv. 7, lxxxviii (inscription).

In the note to Psalm xii. 8 reference to the interpretation of Kimchi and A. Ezra is given in Bucer as well as in Olivétan and Matthew. It is interesting to note that Bucer in a later edition of his Commentary (1547) includes notes of Olivétan, which are not to be found in the original edition. e.g. on Hebrew terms in the superscriptions of Psalms v-viii, and xvi (Schigaion, Michtam, etc.). Those notes from Olivétan are incorporated in the 'Matthew Bible'. Another note to cvii. 3, which is also taken over by the 'Matthew Bible', occurs also only in the 1547 edition of Bucer's Commentary:

Olivét.: Ebri. mer | ascauoir | vers Arabie | qui est es parties de Midy.

[1] cf. Adam, Melchior: *Vitae Germ. Theol.* (Francf., 1653), p. 90. cf. also Bucer's reference to Lefèvre, in his Psalm-Com. (1529), fol. 3 verso.

hostis elephanto cornu ad saxa limato praeparet se pugnae, in dimicatione alvum maxime petens, quam scit esse molliorem. . . . (*Nat. Hist.* VIII, 71.)
The marginal note by Lefèvre on Deut. xiv. 5 (cf. Laune, op. cit., p. 44) is also from Plinius (*Nat. Hist.* VIII, 69). Also that on Lev. xi. 22, from Plinius (*Nat. Hist.* XI, 102). It is thus not correct when Laune (p. 45) says that Lefèvre had 'notions au moins singulières en histoire naturelle'. (Laune, Alfred: *La traduction de l'ancien testament de Lefèvre d'Étaples.* Le Cateau, 1895. Université de France – Académie de Paris.) Some woodcuts in 'Matthew's Bible' suggest close affinity to those of Lefèvre's Bible, being reproductions of those in Lefèvre's Bible.

Matth.: Hebr. See: that is to saye | towarde Arabia whych is in the Southe partes.

1547-*Bucer:* Nam sinus Arabicus ei est ad meridiem, quod mare hic designatum.[1]

(2) BUCER — LEFÈVRE — MATTHEW

Psalm xv. 2:

Bucer: Loqui veritatem in corde suo, nihil aliud est . . . fide optima, . . . promissis nunquam deesse, neque aliud simulare verbis, aliud spectare animo . . . ut Psalmo duodecimo.

Lefèvre: (xiv. 2) Parler verite en son cueur | est en bonne foy faire ce q̃ lon promet & non simuler p. parolle autre chose q̄ lon nepese au cuer. s̄. 11.a.

Matth.: To speake the trueth frō hys hert | is | to meane good fayth and to do that he promeseth | so that he fayne not in worde another thynge then he thyncketh in hert. Psalme xij.a.

Psalm xxvi. 2:

Bucer: Cor & renes pro intimis cogitationibus & adfectibus poni . . . & in versu 7 Psal. xvi.

Lefèvre: (xxv. 2) Par le cueur & les reins veult signifier les delectations & affections de la chair retirās de suyuir Dieu. s. 15.b.

Matth.: By the hert & reynes wyll he sygnifye the delectacions & affeccyons of the flesshe | whych let hym to folowe God . . . Psal. xvi.b.

Psalm cxxxiii. 2: All three refer to Exod. xxx.

Bucer, Olivétan, Lefèvre provide the material for the marginal notes to the Psalter of the 'Matthew Bible'. Chester's statement on the marginal notes in the 'Matthew Bible':

> there is no reason to suppose that he had any immediate assistance in their preparation. He made, perhaps, some use of the notes of the various German editions, particularly those of Luther and Melanchthon, but, with regard to the great portion of them, there is no cause for believing that he drew upon any resources save those of his own mind.

needs therefore some correction.[2]

[1] Notes in Bucer and Olivétan only: to Ps. xx. 30, xxix. 7, xxx. 13.

[2] Chester, Joseph Lemuel: *John Rogers: The Compiler of the First Authorised Bible* . . . London, 1861, p. 47.

ON PSALMS AND ENGLISH PSALTER

§ V

APPENDIX I

WORDS AND EXPRESSIONS

SELECT list of characteristic Words and Expressions occurring in the English version of Bucer's Commentary on the Psalms taken from the Strassburg and Godfray edition, and from the edition of the Primer.

abate	Psalm cii. 23
abiect	xxii. 6; cxix. 141
addict	cxix. 38
botch	xxxviii. 5
bounteous	cxix. 156
bray	xxix. 8
bridle	lxxvi. 10
buckler	xxviii. 8; xci. 4
bugg	xc. 5=Coverdale
bulwark	xxxi. 3
canvas (to)	xxvi. 10
chide (to)	xcv. 10
churlish	cxx. 4
congele (to)	cxix. 70
cumber	xl. 15
dassle	cxix. 82
at debate	xc. 10
deiect	xlii. 8; xlii. 13
dike	vii. 16
doe	xxix. 8
drest me to my grave	xxii. 15
fester	xxxviii. 5
fie, fie = Cov. 1539	xl. 18
foreporches	c. 3
fourscore = Cov.	xc. 10
fowler = Cov.	cxxiv. 6
frantic	cxix. 113
fret	cxix. 53
garnish	xxiii. 5
hamper	cxvi. 3
havoc	lxxvi. 6
homage	xxii. 29
irk	cxix. 158
juniper coals (cf. Geneva Bible 1560 to same passage)	cxx. 3
leisure	xxiii. 2
lot	cxix. 57
lucre	cxix. 36
lurking place	cxix. 114
merciable	lxxvii. 42
merciably	cxix. 124
mugger up	lxii. 10
neat	viii. 7
nurture	cxix. 64
opprobry	xxii. 6; xlii. 12
and if they pitch field	xxvii. 3
pitfall	cxix. 85
potsherd = Cov.	xxii. 15
quitch	lxxvi. 8
quiver	cxxvii. 6
ravish	vii. 2
refection	cxxvii. 3
retch	xxiii. 2
reviler	cxix. 42

savour	cxix. 66	taberet = Cov.	cxlix. 3
scourge	cxix. 75	tallow	cxix. 70
seed-cods (seede koddes)	cxxvi. 7	thack	cii. 7
sheephock	xxiii. 4 = Cov. 1535	toasted (toosted)	xxxii. 4
shield	xci. 4	vernacle (only 1535 Prim.)	xxvi. 8
shrewdness	xxviii. 3		
staff	xxiii. 4	wag	xxii. 7
stagger	cxxv. 1	waver	xxvi. 1
supplant	xli. 9	weaned = Cov.	cxxxi. 3
supple (souple)	xxiii. 5	whetteth	xix. 2
swerve = Cov.	cxix. 110	wither = 1539 Cov.	i. 4 [cxxix. 6 = 1535/9 Cov.]
tabernacle = Cov.	xix. 5 = xxvii. 5 [xxvi. 8 (undated Primer)]	wont me to	xxv. 3
		woodnes	xxii. 20
		wrap	cxxiv. 3

§ VI

APPENDIX II

SOME PSALMS OF THE ENGLISH VERSION OF BUCER'S PSALTER[1]

Quare fremuerunt gentes. psal. ij

WHerfore do the gentyles thus swelle and cluster togyther? wherfore do the people of the Jues thus gnaste in vayne?

wherfore conspire the kynges of therthe: and ye chiefe preestes thus caste theyr heddes togyther agaynst the lorde and his anoynted?

Sayenge, let vs breake theyr bondes: and let vs caste of theyr yokes.

But he y^t^ hath his residence in heuen mocketh[2] them: it is the lorde that scorneth them. Than shal he thrust them downe in his wrathe: and in his indignation shall he all to trouble them.

I haue cōstituted and ordeyned my kynge: to be ouer Syon my holy hylle.

I shall shewe forthe the lordes cōmaūdement: for he sayde vnto me, thou art my sonne, whom I haue nowe openly declared.

Aske of me, and I shall gyue the, the nacions into thy heritage: and to be thyne owne possession thrughout all the worlde. Thou shalte smyte them togyther w^t^ an yrne sceptre: and shalte breake

[1] Printed here (without the summaries) from the Strassburg—and Godfray—edition and from the Primer—editions.

[2] 1530, Strassburg edition: derideth.

them lyke erthen vessels. Nowe therfore ye kynges, be wyse and vnderstande: ye rulers of the erth be cōtent to be monyshed & lerned.

Serue ye the lorde besely: study to gyue hym his honour ioyfully with reuerence. Kysse ye the sonne: leste (he beinge wrothe) your lyfe peryshe: for his angre shall be shortely kendled. And than blessed are all men that truste in hym.

('Marshall's Primer' 1535 (Evensong) fol. Jj verso)

Domine quid. psal. iij

LOrd, se what a sorte there are that trouble me: full many there are that ryse agaynst me.

Many there are y^{t} thynke thus vpon my soule: surely ther is no helth to be loked for from god, vnto this mā.

But thou lorde, thou arte my helpe and my glorye: thou lyftest vp my heed.

The lorde I called vpon with my prayer: and he answered me euyn from his holy hylle, so he dyd.

I shall lye downe and slepe, I my selfe shall vpwake me: for the lorde susteyneth me.

I shall not feare, yea thousandes of folke: although they besege me rounde aboute.

Aryse (lorde) saue me my god: thou shalte gyue all myn enemyes suche a clappe on theyr chekes, y^{t} anone the tethe of these vngodly shall be broken.

It is the lordes proprетie to saue: and thy people it behoueth to be holpen and endued with thy benefites.

('Marshall's Primer' 1535 (Evensong) fol. J ij)

Psalm viii

LOrde | ye | ower lorde | howe woundrefull reverēte is thy name ī every lāde? which haste lyft vp thy highe magnificense above the hevens.

Ye and that of the mouthes of ye lytel souklinges haste thou stablesshed thy myghty prayse ageinste thy enymes: to smytdowne aduersary | & hym that will avenge hymselfe.

I shall therfore lokevp and wondre at thy hevens: lo | theis are the workes of thy fyngres | the mone | and starres | thou haste set them so goodly.

And lo | what thīge is mā mortall that thou thus remembrest hym? what is the sonne of Adam y^{t} thou regardeste hym so gretly?

Thou haste made hym not mych lesse ād inferior then Angels: with so grete dignite & glory haste thou endued hym.

Thou haste made hym lorde of thy handy workis: thou hast cast all thinges vnder hys fete.

As flocks of shepe all herdis of nete: and also the wylde bestis.

Foules of the aier and fysshes of the see: ād what so ever swymmeth in the water.

Lorde | ye owre lorde: howe woundrefull reverent is thy name in all the erthe?

(1530 Strassburg edition)

This version has been altered in the Primer (undated, and 1535) as follows:

verse 1 reverent, and clear . . . over all the earth . . .

2 . . . and that by the mouths of thy sucking babes, that cannot yet speak, hast thou set up the praise of thy might against thy enemies, to confound thy adversary that will avenge himself.

5 . . . not much inferior than angels.

9 . . . reverent, and clear . . . over all the earth.

Psalm xix

CEli enarrant. The heuens declare the maiestye of god | and the fyrmamente sheweth what are his workes. One daye succedynge another | whetteth contynually our thoughtes | & one night folowyng another | encreaseth our knowlege. These creatures haue nether spech nor wordes | neyther is their voyces any where herde. And yet their poyntinge & shewynge hathe taught all the worlde | & their dōme speche hath gone forth īto all the costs of yͤ worlde. He hath fastened in thē a tabernacle for yͤ sōne | this sōne cometh forth of his clouds like a bridegrōe ye lyke a fresshe valyant knyght to make his course. From the farthest eest parte of the heuyns cometh he forthe | hauynge his recourse vnto the other extreme | neither is there any man that maye hyde hī from his heat. The lawe of the lorde is perfyte | refresshynge the soule | the testymonye of the lorde is faithful | ministrīg wysdome to the vnlerned. The cōmaundemētes of the lorde are right | makynge glad the herte. The thinges whiche god cōmaundeth are playne & pure | & lyghtē the eyes. The feare of the lorde is pure and holy abidynge for euer | the plesures of the lorde ar true & right in euery parte. More worthy to be desyred than golde &

precyouse stones | sweter than the honye combe whan it dropeth. And thy serūāt is taught & monisshed by thē | that same obseruynge of them is a great rewarde. Who maye perceyue and consyder what thynge is synne? purge me from secrete euyls. Also turne thou these great synnes from thy seruant | leste they haue domination ouer me | & than shall I be pure and clere from euery great synne. Let ye speches of my mouth & the thoughtes of my herte be plesaunte & accepte vnto the lorde my defender and my redemer.

(Godfray's edition)

verse 7 1529 text: absoluta: (in commentary (1529), p. 112: Ea enim perfecta & absoluta est, nihil mutationis admittens . . .)
1547 text: sincera

Primer (undated, and 1535):
verses 1 the glorious majesty
2 One day following another
5 and he cometh forth
11 is a great gift
12 Who may attain to the knowledge of his sinful nature? . . . from my secret sins.
13 Yea and turn thou . . . dominion
15 and redeemer

Psalm xxiii. Dn̄s regit me

THe lorde is my pastoure and feader: wherfore I shall not wante. He made me to feade in a full plentuous batle groūde:[1] and dyd dryue & retche me at leyser by the swete ryuers. He restored my lyfe, and led me by the pathes of ryghtwisnes: for his names sake. Ye yf I shold go thorowe the myddes of deth: yet wolde I fere none euyll: for thou art with me: thy staffe and thy shepe hoke conforte me.

Thou shalt sprede & garnysshe me a table | ye and that in the syght of myn ennemyes: thou shalt souple my heed with oyntment | and my full cuppe shall laugh vpon me. Ye and thy mercy and gentylnes shall folowe me al my lyfe: I shall syt in the house of the lorde a longe tyme.

('Marshall's Primer', undated edition, fol. Q iij verso)

[1] In Bucer's Latin Commentary of 1529: In conseptis soli herbidi.

Psalm lxxxiv

HOwe goodly and amyable are thy tabernacles: O lorde of hostes!

My soule brennethe ād fainteth for desier to come into the porches of the lorde: my harte and my flesshe kried vnto the lyvynge god.

Even the littel sparowe there founde hyr an house: and the swalowe a neste to ley in hyr yonge: and shal not J come vnto thy altaris (O lorde my kynge and my god)?

Happe are they that maye dwell in thy house: for thei shall praise y[e] for ever. Selah.

Happe are theis men whos strengthe is set in the: to whom also thy pathes are plesaunte.

Men shall make plentous fountaines for the goers thorowe y[e] wailynge valey: and rayne shall fyll theyr cesternes.

And men shall goo thicke | flocke aftyr flocke: of y[e] which every won shall apere before god in Zyon.

Oh lorde | God of hostes | heare my prayer: lysten vnto me | god of Jacob. Selah.

Beholde god | which arte ower shylde: beholde the face of thy anoynted.

It ys beter to be won daye in the foreporches of thy temple: then here a thousande. I had lever sit at y[e] thressholde of the house of god: then to dwell longe in theis troublous tabernacles.

For the lorde god is bothe sonne & shylde: the lorde shall geve grace & dignite. He shall not turne that at good ys: from theis men which lyve harmlesse. Oh lorde of hostes: blessid is y[t] man whiche trusteth in the.

(From the Strassburg edition)

Psalm cxxi

LEuaui oculos. I lyfte vp my eyes into the hylles | from whence helpe might come vnto me. My helpe cometh frō the lorde | the maker of heuens & erthe. He shall nat suffre thy fete to slyde | neyther he beynge thy keper shall slepe. Lo | neyther wyll he slepe | nor yet wynke that kepeth Jsrahell. The lorde is thy keper | the lorde is thy defence | and is euer at thy right hande. The sone shall nat smyte the by day neither yet the mone by night. For y[e] lorde shall kepe the from all euyll ye | he shall kepe thy soule. The lorde shall kepe both thy outgoinge and thy incommynge | from thys tyme vnto euerlastynge.

(Godfray's edition)

Sepe expugnauerunt. psal. C.xxix.

GReuously haue they vexed me euyn from my yonght[!]: nowe let Jsraell speake.

Greuously haue they vexed me euyn from my yōght: but yet they preuayle not agaynst me.

Upon my backe these ploughmen ploughed: & haue cutte forthe theyr longe forowes.

But the ryghtwyse lorde hath cut awaye the bondes of these vngodly.

They shalbe shamed and put to flyghte: wo soeuer hateth Syon.

They shall be as grasse that groweth vpon the house rydges: whiche is wythered before it be pulled vp.

With the whiche, neyther ye reaper fylleth his hands: nor yet the gatherer fylleth his armes.

Neyther the goers foreby so regarded them, as to say ons, god blesse you: or we wyll wysshe you in ye name of the lorde.

('Marshall's Primer', 1535, fol. J iiii verso)

The argument in to the. C.xlix. psalme. In this psalme the prophete exhorteth Israell to prayse god.

SYnge ye to the lorde with a newe ditie, his prayse shalbe in the cōgregation of ye saynts.

Israell shall reioyse of his maker, and the citezens of Sion of theyr kynge.

They shall prayse his name with trumpet, synge ye vnto hym with taberet and harpe.

For the lorde well pleased w^t^ his people, shall exalte lowlyons with his helpe.

Sayntes shall reioyse euyn from their hertes, and the nobles shall triumphe in theyr couches.

The exaltynge of god is in theyr throtes, and in theyr handes a twoedged swerde.

To take vengeaunce vpon ye gentyles, and to correcte the people.

To bynde theyr kynges in chaynes, and theyr moste noblest rulers in feters of iyerne.

To execute iudgement amōge them, as it is wryten, this glorie shalbe vnto all that are his payntes.

('Marshall's Primer', 1535, fol. P iij verso)

§ VII

APPENDIX III

MARGINAL AND TEXTUAL NOTES OF THE PSALTER IN 'MATTHEW'S BIBLE' COMPARED WITH BUCER'S COMMENTARY

BUCER	MATTHEW
Psalm iv (*Superscription*) (*Bucer in the introduction*): . . . למנצח, quod Graeci reddunt, εἰς τὸ τέλος, id est, in finem . . . alij reddunt, uincenti, alij, ad uictoriam . . . sententia A. Ezrae & D. Kim. qui putant per מנעה significcari praefectum cantorum, unde reddidi Praesuli.	That is here translate | To the Chaunter | is in Hebrue Lamnazeah: which worde after the mynde of Abrah. Ezra & Dauid Kimhi | . . . signyfyeth | To the cheafe of the syngers: . . . Some saye that it signyfieth | To the victour or ouercomer: . . . some interprete | vnto the ende | . . .
Neginoth, modulationes . . .	Neginoth . . . the tune or note.
Psalm vii (*Superscription*) *Schigaion:* (commentary): R. D. Kim. . . . Shiggaion fuisse ex instrumentis, ad quae psalmi fuerint decantati, aut certum genus melodiae . . .	Sigaion: . . . an ignoraunce. . . . Some saye that it was one of the instrumentes | wherat all the Psalmes before which it is sett | were songe . . . a certayne kynde of melodye. (cf. Olivétan.)
Psalm cxx (*Superscription*): שיר מערלות alij canticum graduum uertunt, & dicunt, fuisse gradus quindecim, quibus ab aede, in qua conueniebant mulieres, ad eam, in qua uiri, ascendebatur, & in illis leuitas hos psalmos decantasse. . . . A. Ezra, . . . putat fuisse initium aliquod carminis, ad cuius modos sint hi psalmi modulati	In Hebr. Maheloth. Abr. Ezra thyncketh it to be the begynnynge of some songe | after whose tune the Psalmes that haue this tytle were songe. Other expounde it to sygnifye: in a hyghe place. Some ther be which saye | that the Leuytes sange all these Psalmes in Dauids house | vpon the steares which went frō the chamber where the men assembled | to the chamber where the wemen commenly abode.
Note to Psalm lxiii (*description*): Desertum Iehudah, cuius meminit, desertum Ziph est, . . . Ziph enim ad sortem Iehudah attinebat.	He meaneth the wyldernes of ziph, which fell to the lott of Juda. (marg. note)

BUCER	MATTHEW
to lxv. 12 ... has Kim. interpretatur nubes ... A. Ezra scaturigines aquarum intelligit.	(sc. footsteps): Rab. Kim. vnderstandeth this of the cloudes. Rab. Ezra of rūning waters. (marg. note) (cf. Olivétan)
to lxxv. 7 Desertum magnum a meridie Iudaeae est, ideo pro meridionali plaga usurpatur. *text:* a meridie	(sc. wilderness): That is | the South: because Jewrye hath a wyldernesse towarde the South. (marg. note) (cf. Olivétan)
to lxxxvii. 3 Aegyptus uocatur & Iesha. 51.	Rahab ... [*marg. note:*[That is | Egypt: which is so called in Esa. li. (cf. Olivétan)
to lxxxviii (*Inscription*) ... id uertunt quidam: de infirmitate propter adflictionem ... Heman, i Paral. 6 & 26 inter Principes Cantorum numeratur.	(affliction): Some reade | as touchynge dysease for affliccyon. (marg. note) Of that Heman | whych was one of the chefe syngers. i. Para. vi. and xxvi. (cf. Olivétan)
to ii. 12 ... *oscultamini filium,* Synecdoche tropus est, qua ex signo, id quod signo repraesentatur, intelligitur, Osculo siquidem manus regiae & hodie in plerisque regnis testantur subditi, se uelle in fide ac potestate regis esse. Filium dicit, eo quod supra patrem induxit dicentem, filius meus es tu ... Graeca editio habet, appraehendite disciplinam ... intelligens, subijcere se regi Christo, & eius disciplinam atque castigationem recipere.	... It is a fyguratyue speach | in whych by the signe is vnderstande that | which is sygnyfyed therby. For by the kysse of the Kinges hande euen nowadayes in many regyons do the subiectes testyfye | that they wyll be in the fayth & power of the Kynge. He calleth hym sonne | because he before brought in the father | sayinge: Thou art my sonne. The Greke readeth: receaue instruccion | or be lerned: meaning therby that they shulde submyt them selues vnto the Kynge Christ | and receaue hys instruccyon and chastenynge.

BUCER	MATTHEW
Psalm iv. 7 . . . Quibus enim fauemus, illos suauiter respicimus, & uultu animi beneuolentiam testante intuemur. . .	. . . For on soch as we fauour loke we amyably | & beholde thē with a countenaūce y^{t} wytnesseth frendshyppe.

Note to xii. 8:

Reference to interpretation of Kimchi and A. Ezra is made in Bucer as well as in Olivétan and Matthew.

Notes to Psalm xviii

BUCER	MATTHEW
to verse 2: . . . uti cornifera animalia, se cornibus defendunt & contra pugnantia repellunt . . .	. . . horned beastes | which w^{t} their hornes defende them selues | & driue awaye thē that feyght agaynst them.
to verse 5: Angustijs enim inferorum & mortis, laqueis mortis . . . pericula & terrores significauit, quae sibi improbitate hostium suorum obuenerant, proximeque mortem saepenumero adduxerunt, ut carnis iudicio iam actum esse de se arbitraretur.	. . . the paynes of hel | & the snares of death: are signified the ieopardous | & terryble feares whych by the wyckednes of his enemyes happened vnto hym | & brought him very often euē to deathes doare: so that by ye iudgemēt of the flesh he thought hymselfe vtterly cast away.
to verses 13-14: His uersibus potentiam Dei canit, quam in tempestatibus declarat, de qua totus Psalmus uigesimus nonus compositus est. . . . Iiob 37. similia ad praedicandam Dei potentiam memorantur. Legimus autem subinde Deum, cum praesentius & reuelatius hominibus suam uoluit potentiam atque uim declarare, tonuisse, fulgurasse & terram concussisse. Ita sane fecit, cum Legem daturus populo primum loqueretur, ut scriptum est Exod. 19 . . . populo . . ., quod regem postulassent: Schmuelis 12 . . . illo (sc. filius Dei) in cruce expirante. Sic cum spiritum sanctum suis seruator mitteret, . . . Act. 2 . . . precationem eorum . . . Act. 4 . . . Talibus crediderim portentis & Dauidi, . . . beneuolen-	By all the thinges here rehersed is described the power | might & maiestye of almyghtye god | whych he declareth in tēpestes | of which the whole. xxix Psal. entreateth | and in Job xxxvij. are like thinges mencyoned to the setting out of his power. Often tymes we reade | that God when he wolde moare openly & moare expressely declare hys power vnto men | caused thūder | lightening | & earth quakes. &c. As in Exo. xix. whē the lawe was geuen. And 1. Regū. xii. when the people desyred a kīg. Mat. xxvij when Christ was on ye crosse Act. ij. whē the holy gost came vpon the Apostles. Actuū. iiij. whē they praied. With soch lyke wondres do some suppose y God did

BUCER	MATTHEW
tiam suam testatum Deum aliquando fuisse, & auxilij promissionem confirmasse, concussa terra, missis fulminibus, fulgetris, grandine & nimbis. Nec obstat quod euenisse haec sacra historia nusquam meminerit, neque enim meminit, & eam tempestatem quam futuram in liberatione Ieruschalaim ab Assyrijs Ieshaiah praedixit, at quis inficias eat, eam uere ita factam.	at one tyme or other shewe his benyuolence to Dauid | and confyrmed hys promes | w^{t} shaking of the earth | sendyng thunder | lightenīg | hayle | cloudes | stormes & other terryble tokens | wherwith he holpe Dauid | & ouerthrue hys enemyes. Nether letteth it that the Scripture mēcioneth not therof in any place. For it mēcioneth not the tempest which Esai prophecyed to come in ye delyueraūce of Jerusalē from the Assyriās | yet who wyll deny but that it was in very deade so done.
Psalm xxxix IEduthun ex principibus Cantorum fuisse legitur, 1 Paralip. 16 & 25. Videtur igitur Kimhi, hunc Psalmum a Dauide fuisse compositum, cantari autem solitum ab eius ordinis cantoribus, cui praefuerit Ieduthun . . . A. Ezra putat aliquod carmen celebre fuisse, . . . ad cuius modulationem, & hic Psalmus cantatus sit.	Iduthun is the name of a chaunter. 1. Paralip. XVI.d. and XXV.a. Kimhi thyncketh that Dauid made this Psalm | and that it was wont to be songe of that kynde of syngars ouer which Iduthun bare rule. Some thynck it to be a certen songe| after whose tyme the Psalme was sunge.
Psalm xliv. 20 . . . idem est, atque damnasti nos in locum draconum. Intelligit autem per locum draconum, seruitutem inter crudeles gentes, quae feritate draconibus similes sint. Eandem uocat umbram mortis: morte enim durius & horrendum magis est, expositum esse per omnia libidini impiorum, audire continuo blasphemari nomen Dei, damnari omnem pietatem, nihil non iniuriarum genus irrogari eius studiosis. Ideo canunt, Vmbra mortis, hoc est, ipsis mortis tenebris, obtexisti nos.	That is | thou has condempned vs to the place of serpētes or dragons: or | thou hast dryuē vs into the place of serpētes or dragons. By the place of serpētes is vnderstande | their bondage amōge the Heithen | whych in cruelnes are lyke vnto serpētes: The same calleth he the shadowe of deeth. for it is worsse then deeth & moare to be feared | to be put in all thinges to the arbytrement & pleasure of the vngodly | to heare continually the name of God blasphemed | & all Godlines despised & all maner of iniuries & wrōges done to the fauourers therof. Therfore sayth he. Thou hast couered vs with the shadow of deeth | that is | with the very darcknes of deeth . . .

BUCER	MATTHEW
Psalm li. 7 In solenni illo sacrificio pro peccato, de quo Num. 19. item in purgatione leprosi, de qua Leuit. 14 hyssopus adhibebatur. Vt ergo aspersione illa, uera animae puritas significata fuit, ita pro illa hic precatur, plena scilicet remissione peccati, qua percepta, & restituto fauore Dei, indicibili animus gaudio exultat . . .	In the solempne sacrifice for synne | of which Nu. xix. a & in the clensynge of the lepre | of which Leui. xiiij. ther was ysope annexed & ioyned to. By that sprinckling was sygnifyed ryght purenes of hert: for that praieth he here | that is | for full remyssyō of his synne: whych ones had | & the fauour of God obtayned | the mynde reioyceth with vnspeakable ioye | . . .
Psalm lvi Hoc putat A. Ezra carminis cuiusdam fuisse initium, ad cuius numeros sit hic Psalmus compositus. Kimhi & alij existimant, Dauidem, seipsum columbam mutam & longe auolantem, uocasse, propterea, quod omnia Deo committens, & nihil aduersarijs suis respondens, longe a suis fugisset, nimirum ad Philistaeos usque, gentem, non solum alienigenam, sed & hostilem. Historia haec legitur 1. Reg. 21 . . .	Abra. Esra thincketh that the dome stocke dowue was the begynnynge of a songe | after whose tune this Psalme was songe. Kimhi and other suppose that Dauid called him selfe | a dōme stockdowue which flewe farre | because he commytted hym selfe wholy vnto God | and geuyng none answere to his aduersaryes fledde farre from his awne nacyō vnto the Philistines | which were not only strañgers | but also enemyes. The story here of is reade. 1. Reg. xxi.
Psalm lxxviii. 26 Alij angelorum legunt, quod tamen non ita intelligendum est, quasi eo cibo angeli uescantur, sed quod e coelis, angelorum domicilio, descenderit.	Manna is called the fode of angels | not that the angels vse soche fode | but because it came doune frō heauen | whych is the dwelling place of the angels.
Psalm xci. 4 . . . simile integentium alarum ob auibus mutuatum, pullos obiectu proprij corporis defendentium | repetit, adiecto simili scuti & parmae. (cf. similar note to Ps. xvii. 8 with reference to Matt. xxiii. 37): (. . . aues pullos suos, quos imminente periculo subter alas suas abscondunt . . . Seruator quoque hac similitudine usus est, Matt. 23: Quoties . . . Nos ineffabilem Dei super nos bonitatem, hinc consideremus).	That is | he shal succoure & defende the by his proteccyon and kepe the in safetye. They be speaches borowed of the nature of a hēne | whych w[t] her winges and fethers defēdeth and saueth her chekyns. (cf. the similar note to Ps. xvii. 8 with ref. to Matt. xxiii. 37).

BUCER	MATTHEW
Note on Psalm cxiv. 6 Montis Sinai concussionem ac tremorem, qui uisus est, cum *Dom*inus daturum legem in eum descendisset, qui indubie non in uno monte, sed omnibus uicinis, uisus est.	. . . some | . . . excellently lerned | vnderstande it of the shakyng | tremblyng & leapynge of the hyll Sion | when the Lorde came downe to geue the lawe . . . which shaking (saye they) was not onely sene in that hyll alone | but also in all the hylles nye vnto hyt.
Psalm cxxx. 1 Per profunda, . . . intelligit aduersa, in quibus erat populus, cum exularet apud Chaldaeos. Intelligi autem per ea possunt & quaeuis sanctorum mala, quibus ob peccata sua diuinitus addicuntur.	By the depe is vnderstande the aduersytye wherin ye people of Israel were | whē they were scatered amōge the Chaldees. Unto vs Christen it signifieth the aduersytie | trouble & mysery which happeneth to vs for oure offenses & synnes.
Note to Psalm cxxxix. 24 . . . interpretantur quidam illud, duc me in via עולם, id est, seculi, pro, occide me, quasi diceret, Si deprehenderis quicquam in me peruersum, perde me.	Some reade: then leade me by the waye of the worlde/that is/destroy me. (*marg. note*)

§ VIII

APPENDIX IV

DESCRIPTIVE ARGUMENTS TO SOME PSALMS IN BUCER'S PSALTER AND IN THAT OF 'MATTHEW'S BIBLE'

BUCER	MATTHEW
Psalm xix In this psalme Dauid declareth the excellent vertue & power of god | expressed in the meruelouse creation of this present worlde aboue: and than he sheweth the preciousnesse of goddes law at the last he prayeth to be preserued from synne & that what soeuer he thīketh or speketh myght be plesante and accepte before god.	He describeth the power of God | wonderfully declared by the worckmāshipe of the heauēs. He sheweth the excellentnes of the lawe of God | desyreth to be saued from synne | and wissheth that whatsoeuer he ether thyncketh in hert or speaketh w^t mouth | maye be good and acceptable to God.

BUCER	MATTHEW
Psalm xxii Here Dauid declareth him selfe plainly to be the very fygure of Christ. Wherfore first of al he syngeth & expresseth his great deiectyon and downe fall: & anon after his exaltatyon | his encrease & purchasynge of his kingdome | euen to the vttermost part of the lande | & the contynuance therof vnto the worldes ende.	Dauid declareth very euydently in thys Psalme that he was a fygure of Christ. First he declareth Christes deieccion & small eastymacyō | & then the exaltacyon and dylatacyon of his kyngdome | euē to the coastes of the earth and ende of the worlde | & all vnder the fygure and shadow of him selfe.
Psalm lviii This psalme is an inuectyue agaynst the flatterers of Saule | thorowe the punysshemente of whom he prophesyeth the rightwyse to be merueilously made glad . . .	An inuectyue agaynst the flatterers and adherētes of Saul | with whose punysshement he prophecyeth that the ryghtuous shalbe wonderfully reioysed·
Psalm lxviii (Latin 1529) . . . In quo uerbis plane heroicis, Dei in suum populum, in sanctam ciuitatem Ierusalem, bonitatem, & mirifice pro illis exertam uirtutem praedicat, aperte simul Christi regno in his deliniato, cui nimirum totum orbem nomen daturum praeuidit, quare & laudem DOMino canere uniuersos hortatur.	He sheweth the great goodnes & wonderfull power which the Lord exercised toward his people & the holy citie Jerusalem | . . . fyguringe openly therin the kyngdome of Christ | vnto whom he sawe by the sprete that the hole worlde shulde obeye: wherfore he exhorteth all men to geue prayse vnto the Lorde.
The argument into the C.xix. Psal. This Ps. declareth in how gret price & reuerence | the sayntes or holy men haue the lawes of god: how ernestly they are occupyed in thē | howe they sorowe to se thē broken & sayd agaynste of the vngodly: howe they pray to be taught them of god: and to be acquaynted and accustomed with them | and (to be shorte) howe they desyer those men to be destroyed (what so euer they be) which breake and sye agaynste them.	*The. CXIX. Psalme* This Psalme declareth how moche the saynctes & Christen set by the lawes of God | and how greatly they endeuour thēselues vnto them: in so moche that they sorowe them to be transgressed & withstanded of the wycked: And how they praye to be taught thē frō aboue | & to be accustomed with thē: & wyshe as many as transgresse & withstande them | to be destroyed and made awaye.

BUCER | MATTHEW

The argument into the C.xx. Psal.
This Ps. is a cōplainte full of affectes | it is a cōplaint of an holy mā banished īto amōge the vngodly doynge althīge with disceyt & vyolence. The tytle of these. xv. Psal. folowynge is only this The songe of Maehloth | whiche worde cōmenly is interpreted stayres or degrees | supposynge these xv. Psalmes to haue be songe in an higher tune.

The. CXX. Psalme
An affectuous complaynte of the prophete | beynge dryuē oute of the lande & abydyng amonge the wycked that dyd all thynges by fraude and violence.

The songe of the steares.
In Hebr. Maheloth. Abr. Ezra thyncketh it to be the begynnynge of some songe | after whose tune the Psalmes that haue this tytle were songe. Other expounde it to sygnifye: in a hyghe place. Some ther be which saye | that the Leuytes sange all these Psalmes in Dauids house | vpon the steares which went frō the chamber where the men assembled | to the chamber where the wemen commenly abode.[1]

The argument into the C.xxi. Psal.
This Psalme declareth that of god onely | helpe is loked and taryed for | of the faythefull men: and that he onely bringeth it presently.

The. CXXI. Psalme
He sheweth that the godly must loke for their helpe of God only | & that he geueth it very readely.

The argument into the Cxxii. Psal. (*Latin: 1529; and English*)
sub typo Hierusalem, Ecclesiae Christi foelicitatem, & vota sanctorum, illam semper prouehi optantium, describit. Here vnder the fygure of Jerusalem are descrybed the felycyte of Christes Churche | and the desyers of the saayntes therof.

The. CXXII. Psalme
Under the shadow and fygure of cerusalem he describeth the felyJytie of the congregacyon of Christ | and the desyres of the saynctes | wyshyng euer the furtheraunce of it.

The argument into the C.xxiii. Psal.
Here the sayntes layde in the mouthes of the welthy vngodly doynge all amysse | praye to god for their delyueraunce | commyttynge them selfe to his cure.

The. CXXIII. Psalme
The godly subdued to the wycked | do affectuously desyre God to delyuer them | for vnto hym they wholy commyt them selues.

[1] cf. here p. 240.

BUCER	MATTHEW
The argument into the C.xxiiii. Psal. Here the sayntes of god gyue thankes and reioyse | that they ar delyuered by goddes helpe frō so present peryls.	*The. CXXIIII. Psalme* The godly reioyse that they are rydde | by the helpe of God | frō a Jeopardy wherevnto they were very nye.
The argument into the C.xxv. Psal. Here is declared | the congregation of god to be sure | god defendynge them and to prospere | the lorde fauorynge | and weedyng the vngodly out of them.	*The. CXXV. Psalme* The churche or congregacyon is in safetye when the Lorde defendeth it | and shalbe prosperous when he fauoreth it | and purgeth the wycked theroute.
The argument into the Cxxvi. Psal. Here is declared the gladnes of the people returned from Babylon: and vnder this fygure is it shewed also the gladnes of the faythful whō | Christe hath verily delyuered from the captiuyte of synne and dethe.	*The. CXXVI. Psalme* He descrybeth the gladnes of the people returning agayne from Babylon | & vnder the fygure herof the reioysynge of the Christen | whom the sonne of God hath made fre from the captiuyte of synne and deeth.
The argument into the C.xxvii. Psal. (Latin: 1529; and English) Sola Diuina benignitate donari domum & familiam, custodiri ciuitatem, cibum summa facilitate suppeditari, liberos, & eos frugi, contingere. This Psalme teacheth vs: the house and family: the sure custody of the cyte | to haue meate | rest | and chyldren well dysposed and towarde | all cometh of the grace of god.	*The CXXVII. Psalme* By the only liberalyte & gyft of God is the house and housholde geuen | the cytye defended | meate mynystred | chyldren & those toward and thryftye obtayned.
The argument into the C.xxviii. Psal. This Psal. techeth vs that the worshyppers of god shall prospere both priuatly and openly.	*The CXXVIII. Psalme* He that feareth God shall do well and fortunately at all ceasons.

BUCER	MATTHEW
The argument into the C.xxix. Psal. This Psalme sheweth vs | that the vngodly although they vexe longe and sore the people of god: yet shall they nat preuayle | but at the laste to perisshe | goddes people beynge free and safe.	*The CXXIX. Psal.* Althoughe the wycked do longe and greatly persecute the godly | yet shall they not preuayle ouer them: yee they shall at the length perish | when the godly shal be in safetye.
The argument into the C.xxx. Psal. This Psalme is an ernest prayer full of affectes of a man here oppressed with aduersytie for his sines | but yet promisynge him selfe with fast fayth & hope frō god | to haue both forgyuenes of his sīnes: & delyuerance frō his afflictiōs.	*The CXXX. Psalme* An earnest prayer of him that is oppressed with aduersitie for his sinnes | & that surely hopeth to obtayne of God bothe forgeuenes of his synnes & delyuraunce from hys aduersytyes.
The argument into the C.xxxi. Psal. Here in this Psal. the prophet sheweth him selfe to be without all pride | & to haue folowed humilite: wherfor he trusted to be exalted of god.	*The CXXXI. Psalme* He sheweth y^t^ he was not proude | but meake & lowly.

NOTE ON SELAH

BUCER[1] (Latin, 1529)

. . . Selah:. Kim. scripsit . . . nimirum notam fuisse uocis exaltandae, eoque monitorium, cogitationis animi intendendae, . . .

BUCER[2] (Engl.)

This word Selah / sygnifyeth the sentence before to be pondred with a depe affecte / long to be rested vpon / & the voyce there to be exalted . . .

COVERDALE[3] (1535)

. . . Selah . . . (after the mynde of the interpreters) it is asmoch to saye as, . . . a liftinge vp of the voyce, . . . and earnestly to consider, and to ponder the sentēce.

MATTHEW[4] (1537)

Selah. This worde after Rab. Kim. was a sygne or tokē of lyfting vp the voyce / & also a monyciō & aduertissemēt to enforce the thought & mynde earnestly to geue hede to ye meaning of the versse vnto which it is added. Some will that it sygnifie perpetually or verely.

OLIVÉTAN[5] (French Bible, 1535)

. . . selon Ra. Kim. vng signe des leuer la voix / & aduertissemēt de pēser. Aucūs / ꝑpetuellemēt / ou veritablement

[1] Selah, p. 8v.
[2] fol. Aiii.v. (at the end of the 3rd Psalm).
[3] Coverdale at the end of the Psalter in his Bible (1535).
[4] Marginal note to Ps. iii.
[5] Marginal note to Psalm iii in the French Bible of 1535 (Olivétan) 'Neufchastel', 1535.

APPENDIX

CORRESPONDENCE

I

Extract from a letter of Martin Bucer to John Schwebel 1535[1]

... Angliae Legatus, Vir doctissimus, & peritissimus, Episcopus Herefordiensis. Edoardo Foxaeo nomen est. Hic nihil egit, transiit modo, jam per Gallias venit Schmalcaldiam abijt, & ad singulos Principes nostrae Societatis, Legationem habet. Capita Legationis nobis exponere non debuit, judicatur tamen praecipua pars esse, ut certum Genus Doctrinae sanctae constituatur, *ne existant inter nos ipsos dissensiones*: Offendi enim Regem nostrorum Hominum varietate & dissensionibus. (p. 283). Hac de causa cum audiret de nostro Conventu, optabat illum maturari, quo ei interesse liceret. Lege Curiata, abrogatus est Primatus super Ecclesias, jure, Domino Papae in Anglia, Ei Legi subscripserunt universi Regni Ordines, Archiepiscopi, Episcopi, Scholae, Principes, Respublicae. Paena Legis est. Si quis constanter Papae suum Primatum defendere conetur, primum, erit Carcer perpetuus & Confiscatio Bonorum. Deinde si quid adhuc moliatur, decollatio. Hac Lege utraque paena scripta est de Roffensi & Moro; uterque enim deprehensus est hac de causa gravia moliri in Regnum.

De Matrimonio ajebat nunc esse in Anglia omnia placata: Biennio nunc perstitit. De quo consulti sumus ante quatuor annos. Sic Res habet, Rex natus annos xviii. jussu Patris dispensatione, Iulio Pontifice, & sic Regno ferente, duxit Catharinam, materteram Caroli, quae paucos dies nupta fuerat fratri eius Arturo.

Is enim fuerat primogenitus. Dos & Donatio propter Nuptias cum ingentes essent & alias quoque ob causas, maxime propter Gallum, Anglus, Pater huius Regis, Henrichus vii, vir iratus & vehemens, cuperet contractam cum Hispanis Affinitatem consistere, voluit ut Fratris relictam, Filius superstes, duceret.

Aiunt Filium hoc gravatim fecisse. tamen ductam admodum regie semper habuisse, maximaque veri amoris indicia in eam declarasse ferunt, usque hinc sexennio ibi, qui Regem defendunt, dicunt motum

[1] *From* CENTVRIA EPISTOLARVM Theologicarum ad IOHANNEM SCHWEBELIVM ... A Philippo Melancthone, Bucero, Capitone, Hedione ... BIPONTINA M.D.XCVII, and later edition of 1605, no. LXXIX, pp. 282 ff. cf. here p. 195.

Lege Dei, quae orbitatem intentat ei, qui Fratris vxorem ducat, alij desiderio Masculae prolis, iusti Haeredis Regni: removit a se Regimen, & Consilia a multis petijt, quaestione hac proposita, *an possit quis intercedente Dispensatione Pontificis ducere vxorem Fratris Defuncti, vel ductam retinere.* Academiae Perusina, Aurelianenſis, Andegavensis in Gallia: Bononiensis & Patavina in Italia responderunt, *non posse*: Lovaniensis Consilia, & Regina, quae semper repugnavit conatui Regis, respondit, *posse*: Cum hac consensit Lutherus, Philippus & nos hic. Cum illis Zvvinglius & Oecolampadius: Luthero & Philippo rationes sunt: In his externis rebus Moses nos non ligat, & tuta conscientia stare placito Magistratus.

Hoc Regi accessit ad suas Nuptias, alias incestas. Ergo Propitio Deo, initae sunt, nec possunt nisi Deo irato dissolvi.

Nobis ratio fuit, nam nondum videramus Responsum hoc: Quod Deus unquam justum habuit, non est. per se impium, & adeo quibuscunque Legibus prohibeatur, nec manet Dispensabile, ducere Vxorem defuncti Fratris. Deus aliquando justum habet, sic enim praecepit etiam ut nosti.

Ergo est dispensabile. Cum itaque dispensatum sit per omnes nos, qui tamen credi potuerunt huius habere potestatem: tenet dispensatio, & est ratum apud Deum Matrimonium. Ratio Academiarum illarum, & Zuinglij atque Oecolampadij fuit. *Levi.* 18 praestat has nuptias prohibitas esse, ideo esse iniustas iure Divino, eo quod nulla potest valere Dispensatio creaturae. Hi habent pro se praejudicium Ecclesiae, & Leges Principum. Nos perstamus in nostra sententia, *non debuisse condemnari: incestus, prius Regis Matrimonium, eoque nec dissolvi.*

Quod non ita sit iure divino prohibitum, quia admittit Dispensationem Magistratus & Ecclesiae. Extat item Lex in Iustiniani Codice, tales nuptias Gentibus olim, quae sic contractae essent, permissas esse.

Id parum in nobis placuit Episcopo isti.

Verum nunc secundis Nuptiis initis & prioribus solenni judicio Regni abrogatis, sic audimur. Quae res perplexa est: & Ecclesiae purioris iudicium pro Rege est: Nos & quoslibet Christianos debere hac in causa, Regem iudicio Christi, Ecclesiae suae, & Regno, Propriaeque conscientiae relinquere, utcunque nos non dubitemus aliter iudicandum fuisse. Nosti ut olim, semper volunt in causa dubia, uti Foro externo & interna sententia duorum aut trium probatorum Doctorum ita hac etiam in causa Regis Angliae. . . .

II

A Letter of Martin Bucer to Farel
Cambridge, January 12th, 1550[1]

S D Et optatum annum charissime collega, plurima certe debeo tibi, et optimo Caluino nostro, pro literis uestris, quibus me tam praeclare consolamini in hac mea non simplici afflictione et tam salubriter in fide et obsequio Christi seruatoris instauratis, verum scito, mi Farelle, necquicquam dubites, me per omnia consentire tibi de simplici puroque obsequio regis et seruatoris nostri Jesu Christi, ut in eius ecclesia, et administratione sacrorum eius nulla omnino re utamur quam ipse non praecepit et commendauit. Nimis enim saepe expertus sum, quam horribiliter suis euanescant cogitationibus, qui uel minimum aliquid praeter Christi mandatum usurparint. Sed ut antea tibi scripsi, non modo ego sed nec Doctor Petrus Martyr nec Doctor Bernhardinus, aut quisquam nostri ordinis homo, in consilium adhibetur, de constituenda religione, nos tamen apud Patronum nostrum, non cessauimus monere uerbis et scriptis de uera et solida regni Christi restitutione. Ille autem se maximas agere Deo gratias, quod tantum obtinuerunt uestibus et alijs huiusmodi retentis, non agnoscit aliquid Antichristi retentum esse, cum doctrina Christi pure administretur, et obijcit nostras ecclesias Saxonicas et alias plerasque, assentitur tamen libenter ueritati atque satagit, ut eandem, et alij primores intelligant. Scripsi alias tibi, hic ecclesiae rudia quaedam esse noualia, quae uerba ponderes. Rex heinricus octauus et qui interim primas obtinuerunt, nimis diligenter exempla nostrorum principum sunt in eo seculi, ut ministerio uitae aeternae, ad eos qui minimam acciperent relegato prouentus ecclesiasticos, gratiosi et utiles in aula reciperent hinc uenit ut si quando parrochia uacaret praefectus ei sit, aliquis ex illis, qui in coenobijs fuerunt, ut eo pacto pensione 'persoluenda' talibus propter relictum coenobium aerarium regium liberaretur. Atque hi, ut nostri saeculi coenobitae fere solent, sunt homines ab omni honesta institutione et literis nimium alieni. Abesse certo et ego uelim, ubi iussis Domini nostri Jesu Christi, non per omnia obtemperatur. Sed quid facias, hic sum et nunc quintum mensem ago sub eruditione Domini per morbum non acrem adeo, nisi primo mense, sed mire tenacem et inutilem me reddentem. Pituita lenta et frigida incidit a capite in iuncturas et

[1] For the first time published from the MS. at the *Bibliotheque Des Pasteurs, Neuchatel* (Switzerland). Reference to the letter is made in: *Guillaume Farel*, 1489-1569. *Biographie Nouvelle* (Neuchatel-Paris, 1930), p. 591 and note; and in Kirchhofer, Melchior: *Das Leben W. Farels* (Zurich, 1831-1833), vol. ii, p. 107.

The letter is written the same day as the letter discussed here on pp. 62-63. The italicized words at the end of the letter are in Bucer's own handwriting.

musculos, etsi non dolorem multum, stuporem tamen et inutilitatem adfert, aluum sistit et arenam renum commouet et ter nunc colico malo adflixit satis acriter sed gratia Domino, iam indies Dominus uires magis reficit adeo, ut domi primum exposuerim studiosis psalmum 119; agnoscis, quid spectarim, nunc ad publicas quoque disputationes prodij, et praelectiones publicas confido me posse ordiri die lunae proximo, nec certe uideo, qua omnino re queam ad regnum Christi utilius adseruire, sunt enim hic plurimi adolescentes et iuuenes doctrinae Christi admodum sicientes, quorum ministerio confido regnum Christi, non parum promouendum. Nunc enim paucissimi populi idoneos habent doctores. Rex religiosissimus, cupit omnia ad purum Dei uerbum exigi, et restitui, sed gubernacula regni nondum tenebit, ingressus primum tredecimum annum, octauo octobris praeteriti. Qui me inde calumniatur, quod ibi adsum, ubi nonnihil ueteris fermenti retinetur, cogitent, quid uera iubeat charitas, iudicare de fratribus, et quod sine charitate nihil sumus. Quae mea sententia sit, de sequendo omnibus in rebus uerbo Domini, quam simplicissime, satis multi norunt, et maxime ij, qui me ad repurgandas ecclesias suas in consilium adhibuerunt, nec uspiam fui repurgandis ecclesijs adhibitus ubi Dominus non dederit, ut ad simplicitatem Christi propius accederetur. Quod uero ubique non omnia obtinui, cogitent, quod nusquam solus sum consultus, sed semper fere maioris authoritatis uiri adfuerunt. An autem debuerim, quia non puram simplicitatem in caeremonijs obtinere, discedere, et ab omni me ecclesiarum reformatione abstrahere, certe uidere non potui, cum prouiderem res adhuc longius a Christi simplicitate abituras, siquidem non adfuissem. Equidem certe, multo arbitror ecclesijs esse pernitiosiorem communionis et disciplinae Christi neglectum, quam sit in plaerisque Ecclesijs, qui pios habent auditores, retenti aliquot ritus ex ueteri consuetudine. Et tamen, multi sancti, et docti pastores propter rem tantam imo alteram partem totius Euangelij, Christi communionem, et disciplinam neglectam, ecclesias suas non deserunt, imo plaerique qui praecipuam authoritatem obtinent apud plaerosque Christi communionem et disciplinam non existimant reuocandam nunc esse, et quicquid moliuntur, eos ab instituto reuocant. Haec cum consydero taedet me uitae meae et ab ecclesiarum administratione summopere abhorreo, cum uideam adeo nunquam posse obtineri, ut saluificum Christi regnum totum admittatur. Indubie enim monet nos ira Dei horrenda, quod Euangelium salutis aeternae tantum ad reiectionem iugi Antichristi, licentiam carnis, et spolia ecclesiarum usurpatur, et iugo Christi tam commodo nemo ceruicem suam uult penitus submittere. Scio unde me de hoc consolari debeo, quis tamen non doleat et metuat, quod nostri homines, quae sunt pacis, tam parum perpendunt quae sunt in hac die sua.

Si posset conscientia mea ferrem admiscendi Euangelio ueteris fermenti aliquid, certe tam commodam habitationem, quae altera fere pars est sustentationis uitae corporalis, tamquam commodam iuuendi rationem, quod attinet ad coelum meritum[?] amicos scholam et ecclesiam nunquam commutassem, cum praesenti uiuendi ratione, ubi coelum[,] lingua, uictus, mores, habitatio et omnia prope diuersissima sunt, ab ijs, quibus assueui a puero, quanquam, patronus meus et pia foemina Dux Suffolciae utque alij nonnulli, ea me beneuolentia et benignitate prosequantur, ut me magno pudore adficiant, postquam adhuc ecclesiae Christi nihil commodarim cuius tamen gratia omnis illa in me beneuolentia et benignitas exhibetur.

Experiar, uolente Domino dum modo aliud non possum, quod nam Dominus operae pretium uelit dare ministerio meo, in hac Academia, si uidebo me frustra sudare, nam Papistarum et Epicureorum nihil uspiam desyderes, conabor me in aliquem lugendi angulum abscondere donec me Dominus ex hoc perdito saeculo liberare dignetur. Magnum quoque uulnus animo meo inflictum morte Pauli Fagij uiri ad regnum Christi uere docti, adeoque periti sacrae linguae et omnium scriptorum haebraicorum, ut neminem uiuere inter Christianos non dubitem qui sit eo in his progressus longius. Fuit praeterea ingenij humanissimi atque communicationi et disciplinae Christi studiosissimus. Hic, ut quondam me ageret in Academia (destinatus enim erat Oxoniensi) improbis precibus impetrauit, nosti enim, quam sim cupidus consuetudine eorum, qui regnum Christi totum et ipsi recipere, et praedicare alijs fideliter ac constanter student. Nolim hunc propter meum solatium, gaudijs non perfrui coelestibus, cruciat autem me, quod uiri tales in sua colliguntur cubilia, tam praemature, diem enim malam portendere hoc, quis nesciat, cumque tam pauci Christi communionem et disciplinam uel intelligunt, etiam ex primarijs ecclesiarum gubernatoribus, qui non acerbissime affligat me, eripi nobis, qui huius alterius partis regni Christi, non intelligentes modo sunt, sed etiam constantissimi zelotes. Quod quereris de magistratuum praepostera seueritate, et lenitate, et ego semper questus sum, et queror, sed hi non sunt contenti munus suum tam praepostere administrare, uerum etiam ecclesiasticam fidelem administrationem impediunt et peruertunt, quae etiam ex praecipuis caussis est, cur mori malim, quam uiuere in hoc tam stupido, ad res salutis suae, saeculo, tamque astuto, et callido, ad sui perditionem. Fons unus malorum omnium est, ut pie et experienter scribis, quod homines nolunt Christum super se regnare. Quod ad bellum attinet certe regno huic damnosissimum, nihil possum scribere, audiui quidem, ut quisque ex proceribus sapientior est, et magis religiosus; plurimum ab hoc bello abhorrere, dici enim uix potest, quantam uoret pecuniam, et sine spe utilitatis. cum huc proficiscerer, magna erat spes, pacis cum Gallo paciscendae, quid interim acciderit, ut nunc recrudescat bellum, nescio, magis autem existimo caussam a Gallo existere, qui forsan regnum hoc non suo bono contemnit nimium, minus enim se munit contra eos, a quibus ei longe grauiora impendent. Sed regit haec Dominus, ego de conditionibus pacis utrimque oblatis, nihil noui, et si nouissem, nihil tamen possem melioribus consilijs momenti afferre. Oro itaque Dominum, ut gubernare ipse dignetur eorum animos, quos utrique regno ipse praefecit. Quo enim bellum hoc pertineat, quis non uideat Pontificios enim suffundere frigidam Gallo, quis dubitet. Hoc tamen boni nostris accessit, quod septennales indutias cum Scotis constituerunt. Mei homines Argentinae iam in quartum mensem nullas mihi miserunt literas, cum singulis proper possent septimanis, aut ad summum alteris, ita, tanquam instrumentum mutile passim expectoror [*sic*], etiam ab ijs, quibus ego multa opera, et magna inuidia studui commodare. Verum, haec Domini iudicia non sustinerem, si ipse me semper dijudicassem, et omnia opera mea. Benedictus sit Dominus in saecula, qui in his omnibus aduersis rebus, mirifica semper consolatione subleuat, per multos uere pios homines. Ego me, et meum ministerium, uestris commendo precibus. Dominus consoletur, et calumnijs eripiat, sanctissimum uirum, Viretum nostrum. Et quis non despondeat animum, de religione istorum hominum, qui zelo tam nefario, persequuntur tam eximios Christi ministros. Christi spiritus summe lenis est, et ab omni horrens contentione. Quid enim contra tam sanctum uirum, et sanctam eius doctrinam, incitat tot homines, quam turpissima *φιλονικεία*, et furor diaboli incitatus contra molitionem disciplinae. Dominus det, ut uideamus aliquando euangelium in uirtute, et non in sermone tantum aut transferat nos ad se, ubique est, quod fugias, quo confugias, nusquam apparet. Patiamur ergo cum Domino pressuram a mundo, et falsis fratribus, et oremus, ut tandem nos eripiat e mundo. Opto te rectissime ualere cum omnibus collegis regnum Christi solidum expetentibus. Si referre putaueris, Caluinus literas has, quoque legat. *Opto uos omnes Domino feliciter uiuere & agere ac uestris me literis semper viuificare. Cantabrigie* 12 *Ianuarij* 1550

M. Bucerus totus
tuus in Dño

APPENDIX

III

John Banck's Letter to the Marquis of Dorset, Henry Grey
Cambridge, July 1552[1]

The MS. notes are a beautifully bound little volume (approximately 8 × 6 inches). The text is written on 29 fols. (The 29th is only half.) The title on one leaf. The letter following the title-leaf is written on two leaves (the second only half), and on the back of the second half the address is to be found.

The title runs:

> De priuato ministerio, quod clericale uulgo appellatur, deque ui ministerij publici, et administrationis uerbi, et baptismatis cum quibusdam, quae de efficacia caenae Dominicae tractantur, locus communis ad illustrissimum principem. D. Marchionem Dorcestriae

The handwriting throughout the MS. is perfect and clear. The usual contractions and abbreviations occur (e.g. cũ = cum, Dñi = Domini, oĩa = omnia), which have been expanded here. There is no pagination throughout the volume; a new page is indicated in our text by ||.

Illustrissimo, ac nobilissimo principi D. Marchioni Dorcestriae summo studiosorum patrono, et Domino suo clementissimo S in Domino p.D.

Quoniam ante menses aliquot eam partem disputationis quae est habita de publico ministerio ab excellentissimo, et sanctissimo viro D. Martino Bucero ad Dominationem tuam perscripseram, illustrissime princeps, et Domine clementissime, eamque non ingratam tibi fuisse intelligo: ob eam causam visum est et illa adiungere, quae postea disserebat magna cum eorum, qui audiebant, admiratione de priuato ministerio, quod pastorale appellatur, deque verbi administrationis, itemque baptismatis, et coenae Dominicae vi, et efficacia. Quam quidem tractationem quo minus perficeret, etsi sibi matura, nobis praematura morte effectum est, quae tamen ijs ipsis de rebus tractata ab eo, et disputata sunt, quoniam eius generis sunt, ut non minus splendida sint propter magnitudinem, et excellentiam rerum, quas continent, quam necessaria propter dilucidam tractationem, et explicationem, quam eisdem ipsis de rebus instituerat, facere // equidem non possum, quin quem admodum[?] illa, ita haec quoque, quoad eius fieri possit, ad Dominationem tuam pertexam. Atque quidem quae de uerbi administrationis, et baptismatis energia instituta tractatio est, eam ad exitum adduxerat, et ad postremum in grauissimam illam de coena Domini quaestionem, quae hodie maxime agitatur, ingressus erat. De qua quidem, quia perdifficilis, et ardua uidebatur, quaedam prefatus est, et plurima disserebat cum de distributione totius causae, tum de ijs hominibus, qui anxie de hoc mysterio quaerebant. De eo enim qui disceptabant, omnes in duplice

[1] MS. Coll. Gonv. et Caius (Cantab.) 423, see here p. 20.

genere ponebat. Eorum namque aut in rebus errorem, aut in uerbis cerni dicebat. Quorum autem in re ipsa uersabatur error, eos vel papistas esse, qui monstrosam naturae panis, et uini commutationem introducebant, uel anabaptistas, qui mysterium hoc exinanibant, conformabat. Qui uero de uerbis errabant, eorum alij, cum de hoc mysterio loquerentur, nimia quadam uerborum granditate vtebantur, troposque scripturarum nimis exaggerabant: alij uero de eo nimis exiliter disserebant, et omnem tropicam locutionem reformidabant. Qui igitur, cum de rebus conspirarent, omnem de uerbis disceptationem suscipiebant, eos coniungere inter se, conciliareque studebat, huiusque item distractionis causas paulo altius repetebat. Haec quidem cum breuiter attigisset, et grauissimis quibusdam rationibus, vt omnem in his mysterijs contentionem deuitaremus, commonuisset, tripertito // vniuersam hanc rationem distribuit. primo enim, quae in coena nobis beneficia per ministrum tributa sunt, persecutus est: Deinde propositum hoc erat, vt omnem de uerbis coenae litem dirimeret: Ad postremum uero vt qualis adhiberi interpretatio ex S. patribus deberet, demonstraret. Ac ad primam quidem partem accomodare uoluit D. pauli, et omnium euangelistarum testimonia, sed cum locum in Matthaei 26 de coena explicasset, fatali correptus morbo non sine maximo omnium dolore, et lamentatione vita est priuatus. Quae igitur in ipsius ego praelectionibus obseruaui, ea quia illi, quam ante Dominationi tuae de publico ministerio dederam, tractationi finitima sunt, atque coniuncta: licet omnia non complexus sim, et ipsa sit explicatio manca quodammodo, et imperfecta, tamen existimaui fieri a me oportere, vt quae habebam, omnia complecterer, ad tuamque Dominationem mitterem, et eo quidem maxime, vt et qualis futura tractatio esset, si perfecisset, cognosceret, et haec etiam ratione mea erga ipsam obseruantia testatior esse posset: cui certe, cum omnia mea debeantur, existimo, quicquid a me proficisci possit, id iure quodam Dominationi tuae ditari debere. Vale illustrissime princeps, et domine clementissime.

Cantabrigiae e Collegio Trinitatis anno Domini 1552 mense Julio:[1]

verso: Amplissimae dominationis tuae humillimus seruus, et precator assiduus

Jωannes Banchus

[1] The date of the letter given in the MSS.-Catalogue of Coll. Gonv. et Caius is 1551.

CONCLUSION

THE attempt has been made to show that Bucer's contribution to the English Reformation is not confined to the story of the Revision of the First Edwardian Prayer Book, or to the fact that as he had been in England for two years, obviously links with Englishmen and their thoughts could be traced.

Research revealed a far more composite and detailed contribution of intrinsic value.

The fact that Bucer influenced the Notes and Superscriptions of the Psalter in 'Matthew's Bible', and the fact that the English Version of Bucer's Commentary on the Psalms provided the text for the first printed English Primer, connects him even more intimately with the History of the English Reformation and with the men who gave England its Bible and to whom the English Church is always indebted. Thus Bucer's contribution could be traced back to a time long before he came to England.

The Reformer's attitude in the Vestiarian Controversy as expressed in his Correspondence impressed English theologians in their judgement and affected the course taken by the Church in the Elizabethan controversy on the same subject with the Puritans.

Bucer's interest in ecclesiastical and social problems of his time, as found in his *De Regno Christi*, affected to a certain extent English legislation, as e.g., laws for relief of the poor.

It has been attempted to trace Bucer's relations with English thought by approaching the task from various aspects, thus venturing to show and prove that the Reformer's share in the English Reformation is to be found in further and other sections of the history of the Reformation than usually realized.

To substantiate our claim, the material, already known but scattered in many works on the English Reformation, had to be collected, and other still unknown material added. A detailed study of certain aspects of Bucer's theology, character, interests and dependence on ideas of his time is thus wanting. Bucer as humanist and his dependence on the classics, his conception of the Church, his influence on Calvin, Bucer as politician, Bucer's doctrine of predestination, those are a few headings which, although not coming into the scope of this work, will be found helpful towards a fuller apprehension of his character, work and theology.

In the Arminian controversy the Reformer's writings were repeatedly quoted and adduced to substantiate arguments of men like Robert Abbot, William Prynne and Richard Thomson. His conception of Predestination was ranked next to — or above — that of Calvin.

The discussion in the nineteenth century on Regeneration in connection with Baptism (Gorham, Goode, Laurence, Wilberforce) recalls once again Bucer's teaching. Any discussion on the validity of Anglican Orders is characterized by references to Bucer's Ordinal (Le Courayer, R. T. Smith, W. H. Frere, Firminger, Constant, Messenger).

The Marian reaction against Protestantism could not succeed in suppressing permanently ideas and doctrines, which already had gained influence. English refugees to the Continent had taken with them as heritage the teaching and theology of the Reformers. Returning to England under Elizabeth they continued the interrupted work of their teachers, thus carrying on the task which men like Bucer and other reformers had set themselves. William Whitaker, in a sermon at Cambridge in 1595, points out how much English theology of his time is indebted to Bucer, and how his spiritual heritage was alive, as many bishops and ecclesiastical leaders of the Church in Whitaker's time, had once been the auditors and pupils of the Reformer, Martin Bucer:

> This [i.e. the doctrine of Election and Reprobation] *Bucer* (*saith he*) in our Vniuersity; *Peter Martyr* at Oxford haue proffessed: two eminent Diuines, who haue most abundantly watered our Church with their streames, in the dayes of King *Edward*; whose memories shall be alwayes honourable among vs, vnlesse we will bee most vngratefull: This opinion their Auditors in both our Vniuersities; the Bishops, Deanes, and other Diuines, who vpon the aduancement of our famous Queene *Elizabeth* to the Crowne, returned either from exile, or were released from the prisons into which they had beene thrust for the profession of the Gospell: or saued from the hands of persecuting Bishops: those by whom our Church was reformed, our Religion established, Popery thrust out and quite destroyed . . . This opinion (I say) they themselues haue held. and commended vnto vs: in this faith haue they liued, in this they dyed, in this they alwayes wished that we should constantly continue . . . Lastly, I appeale (*saith he*) to our Confession; in which I am perswaded the same Doctrine which I haue this day handled is not obscurely deliuered: not onely because all our Articles were composed by the Disciples of *Bucer* and *Martyr*, but euen out of the very words & meaning of the Confession it selfe: . . .[1]

[1] English translation (in Prynne, William: *Anti-Arminianisme* . . . (2nd ed., 1630, pp. 261-262) of *G. VVitakervs* . . . *Cygnea Cantio* (pp. 44 ff.: Petri Baronis Summa Trium De Praedestinatione Sententiarum . . . 1613, pp. 65 ff.).

CHORVS ALTERNATIM CANENTIVM

Nos Dominus, subdens impia colla iugo,
Hi sunt ecce canes, Bucerus *Apostata* Petrus
Quos sequitur comites vltimus iste canis,
Vltimus iste Canis binos cantare magistros
Tentat, præ reliquis, vltimus iste Canis
Namque canum dives, vasto & circundata Ponto,
Mordaces habuit hos quoque terra Canes
Vltimus iste canis lacerat quia dente ministros
Ecclesiæ, illius lingua canina fuit
Quodque pios Domini sua mordet Epistola Christos
Et canones sacros, lingua canina fuit.
Lingua canina fuit, qua religionis honores
Denigrare audet, lingua canina fuit
Lingua Canina fuit, qua tollit perfidus hostis
Ecclesiæ ritus: lingua canina fuit,

Votaque disrumpit, lingua canina fuit
Lingua canina fuit, quæ dogmata falsa Lutheri
Impie decantas: lingua canina fuit,
Lingua canina fuit qua mordet dogmata Christi
Quaque pios rodit: lingua canina fuit
Lingua canina fuit qua tu Gualtere *magistros*
Hereticos laudas, lingua canina fuit.
Lingua canina fuit, qua sacras destruit ædes,
Qua ruit in Divos, lingua canina fuit,
Lingua canina fuit, qua Purgatorius ignis
Tollitur, & Sacrum, lingua canina fuit
Lingua canina fuit, qua Pontificalia spernit
Munia, sacrilegi lingua canina fuit,
Lingua canina fuit, qua tot mendacia scriptis
Miscuit in sacris, lingua canina fuit

Introducta Dei, lingua canina fuit
Lingua canina fuit qua scisma extollit, & ipsos
Scismatis authores, lingua canina fuit
Lingua canina fuit qua vult peruellere sanctas
Pontificum leges, lingua canina fuit
Lingua canina fuit, qua maximus ille sacerdos
Roditur, HADDONI *lingua canina fuit*
Lingua canina fuit qua cultum respuit omnem
Diuinum in templis, lingua canina fuit
Lingua canina fuit qua vertit sæpe latinam
Maternam in linguam, lingua canina fuit
Lingua canina fuit, qua libera nostra voluntas
Stringitur in vinclis, lingua canina fuit
Non igitur mirum si currum baiulat istum
Victoremque vehat tempus in omne suum.

Auriga

Festinate Canes quoniam via restat eundi
Longa, per anfractus, accelerate pedes
Maturate fugam, siquidem post terga sequuntur
Qui jam iam vobis cantica digna canunt,
Maturate fugam, nec vos obstacula tardent
Aut pingent vestras crebra flagella nates.

Argumentum infrascriptæ tabulæ.

Quam videt effigiem, celebrem præcedere currum
Hic lector, turbam denotat ipsa Canum.
Turba canum illa sequens, designat ritè cohortē
Quam iunxit magno littera scripta cani

Perque triumphantem, signatur Osorius *ipse,*
Per fratres: sanctæ Religionis honor
Per binosque canes, Bucerus, *Apostata* Petrus:
Lis contestata est cum refremente Cane.

At monstrat sydus digitus auriga caninum,
Vt benè conueniant sydus, & ipse Canis
Vtque canum cecinit cunctorum nomine quondam:
Sic nunc pro cunctis vlulet iste canis.

Portrait of Bucer
in Heinrich Pantaleon's *Prosopographiae*

From the Whitchurch Edition of Bucer's
Psalter in English
(cf. p. 221)

NOTE ON THE BIBLIOGRAPHY

The spelling in our quotations from sixteenth-century English or Latin texts has been modified in a few instances by adopting present-day spelling. (In Latin, for instance, in the usage of v and u: ut for vt, vocavit for uocauit, etc.)

Although there exists a most extensive literature on Martin Bucer and his theology, only research more recently carried out paid special attention to Bucer's relations with England.

To the two special monographs by A. E. Harvey and W. Pauck, already mentioned, the chapter on 'Cambridge and Bucer' in C. H. Smyth's *Cranmer and the Reformation under Edward VI* (Cambridge, 1926, pp. 139 ff.) ought to be added.

The works and correspondence of the Bishop of Winchester, Stephen Gardiner, provides also indispensable material to our subject: cf. Pierre Janelle's *Obedience in Church and State* (Cambridge, 1930) and his *La Controverse Entre Étienne Gardiner et Martin Bucer* (Strasbourg, 1927); and Muller, J. A.: *Stephen Gardiner and the Tudor Reaction* (London, 1926) and *The Letters of Stephen Gardiner* (Cambridge, 1933). F. E. Brightman's *The English Rite*, Procter and Frere's *A New History of the Book of Common Prayer*, and Aidan Cardinal Gasquet's and Edmund Bishop's *Edward VI and the Book of Common Prayer*, contain valuable material for Bucer's relation to the Prayer Book. Abbé G. Constant's *La Réforme en Angleterre* ought to be read in conjunction with Brightman and Frere. J. Collier's *An Ecclesiastical History* and Canon R. W. Dixon's *History of the Church of England* also give a careful and minute account of Bucer and the Prayer Book.

The biography by J. W. Baum (1860) and the short monograph by G. Anrich on Bucer (1914) in connection with the modern monograph on Bucer by H. Eells (1931) and Eells' *The Attitude of Martin Bucer towards the Bigamy of Philip of Hesse* (1924) acquaint the student with the story of the life work and theology of the Strassburg Reformer in general, with only few references to the special period with which we are concerned.

A. Lang's *Der Evangelienkommentar Martin Butzers und die Grundzüge seiner Theologie* has still to be regarded as the standard work on Bucer's theological conceptions.

Georg Klingenburg's *Das Verhältnis Calvins zu Butzer* should be consulted by any student on the question, which has occupied a considerable space in modern research, of Bucer's influence on Calvin.

John Strype's various works on the English Reformation and his biographies on English Reformers are also valuable sources of information, although not always reliable.

To consult Bucer's own works means to work at libraries like the Bodleian, the British Museum, or at the Cambridge University Library, etc., as they are extant only in sixteenth-century editions, thus being not easily accessible to the reader. The volume of *Scripta Anglicana* (Basle, 1577), containing writings of the Reformer during his time in England and before he came to this country, is the only attempt which has been made to edit a collection of his works.

Indispensable material for information is contained in Bucer's extensive correspondence. The great proportion of that correspondence is still only extant in manuscripts kept at Strassburg, Zürich, Corpus Christi College, Cambridge, the Bodleian Library at Oxford, and other places.

His letters concerning his work under Philip, Landgrave of Hesse, have been edited by Max Lenz in three volumes. Apart from this collection referring to a special period of the life of the Reformer, his correspondence is scattered in collections of letters of that period, in editions of the Correspondence of the Reformers, Calvin, Luther or Zwingli. A. L. Herminjard's *Correspondence Des Réformateurs* . . . and Traugott Schiess's *Briefwechsel der Brüder* . . . *Blaurer* and the many volumes of the *Corpus Reformatorum* deserve, apart from many other works, special mention, as containing many letters of Bucer.

The volumes of the Parker Society *Epistolae Tigurinae* and the *Original Letters* (English translation of the former) and C. Gorham's *Gleanings* . . . acquaint the English reader with correspondence of the Reformer.

Ferdinand Mentz's *Bibliographische Zusammenstellung* of Bucer's writings is still a standard work, although the literature on Bucer since then has considerably increased.

In a few instances in this work, when it seemed not of vital importance to refer to a first edition of a work, quotations have been taken from editions which are also easily available to the student (e.g., Hallam's *Constitutional History*; *The First and Second Edwardian Prayer Books*; F. Seebohm's *The Oxford Reformers*; Thomas More's *Utopia*; have been quoted from the Everyman's Library editions. Milton's Prose Works from the edition in Bohn's Library and R. H. Tawney's *Religion and the Rise of Capitalism* from the Pelican book edition).

An asterisk before author and work in our bibliography indicates that special references to Bucer or material relevant to the Reformer's relation with England will be found.

BIBLIOGRAPHY

MSS. CONSULTED

At the Bodleian Library, Oxford:

MSS. Rawlinson D 346 (Correspondence concerning the Vestiarian Controversy).

MS. Rawlinson D 858: Consilium theologicum in cujusdam viri gratiam privatim conscriptum, quo auctoritate sacrarum literarum ostenderet an, et quatenus, Christiani in ecclesiis pontificia tyrannide adhuc pressis degentes, illarum ritibus et per-actionibus communicare possint; quis quoque uniuscujusque ritus sit fons verus, usus, atque abusus: autore sanctissimo et celeberrimo sacrarum literarum professore M. Bucero.

Other MS. copies of the same work:

1. MS. Rawlinson C 373 (Joannis Lenglini liber. *not:* Lengbiri).
2. Cambridge University MS. Mm, iv, 5.
3. Corp. Chr. Coll., Camb. MS. 185.
4. Harleian MS. 1854, fol. 1.

MS. Rawlinson D 858 (Bucer's letter to Italian Brethren; second part printed in: *Scripta Anglicana*, pp. 689-691; first part now printed in *Journal of Theological Studies* (January-April, 1943; No. 173-4, pp. 67-72). *A Letter of Martin Bucer*).

MS. New College 343 (Correspondence concerning the Vestiarian Controversy).

MS. New College 317 (MS. copy of Bucer's *Censura*).

MS. Add. C. 97 (=Summary Catalogue 30255) MS. of Bucer's *Constans Defensio* . . .

MS. Lat. Th. e. 4 (=Summary Catalogue 29808) Thomas Sampson's MS. translation of Bucer's reply to the *Antididagma*.

MS. Smith 67 (=Summary Catalogue 15673) sixteenth-century letters.

MS. Clar. Press c. 5 (=Summary Catalogue 41549): S. Hess, about 1823: Annales reformationis ecclesiae anglicanae sive commentarius chronologicus chartarum diplomaticarum . . . ecclesiae helveticae ut et in primis anglicanae reformationem spectantium, Henrici Bullingeri . . . temporibus, inde ab anno 1534 ad annum 1574.

MS. Mm. iv, 14. Correspondence concerning the Vestiarian Controversy. (*At Cambridge University Library.*)

MS. Coll. Gonv. et Caius, 423.

MS. Lambeth 306, *fol. 65*. List of prohibited Books, by Stokesley, Bishop of London.

MS. Bibliotheque Des Pasteurs, *Neuchatel*.

BIBLIOGRAPHY

PRINTED BOOKS

*ABBOT, ROBERT (Bishop of Salisbury): *De Gratia . . . Quibus Accessit Eiusdem In Richardi Thomsoni . . . Diatribam* . . . (London, 1618).

*A briefe examination for the tyme, of a certaine declaration, lately put in print in the name and defence of certaine Ministers in London . . . (Imprinted, London, by Richarde Iugge . . .) (1566).

*A briefe treatise concerning the burnynge of Bucer and Phagius, at Cambrydge, in the tyme of Quene Mary, with theyr restitution in the time of our moste gracious souerayne Lady that nowe is; . . . *translated* by Arthur Goldyng (London, 1562).

*ADAM, MELCHIOR: *Vitae Germanorum Theologorum* . . . (Heidelberg, 1620). *Vitae Germanorum Medicorum* . . . (Heidelberg, 1620).

*ALESIUS, ALEXANDER: *Primvs liber Psalmorvm et Divi Hieronymi . . . in celebri Academia Lipsensi* (1554).

ALLEN, J. W.: *A History of Political Thought in the Sixteenth Century* (London, 1928).

*ALLEN, P. S.: *Opus Epistolarum Des. Erasmi Roterodami* . . . (Tome I, 1484-1514, Oxford, 1906) and following volumes.

ALLMENRÖDER: Zur Reformationsgeschichte des Elsass. Zwei Briefe Butzer's und Hedio's an den Grafen Philip IV . . . *Zeitschrift für Kirchengesch.* 1885. Bd. VII. Heft III. pp. 470-477.

ALTHAMER(US), ANDREAS: *Conciliationes Locorum Scripturae, qui specie tenus inter se pugnare uidentur* . . . (Norimbergae. M.D.xlviii).

AMES, JOSEPH and HERBERT, WILLIAM: *Typographical Antiquities*, 3 vol. (London, 1785-90).

*An answere For The Tyme, To The Examination put in print, vvithout the authours name pretending to mayntayne the apparell . . . (Geneva? 1566).

ANDERSON, CHRISTOPHER: *The Annals of the English Bible*, 2 vol. (London, 1845).

*ANRICH, GUSTAV: *Martin Bucer* (Strassburg, 1914).
Ein Bedacht Bucers über die Einrichtung von 'Christlichen Gemeinschaften' — pp. 46-70 in *Festschrift für Hans von Schubert . . . herausgegeben von Otto Scheel.* Archiv für Reformationsgeschichte, Ergänzungsband V (Leipzig, 1929).

**Antididagma*, seu Christianae et Catholicae Religionis, . . . propugnatio . . . (1549).

*ARBENZ, EMIL: *Die Vadianische Briefsammlung der Stadtbibliothek St. Gallen.* V. II. Hälfte (1536-1540); Herausgegeben von Emil Arbenz und Herman Wartman (St. Gallen, 1905).

*ASCHAM, ROGER: *Rogeri Aschami Epistolarum, libri quatuor* . . . (Editio Novissima, Prioribus auctior . . . Oxoniae . . . MDCCIII).
Early edition with Epistles of John Sturm and others and poems of Ascham (Londini, 1590).

BIBLIOGRAPHY

BARCLAY, ALEXANDER: *The Protestant Doctrine of the Lord's Supper. A Study in the Eucharistic Teaching of Luther, Zwingli and Calvin* (Glasgow, 1927).

BARROW(E), HENRY: *A petition directed to her most excellent Maiestie, wherein is deliuered* . . . (anon., no place or year).

*BAUM, ADOLF: *Magistrat und Reformation in Strassburg bis 1529* (Strassburg, 1887).

*BAUM, J. W.: *Capito und Butzer* (Elberfeld, 1860).

**Thesaurus Baumianus, Verzeichnis der Briefe und Aktenstücke* . . . Herausgegeben von Johannes Ficker (Strassburg, 1905). (Kaiserliche Universitäts-Und Landesbibliothek, Strassburg).

*BAUMGARTEN, HERMANN: *Sleidans Briefwechsel* (Strassburg-London, 1881).

*BEARD, CHARLES: *The Reformation of the Sixteenth Century* . . . Hibbert Lectures, 1883. (New Impression, with an Introduction by Ernest Barker, London, new edition, 1927.)

*BELL, THOMAS: *The Regiment of the Church* . . . (London, 1606).

*BEZA, THEODOR: *Icones, id est Verae Imagines* . . . (Geneva, 1580).

Biographie Nationale . . . De Belgique (Bruxelles, 1866).

*BIZER, ERNST: Martin Butzer und der Abendmahlsstreit. Unbekannte und unveröffentlichte Aktenstucke . . . pp. 203-237, in *Archiv für Reformationsgeschichte, Jahrgang* 35 (Leipzig, 1938), pp. 68-87, and pp. 214 ff. in: op. cit., *Jahrgang* 36 (Leipzig, 1939).

*BOISSARDUS, JANIUS JACOBUS: *Iconum Viros Virtute Atque Eruditione Illustres repraesentantium* . . . Pars IV . . . per haeredes Theodorj de Bry . . . (Francf., 1599).

BONNER, RICHARD: A treatyse of y[e] ryght honourynge and wourshyppyng of our sauiour Jesus Christe in the sacramēt of breade and wyne, when it is ministred wyth thankes geuing at the holy supper: sette forth by Rycharde Bonner priest, in ye yeare of our lord god. M.cccccxlviii. and the. xii. of Nouember. Jmprinted at Londō for Gwalter Lynne dwellyng on Somers kaye by Byllynges gate. Cum priuilegio ad imprimendum solum.

*BOSSUET, JACQUES BÉNIGNE: Traité de l'usure. in vol. xxxi, pp. 21 ff. of: *Oeuvres complétes de Bossuet* (Paris, 1866).

*BOYS, JOHN: *An Exposition of the Proper Psalmes used in our English Liturgie* . . . (London, 1616); 2nd part . . . London, 1617. *An exposition of al the principall scriptures used in our English Liturgie* . . . (London, 1610).

*BRADFORD, JOHN: *The Writings of . . . Sermons, Meditations* . . . (Parker Society, Cambridge, 1848).

The Writings of . . . Letters, Treatises, Remains (Parker Society, Cambridge, 1853).

*BRERELY, JOHN (pseudonym for Anderton, James): *Luther's Life collected from the writings of himself, and other learned Protestants, together with a further shorte discourse, touchinge Andreas Melanchton, Bucer* . . . (At S. Omers, Anno 1624).

*BRESCH, FREDÉRIC: *Strasbourg et la Querelle Sacramentaire, ou rapports de Bucer a ce propos avec Luther, Zwingle et Calvin* (Montauban, 1902).

*BRIGHTMAN, F. E.: *The English Rite*, 2 vol. (2nd ed. Rev., London, 1921).

BUCER, MARTIN (Works only more frequently referred to):

Scripta Anglicana fere omnia a Conr. Huberto collecta (Basle, 1577).

Epistola in evangelistarum enarrationes nuncupatoria . . . (s.l. 1530).

Enarrationes perpetuae in sacra quatuor euangelia . . . (Argent., 1530).

In sacra quatuor euangelia, enarrationes perpetuae . . . (Jo. Hervagen) (Basle, 1536).

Metaphrases et enarrationes epistolarum Pauli . . . vol. I (Romans) . . . (Argent., W. Rihel. 1536).

Sacrorum psalmorum libri quinque . . . per Aretium Felinum . . . (Strassburg, Georg. Vlrich Andlan. 1529). (Basle, Jo. Hervagen, 1547) editio cum commentar. in librum *Judicum* & in *Sophoniam* . . . (Oliua, Robert. Stephan. 1554).

Declaration familiere sur le second liure des Pseaumes (s.l. 1553).

Praelectiones in Epist. ad Ephesios . . . (Basle, 1562).

(*Epist. Pauli ad Ephesios* . . . (Argent, 1527)).

De Caena Dominica Ad obiecta, quae contra ueritatem Euangelicam Murnerus, partim ipse finxit, partim ex Roffensi ac alijs pietatis hostibus, sublegit, Responsio Martini Buceri. (s.l. & a.)

Defensio adversus Axioma Catholicum, id est criminationem R. P. Roberti Episcopi Abrincensis . . . (Argentor., 1534).

Sententiae Philip. Melanthonis, Martini Bvceri . . . *de pace Ecclesiae* . . . (1534) . . . in Goldast, M.: *Politica Imperialia* . . . pp. 1280-1284, 1291.

Acta colloquii Ratisponae habiti . . . W. Rihel . . . (Argent., 1542).

Scripta Duo Adversaria D. Bartholomaei Latomi . . . see LATOMUS.

De vera ecclesiarum in doctrina, ceremoniis, et disciplina reconciliatione et compositione; responsio ad calumnias Alberti Pighii . . . (s.l. & a.).

Gratulatio ad ecclesiam Anglicanam . . . (s.l. 1548).

Disputata Ratisbonae, in altero colloquio anno xlvi . . . (s.l. 1548).

De Regno Christi (Basle, 1557).

Du royaume de Jesus Christ . . . Jacques Berthet (Geneva, 1558).

BIBLIOGRAPHY

WORKS OF BUCER TRANSLATED INTO ENGLISH

The Psalter of Dauid . . . (Francis foxe, Argentine, 1530).
The Psalter of Dauid . . . (Thomas Godfray, London).
The Psalter of Dauid . . . (Edward Whytchurch, London).

AND THE PSALMS IN

A Prymer in Englyshe . . . William Marshall (John Byddell, London),
another edition (John Byddell, London, 1535).
The prymer with the pystles . . . (John Byddell, London).
A treatise declarying & shewing dyuers causes taken out of the holy scriptur | of the sentences of the holy faders, & of the decrees of deuout Emperours, that pyctures & other ymages which were wont to be worshypped | are in no wise to be suffred in the temples or churches of Christen men. By the whiche treatise the reder that is indifferent, shall se and perceyue, how good and godly a dede it was of the Senatoures of Argentine, that of late daies they caused all the ymages with their auters to be cleane taken out of their churches.

The authours of this little treatise ar the open preachers of Argtēyne . . . (Printed for W. Marshall. 1535?) (by Thomas Godfray(?). as the designs are the same as in the Psalter printed by Godfray).

The actes of the disputacion in the Cownsell of Regenspurg . . . (translated by Myles Coverdale, no place, 1542).
The Gratulation of . . . *Martin Bucer* . . . *vnto the churche of Englande* . . . (translated by Sir Thomas Hoby) (R. Iugge, London, 1549?).
A Treatise, How by the Worde of God, Christian mens Almose ought to be distributed . . . (no place, or year).
The mynd and exposition of that excellente learned man Martyn Bucer | vppon the wordes of S. Mathew; Woo be to the wordle [sic] . . . (Printed at Emden, 1566).
Bucer's letters to:

Cranmer, Hooper, à Lasco: 1. in Whether it be mortall sinne . . . (R. Iugge, London). 2. in A briefe examination for the tyme . . . (R. Iugge, London).

His judgement touching the originall of bishops and metropolitans . . . (p. 45 of Certain briefe treatises concerning the ancient and modern government of the Church) (London, 1641).
The Ivdgement Of Martin Bucer, Concerning Divorce, Writt'n to Edward the sixt, in his second Book of the Kingdom of Christ. And now Englisht (by John Milton) . . . (London, 1644).

*BUGENHAGEN, JOHANNES: *Psalter wol verteutscht* . . . (Basel, 1526). Der cxi. psalm . . . 1526.

*BURNET, GILBERT: *The History of the Reformation of the Church of England.* 2 vol. (ed. London, 1841).

*BURTON, EDWARD: *Three Primers Put Forth In the Reign of Henry VIII* (Oxford, 1834).
2nd ed., without preface by Burton (Oxford, 1848).

*BUTTERWORTH, CHARLES C.: *The Literary Lineage of the King James Bible 1340-1611* (Philadelphia, 1941).

CAEMMERER, HERMANN VON: *Das Regensburger Religionsgespräch im Jahre 1546* Inaugural Dissertation (Berlin, 1901).

*CALDERWOOD, DAVID (pseud. Edward Didoclavius): *Altare Damascenvm* . . . (1623).

*Calendar of State Papers Domestic, 1547-1580 (London, 1856).

Calendar of State Papers Foreign, 1547-1553 (London, 1861).

Calendar of State Papers Spanish, 1550-1552 (London, 1914).

Calendar of State Papers Venetian, 1534-1554 (London, 1873).

*CALVIN, JOHN: *Joannis Calvini Epistolae et resp.* Editio Secunda (with Life of Calvin by Th. Beza), Geneva, 1576.
The psalmes of Dauid and others. With M. John Caluin's Commentaries (1571). Jmprinted at London by Thomas East and Henry Middelton . . . (1571).

*CASTALIO (CASTELLIO), SEBASTIAN: *Biblia, interprete Sebastiano Castalione* . . . (Basle, 1551).

*CENALIS, ROBERT, Bishop of Avranches: *De utriusque gladii facultate, usuque legitimo* . . . (Parisiis, 1546).
Pro Tuendo Sacro Coelibatu Axioma Catholicum. (Parisiis, 1545).

*CHEKE, JOHN, and CARR, NICHOLAS: *De obitu Mart. Buceri Epistolae duae, item epigrammata varia cum Graecae tum Latine conscripta in eundem.* (Lond. Res. Wolfii, 1551).

CHESTER, JOSEPH LEMUEL: *John Rogers . . . The Compiler of the First Authorised Bible* . . . (London, 1861).

**Chorus* alternatim canentium. Cantemus, quoniam mordaci a dente redemit Nos Dominus, subdens impia colla jugo, Hi sunt ecce canes, Bucerus Apostata, Petrus. Quos sequitur comites ultimus iste canis . . . (Antwerp? 1563? broadsheet).

**The Church Quarterly Review*: The Anglican Order of Ordination (pp. 261-290), N.X., January 1878.
The True History . . . (pp. 123 ff.) April 1897.

CLAPTON, ERNEST: *Our Prayer Book Psalter containing Coverdale's Version from his 1535 Bible and the Prayer Book Version by Coverdale from the Great Bible 1539-41* . . . (S.P.C.K., London, 1934).
Coverdale And the Psalter, in *Church Quarterly Review*, January 1929, vol. CVII, No. 214, pp. 288-307.

*Clemen, Otto: *Der Gothaer Briefcodex A 406* . . . (pp. 119-145; 238-251) in *Archiv für Reformationsgeschichte. Jahrgang 35* (Leipzig, 1938).

*Clement, David: *Bibliotheque Curieuse Historique Et Critique* . . . Tome V (Hannover . . . 1754).

*Cochlaeus, Johan: *In XVIII. Articvlos Mar. Bvceri* . . . (1546).

*Collier, Jeremy: *An Ecclesiastical History of Great Britain*, vol. II (London, 1714).
New Ed. in 9 vol., vol. V (London, 1845).

Colomesius, P., *Epistolae aliquot Singulares* (London, 1695).

*Constant, Abbé G.: *La Transformation Du Culte Anglican Sous Édouard VI.* pp. 38-80; 242-270; 474-495 in *Revue D'Histoire Ecclésiastique*, vol. XII (1), Université Catholique De Louvain (Louvain, 1911).
La Réforme En Angleterre. I. Le Schisme Anglican. Henry VIII, 1509-1547 (Paris, 1930).
English Translation: (by R. E. Scantlebury), *The Reformation in England, I. The English Schism, Henry VIII, 1509-1547* (London, 1934).
La Réforme En Angleterre II, L'Introduction De La Réforme En Angleterre. Edouard VI, 1547-1553 (Paris, 1939).
English Translation: (by E. I. Watkin): *The Reformation in England. II. Introduction of the Reformation into England. Edward VI, 1547-1553* (London, 1941).

Cooper, Charles Henry: *Annals of Cambridge.* vol. II (Cambridge, 1853).

*Cooper, Charles Henry and Cooper, Thompson: *Athenae Cantabrigienses*, vol. I, 1500-1585 (Cambridge, 1858).

Cope (Copus) Alan, *Dialogi Sex* . . . (Antwerp, 1573).

**Corpus Reformatorum*, edit. Carolus Gottlieb Bretschneider, Halis Saxon. (1834-).

**Corpus Reformatorum*, vol. XLI. Ioannis Calvini Opera, vol. XIII (Ed. W. Baum, E. Cunitz, E. Reuss, Brunsvigae, 1875).

*Cosin, John: *The Works of the Right Reverend . . . John Cosin, Lord Bishop of Durham*, vol. V (Oxford, 1855). Library of Anglo-Catholic Theology.

*Cotton, Henry: *Editions of the Bible and Parts thereof in English from the year 1505-1850*, with an Appendix, 2 vol., 2nd ed. (Oxford, 1852).

*Le Courayer, Pierre François: *Défense de la Dissertation sur la validité des Ordinations Des Anglois.* Tome II, Pt. I (Bruxelles, 1726).

*Courvoisier, Jaques: *La Notion D'Eglise Chez Bucer* . . . (Paris, 1933).

Une Traduction Française Du Commentaire De Bucer Sur l'Evangile Selon Saint Matthieu in No. 26 of *Cahiers De La Revue D'Histoire Et De Philosophie Religieuses* (Paris, 1933).

*COVERDALE, MYLES: *Works of Bishop Coverdale. Remains* . . . (Parker Society, Cambridge, 1846).

*CRAMER, S. EN PIJPER, F.: *Bibliotheca Reformatoria Neerlandica. Vijfde Deel* . . . ('S-Gravenhage . . . 1909). (pp. 199-314): . . . Handelinge van der . . . disputacie in Synodo te Straesburch teghen Melchior Hoffman door die Predikanten derseluer stadt . . . Anno Dom. MCCCCC. xxxiij.

*CRANMER, THOMAS: *Miscellaneous Writings and Letters of Thomas Cranmer* (Parker Society, Cambridge, 1846).

Writings and disputations of Thomas Cranmer . . . Relative to the Sacrament of the Lord's Supper . . . (Parker Society, Cambridge, 1844).

*CROWLEY, ROBERT: *A briefe discourse against the outwarde apparell and ministring garmentes* . . . (Emden? 1566).

DAICHES, DAVID: *The King James Version of the English Bible* (The University of Chicago Press, 1941).

DAKIN, A.: *Calvinism* (Duckworth, London, 1940).

DALTON, HERMANN: *Johannes à Lasco* (Gotha, 1881).

DARMESTETER, ARSENE: *Les Gloses Francaises De Raschi Dans La Bible* (Paris, 1909).

DELONEY, THOMAS: *The Works of Thomas Deloney* . . . (Ed. Francis Oscar Mann, Oxford, 1912).

DIBDIN, THOMAS, F.: *Typographical Antiquities* . . . (London, 1810-19).

DIBDIN, SIR LEWIS T. and SIR CHARLES E. H. CHADWYCK HEALEY: *English Church Law and Divorce* (London, 1912).

Dictionary of National Biography.

*DIXON, RICHARD WATSON: *History of the Church of England* . . . vol. III (London, 1893).

*DODINGTON, BARTHOLOMEW: Letter to Sir Walter Mildmay, 'Cantabrigiae pridie Calend. Nouembris 1570' in NICHOLAS CARR: *Demosthenis, Graecorum Oratorum* . . . (London, 1571).

*DOWDEN, JOHN: *The Workmanship of the Prayer Book* (2nd rev. ed., London, 1902).

Further Studies in the Prayer Book (London, 1908).

DRIVER, S. R.: *The Parallel Psalter* . . . (2nd ed., Oxford, 1904).

DRUFFEL, AUGUST VON: *Beiträge zur Reichsgeschichte 1546-*, vol. I (München, 1873-).

*DRYSDALE, A. H.: *History of the Presbyterians in England* (London, 1889).

*DUREL, JOHN: *Sanctae Ecclesiae Anglicanae Adversus Iniquas atque inverecundas Schismaticorum Criminationes Vindiciae* . . . (Londini . . . MDCLXIX).

EADIE, JOHN: *The English Bible* . . . 2 vol. (London, 1876).

*ECK, JOHANN VON: *Replica Ioan. Eckii adversus scripta secunda Buceri apostatae super actis Ratisponae* . . . (Ingolstadii, 1543).

*EELLS, HASTINGS: Martin Bucer and the conversion of John Calvin, pp. 402-419 in *The Princeton Theological Review*, July 1924.

The Attitude of Martin Bucer toward the Bigamy of Philip of Hesse (Yale University, 1924).

Sacramental Negotiations at the Diet of Augsburg, 1530, pp. 213-233 in *The Princeton Theological Review*, 1925.

The Genesis of Martin Bucer's Doctrine of the Lord's Supper, pp. 225-251 in *The Princeton Theological Review*, 1926.

The Origin of the Regensburg Book, pp. 355-372 in *The Princeton Theological Review*, 1928.

Martin Bucer (Yale University, 1931).

ENDERS, ERNST L.: *Luther's Briefwechsel. Bearbeitet u.m. Erl. vers. von E. L. Enders* . . . vol. VIII (Calw u. Stuttgart, 1898).

**Epistolae Tigurinae* (Parker Society, Cambridge, 1848).

*ERBKAM, H. W.: *Geschichte der Protestantischen Sekten im Zeitalter der Reformation* . . . (Hamburg und Gotha, 1848).

*FECHT, JOH.: *Historiae Ecclesiasticae Seculi A.N.C. XVI Supplementum* . . . (Durlaci, anno 1684).

FELINUS, ARETIUS, i.e. BUCER, MARTIN.

*FICKER, JOHANNES und WINCKELMANN, OTTO: *Handschriftenproben des Sechzehnten Jahrhunderts.* 1 Band (Strassburg, 1902). 2 Band (Strassburg, 1905).

FINCH, R. G. and BOX, G. H.: *The Longer Commentary of R. David Kimhi on the First Book of Psalms* . . . Translated from the Hebrew by R. G. Finch, with an Introduction by G. H. Box (S.P.C.K., London, 1919).
(Translations of Early Documents, Series III, Rabbinic Texts).

*FIRMINGER, WALTER KELLY: The Ordinal. Article in *Liturgy and Worship* (London. Reprinted 1936).

*FOXE, JOHN: *Acts and Monuments* . . . (1563) . . . (Ed. A. Townsend, vol. VIII, London, 1849).

French Bible editions:

(LEFÈVRE). La saincte Bible en Francoys . . . En Anuers | par Martin Lempereur, 1534.

(OLIVÉTAN). La Bible Qui est toute la Saincte escripture. En laquelle sont contenus | le Vieil Testament & le Nouueau | translatez en Francoys.
col. Acheue dimprimer en la Ville et Conte Neufchastel . . . 1535.

*FRERE, W. H.: The English Church in the Reign of Elizabeth and James I (1558-1625) vol. V in *A History of the English Church* (London, 1904).

Puritan Manifestoes. A Study of the Origin of the Puritan Revolt. (*The Church Historical Society*, LXXII), London, 1907.

FRERE, W. H. and KENNEDY, W. MC. C.: *Visitation Articles and Injunctions of the Period of the Reformation.* 3 vol. vol. II with the assistance of Kennedy W. Mc. C. (London, 1910). (Alcuin Club Collections, n. xiv, xv, xvi).

*FRERE, W. H. and PROCTER, FRANCIS: *A New History of the Book of Common Prayer on the Basis of the Former Work by Francis Procter*, Revised and rewritten by Walter Howard Frere (London, 1941).

*FULLER, THOMAS: *The History of the University of Cambridge* . . . (New ed., with Notes by James Nichols, London, 1840).

FURNIVALL, FREDERICK J.: *Political, Religious and Love Poems* . . . Early English Text Society, Original Series 15 (London, 1866, re-ed., 1903).

*GABBEMA, SIMON ABBES: *Illustrium & Clarorum Virorum Epistolae* . . . (Harlingae Frisiorum, 1669).

GAIRDNER, JAMES: *Three fifteenth-century Chronicles* . . . (Ed. by James Gairdner, Camden Society, 1880. New Ser. 28).

GAIRDNER, JAMES: The English Church in the Sixteenth Century from the Accession of Henry VIII to the Death of Mary . . . vol. IV in *A History of the English Church* (London, 1924).

GAMS, P. PIUS BONIFACIUS: *Series Episcoporum Ecclesiae* (Ratisbonae, 1873).

*GARDINER, STEPHEN: *Stephani VVinton. Episcopi Angli, ad Martinvm Bvcerum, De Impudenti eiusdem Pseudologia Conquestio* (Lovanii . . . 1544).

Stephani VVinton. Episcopi Angli ad Martinvm Bvcervm Epistola . . . (Louanii . . . 1546).

Exetasis testimoniorum, quae Martinus Bucerus ex Sanctis Patribus non sancte edidit . . . (Louvain, 1554).

GARRETT, CHRISTINA HALLOWELL: *The Marian Exiles* (Cambridge, 1938).

*GASQUET, AIDAN, CARDINAL and BISHOP, EDMUND: *Edward VI and The Book of Common Prayer.* (Rev. ed., London, New Impression, November 1928).

*GERDES(IUS), DANIEL: *Scrinium Antiquarium* . . . (8 vol. Groningae et Bremae, 1749-65).

GERLACHIUS, STEPHANUS: *Antidanaeus* . . . (Tvbingae . . . 1580).

*GOLDAST, MELCHIOR: *Politica Imperialia* . . . (Franc., 1614).

Monarchia Sancti Romani Imperii . . . Tom. I. (Hanoviae . . . 1612).

GOODE, WILLIAM: *Altars Prohibited by the Church of England*, 2 parts (London, 1844).

An Unpublished Letter of Peter Martyr to Henry Bullinger . . . (London, 1850).

The Doctrine of the Church of England as to the Effects of Baptism . . .

With an Appendix . . . The Baptismal Services of Luther and the Nuremberg and Cologne Liturgies. (2nd ed., London, 1850).

*GORHAM, GEORGE CORNELIUS: *Gleanings of a few scattered ears during the period of the Reformation in England* (London, 1857).

*GOUGH, HENRY: *General Index* (to the volumes of the Parker Society) (Parker Society, Cambridge, 1855).

GRINDAL, EDMUND: *The Remains of* . . . (Parker Society, 1843).

*GROTIUS, HUGO: *Votum Pro Pace Ecclesiastica* . . . (s.l. 1642).

GUPPY, HENRY: Myles Coverdale and the English Bible, 1488-1568. Reprinted from the *Bulletin of the John Rylands Library*, vol. 19, n. 2, July 1935. (Manchester, 1935).

*HADDON, WALTER: *Lucubrationes . . . collectae et editae studio Th. Hatcheri* . . . (Lond. apud Gul. Seresium, 1567).

*HADDON, WALTER and WILSON, THOMAS: *Vita et Obitvs Dvorvm Fratrum Suffolciensium* . . . (London, no year).

*HAKEWILL, GEORGE: *The Auncient Ecclesiasticall practise of Confirmation;* . . . (London, 1613).

*HALLAM, HENRY: *The Constitutional History of England* . . . 3 vol. (London, 1855).

HARDWICK, CHARLES: *A History of the Articles of Religion.* (Cambridge-London, 1851.)

*HARRISON, BENJAMIN: *An Historical Inquiry into the True Interpretation of the Rubrics* . . . (London, 1845).

*HARVEY, A. E.: *Martin Bucer in England* (Marburg, 1906).

HASENCLEVER, ADOLF: *Sleidan Studien* . . . (Bonn, 1905).

Martin Bucer als Verfasser eines bisher anonymen Berichts über das Regensburger Kolloquium vom Jahre 1546. in *Zeitschrift für die Geschichte des Oberrheins.* Neue Folge 26, pp. 491-500. (Karlsruhe, 1911).

*HASSENCAMP, F. W.: *Hessische Kirchengeschichte seit dem Zeitalter der Reformation* (Frankfurt.a.M., 1864, 2 vol. 2nd ed.).

HAUCK, ALBERT and HERZOG, J. J.: see *Realencyklopädie* . . .

HERFORD, CHARLES H.: *Studies in the Literary Relations of England and Germany in the sixteenth century* (Cambridge, 1886).

HERGANG, K. T.: *Das Religionsgespräch zu Regensburg 1541 und das Regensburger Buch* (Cassel, 1858).

HERMAN VON WIED, Archbishop of Cologne: *Von Gottes Gnaden, unser Hermans Erzbischofs zu Köln . . . einfältiges Bedencken* . . . (1543).

Nostra Hermanni ex Gratia Dei Archiepiscopi Coloniensis . . simplex ac pia deliberatio . . . (Bonn, 1545).

A simple and religious consultation of us, Herman . . . (London, 1547, amended ed. 1548).

Bestendige Verantwortung auss der Heiligen Schrifft . . . (Bonn, 1545).

see: BUCER, MARTIN: *Constans Defensio* . . .

*HERMINJARD, A. L.: *Correspondance des Réformateurs dans les Pays de Langue Française* . . . (Genève, 1866).

*HESSELS, JOANNES HENRICUS: *Epistulae . . . Ecclesiae Londino-Batavae Archivum* . . . Tomus secundus . . . (Cantabrigiae . . . 1889).

*HEYLYN, PETER: *Ecclesia Restaurata, or The History of the Reformation of the Church of England* (London, 1661).

**Historia uera:* De Vita, Obitv, Sepvltvra, Accvsatione haereseos, condemnatione, combustione . . . D. Martini Bvceri . . . (Argent, 1561-62).

Historical Manuscripts Commission. Fourteenth Report, Appendix, Part VIII. The Manuscripts of Lincoln, Bury St. Edmund's . . . (London, 1895).

*HOBY, THOMAS: *The Travels and Life of Sir Thomas Hoby, Knight, 1547-1564.* (Ed. for the Royal Historical Society by Edgar Powell. The Camden Miscellany, 3S.IV(2) (London, 1902).)

HOLL, KARL: *Gesammelte Aufsätze zur Kirchengeschichte.* 3 vol. (Tübingen, 1927-28).

Homilies: Certain Sermons or Homilies . . . in the Time of Queen Elizabeth . . . (New ed., S.P.C.K., London, 1843).

HOOPER, JOHN: *Early Writings of* . . . (Parker Society, Cambridge, 1843).

Later Writings of . . . (Parker Society, Cambridge, 1852).

HOSKINS, EDGAR: *Horae Beatae Mariae Virginis* . . . Sarum and York Primers (London, 1901).

*HORAWITZ, ADALBERT and HARTLEDER, KARL: *Briefwechsel des Beatus Rhenanus* (Leipzig, 1886).

*HOSPINIAN, RUDOLPH: *Historiae Sacramentariae* . . . Pars II (Geneva, 1581).

*HUMPHREY, LAURENCE: *Ioannis Iuelli . . . vita et mors* . . . (Londini . . . 1573).

*HUNDESHAGEN, C. B.: *Epistolae aliquot ineditae M. Buceri ad Hist. Magn. Brit. pertinentes* (Bernae, 1840).

ISAACS, J.: The Sixteenth-Century English Versions (pp. 146-195). The Authorized Version and After (pp. 196-234). in *The Bible in its Ancient and English Versions.* (Ed. by H. Wheeler Robinson, Oxford, 1940.)

*JAMES, MONTAGUE RHODES: *A Descriptive Catalogue of the Manuscripts in the Library of Corpus Christi College, Cambridge:* 2 vol. (Cambridge, 1911-12).

*JANELLE, PIERRE: La Controverse Entre Étienne Gardiner Et Martin Bucer sur la Discipline Ecclésiastique (1541-48). In *Revue Des Sciences Religieuses*, Tome VII, pp. 452-466 (Strasbourg, 1927).

Le Voyage De Martin Bucer Et Paul Fagius De Strasbourg En Angleterre En 1549, pp. 162-177 in *Revue D'Histoire Et De Philosophie Religieuses* . . . (Strasbourg, 1928).

L'Angleterre Catholique a la Veille du Schisme (Paris, 1935).
Obedience in Church and State . . . (Cambridge, 1930).

JENKINS, CLAUDE: Sixteenth Century Studies . . . pp. 96-114, in *Church Quarterly Review* (October, 1926).

*JEWEL, JOHN: *The Works of John Jewel . . . The First Portion . . . Sermon . . . The Reply to Harding's Answer* . . . (Parker Society, Cambridge, 1845).

*JOYE, GEORGE: *The letters which Johan Ashwel Priour of Newnham Abbey besides Bedforde | sente secretely to the Bishope of Lyncolne | in the yeare of our lorde M.D.xxvii* . . . (At Strassburg the 10 day of June (1528?)).
An Apology made by George Joy, to satisfy, if it may be, W. Tindale. (February 27th, 1535). Edited by Edward Arber, 1882, in *The English Scholar's Library*, nr. 13.

KATTERFELD, ALFRED: *Roger Ascham* (Strassburg-London, 1879).

KAWERAU, WALDEMAR: *Thomas Murner und die Deutsche Reformation* (Halle, 1891).

*KEIL, LEONHARD: BARTHOLOMAEUS LATOMUS: *Zwei Streitschriften gegen Martin Bucer* (1543-45). Herausgegeben von Leonhard Keil. (Corpus Catholicorum) (Münster, 1924).

KIRK, K. E.: *Marriage and Divorce* (London, 1933).

*KLINGENBURG, GEORG: *Das Verhaeltnis Calvins zu Butzer* . . . (Bonn, 1912).

*KUYPER, ABRAHAM: *Joannis à Lasco Opera* . . . 2 vol. (Amsterdam, 1866).

*LAMB, JOHN: *A Collection of Letters, Statutes and other Documents, from the MS. Library of Corpus Christi College, Cambridge* (London, 1838).

*LANG, A.: Der Evangelienkommentar Martin Butzers und die Grundzüge seiner Theologie, in *Studien zur Geschichte der Theologie und der Kirche*, II, Heft ii (Leipzig, 1900).
Martin Bucer. pp. 159-165 in *The Evangelical Quarterly* (London, April, 1929).

*LATOMUS, BARTHOL.: *Scripta Duo Adversaria D. Bartholomaei Latomi . . . et Martini Buceri* . . . (Argentorati . . . 1544).

*LAUD, WILLIAM: *The Works of . . . William Laud, Archbishop of Canterbury.* (Library of Anglo-Catholic Theology), vol. III (Oxford, 1853).

LAUNE, ALFRED: *La traduction de l'ancien Testament de Lefèvre D'Étaples* (Dissertation: Université de France Académie de Paris) (Le Cateau, 1895).

*LAURENCE, RICHARD: *An Attempt to illustrate those Articles of the Church of England* . . . Bampton Lectures for the year MDCCCIV. (3rd ed., enlarged, Oxford, 1838).
(4th ed., Oxford, 1853).

*LEE, SIDNEY: Article on 'George Joye': in *D.N.B.*
The French Renaissance in England (Oxford, 1910).

LE LONG, JACOB: *Bibliotheca Sacra . . . Continvata ab Andrea Gottlieb Masch* . . . 2 vol. (Halae, 1778-).

*LENZ, MAX: Briefwechsel Landgraf Philipp's von Hessen mit Bucer. in *Publicationen aus den K. Preussischen Staatsarchiven:*
1. Theil: vol. V (Leipzig, 1880).
2. Theil: vol. XXVIII (Leipzig, 1887).
3. Theil: vol. XLVII (Leipzig, 1891).

LEONARD, E. M.: *The Early History of English Poor Relief* (Cambridge, 1900).

L'ESTRANGE, HAMON: *The Alliance Of Divine Offices*. 4th ed. (Library of Anglo-Catholic Theology, Oxford, 1846).

Letters & Papers, Foreign & Domestic, Henry VIII, 1509-46 (21 volumes. London).

LEUBE, HANS: *Reformation und Humanismus in England* . . . (Leipzig, 1930).

LEWIS, JOHN: *A Complete History of the Several Translations of the Holy Bible* . . . (London, 1739).

**Liturgy and Worship*: A Companion to the Prayer Books of the Anglican Communion, Ed. by W. K. Lowther Clarke, with the assistance of Charles Harris. (S.P.C.K., London. Reprinted 1936).

*McCRIE, C. G.: *Beza's 'Icones'* . . . (2nd imp., London, 1909).

*McCRIE, THOMAS: *History of the Progress . . . of the Reformation in Italy* . . . (Edinburgh-London, 1827).

MACHYN, HENRY: *The Diary of Henry Machyn . . . 1550-1563* (Ed. by John Gough Nichols. Camden Society, n. xlii, London, 1848).

MAITLAND, S. R.: *Essays on Subjects Connected with the Reformation in England*. (Reprinted . . . London, 1849).

*MASSINGBERD, F. C.: A Letter to the Rev. William Goode . . . showing that the opinion of Cranmer, Ridley and Bucer, concerning Holy Baptism . . . (pamphlet) (London, 1850).

*MASSON, DAVID: *The Life of John Milton* . . . (6 vol.), vol. III (London, 1873).

MATTHEW, THOMAS: *The Byble* | which is all the holy Scripture: In whych are contayned the Olde and Newe Testament truly and purely translated into Englysh by Thomas Matthew . . . M,D,xxxvii.

*MENTZ, FERDINAND: 'Bibliographische Zusammentstellung der gedruckten Schriften Martin Butzers' in *der Schrift* Zur 400 jährigen Geburtsfeier Martin Butzers (Strassburg, 1891).

*MESSENGER, ERNEST C.: *The Lutheran Origin of the Anglican Ordinal* (London, 1934).
The Reformation, The Mass and the Priesthood. 2 vol. (London, 1936-37).

METCALFE, WALTER: *The Visitation of Suffolk* . . . (Exeter, 1882).

Meyer, Arnold Oskar: *Die Englische Diplomatie in Deutschland zur Zeit Eduards VI. Und Mariens.* Dissertation (Breslau, 1900).

*Milton, John: The Judgment of Martin Bucer, Concerning Divorce . . . (pp. 274 ff.) in *The Prose Works of John Milton*, vol. III (Bohn's Libraries. London, 1916).

More, Thomas: *Utopia* (Everyman's Library, n. 461. Reprint, 1937).

The cōfutacyon of Tyndales answere made by syr Thomas More . . . (London, 1532).

*Morton, Thomas: *A Defence Of the Innocencie Of the Three Ceremonies Of the Church Of England.* (2nd imp., London, 1619).

Mozley, J. F.: *William Tyndale* (London, 1937).

Muenster, Sebastian: Aruch, Dictionarium Chaldaicum . . . (Basle) editions: 1523, 1525, 1527 . . .

in *Liber Precum Publicarum . . . (Elizabethan Latin Book of Common Prayer) Londini* . . . per Assignatum Francisci Florae, pp. 188-299: Liber Psalmorum Davidis . . . a Sebastiano Munstero . . . 1574, p. 299: Excudebat Thomas Vautrollerius 1574.

*Muller, James Arthur: *Stephen Gardiner and the Tudor Reaction* (S.P.C.K., London, 1926).

The Letters of Stephen Gardiner (Cambridge University Press, 1933).

Mullinger, James Bass: *The University of Cambridge from the Royal Injunctions of 1535* . . . (Cambridge University Press, 1884).

Murdin, William: *A Collection of State Papers relating to affairs in the Reign of Queen Elizabeth* . . . (London, 1759).

Nasmith, Jacobus: *Catalogus Librorum Manuscriptorum quos Collegio Corporis Christi . . . In Academia Cantabrig . . .* (Cambridge, 1777).

*Nausea, Frederick: *Epistolarum Miscellanearum ad Fredericum Nauseam* . . . (Basileae M.D.L.).

Neal, Daniel: *The History of the Puritans* . . . (2nd ed., London, 1732).

Nègrier, Charles-Abel: *Pierre Robert dit Olivétan.* Thèse. (Montauban, 1891).

**Original Letters Relative to the English Reformation* . . . 2 vol. (Parker Society, Cambridge, 1846-47).

Page, W.: The First Book of Common Prayer and the Windsor Commission in *Church Quarterly Review*, April, 1924, pp. 51-64.

*Pantaleon, Heinrich: *Prosopographiae Herovm Atqve Illvstrivm Virorvm Totivs Germaniae.* Pars tertia . . . (Basileae . . . 1566).

*Parker, Matthew: *Correspondence* . . . (Parker Society, Cambridge 1853).

Howe we ought to take the death of the godly. A sermon made in Cambridge at the buriall of the noble clerck D. M. Bucer. R. Iugge (1571?).

A funerall sermon preached 1551 at the buriall of M. Bucer. T. Purfoote (1570?).

*PARKER, ROBERT: *De Politeia Ecclesiastica Libri Tres* . . . (1616).

*PAUCK, WILHELM: *Das Reich Gottes auf Erden. Utopie und Wirklichkeit eine Untersuchung zu Butzers De Regno Christi und zur Englischen Staatskirche des 16. Jahrh.* (Berlin und Leipzig, 1928).
Martin Bucer's Conception of a Christian State, pp. 80-88 in *The Princeton Theological Review*, vol. XXVI, 1928.

PAULUS, NIKOLAUS: *Luther's Lebensende* (I Bd. I Heft. Erläuterungen . . . zu Janssen's Geschichte des deutschen Volkes. Herausgegeben von Ludwig Pastor. Freiburg i. Br. 1898).
Die Strassburger Reformatoren und die Gevissensfreiheit, II. Bd. in II. Heft: *Strassburger Theologische Studien* (Strassburg, 1895).

PEARSON, ANDREW FOREST SCOTT: *Thomas Cartwright and Elizabethan Puritanism* (Cambridge, 1925).

*PEEL, ALBERT: *The Seconde Part of a Register Being a Calendar of Manuscripts under that title intended for publication by the Puritans about 1593* . . . 2 vol. (Cambridge, 1915).

*PIGHIUS, ALBERT: *Apologia Alberti Pighii Campensis aduersus Martini Buceri calumnias* . . . Moguntiae, 1543 (against Bucer's: De vera ecclesiarum in doctrina, caeremonii, et disciplina, reconciliatione & compositione).

PIJPER, FREDERIC: *Jan Utenhove* (Leiden, 1883).

*PILKINGTON, JAMES: *The works of* . . . (Parker Society, Cambridge, 1842).

*POCOCK, NICHOLAS: *Troubles connected with the Prayer Book of 1549.* (Ed. by N. Pocock, Camden Society, 1884. New Series xxxvii).

**Politische Correspondenz der Stadt Strassburg:*
1. 1517-30 Hans Virck (Strassburg, 1882).
2. 1531-39 O. Winckelmann (Strassburg, 1887).
4(1) 1546-49 Vierter Band. Harry Gerber. 1 Halbband 1546-47 Jul. 12. (Strassburg, 1931).
4(2) 1546-49 2. Halbband 1547 Jul. 20 — 1550, Jun. 12 (Strassburg, 1933).

POLLARD, ALBERT FREDERICK: *Thomas Cranmer and the English Reformation* (in the series: Heroes of the Reformation) (New York—London, 1904).

POLLARD, A. W. and REDGRAVE, G. R.: *A Short-Title Catalogue of Books printed in England* . . . 1475-1640 . . . 2 volumes (London, 1926).

*POLMAN, PONTIEN: *L'Élément Historique dans la Controverse religieuse du XVIe Siècle* . . . (Universitas Catholica Lovaniensis) (Gembloux, 1932).

PONET (POYNET) JOHN: *A Shorte Treatise of politike pouuer, and of the true Obedience which subjectes owe to Kynges* . . . 1556.

*POULLAIN, VALERAND: *Antidotus Valerandi Pollani Flandri, Aduersus Ioachimi Vuestphali* . . . *Aphorismi D. Martini Buceri de S. S. Coena Domini* . . . (1557).

POWICKE, F. J.: *Henry Barrow* . . . (London, 1900).

*POWICKE, F. M.: *The Reformation in England* (Oxford, 1941).

*PRATEOLUS, GABRIEL: *De Vitis, Sectis, Et Dogmatibus Omnium Haereticorum* (Cologne, 1569).

*PROCTER, FRANCIS: see FRERE, W. H. and PROCTER, FRANCIS: *A New History of the Book of Common Prayer*.

*PRYNNE, WILLIAM: *Anti-Arminianisme. Or the Church of England's Antithesis to New Arminianisme* . . . (2nd ed., enlarged, 1630).

Realencyklopädie für Protestantische Theologie und Kirch. 3. Auflage. (Leipzig, 1896-). begründet von J. J. Herzog. Herausgegeben von Albert Hauck.

Reformatio Legum Ecclesiasticarum . . . (Londini . . . M.DCXL). De Adulteriis et Divortiis (pp. 47-56, 21 chap.).

*REUSNER, NICOL.: *Icones sive Imagines Virorvm Literis Illvstrivm* . . . (Argent., 1587).

*RIDLEY, GLOCESTER: *The Life of Dr. Nicholas Ridley* (London, 1763).

RIDLEY, NICHOLAS: *The Works of Nicholas Ridley* . . . (Parker Society, Cambridge, 1843).

RIGGENBACH, BERNHARD: *Das Chronikon des Konrad Pellikan* (Basel, 1877).

*RITSCHL, OTTO: *Dogmengeschichte des Protestantismus.* III. Bds (Göttingen, 1926), Kapitel xlvi, pp. 122-156: Martin Bucer. Theologie und ihre dogmengeschichtliche Bedeutung.

*RIVETUS, ANDREAS: *Andreae Riveti Apologeticus, pro suo de verae & sincerae pacis Ecclesiae propositio. Contra Hugonis Grotii Votum.* (Lugd. Batavor . . . 1643).

*ROBERTS, ARTHUR: *A Review of the Book of Common Prayer by Martin Bucer*, briefly analysed by A. Roberts. (London, 1853.)

ROBINSON, H. WHEELER: *The Bible in its Ancient and English Versions.* (Ed. by H. Wheeler Robinson, Oxford, 1940.)

*ROCKWELL, WILLIAM WALTER: *Die Doppelehe des Landgrafen Philipp von Hessen* (Marburg, 1904).

*RÖHRICH, TIMOTHEUS WILHELM: Martin Butzers Testamente, nach dem Original herausgegeben . . . pp. 193-230 in *Beiträge zu den theologischen Wissenschaften . . . herausgegeben von Dr. Eduard Reuss und Dr. Eduard Cunitz.* Zweites Bändchen (Jena, 1851).
Mitteilungen aus der Geschichte der evgl. Kirche des Elsasses. (Strassburg-Paris, 1855).
Geschichte der Reformation im Elsass. 3 Theile (Strassburg, 1830-1832).

ROGERS, THOMAS: *The Catholic Doctrine of the Church of England, An Exposition of the Thirty-Nine Articles.* (Parker Society, Cambridge, 1854.)

*ROLT, RICHARD: *The Lives of the Principal Reformers* . . . (London, MDCCLIX).

ROTT, JEAN: *Jean Sturm, Classicae Epistolae . . . Quatrienne Centenaire du Gymnase Protestant de Strasbourg* (Paris-Strasbourg, 1938).

ROY, WILLIAM and BARLOWE, JEROME: *Rede me and be nott Wrothe* . . . (at Strassburg, 1528) in English Reprints, 14 (Ed. by Edward Arber. London, September 20th, 1871).

RYMER, THOMAS: *Foedera, Conventiones, Literae . . . Acta Publica* . . . vol. XV. (London, 1713).

SALZMAN, L. F.: *England in Tudor Times* (London, 1926).

*SCHELHORNIUS, J. G.: *Amoenitates Literariae,* . . . Tomvs Quintvs . . . (Francofvrti & Lipsiae . . . MDCCXXVI).

*SCHELVEN, A. A. VAN: Zur Biographie und Theologie des Valérand Poullain. *Zeitschrift für Kirchengeschichte,* Neue Folge X, Band xlvii. II. Heft (1928), pp. 227-249.

*SCHIESS, TRAUGOTT: *Briefwechsel der Brüder Ambrosius und Thomas Blaurer* (Freiburg, i.B. 3 vol. 1908-12).

*SCHMIDT, C.: *Peter Martyr Vermigli* (Elberfeld, 1858).

*SCHMIDT, GERHART: *Martin Butzer als protestantischer Politiker.* Inaugural Dissertation. (Leipzig, 1936.)

*SCHNEIDER, JOHANNES: *Ein Brief M. Butzers an den Ritter Hans Landschad von Steinach über das heilige Abendmahl, 1526* . . . (Archiv für hessische Geschichte . . . Neue Folge. Ergänzungsband 3, pp. 105 ff.). (Darmstadt, 1906.)

*SCHROECKH, JOHANNES MATTHIAS: *Abbildungen und Lebensbeschreibungen* . . . vol. III (Leipzig, 1767).

*SCHUBERT, HANS VON: Zwei Predigten Martin Bucers . . . pp. 192 ff. in *Beiträge zur Reformationsgeschichte* (Gotha, 1896) (Festschrift zum 70 sten Geburtstag von Köstlin . . .).

*SCHULTING, CORNELIUS: *Bibliothecae Ecclesiasticae, seu* . . . Tomi Quatuor . . . Coloniae Agrippinae (Anno M.D.xcix).
Hierarchica Anacrasis . . . Coloniae Agrippinae (Anno M.DC.iiii).

*SCHULTZ, RUDOLF: *Martin Butzer's Anschauung von der Christlichen Oberkeit, dargestellt im Rahmen der reformatorischen Staats und Kirchentheorien.* Inaugural Dissertation (Zella-Mehlis, Thür. 1932).

SCHWEBEL, JOHAN: *Centvria Epistolarvm Theologicarum ad Iohannem Schwebelivm* . . . (Bipontina, 1597), and *Dn. Iohannis Schwebelii . . . Scripta Theologica, . . . Addita est, Epistolarvm . . . Centvria.* (Biponti, 1605).

*SECKENDORF, V. L.: *Commentarius historicus et apologeticus de Lutheranismo* (Francofurti et Lipsiae, 1692-).

*SEEBERG, REINHOLD: *Lehrbuch der Dogmengeschichte. Zweite Hälfte: Die Dogmengeschichte des Mittelalters und der Neuzeit* (Erlangen-Leipzig, 1898).

SEEBOHM, FREDERIC: *The Oxford Reformers* (ed. Everyman's Library, no. 665, reprinted, 1938).

*SENARCLAEUS, CLAUDIUS: *Historia vera de morte . . . Ioannis Diazij Hispani . . . per Claudium Senarclaeum* . . . (1546). Prefatory Letter of Bucer to Prince Otto Heinrich, Palatine . . .

SLEIDANUS, JOHANNES: *De Statu religionis et reipublicae Carolo V* . . . Commentarii . . . (Argent., 1555).

SMELLIE, ALEXANDER: *The Reformation in its Literature* (London, 1925).

*SMITH, RICHARD TRAVERS: *We ought not to alter the Ordinal* . . . with an Appendix Shewing the Process by which the Ordinal of 1549 was framed in Episcopal Form on the Basis of a semi-presbyterian Draft by Martin Bucer (Dublin, 1872).

*SMYTH, C. H.: *Cranmer & the Reformation under Edward VI* (Cambridge, 1926).

SPAHN, MARTIN: *Johannes Cochläus* (Berlin, 1898).

*STAEHELIN, E.: *Oekolampad und Butzer in Französischer Übersetzung. Zeitschrift für Kirchengeschichte* (1928), Neue Folge X, Band xlvii, I. Heft. pp. 57-63.

Statutes of the Realm 1547-84-5, vol. IV. (London, 1819).

STEELE, R. L.: Humphrey Dyson. (In *The Library*, 1910, 3rd series, N. 2, vol. I. April, 1910. London, 1910-19).

STEELE, ROBERT: *A Bibliography of Royal Proclamations . . . Bibliotheca Lindesiana*, vol. V, vol. I. (Oxford, 1910).
Notes on English Books printed abroad. *Transactions of the Bibliographical Society*, vol. XI (London, March, 1912).

STOW, JOHN: *A Survey of the Cities of London and Westminster* . . . (Ed. by John Strype . . . London, 1720).

STRASSER, OTTO ERICH: *Capitos Beziehungen zu Bern.* Dissertation (Gräfenhainichen, 1927).

*STROHL, H.: Deux études sur Bucer, in *Revue D'Histoire et de Philosophie Religieuses.* (Strasbourg, 1930. November-December), pp. 571-578.
La notion d'Eglise chez Bucer dans son développemente historique, in *Revue D'Histoire et de Philosophie* . . . (Strasbourg, 1933), pp. 242-249.
Théologie et Humanisme à Strasbourg au moment de la création de la Haute-Ecole, in *Revue D'Histoire* . . . (Strasbourg, 1937), pp. 435-456.
Un aspect de l'humanisme chrétien de Bucer, in *Revue D'Histoire* . . . (Strasbourg, 1938), pp. 432-447.
Bucer Interprète De Luther, in *Revue D'Histoire* . . . (Strasbourg, 1939), pp. 223-261.

*STRYPE, JOHN: *The History of the Life and Acts of . . . Edmund Grindal* (Oxford, 1821).
Ecclesiastical Memorials (Oxford, 1822).
Annals of the Reformation (Oxford, 1824).
Memorials of Archbishop Cranmer (Oxford, 1840).

STUBBS, WILLIAM: *Registrum Sacrum Anglicanum*, 2nd edition (Oxford, 1897).

*STUPPERICH, ROBERT: Die Kirche in M. Bucers Theologischer Entwicklung, pp. 81-101, in *Archiv für Reformationsgeschichte . . .* Jahrgang 35. (Leipzig, 1938).

STURGE, CHARLES: *Cuthbert Tunstal* (London . . . 1938).

*TANNER, THOMAS: *Bibliotheca Britannico-Hibernica* . . . (Londini, 1748).

*TAWNEY, R. H.: *Religion and the Rise of Capitalism* (ed.: Published in Pelican Books, 1938).

*THOMSON, RICHARD: *Richardi Thomsonis Angli Diatriba de Amissione et Intercisione Gratiae* . . . (Lugd. Batav., 1616).

*TOLLIN, H.: *Servet und die Oberländischen Reformatoren* . . . Band I. Michael Servet und Martin Butzer. (Berlin, 1880.)

TOMLINSON, J. T.: *The Prayer Book, Articles and Homilies* . . . (London, 1897).

*TURNER, WILLIAM (Pseud. Wraghton): *The huntyng and fyndyng out of the Romyshe foxe* . . . (Basle, 1543).
The Rescvynge of the Romishe Fox . . . The Seconde Covrse of the Hvnter . . . (Jmprynted haue at winchester . . . 1545).

*USTERI, JOH. MARTIN: Die Stellung der Strassburger Reformatoren Bucer und Capito zur Tauffrage, pp. 456-525, *Theol. Studien und Kritiken* (Gotha, 1884).

*VARRENTRAPP, C.: *Herman von Wied und sein Reformationsversuch in Köln.* (Leipzig, 1878).
Zur Charakteristik Hermanns von Wied, Bucers und Groppers. (*Zeitschrift für Kirchengesch.*, Bd. XX. I. Heft. Gotha, 1899).

VERGIL, POLYDOR: *Polydori Vergilij Vrbinatis De Rerum inuentoribus libri octo* (ed. Basileae, apud Isingrinum, 1546).

*VERHEIDEN, JAC.: *Praestantium aliquot Theologorum, qui Rom. Antichristum praecipue oppugnarunt, Effigies* . . . (Hagen, 1602).

*VERPOORTENN, ALBERT MENON: *M. Alberti Menonis Verpoortenns Commentatio Historica, De Martino Bucero, Eiusque de Coena Domini* . . . (Coburg, 1709).

*VOSSIUS, GERHARD JOHAN: *Gerardi Joan. Vossii Clarorum Virorum ad eum Epistolae.* Collectore Paulo Colomesio Ecclesiae Anglicanae Presbytero (London, 1690).

*WALCH, JOHANN GEORG: *D. Martin Luthers . . . Sämtliche Schriften* . . . (Halle, 1745).

WALTER, HENRY: A Letter to the Right Reverend Herbert, Lord

Bishop of Peterborough . . . on the Independence of the Authorized Version of the Bible. (London, 1823.)
A Second Letter . . . (1828).

*Ward, A. W.: Article on Martin Bucer in *D.N.B.*

*Waterland, Daniel: *The Works of the Reverend Daniel Waterland* . . . vol. X (Oxford, 1823).

Watson, Edward William: *The Church of England.* The Home University Library, 2nd imp. (London, 1935).

Watt, Robert *Bibliotheca Britannica* . . . (Edinburgh-London, 1824-).

Wernham, R. B. and Walker, J. C.: *England under Elizabeth* (London, 1932).

Westcott, Brooke Foss: *A General View of the History of the English Bible.* (3rd ed., revised. London, 1905.)

Wette, W. M. de: *Dr. M. Luther's Briefe* . . . (Berlin, 1828).

*VVhether it be mortall sinne to transgresse ciuil lawes, which be the commaundementes of ciuill Magistrates . . . (Imprinted, London, by Richarde Iugge).

*Wilberforce, Robert Isaac: *The Doctrine of Holy Baptism*, with Remarks on the Rev. W. Goode's 'Effects of Infant Baptism' (London, 1849).

Wilkins, David: *Concilia Magnae Britanniae* . . . in 4 vol. (London, 1737-).

*Wilson, H. A.: *The Order of the Communion, 1548.* (Ed. by H. A. Wilson. London, 1908.) Henry Bradshaw Society, vol. XXXIV.

*Whitaker, William: *G. VVitakervs Viri Clar. Cygnea Cantio, hoc est, ultima ejus concio ad Clerum Cantabrigiae habita: Octobr. 9. Anno Dom. 1595* pp. 44 ff. in *Petri Baronis Summa Trium De Praedestinatione Sententiarum* . . . (1613).

Whitby, E. O. Humphrey: *The End of Sacrifice* (S.P.C.K., London, 1942).

*White, Johan: *Diacosio-Martyrion . . . Ioanne Whito* . . . (Londini . . . Mense Decembri Anno 1553).

*Whitgift, John: *Works of* . . . 3 vol. (Parker Society, Cambridge, 1851-53).

**Zurich Letters, The*, 1558-1579 (Parker Society, Cambridge, 1842).
2nd Series, 1558-1602 (Parker Society, Cambridge, 1845).

*Zwingli, H.: *Huldrici Zuinglii Opera.* Ed. Melchior Schuler and Io. Schulthess. vol. VIII. (Zurich, 1842.)

INDEX

INDEX

INDEX